Unreached Peoples '81

The Challenge of the Church's Unfinished Business

With Special Section on the Peoples of Asia

Unreached Peoples '81

Unreached Peoples '81

C. Peter Wagner
and
Edward R. Dayton,
editors

David C. Cook Publishing Co.

The material contained in the Unreached Peoples Registry may be reproduced
or copied in any form provided appropriate credit is given. Portions of the rest of
this book may only be used with written permission from the David C. Cook
Publishing Co., 850 North Grove Avenue, Elgin, IL 60120, U.S.A.

Design by Graphic Communications, Inc.
Printed in U.S.A.

ISBN: 0-89191-331-9
LC: 80-69556

Contents

LINCOLN CHRISTIAN COLLEGE AND SEMINARY

79885

Introduction

BACKGROUND OF THE UNREACHED PEOPLES SERIES

The *Unreached Peoples* series began in 1979. This is the third volume in the series, which has been sponsored by the Strategy Working Group of the Lausanne Committee for World Evangelization (LCWE). (See page 8.) The series finds its genesis in the work that was done for the International Congress on World Evangelization held at Lausanne, Switzerland, in 1974, from which the LCWE found its beginning. The Missions Advanced Research and Communication Center (MARC) was asked by the 1974 program committee to prepare a picture of the current status of world evangelization. As the MARC staff corresponded with Christian leaders around the world, it became apparent that the terms *evangelized* or *unevangelized* were inadequate to describe the task before us. We found two extremes. On the one hand, there were many places in the world where people described themselves as Christians but their lack of attendance at worship and their other Christian practices and life-style indicated that they had little or no commitment to Christ. They may be evangelized, but they need a fresh call to turn to God and accept Christ as Savior and Lord.

On the other hand, there were places where there was a Christian presence, but no apparent response. Were these people evangelized?

Out of these discussions emerged the concept of *unreached,* rather than unevangelized. But again it was seen that the formerly standard terminology of geography—country or field—was not adequate. A more useful way of looking at the world was the *people group.*

The report prepared by MARC and given to each of the participants at Lausanne was called an *Unreached Peoples* Directory. It listed 434 people groups that reports from around the world indicated were unreached.

Subsequent to Lausanne, the LCWE was formed and constituted four working groups (Communications, Intercession, Theology and Education, and Strategy). The Strategy Working Group (SWG) requested World Vision International, the parent agency of MARC, to make the services of that research and strategy organization available to work with SWG. World Vision was pleased to accede to that request. The result has been a series of publications that focused on unreached peoples and developing strategies to reach them. *Planning Strategies for Evangelism* is a workbook which has gone through six revisions as it has been field-tested. *World Christianity* is a series of regional status-of-Christianity country profiles, which at this writing includes the Middle East, Eastern Asia, Central America, and Southern Asia. *That Everyone May Hear* is a small study book which attempts to spell out the theory behind a people-group approach to world evangelization. It has been translated into Spanish, Chinese, Japanese, and French. An audiovisual based on the book has had wide distribution in English, French, Spanish, Tamil, Karen, German, Korean, Chinese, and Portuguese. (For information on these and other LCWE and MARC publications, write to MARC International, 919 W. Huntington Drive, Monrovia, CA 91016, U.S.A; MARC/Canada, 6630 Turner Valley Road, Mississauga, Ontario, L5N 2S4, Canada; MARC/Australia, Box 399-C, G.P.O. Melbourne, 3001 Victoria,

Australia; MARC/New Zealand, P.O. Box 1923, Auckland, New Zealand; or MARC/Europe, 146 Queen Victoria Street, London EC4, England.)

These, and other materials, were utilized by LCWE in preparing for the Consultation on World Evangelization held at Pattaya, Thailand, June 16-26, 1980. The primary purpose of the Consultation was to evaluate the work of LCWE and to prayerfully consider whether LCWE should continue.

In preparation for COWE, seventeen coordinators were appointed in the major categories of Muslims, Hindus, Buddhists, Mystics and Cultists, Marxists, Traditional Chinese, secularists, traditional religions (in Africa, Asia and Oceania, Latin America and Caribbean), refugees, nominal Protestants, nominal Catholics, nominal Orthodox, Large Cities, and Inner-city. These coordinators in turn appointed conveners all over the world who were asked to discuss the challenge of reaching specific people groups in these larger categories. Hundreds of study groups were convened, and their reports were synthesized into a major report by the coordinator. The COWE then discussed each of these areas in a series of mini-consultations, as well as regional groups. A great deal of new information and new insight was gained which will be reflected in a series of LCWE publications, as well as subsequent editions of this series.

THE CURRENT DIRECTORY

The editors wish to express appreciation to the Reverend James Wong, a member of the Strategy Working Group and a citizen of Singapore, for acting as Special Consultant on *Unreached Peoples '81,* which features the peoples of Asia. Reverend Wong was the director of the Asia Leadership Conference on Evangelism that preceded COWE.

The articles by Donald McGavran, Christopher Morris, Alex Smith, Gail Law, Tissa Weerasingha, Darwin Sokoken, Jack Rea, Samuel Chao, David Wyma, Cliff Good, James Wong, and Andrew Goh reflect this emphasis on Asia. There are a considerable number of new additions to the Registry of Unreached Peoples, including some groups in China. There have also been some deletions from the 1980 Registry, which reflect the research-in-work nature of the *Unreached Peoples* series. The editors decided from the outset that we would accept information from any apparently reliable source. We recognized that the reporter's own view of a situation would often be different from that of another reporter. We have to indicate in the directory an index of validity. In most cases this is quite subjective. Consequently, when we have received information that leads us to believe that, contrary to a previous report, the group is reached, we have eliminated them from the Registry.

Another problem we have struggled with is how to handle very large groups, particularly those that have a wide geographical distribution. For example, we might have a report that, of forty-four million caste Hindus in Andra Pradesh, only 3 percent are Christian. They therefore appear to be an unreached group. However, in a particular state or locality of India, a large number of these people may have turned to Christ. When one narrows the group down to this region, they are a *reached* group. In discussing this dilemma, it is helpful to remind ourselves of the fundamental purpose of *Unreached Peoples,* which is to enhance world evangelization. *We are less interested in how well we know something than we are in what difference it makes.* We face a similar problem in a place like Hong Kong. One researcher may report that of the four million Chinese in Hong Kong, 8 percent are Christian. His people group is "Chinese Living in Hong Kong." Another researcher may be concerned with "Middle-class Chinese Businessmen in Hong Kong." Obviously, the second group is part of the larger first. It is helpful to know there are four million Chinese in Hong Kong who are only 8 percent Christian. If that is all the data we have, it may well be used by God to send more workers to Hong Kong. It is more helpful to narrow the population down to more meaningful groups such as businessmen, high-rise dwellers in Kowloon, college students, etc.

It is important to note here that we are not attempting to locate and identify every people group in the world. We believe that such a task is probably not only not humanly possible, but that it would serve no immediate purpose.

We are attempting to identify enough people groups to (1) challenge the church to her task of world mission, (2) help the church in a particular country recognize that there are unreached people for whom she is responsible, (3) convince the church that seeing the world as people groups brings new understanding and new hope to the cross-cultural task, and (4) providing demonstrations that approaching cross-cultural evangelism as people groups is actually effective. God honors it. People are won to Christ and made effective members of his Kingdom. It is this approach which makes us not only welcome criticism and correction, but to solicit it. We are only a vehicle that we hope God will use to strengthen his church. At the back of this volume you will find a tear-out page which can be used to mail your comments or corrections to MARC. You will also find a photo-reduced copy of the questionnaire used to gather data on unreached people groups, additional copies of which are yours for the asking.

This edition follows the procedure begun in *Unreached Peoples '80* of indicating in the Registry if an expanded description of the group appears in the 1979, 1980, or 1981 edition. We encourage you, therefore to obtain copies of the complete *Unreached Peoples* series.

Although it is our privilege to be listed as co-editors of this volume, it should be immediately recognized that such a work could never be the product of two people. In addition to our consultant, James Wong, and the hundreds of men and women throughout the world who have given ungrudgingly of their time, we want to recognize each of those who have contributed both missiological articles and case studies. The huge task of managing the unreached peoples data base has been in the hands of R. Boyd Johnson, Research Associate at MARC. Dr. Samuel Wilson, recently appointed Director of MARC, has given valuable oversight. John Pentecost, Senior Research Assistant, has been responsible for the computerization. The members of the MARC staff, especially Kim Allison, have also contributed a great deal to the production of this volume.

Finally, we wish to acknowledge the outstanding cooperation of our publisher, the David C. Cook Publishing Company. It is no mean task to publish a yearly volume such as this in a timely manner. We are grateful.

FUTURE VOLUMES

Unreached Peoples '82 is already in work. Dr. Raymond Bakke, who was Coordinator for Reaching Large Cities at COWE, will be our major consultant. The work that he and others have done for that Consultation will help us understand that the major portion of the world's unreached people now live in urban areas, a fact that both startles us and causes us to think more deeply about people groups in such situations.

The 1982 volume will be edited by Ed Dayton and Sam Wilson, a missionary-researcher and scholar who was appointed to succeed Ed Dayton as Director of MARC in May of this year. The present editors will continue their close collaboration and friendship through the vehicle of the LCWE Strategy Working Group.

C. Peter Wagner
Edward R. Dayton

LAUSANNE COMMITTEE FOR WORLD EVANGELIZATION AS OF 1980

One of the outcomes of the International Congress on World Evangelization held in Lausanne, Switzerland, in the summer of 1974 was a mandate from the 2,400 participants to form an ongoing committee. The "Spirit of Lausanne" was a powerful new thrust for completing the task of world evangelization. It was not to die.

The Lausanne Committee for World Evangelization was born at a meeting in Mexico City, January 20-23, 1975. The committee drew up a constitution, named forty-eight charter members, and elected Leighton Ford president and Gottfried Osei-Mensah executive secretary.

During June 16-26, 1980, the LCWE convened a Consultation on World Evangelization at Pattaya, Thailand, to evaluate the work of the committee and to determine its future. Six hundred participants and 250 consultants, observers, and guests were present. As a result of that consultation, the decision was made to reaffirm the mandate of Lausanne and to continue the work of the movement.

The central offices of the LCWE are located in Nairobi, Kenya (P.O. Box 21225). Four working groups carry out its basic ministries—intercession, theology/education, strategy, and communications. The current listing of committee members follows:

Francisco Anabalon, Chile
Ramez Atallah, Canada
*Saphir Athyal, India, *Deputy Chairman*
Peter Beyerhaus, West Germany
Henri Blocher, France
Vonette Bright, U.S.A.
Michael Cassidy, South Africa
Chongnahm Cho, Korea

*Executive Committee member

13

Robert Coleman, U.S.A.
Mariano DiGangi, Canada
Nilson Fanini, Brazil
Ajith Fernado, Sri Lanka
*Leighton Ford, U.S.A., *Chairman*
*Bruno Frigoli, Bolivia
*Andrew Furuyama, Japan
Emmy Gichinga, Kenya
Geziel Nunes Gomes, Brazil
Billy Graham, U.S.A. *(ex officio)*
Edward Hill, U.S.A.
Fritz Hoffmann, East Germany
C. B. Hogue, U.S.A.
*Donald Hoke, U.S.A., *Treasurer*
*Armin Hoppler, Switzerland
Abd-el Masih Istafanous, Egypt
Festo Kivengere, Uganda
A. T. Victor Koh, Philippines
Gordon Landreth, England
Lamuel Libert, Argentina
Branco Lovrec, Yugoslavia
Billy Melvin, U.S.A.
Stanley Mooneyham, U.S.A.
Agne Norlander, Sweden
Petrus Octavianus, Indonesia
*Samuel Odunaike, Nigeria
*Gottfried Osi-Mensah, Kenya, *Executive Secretary*
Pablo Perez, Mexico
Ted Raedeke, U.S.A.
*John Reid Australia, *Intercession Working Group Chairman*
John Richard, India
Subhas Sangma, Bangladesh
Peter Schneider, Germany
*John Stott, England, *Theology and Education Working Group
Chairman*
*C. Peter Wagner, U.S.A., *Strategy Working Group Chairman*
Ben Wati, India

14

Warren Webster, U.S.A.
James Wong, Singapore
*Thomas Zimmerman, U.S.A., *Communications Working Group Chairman*
Isaac Zokoue, Ivory Coast

Strategy Working Group
The Strategy Working Group of the Lausanne Congress on World Evangelism has the task of discovering unreached groups of people and helping to design strategies to reach them.
C. Peter Wagner, U.S.A., *Chairman*
Fouad Accad, Arabian Gulf
Edward R. Dayton, U.S.A.
David Gitari, Kenya
Tom Houston, England
John Y. Masuda, Japan
George Samuel, India
Douglas Smith, Bolivia
James Wong, Singapore

Part 1
The Unreached and How to Reach Them

The People-Group Approach to World Evangelization

by C. Peter Wagner and Edward R. Dayton

In this article, the editors review the concept of unreached people groups, explain the rationale behind the definition of less than 20 percent Christian constituting an unreached group, and give the advantages of utilizing the concept of unreached people groups as a way of thinking about the task of world evangelization.

EVANGELIZATION: WHAT IS THE GOAL?
Because world evangelization is a task, it is essential to have a clear understanding of the goal of that particular task. The *nature* of world evangelization, in our opinion, is the communication of the good news. The *purpose* of world evangelization is to give individuals and groups a valid opportunity to accept Jesus Christ. And the *goal* of world evangelization is the persuading of men and women to accept Jesus Christ as Lord and Savior and serve him in the fellowship of his church.[1]

According to this definition, then, strategies for world evangelization will regard Christian presence among non-Christian peoples and the proclamation of the Gospel of Jesus Christ to them as necessary, but only intermediary, stages of the total evangelistic process. The goal is not fully reached until non-Christians, through the powerful, regenerating work of the Holy Spirit, are persuaded to turn from darkness to light, from unbelief to faith, from serving idols to serving the living and true God. The goal is a growing number of true citizens of the Kingdom of God living out their discipleship in every dimension.

EVANGELIZATION: THE RANGE OF OPTIONS

Several International Congress on World Evangelization presentations at Lausanne 1974, notably that of Ralph Winter, made us aware that all evangelistic tasks are not alike. He stressed especially the important differences between monocultural evangelism and cross-cultural evangelism. Many non-Christians can be evangelized by their culturally near neighbors who speak the same language and dialect, who have the same customs, and who can be understood naturally and easily by those non-Christians. A technical term for such monocultural evangelism is *evangelism one* or E-1.

However, many non-Christians, in fact a substantial majority of them, cannot be reached by E-1 evangelism because there is not yet any viable witnessing Christian group made up of persons of their own culture. In order for them to be reached they obviously need missionaries who are willing to cross cultural boundaries, learn their language and customs, and present the gospel in terms that can be clearly understood. A technical term for this cross-cultural evangelism is *evangelism two* or, if the cultural boundary happens to be a more formidable one, *evangelism three.* In this presentation we will combine the two and use the symbol E-2/3 for cross-cultural evangelism.

We are informed by the U.S. Center for World Missions, for example, that a full 80 percent of the world's non-Christians will initially require E-2/3 evangelism if they are going to become Christians.[2] This leaves only 20 percent of all non-Christians who are proper objects for E-1 evangelism. Thus, the development of strategies for evangelizing the non-Christians of the world does well to give the highest priorities to E-2/3 evangelism, although, as we will see, most individuals have been, and will be, ultimately won to Christ through E-1 evangelism.

EVANGELIZATION: THE PEOPLE APPROACH

If our major task is effectively to evangelize those 80 percent, what is the best way to conceptualize this task? What are the significant units at which we should aim? The essay by Edward Dayton in *Unreached Peoples '79* eliminated three possibilities and concluded that a fourth was the most significant unit.

The 80 percent could be conceptualized as *individuals.* There are something like 2.5 billion of these individuals in the world today. Such a number, however, is staggering and unwieldly. Another option is to use the different *countries* of the world as target units. There are currently 220 of them, and each one contains non-Christians. But the boundaries of today's nation-states, in many cases the arbitrary results of Western colonialism and imperialism, tend to cloud the more essential cultural boundaries between human groups which are more significant for planning evangelization. A third option was to use the *religions* of the world as target units. In a very general way, this has some validity. But there are numerous subgroupings of individuals within the nationality and religious categories that are more helpful for strategy planning.

These groupings are *peoples.* The best way to think about strategies for world evangelization is to think of people groups. Three major considerations have entered into this statement:

1. *The people approach is biblical.* Our Lord's Great Commission, as translated in the Good News Bible reads: "Go, then, to all peoples *(panta ta ethne)* everywhere and make them my disciples . . ." (Matt. 28:19). Jesus himself, during his earthly ministry, concentrated basically on one people: the Aramaic-speaking Jews of Galilee. For example, the comment made by the amazed people of Jerusalem when they heard Jesus' followers speaking in tongues on the day of Pentecost was, "These people who are talking like this are Galileans!" (Acts 1:7).

Although the references were clearly geographical, Jesus' final command that his disciples be witnesses in Jerusalem, Judea, Samaria, and the uttermost part of the earth (Acts 1:8) were also references to locations of peoples. It is interesting to note that at the time Jesus does not mention Galilee, even though it would have fit logically into his list of immediate areas. One could surmise that Galilee was omitted because the Galileans had already been reached. They had been Jesus' principal target group. Jesus' list was a list of what we now call unreached peoples.

When God chose Abraham, he created a people, later known as the people of Israel. God's intention, however, was not to limit the blessings given to Abraham to only that one people. He said, "All peoples on earth will be blessed through you" (Gen. 12:3, NIV). God sent Jonah specifically to one people—the people of Nineveh. The special calling of the apostle Paul was to the uncircumcised, while Peter's call was to the circumcised or the Jews. Paul was basically an E-2/3 apostle while Peter was E-1.

2. *The people approach is reasonable.* It makes sense to think of the world's individuals as peoples because that is how human beings think of themselves. For example, as anyone familiar with African politics knows, it is more important for most citizens of Burundi, as far as self-identity is concerned, to know that they are Tutsi, Hutu, or Twa than that they are Burundi. Most Nigerians find their primary identity as Higi or Magazawa or Ibibio or any of hundreds of other people groups, with Nigerians as a secondary identity and West Africans as a tertiary identity. While many outsiders may think that Hispanic-Americans are one people group, the primary identity of most of them is as Mexican-Americans or Cuban-Americans or Puerto Ricans or other national origin groups rather than as either Hispanics or Americans. In the Middle East, Kurds feel much more loyalty to each other as Kurds than as citizens of Iran or Iraq. They resent the fact that a national border has divided a people. South American Ayores care little whether the United Nations includes them in the population of Bolivia or of Paraguay—they know themselves and each other basically as Ayores.

Of course, national political leaders wish this weren't so. Anglo-Canadian leaders wish the people of Quebec would learn English and stop talking about secession. Many American government officials feel that Navajo Indians are a nuisance—they should have become red white men long ago. Until recently they tried to implement this by punishing Navajo school children if they were ever caught speaking the Navajo language. But despite all the supposed glories of twentieth-century nationalism, people groups simply will not be erased. They will continue to provide a reasonable way of thinking about the world's population probably until Jesus returns.

3. *The people approach is manageable.* A slogan of one of America's well-known preachers, Robert Schuller, is "Inch by inch, anything's a cinch." Most people laugh when they first hear it, but they remember it because it makes sense. Its underlying meaning, of course, is that most any task can be accomplished if it is first broken down into manageable units. No one builds a whole house at once. It must go up board by board or brick by brick or tile by tile. World evangelization is similar. The most manageable way of thinking about evangelizing the world is people by people.

WHAT IS A PEOPLE?
To this point, we have not defined what we mean by a *people.* This was high on the agenda of the first meeting of the Strategy Working Group held in 1977. After a lengthy period of research and discussion, the following definition was agreed upon: *A people is a significantly large sociological grouping of individuals who perceive themselves to have a common affinity for one another.*

WHAT IS AN UNREACHED PEOPLE?
Current mission literature abounds with talk about *unreached people* and *hidden people.* Some missions have specialists set aside to identify unreached peoples. This directory is called *Unreached Peoples.* At the same time many missiologists write about reaching hidden people. Are we talking about the same thing, or is there a difference? Are we somehow confusing ourselves with our terminology?

The phrase *unreached peoples* was first popularized at the International Congress on World Evangelization held at Lausanne, Switzerland, in 1974. MARC prepared the first *Un-*

reached Peoples Directory which listed about 450 unreached peoples. Since that time the attention of mission groups and local churches all over the world has been captured by the phrase and the concept that is embedded in it. There are two parts to the concept:

The first is the idea of the people group. Since its founding in 1966, the Mission Advanced Research and Communication Center (MARC) centered its philosophy of world evangelization around the people group. The analysis that was done jointly by Donald McGavran and Ed Dayton, at the School of World Mission at Fuller Seminary, indicated that the country-by-country approach to missions was no longer viable. It had been a good beginning for the era of modern missions. It pointed direction. It outlined an area for research. But within the national boundaries were thousands of peoples *(ta ethne)*. Often the national boundaries disguised these groups. Often even the church within the country was unaware of their presence.

McGavran and Dayton worked through an analysis of needed world evangelization, based on McGavran's earlier insight gained from people movements—Christward movements of a part or whole of some ethnic group, clan, tribe, caste, or other segments of society. More than two-thirds of the young churches are found in such groups. As the analysis continued, it was obvious that the basic unit of evangelization was not a country, nor the individual, but a vast variety of subgroups. It was also obvious that the Christian world was woefully ignorant about the number and complexity of people groups. We had identified thousands of language groups and seen the power of such definition to attract and motivate cross-cultural missionaries, but the more subtle and diffuse people groups has seldom been defined except by some socioanthropologists and sociologists. The initial report on the work of MARC, issued in July 1966, enumerated the parameters that might be useful in defining a people group for the purposes of cross-cultural communication of the gospel. Since that time those parameters have been sharpened and tested. Those parameters are listed in the *Unreached Peoples* Questionnaire (see Appendix A).

A key idea inherent in the people approach to evangelization comes from the theory of the diffusion of innovation and information. New ideas flow along the lines of natural human relationships. Ideas spread most rapidly within a close-knit group and are often blocked when they reach the boundaries of that group. An analysis of the spread of the gospel during and since New Testament times verifies this dimension of human life. Attempting to discover God's unique strategy for confronting a specific people group with the gospel is not only a comprehendible and believable approach, but it focuses resources in the most effective way *humanly* possible. Once the gospel impregnates a people group, and a viable church is brought into being by the Holy Spirit, that church is an intimate part of its context and has within it the capability to evangelize the rest of the people group. The task of missions—cross-cultural evangelism—is complete for that group.

The second part of the concept is the idea of unreached. During the early seventies there was an extended exchange of correspondence among evangelical leaders around the world. Were we trying to discover *unreached* people or *unevangelized* people? Once we had completed the analysis of the above paragraph the question became moot, for although we could measure and define the degree of "reachedness" by observing the church at work, there was no commonly acceptable measurement of the degree of evangelization that might have taken place. For example, it might be argued that some of the European countries had obviously been evangelized years ago, but that does not change the fact that today in Europe there are millions of people who have had no valid opportunity to accept God's gracious gift. The degree of evangelization might be a *proper* question for some, but for those preparing for the 1974 International Congress on World Evangelization at Lausanne it was not useful. The world that was faced by Lausanne might have been evangelized at some time and place, but it was unreached today.

It was at Lausanne that the *extent* of that unreachedness became apparent. Lausanne rejected the idea that because a church had been planted in a nation-state, the church worldwide had fulfilled its evangelistic mandate for the peoples within that country. It identified over two billion people who were culturally, geographically, or politically isolated from the gospel. It called the Church back to its primary mandate of proclaiming the gospel to all peoples everywhere.

As a result of Lausanne, and the continuing work of MARC and the Lausanne Strategy Working Group, these people were described as unreached people. The phrase caught fire. It is now part of the everyday language of thousands of missions and missionaries. But it needed further refining. When was a people reached? Obviously, when there was a church in its midst with the desire and the ability to evangelize the balance of the group. Sociological theory hinted that the size of such a church might be somewhere between 10 and 20 percent. Twenty percent was selected as being on the safe side. Subsequently the definition was refined to include various degrees of reachedness within the 20 percent figure.

Enter the concept of "hidden people." Ralph Winter, of the U.S. Center for World Mission, coined this phrase to indicate the vast number of people groups within which there was virtually *no* Christian group. It is a useful phrase. It points out the enormity and the demands of the task. If there are well over two billion people living in groups within which there is no effective Christian witness, then the Christian Church needs to know about them and do something about reaching them. Truly they are hidden from us. They need to be found!

The Strategy Working Group thus sought to absorb this valuable term as it further developed a hierarchy of unreached people: if there are virtually no Christians in a group, it is a *hidden people.* If there are as many as 1 percent, it is *initially reached.* Up to 10 percent, *minimally reached.* From 10 to 20 percent, *probably reached.* This can be diagramed (See figure 1: *Categories of Unreached People*).

Some unreached people are hidden people. All hidden people are unreached people. Let's not be confused by the terminology. It forms part of a beautiful whole that God is using to

Categories of Unreached People

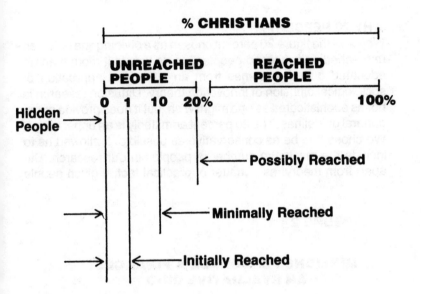

DEFINITIONS:

Hidden People:	No known Christians within the group.
Initially Reached:	Less than 1 percent, but some Christians.
Minimally Reached:	One to 10 percent Christian.
Possibly Reached:	Ten to 20 percent Christian.
Reached:	Twenty percent or more practicing Christians.

FIGURE 1:

awaken his people everywhere to their responsibility to carry the good news across cultural barriers wherever they are found. The important idea is *to see them as people groups,* and to ask what is the strength of the church within the group for the job it must eventually do.

WHY 20 PERCENT?

Why was the figure 20 percent chosen as a dividing line between unreached and reached peoples? In no way is it more than an educated guess. It comes from an attempted application of sociological diffusion of innovation theory. Diffusion research is not as sophisticated as one might wish, but it does provide some general guidelines. The 20 percent admittedly is an upper range. We chose it to be as conservative as possible. It allowed us to include the maximum number of peoples in our research. But apart from theory, as a matter of practical fact, a given people

FIGURE 2

MISSIONS PERSONNEL & FINANCES
AN EVALUATIVE GRID

Cultural Distance ⟶

		1 Same Culture	2 Other	3 Cultures
Major Job Description	**E** EVANGELISM & CHURCH PLANTING	E-1	E-2	E-3
	N CHRISTIAN NURTURE	N-1	N-2	N-3
	S SERVICE	S-1	S-2	S-3

could legitimately be considered reached with substantially fewer than 20 percent of its members practicing Christians. For example, to the degree that Korean city dwellers could be considered a people, that group is probably reached today, although the percentage may not be as high as 20 percent in many cities in Korea. Less than 100 years ago they were still a hidden people, since the gospel had not yet gone there.

In order to explain this in more detail, we will first need to look at some additional technical terminology (See figure 2: Missions Personnel and Financial).

The top line of figure 2 lists cultural distance in terms of 1-2-3. We have already defined them when we introduced E-1 and E-2/3. 1 is monocultural while 2/3 is cross-cultural ministry. Different types of ministry are listed on the vertical column: evangelism (E), Christian nurture (N), and service (S). These terms are also used in figure 3:

The first part of figure 3 shows simple diffusion of innovation theory. A new idea or innovation (such as Christianity) is thought to start at the lower-left corner and move time wise toward the right. The innovation frequently starts slowly, goes through a period of rapid increase, and then may slow down again. Some persons are classified as "early adopters," some as "middle adopters," and some as "late adopters." As you can see, the cutoff point that separates early from middle adopters is loosely around 20 percent. In other words, by the time 10 to 20 percent of the persons of a group accept a new idea, enough momentum may well have been built up so that subsequent increases of acceptance will be rapid. Naturally no actual case would follow the line exactly—it is meant only to be conceptual.

Obviously, the gospel has to take root initially among any given people group by E-2/3 evangelism. And E-2/3 will be the predominant kind of evangelism through the first part of the early adopter period or while the people is initially and minimally reached. Presumably, those who become Christians will soon begin to witness and lead their friends and relatives to Christ, so

E-1 evangelism also appears. Almost all the Bible teaching and instruction in the basics of Christianity, however, will have to be done by N-2/3 at this stage.

By the time the second wave of early adopters comes along, E-1 evangelism will usually have become the most prominent. The common statement that "nationals can evangelize better than missionaries" is very apropos. Notice that E-2/3 drops

FIGURE 3

DIFFUSION OF INNOVATION THEORY

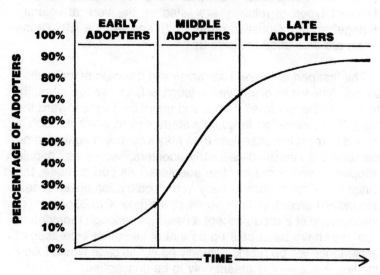

down the list. The role of the cross-cultural workers at this stage may become largely that of N-2/3 nurture, but N-1 also appears.

In the period of the middle adopters ("possibly reached peoples") the E-2/3 is gone. By then cross-cultural evangelists may have moved on to begin evangelizing some other people group. Some cross-cultural workers may still be needed for

FIGURE 4

DIFFUSION OF INNOVATION THEORY

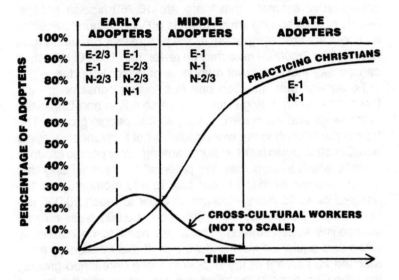

nurture, but most of the ministry is now done by the nationals using E-1 and N-1. When the people group is finally reached (20 percent practicing Christians) cross-cultural workers may play very few major roles, although maintaining a degree of intercultural ministry between reached groups is always healthy. For one thing, outsiders may continue to be useful for stimulating the formation of new missionary sending agencies.

EVANGELIZATION: THE REMAINING TASK

Now that the people approach to world evangelization has been defined, we need to look forward and try to measure as accurately as possible just what remains to be done. No one knows exactly how many peoples are currently living on planet earth. We are working with an estimate of 25,000 to 30,000. Some have said that we will triple or quadruple that number before the research is completed. They may be right. Even the term *people* is an analytical look, not a rigidly scientific category.

How many unreached people groups are there? No one can be really sure. The U.S. Center for World Mission has made a conservative estimate that there are 16,750 *hidden* groups, people groups among which there is no viable church. Precise numbers are not as important as the picture they present. There may well be 25,000. There may be fewer than 16,000. How then can we say that the exact number is of lesser importance?

To answer that question one has to first consider the difference between evangelizing over three billion non-Christians in the world and evangelizing, say, 20,000 people groups. The task of *the Church in the world today* is not to evangelize every non-Christian but to plant a church among every people group, a church, which in turn, has the potential for evangelizing that group. In other words, it is our task to add momentum to the *process* of world evangelization. In order to reach 20,000 unreached people groups we might need 100,000 cross-cultural evangelists (missionaries). These will need to be especially gifted and equipped men and women. If this missionary force reached 20 percent of the people in these unreached groups, then the Christians in those groups can get on with the task of gossiping the gospel to their neighbors.

Seeing the world as made up of people groups who have within themselves the potential to evangelize themselves, once a church is established, is a heartening idea. It puts the task of world evangelization in proper perspective.

WHERE DO WE BEGIN?

Which groups should we begin with? In the past we have usually thought of missionaries (cross-cultural evangelists) as men and women who crossed oceans, or at least national boundaries, to reach the lost. At one time in the 1800s that was a good definition of a missionary. No more. Today we find thousands of missionaries who are crossing cultural boundaries within their own countries. They seldom need permission of their governments to move about. They are used to living within the economic structure of their country. But like every missionary, they have to appreciate and learn the culture they are entering. Sometimes it will be members of a different language group (some countries have hundreds). Other times it will be a similar language but an entirely different socio-religious background.

The first answer to the question "Which groups should we begin with?" is to look at the unreached people groups within your own country and prayerfully consider how they can be reached. All around the world members of local churches are forming mission societies, setting apart some of their members in the tradition of Paul and Barnabas, to reach the unreached in their country.

But there are existing mission agencies who may also be asking the question, agencies that have perhaps been focusing most of their recent efforts on supporting existing churches, but who now want to move to untouched fields. Where should they look? They too need to look first within the countries where they are already working and then at types of people groups with which have been effective in the past. That is one of the values of this directory. It points to possible doorways that need to be opened.

Are we making progress? Since the last edition of *Unreached Peoples* many new mission groups have come into existence, particularly in non-Western countries. In addition, many Western agencies are setting specific goals to reach groups that have been newly identified.

We cannot be content with the status quo. If the *percentage* of professing Christians stays constant, the task of the Church will grow greater every year. Pray the Lord of the harvest to send workers into these harvest fields.

IMPLICATIONS
What are some implications of conceptualizing the remaining evangelistic task like this?

1. It helps God's people to see that the task is not impossible. The figure of 16,750 unreached peoples is a finite number. World evangelization *can* be accomplished. One slogan which

COWE might do well to adopt is "a growing cluster of churches for every people by the year 2000."

2. It impresses us with the continuing need for cross-cultural workers, usually called missionaries. During the seventies we became aware that all missionaries are not being sent by Western countries. The first worldwide survey of Third World missionaries, published by James Wong, Peter Larson, and Edward Pentecost in 1973, identified 2,971 Third World missionaries being sent out by 210 missionary societies. Larry Keyes of O.C. Ministries is currently updating this research under the supervision of the Strategy Working Group. His preliminary results show that there are now at least 8,634 Third World missionaries by actual count being sent out by 430 missionary societies. Asia represents 54 percent of the total, Africa 35 percent, Latin America 8 percent (almost all from Brazil), and Oceania 3 percent. Keyes estimates that it would not be unrealistic to speculate that the actual figure might be nearer to 20,000 Third World missionaries.

An increasing supply of E-2/3 workers, recruited from the churches of every nation, Western and Third World, will be needed to plant a growing cluster of churches among every hidden people by the end of the twentieth century. The age of more effective missions has just begun.

3. Cross-cultural missionaries do not need to win every individual member of a new people group to Christ. As we have seen, in many cases they will personally win relatively few. Most evangelism worldwide has been and will be done by E-1 evangelism—by people who naturally and freely reach out in love to friends and neighbors who share with them the feeling of having a common affinity with each other as one people. Yes, nationals can evangelize better than missionaries, but missionaries will still be needed to get the process started in each new group.

Edward R. Dayton is vice-president for Mission and Evangelism of World Vision International. His early career was in the aerospace industry. In 1967 he received an M.Div. degree from Fuller Theological Seminary. That same year he founded MARC (the Missions Advanced Research and Communication Center), and joined World Vision as director of MARC. He has written many books in the areas of management and missions. The most recent include *The Christian Executive, That Everyone May Hear,* and *Planning Strategies for World Evangelization.*

C. Peter Wagner is Professor of Church Growth at the Fuller Theological Seminary School of World Mission. He served as a missionary to Bolivia for fifteen years, after which he was vice-president of the Fuller Evangelistic Association.

He received the Ph.D. from the University of Southern California. He is a charter member and chairman of the Strategy Working Group of the Lausanne Committee for World Evangelization.

Books by Dr. Wagner include *Frontiers in Mission Strategy* (Moody Press) and *Your Church Can Grow* (Regal Books). He has contributed numerous articles and reviews to *Christianity Today, Eternity, Evangelical Missions Quarterly* and other periodicals.

Reaching South Korea's Rural Fifteen Million People

by Donald A. McGavran

Donald McGavran is the founding dean of the Fuller Theological Seminary School of World Mission in Pasadena, California. This article is an address he delivered to '80 World Evangelization Crusade, a major gathering of Korean pastors in August 1980. It is included as a first-class example of how to look at a specific population segment, in this case rural Koreans, with missiological sensitivity and practical foresight.

The great goal of this Crusade is: FIFTY TO EIGHTY PERCENT OF SOUTH KOREA CHRISTIANIZED BY 1984. This goal is possible. It has been reached in many nations. Today, in the nation of Zaire in the heart of Africa, a huge nation, with rich resources, out of every one hundred citizens, sixty-two are Christians. In Namibia, out of every one hundred, eighty-two are Christians. In the State of Mizoram in northeast India, out of every one hundred citizens, ninety are Christian. In these days, God has caused many whole nations to become Christian.

This goal is possible. God's Word has declared, "Turn to me and be saved, all the ends of the earth. For I am God and there is no other. To me every knee will bow, every tongue will swear allegiance" (Isa. 45:22). The Bible states clearly in Philippians 2 that God has conferred on Jesus the name which is supreme above every other; and that at the name of Jesus every knee will bow, of beings in heaven and of those on earth, and of those under the earth, and that every tongue will confess that Jesus Christ is Lord to the glory of God the Father.

What is the situation in South Korea? How much of South Korea has been Christianized? A few years ago authorities in this city were saying that 15 percent of Seoul was Christian. Today Koreans are saying that 20 or 25 or even 30 percent are Christian. We are probably safe in saying that a quarter of all people living in Seoul count themselves Christian. In the other big cities and towns in Korea the percentage is smaller. Perhaps 15 percent of them are Christian. But in the countryside, the small villages, and the long, twisting valleys leading up into the mountains, the fishing villages along the coast, and in the islands not more than *five in a hundred* are Christian.

The following diagram shows the situation. (See figure 1.) Its total of 5.5 million Christians is a conservative estimate. Some authorities say Korea has 6 million Christians. Others say 7 million. In either case we can all agree that much remains to be done. In the diagram note the urban block of 20 million and the rural block of 15 million. In the first are about 3.5 million Protestants and 1.1 million Catholics. In the rural block only 0.75 million are Christians of any sort. That leaves 15.4 million non-Christians in the cities and 14.25 million in the countryside.

In this article I am considering only the rural population. I am asking how to Christianize the 14.25 million rural population.

A very large part of the population of South Korea lives in the countryside. As long as it remains only 5 percent Christian, we cannot reach our goal of 50 percent to 80 percent of Korea Christianized by 1984. We must increase that 5 percent. Let us look carefully at the rural population.

1. How many people are we talking about? Government statistics show that about 13 million people earn their living by farming. To these must be added those who earn their living in the forests and mines. Then, there are more than 300 islands on

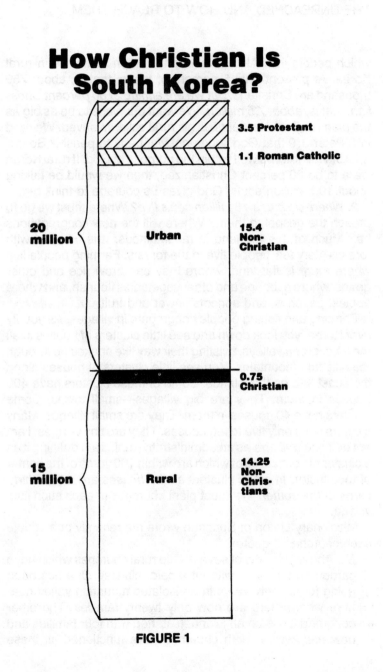

How Christian Is South Korea?

3.5 Protestant

1.1 Roman Catholic

20 million

Urban

15.4 Non-Christian

0.75 Christian

15 million

Rural

14.25 Non-Christians

FIGURE 1

which people live. All told, about 15 million souls live in rural Korea. At present only 5 percent of these, that is, about 750 thousand are Christians. *But we are aiming at 50 percent Christian, that is, about 7.5 million.* We want our plans to be as big as the plans of God. He wants all his rural children saved. We read in 2 Peter 3:9 that God "does not want any to perish." So our goal of 7.5 million is well within the purpose of God. If rural Korea were to be 80 percent Christianized, then we would be talking about 10.5 million souls. God gives us courage to think big!

2. Where do these 15 million souls live? Where must we go to preach the gospel to them? Where will the new congregations be? Much of this fair land is mountainous. It is covered with forests. Very few people live in the forests. Farming people live where there is flat land, where they can grow rice and other grains, where cabbage and other vegetables flourish, and where apples, peaches, and apricots flower and fruit.

Farming and fishing people congregate in villages. As you fly over Korea, you look down and see little clusters of houses in all the long, green valleys, twisting their way like snakes up through the hills and mountains. You see little clusters of houses along the coast and on the islands. Some of these clusters have 400 houses in them. They are big villages—small towns. Some clusters have 40 houses in them. They are small villages. Many clusters have only five to ten houses. They are tiny villages. I am not defining a *village* as an administrative unit. I am defining it as a cluster of houses, all of which are within 100 yards of the center of the cluster. In many clusters *all the houses are within thirty yards of the center.* We must plant churches in each such little village.

Missionary Linton of Sunchun wrote me recently of a couple such churches. I quote:

Mr. Ahn and I know of several little rural churches which have carried on for years without a paid minister. One has been going for seventy years in an isolated mountain valley near here where there are now only twenty families. The other congregation is on an island. It started with four families and now has twelve. Both churches have functioned all these years despite persecution. Both have produced church leaders.

Splendid. Now let us think of thousands of such small communities. As we have been multiplying congregations in our great cities, we have thought of fully self-supporting churches in terms of 100 or 200 or 500 families. Such churches will never be established in rural Korea. We must think in terms of gathering Christians in the actual villages of our land. *Most of these are rather small clusters of houses.*

When I was in Korea a few years ago my host drove along a rough road winding its way up a narrow fertile valley. We stopped at a small church in a cluster of thirty houses. Across the stream, perhaps 200 yards away, was a cluster of fourteen houses. I asked, "How many members of this congregation come from that village?" "None," was the answer. "All the members of this church live on this side of the stream." Our plans for Korea must not stop "this side of the stream." We must Christianize both sides of the stream. We must Christianize villages of thirty houses and villages of fourteen. Of course, we must have churches in large rural centers, but we must also have cells of worshiping Christians in tens of thousands of small villages. We must have worshiping centers within 100 yards and preferably within thirty yards of every front door. This is what it means for 50 to 80 percent of South Korea to be Christianized.

But let me get back to the question I am asking: Where do these 15 million live? They live in clusters of houses. This is where we must go if we are to evangelize them. These natural villages are where the new Christians will gather to read God's holy Word, sing praises to him, pour out their hearts in prayer, and partake of the bread and the wine. We want to have *a worshiping group of Christians in 50 to 80 percent of the natural villages of Korea.*

3. So we must ask, "How many such clusters of houses are there?" We are *not* asking how many big villages are there. We are asking how many clusters of homes are there, where every home is within one hundred yards of its center—where Christians will gather to worship God. How many *such* clusters are there? No one has made this kind of a survey. So there is no firm and correct answer to our question. But we can do a rough calculation. We know there are 15 million men and women, boys and girls in this huge rural population. Perhaps 5 million live in big villages of about 100 houses, 7 million in small villages of about 40 houses, and 3 million in tiny villages of about 10 houses. Since about five souls live in each house, in a village of 100 houses are 500 souls. Consequently the 5 million would be living in 10,000 big villages, the 7 million in about 35,000 small villages, and the 3 million would be living in 60,000 tiny villages. *All told, there would be about 100 thousand villages.*

I would not quarrel with anyone who estimated the number of villages higher or lower. The Government talks about 60 thousand "natural villages." But as we press on toward our goal of Christianizing 50 to 80 percent of South Korea by 1984, let us use the figure of 100 thousand villages. This round number is easy to handle and as correct as any other we could propose.

4. Since our goal is to Christianize 50 to 80 percent of the rural population, *we must put a worshiping group of believing, baptized Christians in 50 to 80 percent of 100 thousand villages.* We can now define our goal more exactly. We want worshiping groups of Christians in 50 thousand to 80 thousand clusters of homes—villages—in rural Korea. That is a very different goal from multiplying churches in our towns and cities; but it is a worthy goal and one which God wants us to attempt. He loves rural people. Remember, our Lord himself grew up, not in a big city, not in Seoul, but in a little hill village. Another way of stating our goal is this: *Let us put a Bible-reading, Bible-loving, Bible-obeying congregation–maybe as small as ten persons–within 100 yards of all rural residences in South Korea.*

5. *Now we turn from houses to kinship webs.* You can see the houses, but the kinship webs you cannot see. They are, nevertheless, very real. This cluster of houses is made up of people all of one clan, one kinship web. They believe they are descended from a common ancestor. It used to be that way in Scotland where my ancestors resided. All the McGavrans lived in one valley in small villages. The Campbells lived in other

villages and other valleys. This is like what I see in rural Korea. In this cluster of houses live people of one kinship web. In that live people of another. In large villages there may be people of several kinship webs—but everyone knows to which extended family he belongs! McGavrans never thought they were Campbells.

Why do I mention kinship webs? Because every web presents a new problem in Christianization. Mr. Linton of Sunchan writes, "It is hard to reach men in another clan if the leaders of the church are all from one clan." We read in Acts that in the beginning very few priests became Christian. Levites, you see, were of a different clan from Judah and Benjamin. Acts 6: 7 says a great many Levites suddenly became Christian. A new kinship web had been won to Christ. In rural Korea many new kinship webs must be won. Discipling is not only winning new houses, but also winning new clans. To Christianize hundreds of winding valleys we must enter both physical doors *and social doors.* We must disciple hundreds of new clans, new extended families. That challenging task is more necessary in rural populations than in urban, for in cities kinship webs are not as distinct and binding as they are in villages.

6. Now that we see the task clearly, *how are we going to do it?* Let me suggest three resources. You will, I am sure, think of others. The Lord's hand is not shortened. The Holy Spirit himself is impelling us to this evangelization. He will provide. When David went out against Goliath, God gave him five small, smooth stones. God will give us what we need. But let us look at three resources.

First, we have very large numbers of soldiers in the magnificent Korean army who have, during the last five to ten years, become Christians. They own Bibles. Probably a third or more of them have come from the villages we have been talking about and are members of those clans. When *they* are discharged from the army, they can go back to their home villages and their loved ones and lead a whole group to Christ. In most villages the returned soldiers will find no Christians. In some they will find a few who walk two or ten kilometers to worship with a congregation in a small town or large central village. *What will the returned soldier do?*

In many cases, his parents will make arrangements for his marriage. His bride will be a non-Christian, and the wedding will take place by Buddhist or traditional rituals. Then what will the Christian soldier do? Some will move to a city. Some will settle down in a non-Christian community with a non-Christian wife, and adjust to a community from which "no one has ever become a Christian." What a tremendous opportunity for the spread of the gospel! Suppose that immediately, in every regiment of the Army, special classes of instruction were instituted. In these would be assembled those Christian soldiers who were within six months of honorable discharge. They would be taught how to begin house churches, how to win other members of one's family, how to appoint an elder for each new cell of Christians, how to study the Bible, worship God, win every member of that particular clan, how to win the new wife to Christian faith, and through her to win her family in a nearby cluster of houses.

Furthermore, suppose that all the existing congregations in that particular section of the countryside were to appoint two vigorous deacons to visit all clusters of homes within 15 kilometers, look up the discharged soldiers, encourage them to start house churches, worshiping groups of local Christians, sister congregations.

The deacons would find that some returned soldiers would already have started small churches. Others would have lapsed back into non-Christian faith. Others would be delighted to be visited and could be launched into effective evangelism of the isolated distant villages. The possibilities are fascinating. The returned soldiers are a great new resource.

Second, we have about 750 thousand rural Christians—of all denominations. Many of these are primary school or high school teachers. Some are businessmen. Among 750 thousand Christians are thousands of dedicated lay leaders who, once they catch the vision, will be a great power in God's hands to Christianize the countryside. Rural Christians now worship in about six thousand congregations in small towns and large villages.

These Christians and congregations can help achieve our goal of 50 to 80 percent of South Korea Christianized by December 31, 1984. But to do this, rural churches must be led to believe that in a cluster of thirty-seven houses, twenty families can become Christians in a single group. Out of that cluster of eight houses, eight whole families can become Christians together. Baptisms of 50 men and women on a single day should become common. Our goal of "50 percent Christian by 1984" necessitates many group decisions for Christ.

Existing congregations in the countryside, from east to west and north to south, will begin to look with new eyes on clusters of houses. Some of these are nearby. Some are far away up in the mountains. But all are potential cells of Christians, worshiping God and counting the Bible as their rule of faith and practice.

All cannot be led by fully paid and highly trained pastors. That is impossible. But all can be led—as the congregations in the New Testament Church were—by serious-minded, unpaid elders, who will gather the brothers and sisters for worship at regular times, and will care for the flock. The Full Gospel Church of Yoido Island, Seoul, has more than four thousand such cells (such house churches, such worshiping groups) led by *unpaid* devout men and women. Dr. Yonggi Cho says that women make excellent leaders of such groups. Rural South Korea has multitudes of Christian men and women who are able to read. The Bible in rural Korea will become, as it did in England and Scotland, the best known book, and a transforming power.

Can such Christian cells thrive under local unpaid elders? Yes they can. Such cells are functioning in many parts of the world. They functioned splendidly in New Testament times. Just read the Book of Acts.

The church in many countries faces exactly the same problems you face in rural South Korea and solves them in various ways: two or three levels of paid leaders, entirely unpaid leaders, circuit pastors, plus strong local leaders. In John Nevius's time, the church in the Shantung peninsula consisted in sixty very small congregations of about ten members each in sixty villages. These were led by unpaid local men. Three paid and ordained men supervised the sixty. One had twenty, one thirty, and one ten in his care. The church of Jesus Christ uses many models for caring for the flock. Under each, Christian cells thrive and multiply.

In China during the last twenty years Christian cells have multiplied exceedingly. The Communist government has been deadly against organized churches: so the Holy Spirit has multiplied house churches by the tens of thousands. Christians have not been able to buy printed Bibles, so they have, by hand, copied out Romans, and Mark, and John, and read from these copies of God's Word. Do not, I beg of you, let the question of what model is best for your denomination in your land at this time bother you. God is sovereign. He uses many models, provided only that each is faithful to the Bible and to the Lord.

A *third* and very great resource is the urban church. Thousands of strong urban congregations led by highly trained dedicated pastors giving full time to their work are a tremendous resource. These are the congregations and leaders which have transformed urban Korea into a largely Christian land. There are probably *seventeen thousand such urban congregations.*

Let us suppose that each urban congregation would covenant before God to plant five village congregations before 1984. One new congregation this year, one in 1981, one in 1982, one in 1983, and one in 1984.

Let us suppose that a national headquarters were to be set up, and by consulting with it, any urban congregation could obtain the name of one cluster of homes in South Korea. The cluster might have ten homes in it, or 100. It makes no difference. Each congregation would then pour out prayer for the conversion of that whole cluster of houses. Each congregation would send a team of specially gifted lay people to that village, no matter how far away. Special meetings would be held there. Leaders of the village would be invited to come to the city church as honored guests and there hear what Christ has done for its members. Literature would be distributed. Christian ex-soldiers living in that village would be regarded as special friends. Inquirers would be enrolled and led on to baptism. A worshiping group would be organized. Delegates from that new, little church would be invited, at the expense of the fathering congregation, to attend the annual meeting of the denomination.

The new churches in each valley or region would be encouraged to hold an annual church festival and revival meeting. South Korea could be divided into perhaps 700 regions. Strong urban churches would see that revival meetings were held in each of these 700 regions each year.

Furthermore, each new congregation would have excellent contacts with several nearby small villages. The congregations started in 1980 would be encouraged to give birth to daughter congregations:

> If we from the city 100 kilometers away can evangelize you, you can certainly plant another Christian cell, a branch church, or a full church in a cluster of homes two kilometers from where you live.

It is impossible for anyone from the outside to draw up an accurate picture of how the 15 million souls in rural Korea are to be discipled and incorporated into Christian cells, Bible study groups, and congregations of Jesus Christ. Indeed, it would be difficult for any of you in this big city to do it for all of South Korea. But the idea I have been laying before you is sound. Forgive, please, any mistakes I have made. And then *covenant with God that,* directed by him and impelled by the Holy Spirit, *you will cooperate with all other Christians in South Korea to evangelize Korea's rural multitudes.* Find out where they live. Go where they are. Tell them of the Savior. Sell them Bibles and New Testaments. Multiply Christian cells, congregations of ten to a hundred members. That is the great goal of all witness, all evangelism, all sharing the gospel, all selling of tracts. Till we get multitudes of new churches, evangelism is incomplete. Multiply churches in rural Korea.

Donald McGavran has served as a missionary to India for thirty-six years under the United Christian Missionary Society. He has taught missions in the United States since 1957 and was the founding dean of the School of World Mission and Institute of

THE UNREACHED AND HOW TO REACH THEM

Church Growth of Fuller Theological Seminary in Pasadena, California. Dr. McGavran has a B.D. from Yale Divinity School and a Ph.D. from Teachers College, Columbia University. He is the father of the Church Growth Movement. Several visits to Korea and numerous studies of this country and its peoples have contributed to this article.

Evangelizing China

by Christopher Morris

Certainly one of the greatest challenges to the gospel today is the nation of China. Much prayer has been focused on this country, and it has intensified as new opportunities have developed.

Christopher Morris urges a comprehensive approach to this great task, one that takes into consideration historical, cultural, political, and religious factors. He explores the pitfalls of simplistic solutions and calls for more thorough research. He also stresses the need for preparation in accord with God's timetable. He reasserts that no one evangelism strategy will work for all of China, since specific people groups must be addressed with strategies tailored to their needs. As information and opportunities grow, modifications will be required.

This should be a model for the kinds of missiological issues that must be squarely faced as Christians strategize for reaching the unreached.

Before evangelizing China can validly move into action, much work needs to be done. This call for proper preparation echoes the recommendations of missionary giants who pioneered evangelization of China over the past 400 years. But it has rarely been heeded by the majority of Christians burdened for China's millions. The result has been one of the most conspicuous missionary failures in mission history.

Today, a wave of excitement has swept through Christian and missionary circles, as the door of China seems to be opening. But in light of the dismal lack of preparation over the last thirty years, the prospects for evangelizing China today are gloomy. Indeed, the most blatant and widely acknowledged errors of nineteenth-century Protestant missionary work in China are being repeated by zealous individuals and respected missions alike today.

Many are asking, "What should we do?" This article proposes three phases of work as a valid answer: First, understanding China and its people. Second, understanding Chinese Christians. Third, understanding the basis for China evangelism by outsiders today. A discussion of these issues will be followed by a specific look at the problem of evangelizing China's minorities, as a case example.

UNDERSTANDING CHINA AND ITS PEOPLES

The millions of China are not one homogenous group. The divisions of Chinese society, now estimated by some to have passed one billion people,[3] are many. Here we will look at just five groups, whose distinctions are highly significant for evangelistic preparations. In a later section, we will look briefly at China's ethnic minorities.

Five Divisions of Chinese Society

Those over forty years of age, who grew up in China's pre-Communist society, make up one group in Chinese society. These may be 200 million of China's people. Many of them had contact with Christians and Christian ideas before "liberation" in 1949. They were the first targets of Communist efforts to re-shape Chinese world views. Today, the understanding of Christianity by this segment is generally confused and inaccurate. Yet they often have a lingering respect for Christianity, perhaps because of mission-school memories or because they admire the advanced state of Western countries.

In contrast is the very small but most influential group of government and party cadres. These approximately 50 million power holders treat religion as a threat to their own authority. Although they claim to be altruistic in "serving the people," in actual practice they have adopted many traditional characteristics of Confucian corruption. Evangelizing them is extremely difficult, and probably impossible by Chinese Christians of lower ranks. But conversions among them could have far-reaching effects.

Another group includes farmers and their families. Their standard of living remains practically the same as before "liberation," the difference being that natural disasters are no longer followed by famine. Poorly educated, but increasingly literate (perhaps 90 percent),[4] their goals are to acquire the basic comforts of life—such as a bicycle, sewing machine, and radio. Most Christians in China today are in this group. Thus, the vast majority of China's population is in fact already within an E-1[5] distance from the gospel!

Urban factory workers make up a fourth group. They have steady work and are paid in cash. Better educated and more politically conscious, these people are being caught up in the materialism of China's current Four Modernizations program for economic development. There are Christians among them, but with limited freedom to proclaim the gospel. However, as urban workers, they are open to outside influence.

A fifth group may be categorized as upper-level students, (those in secondary schools and universities). They are mostly urban, and have always played an important role in shaping popular opinion in China. These 66 million young intellectuals form the base of creative thinking in China, of unrest and dissent, and of disillusionment with their government's performance. They are most impressed with success, and with science and technology. Despite their claims to independent thinking, the Marxist ideas drilled into them since birth form an unconscious conceptual framework. Their understanding of religion is poor or nonexistent, making the evangelistic task formidable. Students in China's universities and those being sent abroad to study are under heavy pressure to maintain their Marxist loyalties. Like the party cadres, the number of students in China is relatively small, but has great influence and potential. And unlike the cadres, many in this group are discontented with the status quo. They should be a special object for evangelism.

The more we can learn about these groups and their subdivisions, the more concretely we can evaluate their distance from conversion, the extent of Christian presence among them, and their potential receptivity to evangelism. Thus, intensive study is a prerequisite to making specifically tailored evangelistic plans.[6]

National Religious Policy Developments
Effective plans for evangelism cannot be made in a vacuum. In China, the religious policies of the government are all important. From the mid-1960s until Mao's death in 1976, the government's religious policy was one of oppressive intolerance. The attacks of the cultural revolution on Christian believers and structures are well-known. But since 1977, this policy has dramatically changed.

In 1978, a number of religious activists, including Protestant pastors imprisoned since 1958, were released. Hundreds of others were restored to full citizenship. A World Religious Research Institute was opened in Peking and held two conferences to discuss the Marxist view of religion. Reports and rumors of churches, mosques, and temples being refurbished and about to open were rife.

On January 1, 1979, the long-closed Nanking Theological Seminary was incorporated into Nanking University as a Center for Religious Studies. It resumed work on a new version of the Bible under the direction of Rev. Ding Guanxun (K. H. Ting). In early 1979, the old United Front Work Department was restored to supervise minority, religious, and overseas Chinese affairs. (The department had been defunct since 1964, and its religious and overseas Chinese work was handled by the Foreign Office in a very limited way.) The UFW Department in turn restored the

Religious Affairs Bureau, and the various associations under it for administering the major religions in China, with the Three-Self Patriotic Movement for Protestants. The Religious Affairs Bureau assembled leading figureheads of China's religions for local and then national conferences in early 1979. Following these conferences, articles were published in Chinese newspapers stating the government's new religious policy.

The main points of this policy were that religious beliefs are categorized in two levels, each of which are to be handled differently. In the higher level are the major religions (Buddhism, Lamaism, Islam, Catholicism, Protestantism, and sometimes Taoism), now given a special toleration under government control. On the lower level are "superstitions," of which the harmless ones are to be eliminated through persuasion, while harmful ones are outlawed.

At the same time, the classic Marxist explanation of religions still defines them as erroneous responses of man to nature, and as tools used by exploiting classes to pacify and control the masses of people. With the progress of science and education, Marxists believe that religions will all die away sooner or later.

In July 1979, China's new law codes were publically announced. Aside from the constitutional provision of freedom of belief for Chinese citizens, the criminal code penalizes officials who infringe on people's normal religious practices. Outlawed, improper religious practices are also spelled out. However, the law leaves many loopholes which could be stretched by anti-religious officials to oppress believers, and the prescribed sentences are generally heavy. Trials held so far under these codes have been irregular by normal legal standards, with heavy sentences imposed.

In August 1979, a new Catholic bishop was elected in Peking, unrecognized by the Vatican. Suddenly in September and October, churches were opened in Shanghai and other cities to overflow crowds of worshippers. Meanwhile, Buddhists were again receiving foreign guests. A large Chinese delegation was sent to the United States for an international religious conference. Hundreds of Muslim mosques were reopened. Koran and

Buddhist scriptures were to be reprinted. Buddhist temples and pilgrimage sites were reopened, staffed with token monks.

This change of religious policy has enabled outside Christians to do some E-3 evangelism in China, although not with the approval of China's government. Much more importantly, it enables Chinese Christians to come out of their rural house groups or lonely urban rooms and reestablish fellowship with other believers through the open churches. The stage is being set for a great movement of E-1 evangelism in China, which has a mind-boggling potential in comparison with E-2 or E-3 work by overseas Chinese or foreign Christians.

UNDERSTANDING CHINESE CHRISTIANS
Thus far, lay Christians in China have been extremely cautious in their response to these changes in China's religious policy. This may reflect the gradual implementation of these changes, which may take years before their final shape becomes definite. Also, Chinese Christians may be reluctant to change their present forms of fellowship and worship, forged from decades of hard experiences under a frequently oppressive regime. Many Christians are now participating in both the official churches and in their house groups.

To avoid detection, these house groups have become congruent with or diffused through other social groups in China—such as families, schoolmates, workmates, etc. Although the number and size of these groups varies from place to place and time to time, the content of their fellowship remains fairly constant: prayer, testimonies, Bible study, preaching, and singing. Offerings are infrequent, and baptisms and Communion are rare because of the traditional requirement that they can only be performed by ordained ministers. Most ministers have been removed from such roles for at least twenty years in China.

Positive Evidences of Evangelism in China
Evangelism with resulting conversions has become a way of life for many Chinese believers. Evangelism sometimes follows the socially accepted lines of relationships. For some it is a way of

life expressed by their living authentic Christian lives and becoming known for their honesty, hard work, and joy. When these Christians can then become production leaders, they are looked to as counselors in their communities.

Christian groups are sometimes called on for help by relatives of the sick or demon-possessed. When the problem is solved through persistent, fervent prayer by the Christian group, new believers are added to the church.

During times of suffering as a result of government antireligious movements, making the issue of their suffering clear has been a special form of witnessing, a testimony that lives on in the memories of those who saw it.

In prison, Christians' diffused forms of witnessing and exemplary conduct continue to arouse interest and gain conversions.

Weddings, funerals, and even visiting the sick are used by some Christians as opportunities for public proclamation of their faith. To observe Christians in their public singing, recitation of Bible verses, prayers, and spiritual joy is for many their first encounter with the reality of Christian faith.

Moving moments of forgiveness as Christians encounter those who betrayed them, and restoration to faith of those who had renounced their beliefs are also ways in which the church in China continues to grow. These are poignant examples of E-1 evangelism.

Negative Influences upon Evangelism

However, all is not victorious heroics for Christians in China. The severe government pressure against religious beliefs and practices in the past has taken a very high toll. These campaigns were conducted in an ambiguous, compromising manner, which eliminated the possibility of religious martyrs emerging who could rally opposition. The campaigns generally resulted in a tremendous loss of face and viability for believers, and the number of those who renounced their faith and denounced other believers was substantial. It created bitterness that could last for generations.

The closing of theological training institutions since 1958 has resulted in a loss of theological awareness today in China. This has had disastrous repercussions for Christian apologetics, for evangelism among China's educated and social leadership for the spiritual virility of Christians, and for the development of visionary Christian leaders. The result has been a serious narrowing of the horizons of Chinese Christians. They lack the richness of interaction with other ideologies and of expression through the symbols of baptism and communion. Their spirituality is strong and refined, but also narrow and brittle.

Another great weakness is the isolation of Christians in China. The generally antiforeign political attitude, plus strict severance with foreign counterparts has put Chinese Christians into a remarkably opaque isolation. In northern Chinese cities Christians who have not dared to see another Christian or say an audible word about their faith for twenty years are not uncommon. That house groups inquired if there were any Christians in Hong Kong or elsewhere in the world is a documented fact. However, this Elijah complex is being dispelled by the opening of official churches in Chinese cities, and by the growing contacts of house group members with outside visitors and information.

These house group Christians, then, are able to do E-1 evangelism in China. They are widely scattered throughout Chinese society, making their potential for evangelistic impact much greater than previously thought. Furthermore, they have experienced the full history of China's Communist government.[7] Their ability to understand the situation, to communicate and empathize with non-Christians in China is unparalleled by any outsiders.

In thinking about the role of Christians coming from outside China, an obvious prerequisite for their work is to adopt the strengths that these Chinese Christians have developed, and to understand their weaknesses as areas in which they may need to be ministered to.[8] Understanding, supporting, and working through this existing group of Chinese Christians to do as much E-1 evangelism as possible is the obvious strategy to develop and promote.

UNDERSTANDING THE BASIS FOR EVANGELISTIC WORK IN CHINA TODAY

When one thinks of possible E-2 and E-3 evangelistic methods for China one might list these tactics:

- evangelizing overseas Chinese and sending them to China
- sending Christian tourists and professionals to China to take literature and do personal work
- writing literature and radio programs for China
- sending literature or personal workers clandestinely
- radio broadcasting
- studying China for increased understanding of its people, their ways, and needs
- praying
- evangelizing Chinese students abroad.

Choosing which programs to implement usually depends on which doors are open and what can be supported financially. During times of relative openness between China and "sending" countries, most of the programs listed are realistic options. During times of political pressure, however, prayer remains as the major item.

But this list of possible tactics ignores two important realities: First, that there is a definite order of logical priority in these options. Second, that building comprehensive strategies is necessary for doing effective work. An example of the first reality is in order here: Literature for China must be written before it can be sent into the country. And prior to that, planners and writers must have been deeply involved in China studies.

In early 1979 when the door for sending literature into China was open, no appropriate literature was available! Materials written for Hong Kong and Taiwan Chinese were sent, in spite of the fact that these were not prepared for Marxist China. Ironically, the necessary study and writing—which could have been done at any time, no matter what the situation in China—was not done. This work had not been funded, probably because its importance was not understood and not communicated by Christian organizations; or because they were waiting until doors for evangelism opened in China to generate donations. In either case, there has been no serious commitment by outside organizations to preparation.

The second reality is the importance of making comprehensive strategies. This can begin with identifying the people group in China to whom the gospel is to be presented, learning about their aspiration, and their needs, and discovering how to communicate most effectively with them. In addition, principles for evangelistic approaches to them by outsiders must be worked out, because of China's unique political situation. Otherwise, all efforts for China could seriously backfire.

Implications of the Sovereignty Principle

The basis of these operating principles lies in two facts of sovereignty: first, the sovereignty of God over historical developments; and second, the sovereignty of China over its people and their quests.[9] Holding these in balance means doing the work in accordance with the Chinese government and people, rather than in spite of them, and observing God's timetable for evangelism. Ignoring this balance is what led nineteenth-century missions to repeatedly violate Chinese laws and treaty terms, which was perhaps the basic historical reason for their total expulsion in 1951. Judging by many of today's activities and publications nearly thirty years of this forced moratorium has brought few observable reforms in mission thinking about China.

In practical terms, maintaining this balance means that when research on China from the outside is all that can be done, then in accord with God's sovereignty, we should enthusiastically be doing research. When basic training of Chinese scholars is all that can be done, then Christian colleges should have Chinese studies programs and be feeding Christians into graduate China studies. This should be sponsored by missions, churches, and educators who take God's sovereignty seriously when China's sovereignty permits no other activities. When it becomes possible to make contacts with religious representatives in China, but literature distribution or evangelism are still frowned upon by Chinese officials, then Christians from outside China should be making contacts, and encouraging the development of religious freedom, but not distributing literature or doing evangelism on their visits. When outsiders are given increased freedom to go into China, then they should go and do as much as they can to spread the gospel, but always respecting China's sovereignty.

Because outside Christians failed to observe these sovereignties over the last thirty years, today we have virtually no Christian China scholars, no inter-mission China study center, no appropriate literature ready, no trained personnel to make contacts in China, and not even any commonly recognized set of principles to guide those who want to do evangelistic work there. As China relaxes her sovereignty by the sovereignty of the Lord, the Christian world is ill-prepared to take up the opportunities, or even to understand them realistically.

Operating Principles
Based on these two principles of sovereignty, several other operating principles become evident. The first is to work with, rather than in spite of, Christians in China. This requires of those who hope to minister in China a period of learning at the feet of those who have undergone the baptism of suffering in China.

The second principle is for long-term commitment to preparation: the training of Christian China scholars; of specialized personnel for radio, literature, and training ministries; and of Chinese Christians for eventual work inside China, including solid theological training in Third World countries. This also means development of an appropriate apologetic, of theological, doctrinal, pre-evangelistic, evangelistic, and Christian growth materials.

The third operating principle is to become familiar with China's legal and religious policies, and to develop plans in harmony with these.

A fourth is to avoid the perpetration of partisanship, both along denominational and organizational lines. An inter-mission approach in both ministering to Chinese Christians and evangelizing Chinese non-Christians is needed in order to maintain the credibility of Christianity as a viable alternative to Marxism.

Analysis-based Evangelism
Finally, we come to concrete evangelism methods. Referring to the tactics listed at the beginning of this section (Understanding the Basis), the lack of focus and direction is immediately obvious. The focus and direction for specific planning today must stem from a growing analysis of China, of the unreached groups and their needs, of the needs of Christians there, and of appropriate operating principles. Obviously, no one set of evangelistic tactics will have permanent validity for China. Such tactics must change as China herself changes. However, as one example of how this process of basing evangelism on analysis might work, what follows is a study of Chinese ethnic minorities.

BASIC QUESTIONS ABOUT CHINESE MINORITIES AND WAYS TO REACH THEM

There are at least four basic questions to ask about China's minorities. The first is "Who are they, and how many of them are there?"

This question is difficult to answer because of lacking data and firsthand studies. The 1953 census in China listed fifty-three minorities, ranging in population from 600 to nearly 8 million. Total minorities in 1953 was estimated at 35 million, or 6 percent of China's total population of 580 million. A "registration" in 1957, and another census in 1964 was made but no statistics released. With China's population passing one billion in 1978, doubling the 1953 figures for minorities should give an acceptable working figure for 1980.

The official list of minorities includes only culturally distinct minorities, not dialect minorities—such as, the Hakkas of Guangdong Province and Taiwan, or the Wu Swatow, the Fukienese, and other primarily dialect groups. Also, not included in the list are minority social-class groups—such as, petty capitalists and businessmen—whose affairs are also handled by the revived United Front Department.

A second question is "What is the Chinese government's policy toward minorities?" Along with the government's religious policy, its minorities policy has undergone a dramatic reversal in the last few years. From the censure of any ideological variants during the Gang-of-Four days, the reestablishment of the United Front Department has meant a renewed emphasis on minority welfare. To the outside observer this is most evident in Chinese publications, where articles on minorities have shifted from occasional references to principal topics of every issue.

This increased attention has meant the revival of minority religious practices, the restoration of minority spiritual leaders, and the reopening of their worship places. Minority customs, often related to their religions, are also being permitted. The press is full of accounts of how these were violated during the Gang-of-Four era. From an attitude of forcing minorities into a Maoist mold, the government is now paternalistically protecting them from other outside influences, while it more gently persuades them to support its Four Modernizations plans as being in their own interests.

The third question is "What evangelistic work among minorities has already been done?" This is a question that requires extensive archival research to answer. Missionary work among Mongolians, for example, started very early. The China Inland Mission worked among minorities in southern China for only some twenty years before "liberation." Scriptures were translated, schools established, converts gathered, and churches started. The work among some groups had amazing breakthroughs, but these only came after years of effort.

For many minorities the breakthroughs never came, and for most minorities the work was never begun. Only twenty of the fifty-odd minority languages were written down before "liberation." But the old school courses, Scripture translations, cultural notes and other pertinent records could still be used in planning evangelistic approaches and materials. Doing field research today is impossible, of course. So gathering the fragments of what has already been done is of chief importance.

The fourth question is "What are the present and future prospects of evangelizing China's minorities?" Obviously, these minorities are at differing distances from the gospel. Some already have Christian believers among them, making them an

E-1 people to such as the Lisu or the Koreans. These groups also have a tradition of Christian training and church life in their memories, and have Christian books in their own languages.

Other minorities had missionary work done among them, but did not respond. At least one case is known where a minority New Testament was completed abroad after the missionaries were forced to leave China. The manuscript was miraculously preserved, but has never been published or broadcast. Although response among this minority was limited, making E-1 evangelism impossible, such materials are available for use in E-2 or E-3 projects.

Most of the minorities, particularly the smaller ones, have never been touched with the gospel. With E-1 evangelism impossible, some of their cultures are so unique that even their closest Christian neighbors are at an E-3 distance. Complicating the picture is the government policy concerning minorities, making it practically impossible for any known Christians to contact them. Their languages are not even known for use on Christian radio programs. Conversions of individuals would be frowned upon or forbidden by the government.

China's minorities are receiving a lot of interest among Christians, but the fact is that they represent only some 6 percent of China's one billion people. To turn China's minorities into a separate priority item in thinking about evangelizing China would be to ignore this statistic. The priorities must be kept clear, as presented earlier in the section on Understanding the Basis for Evangelistic Work in China Today.

Giving attention to China's minorities falls within these priorities. By all means, it is important to be understanding of the situation among minorities; to know what, if any, missionary work was done among them. It is equally important to understand the situation of the Christians among these minorities, to formulate the basis for evangelism among them, and to design tactics for evangelistic action. But to make the minorities into a people target separate from the goals of nurturing Christians in China (including those in minority groups) and from evangelizing non-Christians (including those in minority groups) would be to emphasize the minorities at the expense of evangelizing 94 percent of China's people.

IN SUMMARY

The goal of evangelizing China presents a formidable challenge with small prospects for success unless the task of being prepared is taken seriously by organizations burdened by China's need for the gospel. The requirements for adequate preparation are gigantic but attainable.

"What shall we do about evangelizing China?" is a major issue in modern missions. To develop valid answers an inter-mission approach to research and analysis is a requisite if the blatant bungling and generally recognized errors from the annals of China's mission history are not to be repeated.

Focusing and directing the evangelization task, along with ministering to the Chinese Christians, calls for a variety of strategies suited to the major and the minor segments of Chinese society. It calls for tactics flexible enough to change with a changing China, whose need to know the changeless God and the unchanging good news of the gospel has never been greater.

Christopher Morris is assistant to the director of the Chinese Church Research Center, in Hong Kong. After graduating from Wheaton College, he earned his master's degree in Chinese philosophy and religion at the University of Hawaii. He joined the Center soon after it was founded in 1978. As head of the Center's English Department, he is managing editor of the bimonthly *China and the Church Today* and the widely distributed *China Prayer Letter*.

Reflections on Thailand's Unreached Peoples

by Alex Smith

Although evangelism strategy is best developed by focusing on particular people groups, it helps to occasionally step back and see the larger context in which these groups live. In this article, Alex Smith presents an overview of the unreached peoples of Thailand and applies missiological principles for church growth. His insights speak to missions in Asia as well as in other parts of the world, particularly when he emphasizes that the Church must act quickly in the case of a responsive people group, for this responsiveness to the gospel may not last for long.

Two thousand years ago Jesus said to his disciples, "Do you not say, 'Four months more and then the harvest'? I tell you, open your eyes and look at the fields! They are ripe for harvest. Even now the reaper draws his wages, even now he harvests the crop for eternal life, so that the sower and the reaper may be glad together" (John 4: 35-36, NIV).

This same challenge faces the Church worldwide in the 1980s (Matthew 28: 18-20). Many unreached peoples, like those in Thailand, are ripe for the harvests. Alert harvesters are needed.

THREE CRUCIAL OBSERVATIONS

The term *unreached peoples* refers to those units of population who hold common characteristics and whose practicing Christians are less than 20 percent of that population. The numbers of unreached peoples today are immense. The vast task of evangelization requires our proclaiming Christ and discipling these peoples. Like the apostle Peter, Christians must offer all unreached peoples both the saving name and the helping hand (Acts 4). But discernment is vital in observing and strategizing ways to evangelize the unreached.

First, among the multitude of unreached peoples are large sections that for one reason or another are unreachable except by radio or other similar means. Some peoples are closed off by political barriers, others by social hindrances. But in Thailand, phenomenal freedom still exists to proclaim the gospel to all the unreached. All Thai peoples are presently reachable. None are barred.

Second, receptivity among the various peoples of Thailand's 47-million population differs from people to people. For example, some, like the Karen, are most responsive. Others, such as the Thai Islam, are more resistant.

This matter of receptivity to the gospel is a relative thing. Therefore, it is appropriate to consider David Liao's question as it relates to the many unreached populations in Thailand: "Are the unreached in Thailand resistant because they are unresponsive? Or, because they are neglected?" The answer cannot be known until the Church has effectively proclaimed Christ to all peoples. To neglect this responsibility in Thailand's open door of the present is to reap disappointment and judgment tomorrow.

Third, Thailand's unreached peoples present a great urgency for mission. The swift change of events in the countries of southeast Asia must not deter the Christian mission, particularly while Thailand—strategically straddling the harness of southeast Asia, remains a bastion of freedom. Her doors are, at this writing, wide open; but may be closed at any time by adversaries standing at the portals of this nation which has for centuries retained her sovereignty. Like other nations, the peoples of

Thailand are in the throes of pressing economic, political, and social challenges which may be ingredients in producing dynamics fitting for a movement toward Christ.

Here, indeed, is an urgent harvest, even as philosophies of literal humanism offer psuedosolutions which deny the foundations of godliness, righteousness, and truth.

CURRENT CHRISTIANITY IN THAILAND

Historically Thailand, or Siam as it was known, was the second Baptist mission field entered by the American Baptists in 1833. The American Presbyterians also made it their second field, entering in 1840. So for 150 years Protestant missions have labored to win peoples to Christ in this land, mostly by the one-by-one-against-the-tide method. Their social solidarity stood as a significant bulwark to fend off any major entrance of the gospel.

Some small people movements occurred especially in North Thailand. The Church among the Khow Myang, Northern Thai or Laos as they were then called, grew under Dr. Daniel McGilvary and his associates from 150 members to almost 7,000 between 1884 and 1914. After three decades of slow growth (1914-1944) the church began to advance in post-World War II years. Some small family movements among both Thai and tribes have strengthened local church growth.

However, after all these decades of evangelization, supplemented with much socialization through schools, hospitals, and agricultural or industrial projects, the Protestant Church in 1980 had only 59,000 baptized adults. This is but 0.17 percent of the Thai nation, despite a 30 percent population growth in the last five years (1974-1979). The Roman Catholic community of 175,000 adults and children has followed 450 years of mission endeavor. Much Catholic membership comes from the offspring of former Portuguese or Chinese adherents concentrated largely along the eastern border of former French territories of Laos and Cambodia. Catholics make up 0.4 percent of the population.

So for every 1,000 Thai, only five are Christian in any sense of the word. Truly Thailand is an unreached land, and within it are many unreached peoples.

BROAD CATEGORIES OF UNREACHED PEOPLES IN THAILAND

Thailand is unlike homogeneous Korea, for many peoples, even in broad identification, comprise the Thai population.

First is the dominant Thai. These are divided into four major groups whose linguistic differences differentiate them as separate though closely related peoples: the northern Khon Myanq (Laos), the northeastern Isan Thai, the southern Thai, and the central Siamese.

Second is a significant Chinese minority of more than 2 million. They speak half a dozen dialects, though Teo Chin is the most common. In addition, there is a host of Siamo-Chinese from earlier generations. However, the many full-blooded Chinese born in Thailand, integrated socially and linguistically as full Thai citizens, form an important unreached people who seem destined to guide the nation in the decades ahead.

Third is the 2 million Thai Islam, found primarily in the four southernmost provinces. This group is divided into two major people's blocks, one a Pettani Malay group, the other Thai-speaking Muslims.

Fourth, in Eastern Thailand are 1.5 million Cambodian-speaking Thai citizens. Only one missionary couple speaks their language and works among them. The potential receptivity of this people has not adequately been tested. Here is an urgent call for evangelization.

Fifth, Thailand is adorned with a variety of tribal peoples whose population is over three-quarters of a million. No less than forty-five distinct tribes are broadly categorized under six major linguistic families: Tibeto-Burman, Tai, Karen, Maio-Yeo, Mon-Khmer, and Malayo-Polynesian (Austronesian).

The population of these separate tribes varies from a few thousand, as in the case of the Moken and the Mra Bri (Phi Tong Lyang), to as many as two hundred thousand, such as the Sqaw Karen and the Kui.

Only one-third of the forty-five tribes have any Christians among them. Except for the Sqaw Karen and the Lahu, Christians number less than 1000, often only one or two hundred in each tribe.

This kaleidoscope of peoples in Thailand: Thai, Chinese, Malay, Muslims, Cambodian Thai, and tribes, are all unreached peoples; none has a Christian population of even 20 percent practicing Christians. Herein lies the need that challenges the Church around the world to concentrated prayer, sacrifice, and continuing mission to bring Christ, the Savior of the world, to these people. The mission to disciple these peoples will produce transformed lives that will consequently transform communities and societies. Hundreds of smaller divisions of unreached peoples could be defined, but only the proclamation of Christ and the demonstration of loving service can effectively plant the Church of Jesus Christ firmly among each people and transform the unreached into a reached people. "A church in every community and thereby the gospel to every person" is a good motto and goal.

FIVE PRINCIPLES FROM THAI CHURCH-GROWTH PARADOXES

Like the tantalizing mystery of a diamond's many facets, church growth is always a complex phenomenon, comprising a varigated combination of factors, sociological conditions, spiritual agents, and divine timing. Where the sovereignty of God is matched by the obedience of Christian responsibility at the strategic time, genuine church growth among a people usually occurs.

Five paradoxes gained from examples of church growth in Thailand suggests some basic principles applicable to planting the Church among unreached peoples.

First, peoples of the same broad category may, at the same time, have varying receptivities. For example, the Sqaw Karen have shown exciting receptivity. Their church has tripled in two recent decades from 1,984 members in 1959 to 6,539 in 1978. Their close relatives, the Pwo Karen, on the other hand, have yielded few members to the Church.

A similar illustration is seen among the Lawa (Mountain Lawa) speaking a Mon-Khmer dialect. These now have a growing Christian community of 500; but the Eastern Lawa, using a Tibeto-Burman dialect have no Christians among them.

This paradox shows a principle in church growth: identify the receptive peoples and evangelize them intensely while lightly evangelizing the less responsive.

A second paradox shows that the same people may respond differently in different periods of time. For example, in the late nineteenth century, mainland Chinese traders living in Thailand with Thai wives were often open to the gospel. Hundreds became Christians, though few missionaries concentrated on evangelizing these receptive people. Today, these Chinese are much less receptive as the social pressures under which the Chinese then lived have now been relieved. This points out another principle: It is urgent to evangelize a people while they are responsive and prepared. Procrastination and neglect loses many spiritual harvests.

Third, the same people under changing social stresses often respond differently. During the Japanese era of World War II, the Thai church membership dropped off drastically until only a few thousand remained true to Christ. But as the tide of war turned and the war dealt defeat upon Japan, there was a resurgence of the Thai church growth through restorations and through new converts from non-Christian Thai. By 1952, the Church of Christ in Thailand had 15,000 members. The postwar social conditions had changed and a new advance in growth was possible.

Another current example relates to the displaced persons from Cambodia. Under the old *status quo* Cambodians were satisfied and complacent about change. But the recent devastations of war and famine produced drastic sociopolitical changes which left the refugees with a religious vacuum. In reevaluating their lives under such changed conditions, thousands of Cambodians in the border areas of Thailand have become Christians since 1975.

A principle here calls for evangelists and church planters to be sensitive to changes affecting a dormant people. Drastic changes in social conditions, through mobility or by tragedy, often open those people to a new receptivity. But there are many advocates and harvesters besides Christians ready to take advantage of opportunities, too.

Fourth, different missions working with the same people at the same time sometimes gain widely differing results. This paradox is elucidated in the northeast Thailand province of Ubon. The Christian and Missionary Alliance have labored in this region since 1929 and received some response, but in recent years their churches have more or less stagnated. The Seventh-Day Adventists working in the same province have grown phenomenally from 250 members to 1,000 between 1974 and 1978.

The principle to note here revolves around method and strategy. Missions must evaluate and test their strategy and hone methodology to the appropriate sharpness for harvesting ripened spiritual fields.

A fifth paradox follows on closely. Sometimes different missionaries of the same mission working with the same people in the same region have varying degrees of success. For example, Eugene P. Dunlap, one of the Presbyterian missionaries to Petchaburi in the late nineteenth and early twentieth century saw hundreds come to Christ and planted dozens of village churches. His contemporary fellow workers, Dr. Thompson and Mr. McLure, who followed him, were of a different school and saw the church drop off to a mere shadow of its former strength. Dunlap had a heart for the people, sacrificed himself, took their burdens upon his heart, and had constant contact with the people. His associates stood aloof, were strict and cold towards the people, and believed that principle was more important than feelings.

The principle stands out clearly: those who would win the unreached must themselves be humble and loving. Credibility of the gospel message is essential and comes only through showing the right attitudes and genuine concern for the unreached.

Daniel McGilvary, one of the great missionaries to Thailand, illustrates the point. His success as a missionary was largely founded on two personal characteristics: first, his unswerving devotion to God in faithfully proclaiming Jesus Christ as Lord and Savior; and second, his genuine concern for people. Mrs. Laura B. McKearn, a contemporary of McGilvary, succinctly described McGilvary's true heart in *The Missionary Reaching the World* (p. 370):

> No matter whether he be in the house of a slave or the palace of the prince, he preaches Christ.
>
> He is beloved by all who know him, young and old, native and foreign. He never turns a deaf ear to any who come to him, however trivial their complaint or foolish their request. He seems to be able to enter fully into the lives of the people, understanding their trials and rejoicing with them in their joys. This is one of the sources of his success as a missionary, and an essential characteristic of all who would be missionaries in the fullest sense.

No truer words could be spoken of these who would today take Christ to the unreached peoples of Thailand, or elsewhere. Here is a vital key to reducing the number of unreached peoples: men and women with a true heart for God and for people lost in sin. Such missionaries are always welcome.

IN CONCLUSION

Three words describe the condition that challenges the Christian mission to evangelize and disciple the unreached peoples of Thailand in 1981: great opportunity, dire urgency, possible receptivity. But these will combine to plant and grow churches and to reduce the unreached populations of our day as dedicated servants of Christ go forth to proclaim Christ and to serve by love in his name.

Where are those dedicated to such a mission?

Alex G. Smith has worked with Overseas Missionary Fellowship in Thailand since 1964. He has served as coordinator for evangelism, chairman of the church planning committee, and as acting field superintendent. Smith's Ph. D. dissertation, *History of Church Growth in Thailand: An Analysis,* is published by Fuller Theological Seminary, Pasadena, Calif.

NOTES TO PART 1

1. See *That Everyone May Hear,* Edward R. Dayton. Monrovia, MARC, 1979.

2. Some will recognize that figures such as 87 percent and 83 percent have been used in the past. This data is updated every year and, indeed, the percentage of "hidden peoples" went down from 83 to 80 percent between 1979 and 1980 because of the partial opening of China and the information that the Christian movement is more viable and numerous than previously estimated. Last year 100 million Chinese were removed from the hidden peoples category and perhaps in the years to come, more will be removed. (See the Table in Part 3 of this volume.)

3. China herself gives 970 million as its population, but no census has been taken since 1964. A United States Census Bureau analyst has said that China passed the one-billion mark in 1978, as reported in "World Scene," *Christianity Today,* XXI: 19 (July 21, 1978), p. 54 (1230).

4. China's adults are 95 percent literate, according to "Regional Statistical Indicators," *Asia 1979 Yearbook* (Hong Kong: Far Eastern Economic Review, 1979), p. 16.

5. E-1 and E-2 represent degrees of difference from the evangelist's culture, which in shorthand is called an E-1 culture. E-1, or "monocultural evangelism," is contrasted to "cross-cultural evangelism," for which the symbols E-2 and E-3 stand.

6. This five-group basic analysis has been developed by Jonathan Chao, director of the Chinese Church Resource Center. Other groups and topics desperately needing research are China's children, mass media in China, social mobility, etc. To our knowledge, the Chinese Church Research Center is the only Christian China study center doing professional research work on these topics, and publishing its findings.

7. Information on this history is being systematically gathered by the Chinese Church Research Center, collated, analyzed, and published.

8. Initial conclusions in an analysis of these strengths and weaknesses are to be published in a forthcoming book of the Chinese Church Research Center.

9. The writer is indebted to Jonathan Chao for this basic concept, which is being developed by the Chinese Church Research Center staff in their analysis and reflections on Christian work in China.

Part 2
Case
Studies

Singapore's English-speaking Teenagers: Factors in Evangelization

by James Wong and Andrew Goh

The English-speaking teenagers of Singapore are a people group because they share a common language, situation, set of interests, and background. They are a unique youth culture that will stay in this area even when they move into adulthood.

James Wong and Andrew Goh show how these teenagers are being reached by a variety of methods that have capitalized on their receptivity to the gospel. The article demonstrates evangelization emerging from a situation of sociocultural change that is affecting all the residents of Singapore.

A future goal should be to disciple and nurture these young Christians so that they will reach other people groups that they will eventually become a part of as they enter the mainstream of Singapore society. It is hoped that they will carry their Christian values into new sociocultural groups, and not go back to traditional values because of family pressure or other factors.

SINGAPORE: A CITY NATION

On a typical world map, Singapore is smaller than the dot over the "i" in its name. Located just south of Malaysia, with a land surface of only 626 square kilometers (224 square miles), the

Republic of Singapore is one of the smallest independent nations in the world.

Established as a British colony in 1819, it became a semiautonomous state in 1959 when the ruling People's Action Party was elected. But it wasn't until 1965 that it became an independent sovereign nation.

Singapore has no natural resources of its own so the economy of the nation is supported primarily by its natural, sheltered harbor. Located in the center of southeast Asia, the port is a crossroads for international shipping. In 1970, Singapore surpassed the Port of London to become the fourth busiest port in the world. And, by 1979, it had replaced Yokohama, Japan, as the third largest port, measured by shipping tonnage handled annually. Much of the country's growth since its independence is directly attributable to its mammoth shipping trade. Not surprisingly, the government considers any labor strike within the port area comparable to treason!

Government's Economic Goals
In recent years, the government, which is characterized by strong central leadership with a high level of internal communication, has concentrated its efforts on establishing a broader economic base for the country. Great progress has been made toward advancing the financial, transportation, and communication industries. Further, it is seeking to become a prominent influence in the world money market, particularly the Asian dollar and bond markets. Many feel that one of the government's primary goals during the next decade is to make Singapore an international financial center. Unlike her neighbors in southeast Asia, Singapore's leaders are strongly opposed to the low wage—low skills type of industrial economy. Instead, they are seeking to establish a highly technical society.

The Peoples of Singapore
Also unlike most of southeast Asia, Singapore's population is surprisingly homogeneous. While the population is made up of four distinct groups, religious and racial harmony prevail. The

ethnic Chinese make up the largest portion of the population, accounting for about 76 percent. Malays account for 14 percent and Indians, 7 percent. The remaining 3 percent is composed of Eurasians, Europeans, and others.

At this writing, approximately 43 percent of the total land area has been developed for residential, commercial, and industrial use with another 15 percent reserved for agricultural purposes. The remainder is composed of forest reserves and marshlands. This situation creates a density problem with about 4,000 people occupying each square kilometer. So, while Singapore is nearly the same size and population as Chicago, her people live in about one-quarter of the space.

Three primary factors account for the evident unity within this small city nation: Singapore's strong governmental leadership, the country's compact size, and the adoption of English as a common language. Considering the diversity of the country's peoples and life-styles, its mixture of agriculture and industry, its four languages and its widely disparate religions, its oneness of national purpose is remarkable.

Although the four official languages of the country, Mandarian, Malay, Tamil, and English could easily cause disunity among the people, they do not. In fact, television announcements are routinely made in all four tongues. The use of English as the unofficial common language is a recent trend which ties in closely with the national economic goals of the people.

Importance of the English Language

Primarily influenced by the modern economy of Singapore, many parents have chosen to send their children to English schools, believing that fluency in that language enhances their career opportunities. The choice appears to be a wise one. Many English-educated university graduates command starting salaries at levels which took their parents a lifetime to achieve.

Throughout most of southeast Asia, and much of the rest of the world, English is acknowledged as the official language of commerce. In Singapore, it has become the language of the elite, as well. Even the government has recognized the trend toward English as a positive force within the country and has begun actively recruiting English teachers from Britain, Australia, New Zealand, and the United States to teach at the secondary level. It is hoped that English will evolve into a more standardized version of the language instead of the Singapore English which is presently spoken by nearly everyone.

English is also the language of the young and this is where it is having the biggest impact. English-speaking teenagers are the nation's pacesetters. Along with the language, they have easily adapted to other Western values, styles, thought patterns, and life-styles. In fact, when a famous hamburger chain opened in Singapore recently, they set a new world's record for selling the millioneth hamburger in the shortest period of time!

Most of the English-speaking people of Singapore are still in school. In 1978, it was estimated that there were one hundred and twenty-five thousand of them. Among those who have completed their education, there is little unemployment and they have become an upwardly mobile social and economic influence. English has been the key to their success.

Impact of WOGS and Bananas

While still a minority, the English-educated youth of Singapore are wielding incredible influence throughout the country. Referred to derisively by their peers as "Western-oriented gentlemen" (WOGs), or "bananas" (yellow on the outside but white in the middle), their actions and attitudes are nonetheless emulated. In fact, certain conservative factions fear that the WOGs threaten to wipe out the cultural roots of the country with their Western ways.

Unlike their parents, who usually think of themselves as Chinese, Malay, or Indian first, the English-speaking young people think of themselves only as Singaporean. They have also rejected many of their parents' values. For example, these young people are no longer characterized by thrift as their parents and ancestors always have been. Instead, they have grown up in comparative affluence. It is not uncommon for them to live on credit (based on their future earning capacity) or to take overseas vacations while still in their first year of employment. Because of their broader educations, they often view their parents' traditions and values as backward and they are forward-looking in every way. They are changing the way the country thinks, dresses, eats, spends money, and worships.

Singapore's Youth Open to Christianity

These same young people are turning to the Christian faith in record numbers. It has been estimated that nearly 12 percent of the nation's English-speaking teenagers are Christians—probably the largest segment of the population. (Of those who accepted Christ during the Billy Graham crusade in December, 1978, 37 percent were from the English-speaking minority.)

For many of the same reasons these young people are speaking English, wearing Levi's, and eating Big Macs, they are embracing the gospel for answers to their modern-day problems.

During the past two decades, Singapore's youth have been subjected to more change and to more new ideas than their ancestors experienced in as many centuries. Consequently, they are completely open to all new experiences and ideas. They are not resistant to change like their parents, but have adopted it as their unique life-style. They refuse to accept hand-me-down values as their parents and grandparents did. For example, they regard ancestral worship, which is prevalent among their parents' generation, as backward-looking, and they are far more interested in the future than in the past.

Conversely, it may be that such constant change in their young lives has also caused them to seek the God who does not change. The fast pace of their lives may have dictated their apparent need for something constant in which to place their hopes.

Furthermore, the fact that Christianity emphasizes the exercise of free will and the determination of one's own destiny, is appealing to these assertive young people. Underlying this feeling is a subtle opposition to fatalism which the nation's religions stress.

Again, the broader educational experiences of Singapore's youth have caused them to intellectually challenge their parents' beliefs. And, for the most part, their parents are not prepared to answer their questions. Although many of the Oriental religions have a solid foundation of philosophy beneath them, few have knowledge of it. The religions of their parents most often have been passed on to them through the generations in very simplistic terms. For many, religion has only consisted of a prescribed set of rituals without meaning or explanation. These young people have been educated to seek answers and to question their surroundings at every level. Naturally, they are drawn to a religion which not only provides answers but that encourages their questioning minds to dig deeper.

English also plays a major role in the spread of the gospel in Singapore. As previously noted, the English-speaking young people are the pacesetters but, more importantly, the other religions have done little to translate their teachings and philosophies into English. And, as we've also noted, English is the language of the elite. Even those who have not been educated in English schools are striving to learn English; so, what is written in English is what is being read.

Consequently, due to the significant influence of the English language in Singapore, Christianity has become known as the modern and *with it* religion among the young.

Role of the Christian Church among Singapore's Youth

Para-church organizations have played a vital role in bringing the message of the gospel to Singapore's young people. 80 percent of all the secondary schools have some form of organized Christian witness. Youth for Christ and Scripture Union have ministered at this level since 1957. More recently, Campus Crusade for Christ and The Navigators have had a strong influence. (At eighteen years of age, following graduation from secondary school, all males are conscripted for two and one-half or three years of service in the Singapore Armed Forces, where the Navigator's ministry has had its greatest impact.) Further, the Singapore Armed Forces Committee has received official recognition and support for work among the nation's military personnel.

Organizations like Boys' and Girls' Brigades, Eagles Evangelism, Fellowship of Evangelical Students and other service groups of various kinds also have had a major role. And, for dropouts and drug addicts among teens, the impact of the Teen Challenge ministry has been significant.

Church youth fellowship and Sunday schools have also contributed significantly to winning young people to Christ. According to various surveys, as many as 70 percent of converted teenagers attend church regularly (at least twice a month). Only about 10 percent do not attend church at all. Of these, most do not attend because their parents have forbidden it. Fortunately, this opposition is diminishing and in recent years, only about 1 percent of those who have accepted Christ as their Savior have been asked to leave their homes because of their faith.

Among the churches which have been established during the past twenty years, the congregations consist almost entirely of Christians who are still in their teens and twenties. Many churches have elders who are not yet thirty but who have been committed and active churchmen for ten or more years!

Although little recognition has been given, Christian teachers have also played a major role in bringing the gospel to Singapore's young people. In fact, many Christians have chosen a teaching career because of the great impact they can have toward the furtherance of the gospel. Antiestablishment attitudes are rare among secondary school students and so they are often favorably impressed by the outstanding character traits and testimonies of their Christian teachers. For many students, their introduction to Christ comes from these dedicated professionals.

STRATEGY FOR THE FUTURE

Christianity is an important influence in Singapore today. Churches are constantly springing up with flourishing, youthful congregations. Many new churches have reported annual growth rates exceeding 20 percent! But there is still a need to plant new churches, especially among the various English-speaking youth groups.

Because of the national emphasis on education, schools must continue to have strong ministries. Youth Bible study groups and Christian clubs are of vital importance and must have strong support from the local churches. As these groups become strong and vibrant, they will, in turn, spearhead evangelism among their peers. And, as the national pacesetters, they can expect to have a powerful impact in the years to come.

The churches must stand in readiness to fold these young people into the local congregations and disciple them. Support and cooperation between the para-church organizations and the local churches will be a vital factor in reaching the population of Singapore with the message of the gospel during the next decade.

The church must remain sensitive to the trends of the country as it pushes forward economically and educationally, and be alert to the changing needs of the people. As the economy of Singapore continues to prosper, materialism, as a substitute for spiritual values, is a very real threat.

IN SUMMARY

Of all the elements contributing to the spread of the gospel in Singapore today, the impact of the English language is probably the most important. While visas for missionaries are being routinely denied, English-speaking teachers are being actively recruited by the government. English-speaking Christian teachers probably have the greatest opportunity for ministry ever available.

In conjunction with this, Sunday school materials, evangelistic tools, and other Christian literature printed in English will continue to be vital. This is an area where the church and para-church organizations need to concentrate their resources.

Indeed, the young people of Singapore are eager to hear the gospel and have receptive hearts and minds. We need only continue to keep pace with the growing demands of a young and vital church.

The English language has been the key to material success among the youth of Singapore. It is the church's job to assure that it also continues to be the key to their spiritual success and growth, as well.

Andrew Goh studied at Perth Bible Institute in Australia, and also at Daystar Communications in Nairobi, Kenya. He is presently the National Director of Youth for Christ of Singapore, and also is Regional Director for Southeast Asia. He is married and has one child.

James Wong has served as Anglican Minister in the Diocese of Singapore where his responsibilities included planting new congregations in the high-rise apartments of Singapore for the Anglican Church. He has also served as Chaplain at St. Andrew's Jr. College, and as Pastor of the newly established Chapel of the Resurrection, both in Singapore.

Reaching Chinese Factory Workers in Hong Kong

by Gail M. W. Law

Gail Law identifies the factory workers of Hong Kong as a people group socially isolated from the established middle-class churches. She discusses two approaches to reaching them: first, as subgroups of existing churches, and second, in homogeneous churches of their own.

The needs of this particular people group are unique and require an approach that appreciates their special situation. Ongoing evaluation of this work with the Hong Kong factory workers will be of benefit, especially to those involved in similar ministries in the world's many cities.

Hong Kong is one of the major industrial centers of the Far East. According to statistics released in 1978 by the government, within a total population of 4.7 million, 800,000 were identified as blue-collar workers. These workers and laborers employed in the factories of Hong Kong constitute 17.5 percent of the colony's total population and 42.5 percent of the total labor force. Together with members of their families, factory workers make up a significant segment of the society.

The blue-collars are a people which no church in Hong Kong

can afford to overlook in its outreach efforts. Because most churchgoers there belong to the middle and the upper-middle classes, church programs are generally designed to meet the needs of their members. Evangelization of the factory workers calls for an understanding of these people and the implementation of effective strategies for reaching them with the gospel.

For such purposes this study has been prepared. The intent of this study is briefly to (1) describe the distinctives of these blue-collar workers; (2) give an account of the present evangelistic effort among them; (3) evaluate the effort and suggest methods for future outreach effort. This is not a comprehensive discussion, but will hopefully arouse a widening interest and genuine concern in the blue-collars as a people, with the result that Christians will become committed to winning them for Christ.

THE FACTORY WORKERS' WORLD

Housing

Most blue-collars work in factories and reside in public housing flats built and managed by the Housing Authority of the Hong Kong government. These are high-rise apartment blocks called housing estates and are scattered through the colony. A housing estate may accommodate as few as 3,000 residents, or as many as 129,000. Compared to Western standards, the tiny flats are equipped with subminimal facilities.

These housing estates have become breeding grounds for crime and other major social problems—such as drugs, gang wars, robberies, murders, and sex crimes. The living conditions in most flats are overcrowded, privacy is practically nonexistent, and interpersonal conflict is frequent. As a result, emotional problems are numerous and severe.

Education

A 1976 census showed that approximately 69 percent of these blue-collars have a primary school level education or less; about 19 percent have achieved lower-secondary level; and 10 percent upper-secondary. Most can read and write simple Chinese, but have difficulty dealing with abstract concepts, principles, and doctrines.

Income
The result of a 1979 government survey revealed that 60 percent of Hong Kong's total labor force has a monthly income of less than HK $1,000 and only 6 percent receives more than HK $3,000. It is estimated that most of the factory workers belong to the former group. Although some factory workers may earn over HK $1,000 monthly, blue-collars are generally considered to be in the lower or the lower-middle class of Hong Kong society.

Aspiration and Life-style
Hong Kong is a city that does not offer long-term political security. Although Hong Kong Island and Kowloon became a British colony in 1842, the largest region, New Territories, is held by Britain on a lease from China, a lease scheduled to expire in 1997. To accommodate this uncertainty about Hong Kong's future, her citizens tend to adopt a philosophy of getting as much as they can today. For who knows what will happen tomorrow?

This approach to the future increases the emphasis on a fast return of investment, a preoccupation with immediate gratification of needs, and a focus on pleasure of all kinds. Indigenous folk songs and locally produced tv programs clearly portray and encourage this philosophy which pervades all levels of Hong Kong society. Aspirations of life center around wealth, fame, and education, the latter being a vestige of the respect held for scholars in the traditional Chinese culture.

The monotony of long work hours and the activities offered by the factories are major determinants in the life-style of blue-collars. Workers probably spend from nine to twelve hours a day in a factory. Travel to and from work may take as long as two hours. To keep the workers they have trained, many factories offer weekend outings, picnics, and other types of social functions. The lives of blue-collars center around their work and the friends they have in the factory.

CASE STUDIES

Aware that they belong to the lower or lower-middle class of society, achieving a minimal level of education, and growing up with both parents working in a factory—these are factors that contribute to the factory workers' strong feelings of inferiority and emptiness, and contribute to their strong need for love and acceptance.

A common means factory workers employ in dealing with these psychological needs is attending evening schools. If they can upgrade their skills and qualify for work outside the factories, they can make more money. Of the more than sixty thousand students in Hong Kong's evening secondary schools, the majority are factory workers. Further education and increased income temper their sense of inferiority and insecurity. Nevertheless, wild parties, drugs, and illicit sex are common techniques used to temporarily sublimate the emptiness and monotony of their lives.

Although factory workers have few worries about food and shelter, they do have deep fears and unmet psychological needs. They see superficial causes for many of their problems and often try to deal with life at that level. They seem unaware of their basic problem of sin and separation from God.

Religion

Most factory workers grow up in families which adhere to traditional Chinese folk religion, a complex mixture of Taoism, Confucianism, Buddhism, ancestral worship, and vestiges of animism. Their religion is a blend of customs and festivals, with ancestral worship continuing to be the most commonly practiced.

Because the present generation of factory workers is relatively young, and many of them have been educated in Roman Catholic and Protestant schools, they do not cling as tightly to the traditional Chinese religion as do their parents. Although they continue to enjoy the festivals, their religious rites are almost devoid of mystical meaning.

In Hong Kong today many young people claim no religion. However, this is not to say that they are true agnostics, for they are part of a culture with 5,000 years of religious tradition that cannot be overthrown within one or two generations. Surrounded by superstition, they continue to live with a strong fear of death and of evil spirits.

Attitude toward Christianity

Many of the blue-collars are aware of the Christian faith. Some may even accept the existence of one true and loving God. But they generally have great difficulty in comprehending the concept of absolute value being God himself. That Christians should commit themselves entirely to God is a concept that is too risky to try. To their thinking—which gives money, fame, and pleasure top value—Christianity is impractical and therefore unacceptable.

CURRENT EVANGELISTIC MINISTRY AMONG FACTORY WORKERS

The Integration Approach

Hong Kong churchgoers are made up largely of middle-class, educated members of society and their family members. The need for evangelizing the factory workers has yet to take root in the minds of these Christians. Although some factory workers do attend existing churches, they are few in number. Those who do usually find it hard to make the adjustments for becoming integrated into a congregation with an entirely different background.

The Industrial Evangelical Fellowship (IEF) Approach

The only para-church organization actively engaged in evangelistic work among factory workers is the Industrial Evangelical Fellowship (IEF). This organization started in 1973 with the goal to win factory workers for Christ; also, to incorporate them into fellowship groups in factories and in churches for follow-up, training, and further outreach. To date, the total number of Christian blue-collars is less than 1 percent of the total population of factory workers.

IEF currently has eighteen full-time staff members and is

expanding. The number of contacts the IEF staff can make with Christian and non-Christian factory workers is approximately 3,200 a year. The staff members have established a total of forty-five fellowship groups in the different factories. As of January 1980, thirteen churches in Hong Kong have responded to the IEF ministry by setting up fellowship groups for factory workers in churches. Six other local churches are prepared to do the same.

The work of IEF includes evangelistic work among blue-collars, follow-up of young Christians, developing mass-media tools (i.e., monthly bulletin, gospel songs and messages on cassette tapes), organizing hobby classes, recruiting Christian teachers to teach evening schools, sponsoring social activities with a goal of evangelism, and providing training for lay Christians with a burden to help in ministry among factory workers.

Still in its pioneering stages, the IEF ministry is too young for an accurate evaluation of its approach to be made. However, its success in several aspects is obvious:

1. IEF has aroused the interest and concern of some middle-class, educated Christians in Hong Kong for the ministry to blue-collars. Many IEF board members and volunteer helpers are college graduates.

2. IEF has received a good response from some Christian manufacturers and high-level executives in factories. Through their help, blue-collar fellowship groups have been established in some factories.

3. IEF is beginning to make churches aware of the need for evangelizing the significant blue-collar segment of the society. Some churches have responded by implementing plans for outreach to factory workers, and other churches are preparing to do so.

4. IEF has recruited its staff workers from among former factory workers and expects more IEF leadership to come out from factories to evangelize and church their own people.

Some church-growth experts question the validity of trying to integrate the blue-collars into existing churches because most factory workers belong to a different social class from the average churchgoer. This suggestion indicates that it will be difficult for blue-collars to develop a sense of belonging in the middle-class churches, or to develop their leadership there. They may be sacrificing their potential usefulness in the Christian community by becoming a part of existing middle-class churches and not being free to do what the Lord wants them to do among their own people.

Members of some churches which include blue-collar fellowship groups tend to agree with these concerns raised by church-growth leaders. However, the question remains: "Has the IEF model been given enough time to prove itself?"

STRATEGIZING FOR EVANGELISM

Rationale
Before building strategies and making plans, it is necessary to identify problems and needs in the ministry. Devising solutions to the problems and dealing with the needs then follows logically.

Identifying the Problems
• Basic to the Christian faith are abstract doctrinal concepts that are difficult for the blue-collars to grasp. This element gives Christianity the aura of being foreign and also of being for intellectuals (the educated) who generally seem to understand these concepts. The blue-collars feel inferior when they continue to be puzzled by these same concepts. This lack of abstract thinking experience poses problems when pastors and other Christian counselors talk with blue-collars about principles and doctrines.

• The educational background of most factory workers is too limited for them to make good use of available Christian magazines and books in order to increase their general basis of understanding.

• Factory work is tedious and dull, so workers look for experiences that will give variety and action to their lives. They cannot tolerate solemn, formal meetings and long lectures. Unfortunately, these are the usual forms of meetings and services currently held in the churches.

• Some factory workers attend evening classes, or hold two jobs to earn additional income. Although these involvements usually lessen their feelings of insecurity and inferiority, their full work, travel, and school schedule hinders their attending church meetings.

• IEF suffers from shortage of funds and a relatively high rate of turnover among staff workers. There are neither enough funds nor manpower to develop what needs to be implemented on a long-term basis.

• The majority of Chinese churches in Hong Kong have not yet become sympathetic to the IEF ministry. However, there is evidence that the attitude is changing.

• Some factory workers find it difficult to become adjusted to social and intellectual differences they experience in a middle-class church.

Identifying the Needs

A second step in establishing the rationale is to identify the needs of blue-collars:

• They need a sense of self-worth, security, and purpose in life.

• They need genuine concern and friendship.

• Evening and weekend recreation is needed to provide fun and variety to counteract the dullness of their lives.

• They need opportunities to develop their gifts and talents; also, to grow as persons in an accepting social, intellectual, and spiritual climate.

Solving the Problems

Following an assessment of problems inherent in evangelizing factory workers, and in identification of their needs, the third step calls for a look at some possible solutions to the problems:

• Theologians, biblical scholars, communications people, and staff workers need to engage in research together before launching a ministry to factory workers. Suitable means for conveying the gospel in understandable terms to blue-collars must be worked out, especially the issue of recognizing that absolute value is God himself. Further, an apologetic for defending the Christian faith against a pragmatic, secular mentality should also be derived.

• Mass-media tools suitable for the factory workers' abilities must be developed: gospel songs in the Cantonese dialect, accompanied by indigenous music popular among factory workers; magazines and literature in simple Chinese with ample illustrations and content relevant to the life situation; gospel films, filmstrips, and slides. Pastors, teachers, and staff workers ministering among blue-collar people should familiarize themselves with these media tools and be fluent in the vocabulary used by factory workers.

• Church meetings and evangelistic outreach programs must be conducted in a lively manner and include an appealing variety of events. This requires much planning for those not used to such meetings. The goal is to involve the audience as much as possible in the programs that are relevant to their life situation.

• Christians need to be out where the factory workers are by becoming actively involved as teachers in evening schools, hobby classes, and social events in which they participate.

• A strong conviction to reach factory workers must be firmly planted among church leaders. More effective strategies must be developed for informing and challenging Christians concerning the evangelistic outreach needed to evangelize factory workers. Existing channels for publicizing this need must be well utilized.

Meeting the Needs

The final step in developing a rationale for evangelization of industrial workers moves beyond assessing their needs and suggesting solutions. This fourth process is to implement the plan for presenting the gospel in ways that meet the worker's life needs. To accomplish this goal:

• Christians must make special efforts to affirm factory workers of their worth before God. Teaching on the value of man, eternal life in Jesus Christ, and the Christian's life mission are subject areas that need to be taught with understanding and sensitivity. Blue-collar Christians need to feel the value of being God's person as a factory worker, and of taking pride in their work.

- Christians with a burden for winning blue-collars must take time for them.
- Evening and weekend events should be designed to meet the spiritual, social, and recreational needs of blue-collars.
- Opportunities must be provided for them to develop their talents; and if Christian, their spiritual gifts. They must be allowed occasions to exercise their gifts for building up the church and thereby assuring themselves of their role in the Kingdom of God.

TWO MODELS FOR EVANGELISM

The IEF Model

The IEF model aims at integrating factory workers into existing local churches. Aware of the blue-collars' needs and the problems in outreach to these people, IEF staff members have been testing some of the solutions and methods suggested. Good progress in these areas is expected. However, because this model depends on the cooperation of existing local churches which, in turn, depend on IEF to channel converted blue-collars into them, there are three specific areas in which this work needs increased support and consolidation:

First, a person is needed to promote the IEF vision among leaders of existing local churches. Preferably, this person should be an ordained minister, in his late thirties or early forties, an effective speaker, and able to handle personal relationships well.

Another major need is the development of staff members committed to IEF on a long-term basis and willing to be trained in areas IEF deems necessary.

A third need is for research on philosophical, theological, and cultural problems which hinder factory workers' acceptance of the Christian faith and growth after conversion. IEF should seek help from theologians in local seminaries to aid in this research.

The Homogeneous Unit Model

Some church growth experts have observed that the factory workers belong to a different class than the average churchgoer in Hong Kong. Differences in their social, economical, and educational backgrounds classify them as two different cultures, or homogeneous units. So the pioneer evangelistic ministry to the factory workers can be regarded as cross-cultural.

Inasmuch as the target population of blue-collars is 800,000, the church has sufficient ground to mobilize a missionary organization uniquely equipped to minister among factory workers on mission terms.

To suggest an alternative, distinct divisions could be set up within denominations to develop this specialized ministry. The resources of a denomination may singly, or in cooperation with other denominations sharing similar visions develop a specialized ministry division established for work among blue-collars. The goals, structure, and functions of such a mission or denominational division might follow this pattern:

1. Goals The general goal would be to evangelize factory workers in Hong Kong; and, to plant industrial churches.

```
               Board of Directors/Executive Committee
                              |
                 General Secretary/Division Head
                              |
                        DEPARTMENTS
   ┌──────────┬──────────┬──────────┬──────────┬──────────┬──────────┐
EVANGELISM  TRAINING &  RESEARCH  MASS MEDIA PROMOTION   CHURCH
            FOLLOW-UP                                    PLANTING
```

2. Structure A mission agency or denominational division organized for ministry to factory workers could, when fully developed, be organized as illustrated in the following diagram. (Initially, much of the work would fall on volunteers who share the vision. Staff workers would handle responsibilities not covered by volunteers.)

3. Personnel, Departments, and Functions The board/ executive committee should consist of church leaders/

representatives burdened for ministry to the factory workers.

The functions of this decision-making body are:

- to promote the ministry of the organization;
- to support the work prayerfully and financially;
- to act as the highest policy-making body; and
- to counsel with the secretary/head, who serves as executive officer.

The secretary/head should be a person clearly called to this ministry and committed to develop and direct the work on a long-term basis, to supervise the staff, and to execute decisions of the board.

The department heads should also be called and committed to the work of their departments, the functions of which are described as follows:

- Evangelism: Designs and implements evangelistic programs to factory workers; sends missionaries to these fields; directs and supervises their work.

- Follow-up and Training: Designs and implements follow-up programs for new converts; trains Christian factory workers for outreach; trains volunteers for outreach and follow-up.

- Research: Studies and analyzes philosophical, theological, and cultural problems hindering factory workers' acceptance of Christ and impeding growth after conversion; works out an apologetic to defend the Christian faith and challenge the prevailing secular philosophies; maintains close dialogue with seminaries training future workers and provides suggestions for expanding curricula to meet needs of mission staff.

- Mass Media: Develops appropriate mass-media tools for evangelistic outreach, follow-up, and training.

- Promotion: Designs and implements strategy to promote the vision among local churches; raises funds to support the work; maintains communication with supporting churches and individuals; publishes bulletin to inform constituents of progress and needs.

- Church Planting: Designs and implements strategy for planting churches; recruits suitable pastors for new churches; counsels with pastors and church boards.

Reaching Chinese Factory Workers in Hong Kong

Christian factory workers comprise the most logical and available bridge between their churches and the unchurched blue-collars. Outreach strategies based on the homogeneous unit model must employ this bridging method as a means to establish and grow industrial churches.

When industrial churches have been planted and have demonstrated ability to develop their own outreach plans, the support mission/denomination should be dissolved and the churches be charged with evangelistic and follow-up responsibilities among their own people.

CRITERIA FOR EVALUATION

IEF and homogeneous unit models which become operative should be evaluated periodically by using the following criteria:

1. Number of conversions among factory workers
2. Number of fellowship groups established (IEF model)

Number of industrial churches planted (homogeneous unit model)

3. Financial response of churches to the ministry.
4. Increase of full-time, part-time personnel, and of volunteer involvement.
5. Changes in factory workers' attitudes toward Christianity as a result of contact by or participation in either of these models.

IN SUMMARY

Recognition of the factory workers as a unique people group for which the gospel needs careful packaging has been fairly recent. In fact, the research, philosophy, goals, and functions of a comprehensive evangelistic strategy have yet to become integrated and made operational.

On the basis of the five evaluative criteria suggested above, objective monitoring of the IEF and of the homogeneous unit models can provide significant data about each of these evangelistic strategies. Observers generally agree that until an evaluation process is activated, it is too early to predict which of the models will be the more effective in evangelizing and churching the blue-collars.

CASE STUDIES

The target population of 800,000 factory workers in Hong Kong is unquestionably sufficient to allow both the IEF and the homogeneous unit models to be tested simultaneously. However, the issue is not so much which of these models will get the better results, but rather that the blue-collars are evangelized and churched to the glory of God!

Gail Man-Wah Law is a resident of Hong Kong and director of Chinese in the Diaspora. She is a graduate of the University of Manitoba, where she received the Ph.D. in plant physiology. She has served as director of administration and director of development at the China Graduate School of Theology.

Ikalahan Mission: A Case Study from the Philippines

by Darwin Sokoken

A working strategy for evangelism is dynamic. It is never set in concrete. Ideally, the process involves an ongoing review of the immediate situation as well as the past, and constant tailoring to take advantage of present opportunities.

The Ikalahan case study by Darwin Sokoken is an example of a well-defined people group that has been initially reached with the gospel. This is a situation where Christians within a people group have a vision to reach their own people, and where cross-cultural workers are welcome and needed to train these evangelists.

The process is in motion. The next step is the setting and utilization of goals as meaningful checkpoints so that the church can have a clear understanding of the outcome of its outreach program.

DEMOGRAPHIC INFORMATION ON THE PHILIPPINES
More than fifty million people live in the area of nearly 300,440 square kilometers (116,000 square miles) known as the Philippines. The growth rate of this nation whose people inhabit its more than 7,000 tropical islands is 2.4 percent, one of the highest in the world. Thirty percent of its population is urban and

is heaviest in the coastal areas. Approximately 75 percent of the population is engaged in agriculture and fishing, or related productivity.

Filipino (Tagalog), Spanish, and English are the languages generally taught in the nation's schools. Spanish and English are the languages used primarily in government and business. The number of Philippine residents who can read some language is estimated at 83 percent—one of the highest literacy rates in Asia.

Although the population is largely Fhilipino (Malay), there are more than fifty distinct ethnic groups which contribute to the cultural variety of Philippine society. Among the most evident outside elements are the Spanish and the American cultures; also, some Chinese. Intermarriage is common between the different ethnic groups living in the same areas.

People groups living in the mountainous interior of the islands are descendents of the original Negrito settlers. Today inhabitants of these interior regions may generally be considered by missions as unreached peoples. Among these peoples there are ninety-four known language groups that do not yet have scripture portions available.

A DESCRIPTION OF THE IKALAHAN PEOPLE

Location

The Ikalahan people, about forty thousand, are one of the ethnic groups living in the interior mountain areas of Luzon, the main island in the Philippine group. Also known as Kadasan, Kalangoya, or Kalasan, the name Ikalahan, however recent it may be, seems acceptable to them all.

A mountaineering people, they occupy areas above 2,500 feet in the Caraballo, Cordillera, and Sierra Madre mountain ranges in the provinces of Nueva Vizcaya, Benguet, Pangasinan, and Nueva Ecija on Luzon. Ikalahan communities are invariably scattered, with few areas having as many as thirty families per square kilometer. Standard population density in the mountain areas is less than five families per 1,000 hectares (2,471 acres).

Societal Characteristics

The Ikalahan agriculture is basically swidden (also known as *kaingen*),[1] supplemented with hunting. Recently, however, due largely to the government's outlawing of the traditional farming method, the Ikalahan have begun to build terraces for rice and/or vegetable production.

The Ikalahan people are both communal and individualistic. Concerning their own affairs, they are highly individualistic. Wherever any aspect of their lives adversely touches the lives of others in the community, however, this may be a cause for a *tongtongan* (community council) at which occasion the community decides the matter at hand on the basis of the larger good without sacrificing the good of the individual. In these councils the influence of the elders is strong, but does not necessarily determine the final decision. The outcome is truly a community decision and is enforced by the entire group through the use of social pressures; seldom by force.

Traditionally, the primary cultural value of the Ikalahan is called *li-teng,* meaning wholeness, or total well-being. It is closely related to the Hebrew concept of shalom and includes health, prosperity, happiness, and peaceful relationships with the people and the spirits.

Law, to the Ikalahan, is quite subjective. It is primarily the unwritten compilation of methods found to be effective in maintaining satisfactory interpersonal relationships and preventing improper activities. To the Ikalahan, crimes are actions which destroy the *li-teng* and thereby upset the community.

The traditional life-style of this people is being threatened, however, from several directions. First, population growth increases the pressures of their agricultural society to exist within the confines of the land area available to them. The limitation of land is the result of two factors: the government's declaration of some parts of the Ikalahan ancestral lands to be forest reserves and therefore unavailable for farming; and the settlement of lowland people who have taken over areas of Ikalahan land.

In addition to government pressure to change their farming methods, and encroachment upon their lands by other settlers, the building of roads has further eroded Ikalahan territory and has opened up their formerly isolated areas to the outside world. Other threats have come from education and radio, two elements which have increased pressures for *modernization* upon the Ikalahan society, challenging its ancient beliefs and value systems.

Many of the youth have reacted in frustration and anger to the resulting disruption of old ways. Conflict and other highly irregular behavior, by Ikalahan standards, have become more and more evident in youthful drunkenness and general aimlessness.

RECEPTIVITY TO AND STATUS OF CHRISTIANITY

In 1957 the United Church of Christ in the Philippines (UCCP) established the Ikalahan Mission to evangelize the Ikalahan people near Santa Fe in the province of Nueva Vizcaya on the island of Luzon. The fraternal worker appointed to this work fifteen years ago was the Rev. Delbert Rice, an engineer/anthropologist/theologian who has since lived among the Ikalahan people and guided the planting of six churches.

During the past three years, Ikalahan Christians in the Santa Fe area have received training to help them reach out to the other ethnic groups in the adjacent mountains. An effective base for evangelism has been established among the Ikalahan. Also, two strong branches are now actively reaching out in response to many requests from people of several mountain areas that they be evangelized by their own people and fellow mountaineers. Coming to faith in Christ through the ministry of Ikalahan Christians helps inquirers and new believers feel that they do not lose their identity as mountain people when they become Christians.

A STRATEGY FOR EVANGELISM

Because Ikalahan Christian communities want to do the outreach work to their fellow mountain people, the Ikalahan Mission has designed the Ikalahan Church Multiplication Project as a strategy for evangelizing the Ikalahan by their own people. The outsiders in this work are Delbert Rice and his team of trainers who are faculty members of the Ikalahan Mission high school. This Multiplication Project has established the following guidelines for implementing its evangelism strategy:

Policies and Principles for Evangelism

1. The entire church must be involved in the work of evangelism.

2. In every congregation, however young, God calls leaders (elders) to serve as pastors of congregations. Workers trained in seminary and Bible school must not take over the authority and responsibility of these elders; but must continue to support, assist, and supplement the work of these natural leaders and pastors.

3. The viable church is, from the beginning, involved in regular, consistent, organized, fruitful Bible study and prayer in preparation for its task of evangelism. Therefore, the life-style of the Ikalahan churches must emphasize Bible study and prayer, with evangelism following as the natural outgrowth.

4. Financial subsidy coming from outside a congregation for pastoral services has been found to be damaging to the life and growth of that congregation. Subsidies must, therefore, be specifically limited to and designated for outreach evangelism by that congregation. Further, all types of financial subsidies must be processed directly through local church treasurers.

5. Inter-congregational fellowship has been found to be highly effective in strengthening the spiritual life of the churches and their members. This supportive type of fellowship will be encouraged and stimulated, especially the program of sharing in prayer for the sick and for those who are working at evangelism-related activities.

6. The church, to be effective, must be in close contact with the local culture and must be in effective communication with it. The use of the mountain languages must be encouraged. The use of indigenous hymns must also be encouraged and their preparation promoted. The church must understand the ancient cultural ceremonies and customs, and must be sympathetic to their functions while maintaining its loyalty to the living Christ.

Training Program for Evangelism of the Ikalahan

The basic program of the Ikalahan Mission to the mountain communities is a holistic approach and is based on the preceding six principles and policies of evangelism. To prepare the Ikalahan churches for their evangelistic task, a six-part statement of policies and principles has also been prepared for the implementation and maintenance of a training program. These are stated as follows:

1. To encourage the outreach program, the presently designated three districts will be increased to five in order to decrease the area and number of persons for which each district will be accountable.

2. One trainer-evangelist will be assigned to each district. His responsibility will be to encourage the elders of the local congregations already established; promote the Bible study of each congregation and train the elders in how to promote such Bible study; and to reach out to evangelize new areas as quickly as possible.

3. Basic pastoral services will be provided by local elders and supported by the local congregations. When a congregation grows and desires a trained pastor, one may be provided, but that congregation must continue to support him/her. If that pastor is involved in outreach work, subsidy may be allowed for that specific purpose.

4. It is not the task of the Ikalahan Mission to insist on a unity of customs in the various congregations established. Because congregations will establish their own customs, these will probably be different from those of the nearby lowland churches. This is to be encouraged in order that we might all learn from one another and, in obedience to the Holy Spirit, reach out more effectively to the mountain cultures.

5. In-depth Bible training must be provided for the leaders of the various congregations. This will be done through a central training center in Imugan. Training for pastoral service must also be available. This will be done through the Community Bible School in Imugan. Encouragement of all the members, especially the youth, to a deeper Christian commitment will be en-

couraged through the Bible training incorporated into the curriculum of the Ikalahan Academy, a high school located in Imugan. All of these training programs must remain somewhat mobile, and must not become institutionalized, even though for efficiency they need to be centralized.

6. The Ikalahan Mission should become self-supporting or be supported by the Ikalahan Educational Foundation as early as possible. Local church expenses should be supported entirely by local churches from their beginning. Outreach expenses should be a cooperative effort of the Mission and the local churches. Outside support is necessary, however, to inaugurate this evangelism thrust until such time as the Foundation has its own income and funds.

IN SUMMARY

The Ikalahan Church has been planted by the Ikalahan Mission and has begun to grow, with its chief purpose the evangelization of its own people in the interior of Luzon. The strategy for this evangelistic task has been carefully mapped out. The plan for a basic training program has been thoughtfully delineated in a statement of principles and policies that are in the early stages of implementation. This strategy for evangelism and the development of a basic training program call for the building of a strong indigenous church.

The Ikalahan people are open to the gospel, particularly when presented by the Ikalahan Christians, allowing new believers to become a part of the indigenous church, and at the same time maintain their identity as Ikalahan mountain people.

Genuine evangelism among the Ikalahan will deal realistically with all their ancient culture and value systems that are not contrary to Christianity's scriptural principles. It will also deal realistically with the pressures of secularization now being felt by these people, particularly its serious and destructive effects among the youth.

Genuine evangelism will support the unity of the Ikalahan people, both in the community and in the family. The Ikalahan Christian needs to recognize that his/her status as a child of

Almighty God and as a member of the Ikalahan people is of inestimable value. As such, no Ikalahan has cause to be ashamed either of his/her faith or culture.

Financial responsibility for each church is, from its inception, in the hands of its own congregation. Outside financial aid is available to the Ikalahan churches only for the specific outreach/evangelism tasks required of each congregation. The limitation of outside assistance to this one purpose of outreach/evangelism is a significant means for encouraging an ongoing outreach program within each congregation for the establishment and building up of churches among the Ikalahan.

Darwin Sokoken works on the staff of World Vision. He was born in the Philippines and furthered his education at the Baptist Bible Seminary and Institute in the Philippines, the University of the Philippines, the Asian Theological Seminary, and Fuller Extension. He pastored a Baptist congregation for eight years at the military reservation of the Philippine Air Force, and worked with Philippine Crusades for five years in several capacities.

The Unreached Sinhala Buddhists of Sri Lanka

by Tissa Weerasingha

This article illustrates the background study necessary to begin the identification of people groups. Some dimension of social structure beyond mere religious identification is needed for the formulation of strategy.

This represents just the first step in field selection. The breakdown must proceed further to represent a people group.

The author then proceeds to identify the forces for evangelism present within the vital church, suggesting strategic directions these forces ought to take. The author's suggested stages of conversion could serve as a scale which should provide checkpoints for goals in evangelization.

The world population of 250 million Buddhists consists of two major groups: the Mahayanists and the Hinayanists, or Theravadins. This second group includes the more conservative and earlier form of Buddhists, and are prevalent in the South Asian countries of India, Sri Lanka, Cambodia, Laos, and Burma. The more liberal Mahayanists are found primarily in China, Tibet, Mongolia, Vietnam, Korea, and Japan.

In Sri Lanka, the cradle of Theravada Buddhism, nearly all Buddhists are ethnic Sinhalese, a group that makes up the island's largest community. Although there are other unreached peoples in Sri Lanka, this case study deals with the Sinhalese Buddhists.

A DESCRIPTION OF THE PEOPLE

The Ethnic Sinhalese

The Theravada Sinhala Buddhists form the largest and most influential socioreligious segment of Sri Lanka's pluralistic society. Within the country's 25,000 square miles and total population of 14 million, the Sinhalese number 10 million; 9.2 million of whom are Theravada Buddhists, spanning all classes, castes, and occupations of Sinhala society.

Probably the most distinctive feature of the Sinhalese is their Indo-Aryan mother tongue, Sinhala. According to Sinhalese chronicles, the origin of the people may be traced to a Prince Vijaya and his 700 followers who migrated to the island from Eastern India in 6 B.C.

Buddhism was introduced to the island in 3 B.C. by an Indian, Prince Mahinda, and rapidly became the religion of the Sinhalese. Since that time Sri Lanka's long and dominant tradition of Buddhism and Buddhist culture has served as the cornerstone of its national and religious heritage. Its Buddhists believe that they are a chosen people, and that Sri Lanka is a favored land from which the faith is to be spread to all the world.

For the Sinhalese, Buddhism is not merely a system of religious precepts and practices; it also serves as the unifying theme of the country's history and culture. Sinhalese culture stresses personal discipline and orderliness in behavior, and is group oriented rather than individualistic.

In spite of Western influence and colonial rule (450 years under Portuguese, Dutch, and British), the rural culture has largely remained intact through the centuries. However, among the urban population (the rural-urban ratio is estimated at 80 to 20 percent)—under the influence of Western art, literature, political ideologies, and the advent of tv—there is a gradual trend toward Westernization.

Basic Buddhist Beliefs

Gautama Buddha, born 623 B.C. in Nepal, was the founder of Buddhism. The doctrine *(dhamma)* he preached consists of (1) an analysis of the human situation, nature, existence; (2) the structure of the human personality; and (3) a setting forth of the *way* whereby suffering and mortality, the common lot of mankind, may be transcended and a new state of being achieved.

The basic creed of canonical Buddhism is expressed in the Four Noble Truths which state that:

1. All life is suffering *(duka)*.
2. Suffering arises through ignorant craving or attachment. *(tanha)*.
3. This suffering can be eliminated through cessation of craving *(nirodha)*.
4. Cessation is attained by following the Noble Eightfold Path of right understanding, right thoughts, right speech, right action, right livelihood, right endeavor, right mindfulness, and right concentration. (This path is intended to purify the individual of all defiling thoughts and actions, to work on the mind and to improve one's spiritual condition.)

The first three noble truths form the basic philosophy of Buddhism. The fourth lists the ethical values that stem from this philosophy which forms the basis for all religious practices of Buddhism, from the most popular to the most sophisticated.

To attain salvation, as the Buddha has done, one must escape not only from suffering and death, but also from the desire to live and from the pleasure of living. Only by renouncing the pleasures of life can one attain salvation. This is the one way to salvation and nothing but one's own efforts can achieve it.

There is no recourse to a deity, no prayer, grace, sacrament, predestination, nor even an enduring soul *(anatta)*. To wander through life after life until the goal of salvation is achieved is the individual's only hope. Although Buddhism initially opened a way to salvation for all people regardless of caste or sex, the actual attainment of salvation has always been restricted to a fortunate few, the strong in mind.

For the ordinary Buddhist the achievement of salvation is,

therefore, extremely difficult. It demands arduous meditation; and its ultimate attainment is quite remote because its achievement requires many thousands of rebirths.

Popular Buddhism and the Magico-religious Cults

The relationship between canonical Buddhism, popular Buddhism, and the magico-religious cults has been the subject of much critical and investigative study. The Buddha himself denied that any credit toward salvation could be earned through ritualistic practices. In fact, he openly denounced them. However, contemporary Buddhism cannot be adequately studied apart from the ceremonies and rituals which form a major part of the daily Sinhalese Buddhist's life.

In order to comprehend the complex Sinhalese religious system today, it is important to understand four basic aspects of popular Buddhism.

The pantheon is a hierarchical system composed of the Buddha (god above gods), deities, demons, and spirits. Although the Budda is not worshiped in the conventional sense, he does hold a presiding position in the pantheon. Below the Buddha there are not only guardian deities but also local gods, demons, and spirits.

A second aspect of popular Buddhism is the system of rites and rituals which are currently practiced by Sinhalese Buddhists. First, there are two officially approved rituals involving the monks. One is a devotional rite *(pinkam)* usually conducted in the temple. The other is the most important ceremony performed by monks: the chanting of *pirith* (protection) at important occasions to ward off evil influences.

The system of god worship in the temple shrine provides a second form of ritual. In almost every Buddhist temple a shrine is dedicated to one of the gods of the pantheon. There priest *(kapurala)* presents offerings to the deities to obtain blessings and assistance.

A third ritual system relates to astrology and the worship of planetary deities. In these rites a magician *(baliadura)* mediates to offset the evil influence of the planets.

Finally, there are the rites of exorcism in which an exorcist *(kattadirala)* mediates through offerings and dances to cast the evil spirits out of a patient. Most Buddhists, whether sophisticated or rural, resort to magical animism to promote their emotional and physical well-being. They turn to these practices to deal with their suffering, as well as to gain happiness in the present life.

STATUS OF CHRISTIANITY

Background
Christian missions first came to Sri Lanka with the advent of the colonial powers. The Portuguese brought Catholicism in the fifteenth century; the Dutch brought the Reformed faith in the sixteenth century, followed by the British early in the nineteenth century. During colonial rule, the rights of the Buddhists were denied and Christianity was accorded status as the accepted religion.

Today the Christian population of all ethnic communities in the island is 1,035,000—or 8.4 percent of the total population. Of these Christians approximately 718,000 are ethnic Sinhalese, about 3 percent of the island's total.

Most denominations and several international para-church organizations are represented within the Christian community. It is quite obvious, however, that the Sinhalese as an ethnic group have been the target of very little church planting activity. Currently, the government of Sri Lanka grants no new missionary visas, although replacements for the forty or more missionaries presently working there are permitted. Except for a few charismatic and other evangelical churches, a declining growth rate is evident in most churches of the island.

Receptivity Factors
Historically, the Sinhalese Buddhists have either been resistant or indifferent to the gospel. Because colonialists treated Buddhism as an enemy, the Buddhists continue to feel that Christianity is an ally of Western culture and Western imperialism, and

that it is an obstacle to their objectives.

Furthermore, the current Buddhist revival (initiated in 1880 by the noted American Buddhist, Henry Steele Olcott, and which gives indications of continuing for years to come) has acted as a catalyst in cementing even more firmly the close-knit identification of Buddhism with Sri Lanka's national aspirations. This national religious solidarity is further enhanced by the strong political influence and direct involvement in national affairs of the *sangha* (monkhood) based in more than 6,000 monasteries with approximately 16,000 monks and 14,000 novices.

When the island became a republic in 1972, Buddhism was declared the state religion. Also, the state guaranteed to protect Buddhism and encourage its spread throughout the world. On the basis of this intent, it is a definite advantage to be a Sinhalese Buddhist in Sri Lanka today. And as a result, among the general populace the Christian gospel receives minimal consideration as an option or an alternative to Buddhism.

Forces for Evangelism

At this point it is important to identify four evident resources for evangelizing the Sinhalese Buddhists. These forces are not culturally distant and offer input that could be significant to the conclusions which may be drawn from this case study:

The evangelical Protestant community is estimated at twelve thousand, the large majority of whom are charismatic or pentecostal. How many ethnic Sinhalese are numbered among these evangelicals is not determined.

The Catholic charismatic movement is currently estimated at thirty thousand strong and growing fast. This movement has brought a new vitality to the Church, but it has not yet demonstrated a missionary vision to the non-Christian community. However, if the great resources at their command were harnessed and directed toward evangelizing the Buddhists, a tremendous outreach would be the result. Hopefully, this is a direction the movement will take.

The independent pentecostal and charismatic churches are a third valuable force for evangelization of the Buddhists in Sri

Lanka. Usually meeting as house churches, these groups have an uncompromising commitment to evangelization, and are one of the most potent forces for the fulfillment of the Great Commission among the Sinhalese. These churches have flexible training methods and are geared particularly to rural evangelization.

The para-church organizations are a fourth grouping with potential for mounting an important evangelization thrust to the Buddhists. Although those in this category are not in the forefront of church planting activity, they could provide effective support through their primary tasks in radio and literature distribution.

STRATEGY FOR EVANGELISM

To present the gospel in terms the Sinhalese understand, the following factors should be studied and a strategy for implementation determined:

Christian Ethnotheology

In the past, the gospel has been presented to the Buddhists in Western categories and concepts. The immediate and crucial need now is for the formulation of a Christian ethnotheology which is expressed in terms oriented to the conceptual framework of Buddhism.

Culturally Oriented Literature

Most of the Christian literature distributed among Sinhalese Buddhists today is a translation of material from a foreign source. Such productions do not speak to the Buddhist world view. For instance, the word *god,* as used by the foreign communicators, has a very different meaning to the Buddhist than that which it was intended to convey. In the Buddhist context a god is an inferior person who himself is a seeker of liberation. The term *Son of God* denotes a person even more inferior.

Literature should also be prepared with an eye toward the various groups within Sinhala society—such as the youth (65 percent under thirty years old), the farmers and fishermen (48 percent of the labor force), and other distinct sociological groupings. In the island of Sri Lanka, where the literacy rate is 90 percent, literature is destined to play a significant role.

Indigenous Worship Patterns

Until the Church massively reorients its worship forms to more indigenous patterns—particularly in the rural areas, there will be a limited response among the Sinhalese. In addition, the Christian festivals as generally celebrated by the Western church will receive but a limited response from the Sinhalese until there is an appropriate incorporation of the familiar forms and materials used by the Buddhists in their celebrations.

Obvious questions for consideration here might be, for instance, Why do Christians not set up *pandals* (lighted, open-air stages) for commemoration of the Church's Christmas and Easter seasons, as the Buddhists do during their *Vesak* celebration? And, could the Christian churches not more overtly celebrate the national festivals—such as the Sinhalese New Year, now celebrated almost solely by the Buddhists—in order to create functional substitutes, especially for new converts?

Meeting Needs as a Stimulus to Conversion

Because the majority of Sinhalese Buddhists practice a mixture of Buddhism and magical animism, any evangelistic strategy that does not take seriously the role of the spiritual intermediaries in meeting the Buddhist's psychic needs will have little impact. Fear is clearly the major felt need among Buddhists. This is the logical outcome of the Sinhalese Buddhist's theory of cause that explains all good or ill as determined by supernatural forces: evil mouth, evil eye, demons, and deities, all of which are dangerous and to be feared. Fears of personal pollution, demon possession, sorcery, and witchcraft haunt the Buddhist mind. The one message that can meet the widespread human need among Sinhalese Buddhists is the gospel message of healing, exorcism, and deliverance from demonic powers.

Recognition of Conversion Stages

Experience shows that the idol-worshiping Sinhalese Buddhist usually comes to God in stages. That is, when the person's felt need—whatever that may be—is met, his or her first evident turn from Buddhism is to stop worshiping idols and communicating with spirits. This is a major step. Thereafter, under the ministry of the Word, (s)he realizes (s)he has broken the laws of God and is, therefore, guilty of sin. This recognition and repentance often is a later step in the conversion experience. For this reason, evangelists among Sri Lanka's Buddhists speak of a pre-conversion stage (turning from idols) and a later regeneration experience.

IN SUMMARY

Strategizing to evangelize the Sinhalese Buddhists will require the formation of a Christian ethnotheology to serve as a base from which indigenous literature and worship patterns may be developed. Effective planning for the evangelistic task will also integrate an understanding of the people's needs stemming from the ritualistic systems of Buddhism and an awareness of the multistage conversion pattern (decision, nurture, and regeneration) characteristic of those turning from Buddhism to Christ.

Building the Church of Jesus Christ in Sri Lanka calls for the Christian mission and ethnic leadership to outline, communicate and implement parallel, supportive and, wherever possible, united outreach strategies. Harnessing the island's forces for evangelism from within its present Christian communities is a major determinant in accomplishing this task.

Tissa Weerasingha of Colombo, Sri Lanka, is the pastor of Calvary Church. He has written a book *Morsel of Bread* and many other tracts of booklets. He has traveled and taught in many countries of Europe, North America, Singapore, and Malaysia. His ministry has brought blessings to many people in his country and is one of God's anointed servants in Asia today for the end-time harvest. He has just completed his M.A. program at Fuller Seminary's School of World Mission in Pasadena, California.

Evangelizing Taiwan-Chinese College Students

by Jack C. Rea, Samuel Chao, David Wyma, and Cliff Good

The case of university students is an interesting one. Students seem at first to be a natural grouping on which to base a special strategy for evangelization. The difficulty is that it's hard to imagine student evangelism that would result in a church made up of students only. Fellowship groups may be formed, but they will be only transitory, for the students' experience itself is transitory. The authors wrestle with these and other difficulties.

Some helpful generalizations about students are possible, and the text defines some more distinctive subgroups: Taiwanese aboriginal girls, Catholics whose lives are defined by tradition and family affiliation. These and other definitions could form the basis for special strategies, especially if they further define the students on the basis of geographical location. Students who attend the same college, for example, have a natural affinity for one another that can facilitate evangelization.

DEMOGRAPHIC INFORMATION

Geography and Population of Taiwan

Taiwan is situated about 100 miles off the southeast coast of the People's Republic of China and across the Taiwan Straits from

Fukien Province. Covering roughly 35,900 square kilometers, Taiwan includes approximately eighty-six islands. One-third of the land mass is comprised of coastal plains and foothills that lead to mountains rising to more than 14,000 feet.

The population of Taiwan has grown from more than 6 million in 1946 to over 16 million in 1977, with a present population density of 467 persons per square kilometer. Ninety-five percent of the population lives on the western coastal plain, which is one-third of the island's land mass.

Arranged by age groupings, the population of those up to age fourteen totals 5,705,148 (33.9 percent); from fifteen to sixty-four, a total of 10,464,942 (62.3 percent); and only 643,037 persons over sixty-five years of age (3.8 percent). There are more than twice as many people under twenty-five years of age as there are above twenty-five, with the greater proportion in the five to eighteen year group.

A Profile of Taiwan-Chinese College Students
The age range from fifteen to twenty-eight years is a critical period in many young people's lives. Many are taking exams to gain entrance to higher levels of education. Others have finished their education and are being assimilated into the nation's work force. Some are just waiting until they finish their compulsory military service before they become involved in civilian pursuits. Numerous young women are working and living in the large industrial complexes as they wait for their parents to find the right mate for them. And there are many young men searching for appropriate apprenticeships. These years from fifteen to twenty-eight are times of vocational uncertainty for the young adults of Taiwan.

At no point is societal pressure more evident than in the emphasis placed on university/college/technical school students who represent the nation's intelligentsia and hope for tomorrow. Parents place an inordinate amount of pressure on their young to do well in school because of heavy competition for the few available places in the colleges and technical institutions (20,000 of 100,000 are accepted in college each year).

In Taiwan, education represents the best method of raising one's status in life. Education puts food on the table and serves as the union card for vocational, societal, and geographical mobility. Significant numbers of the young adults, therefore, strive to become a part of the student population and thereby assure themselves good opportunity in the academic, business, or industrial leadership of Taiwan.

With this high-potential population segment in mind, it is crucial that a strategy (goals, methods, and programs) be devised to train people to evangelize students in the secular and the Christian colleges/universities of Taiwan.

Presently, there are approximately 308,500 students in the nation's 102 colleges and universities: 9.5 percent are involved in the humanities; 6.2 percent in education; 3.52 percent in agriculture; 1.3 percent in law; 32.62 percent in social sciences; 4.7 percent in natural sciences; 31.9 percent in engineering; 7.2 percent in medicine; and 3.1 percent in the fine arts. The total student population is grouped with approximately 73,800 in universities; 76,000 in colleges; and 159,000 in junior colleges. These can be considered a people group. How can they be reached?

Religious Attitudes of Students
During the past three years, two major studies have been conducted to examine the religious attitudes and preferences of college-age students. The first was implemented by the local Youth Center. Four thousand students, ranging in age from eighteen to thirty (62.6 percent males, 27.4 percent females) in all kinds of educational institutions were interviewed. The second study was conducted by Dr. Daniel Ross of Fu Jen University in 1978 when he examined the religious values and practices of 2,646 students at a Catholic girls' college.

Ross found that approximately 60 percent of the students felt or reported that they did not have any religious faith. However, when they were asked specifically if they were, for instance, traditional Buddhists, Taoists, or followers of some other religion named, 5.51 percent reported they were Buddhist, 13.26 percent were followers of other popular religions, 11 percent were Protestant, and 8 percent were Catholic. The KMT questionnaire found that 34 percent of the students considered themselves nominal Buddhist, 15 percent Protestant, 7 percent Catholic, and 44 percent felt they did not have any religious affiliation. However, most students hold an informal belief in a god or gods. (This is true of Taiwanese aboriginal girl students, in particular.)

At a Christian college in Chung Li, a survey revealed that course work in religion and in Christianity influenced students' thinking; it also provided opportunity for serious consideration of religious issues.

From the foregoing surveys, several conclusions may be drawn:

1. Most college students are searching for values and religion.

2. Many students, if not all, will listen and study religion if the opportunity is made available.

3. Most non-Christian college students are eager to learn about any kind of organized religion if someone takes the time and effort to present it.

4. Most students enjoyed being interviewed if their ideas were to be recorded or to be in print.

5. Hindrances to accepting the Christian religion are a cover which can be penetrated by the love and personal concern of someone who makes time for honest interaction and allows time for the gospel to soak in.

6. Most students have ethical principles, but do not know how to live them out as an expression of their religion.

7. Most Catholic students are what they are by tradition or family affiliation, not by conversion.

8. Many Protestant students become Christians during high school and early college years. In this period they face many difficult situations—such as exams and heavy parental pressures to pass college entrance requirements.

9. Christian education within the church or in the family is the single most important contributor to personal religious beliefs, and correlates positively with church attendance, personal de-

votions, mate selection, and continuing involvement in the church.

AN ANALYSIS OF TAIWAN-CHINESE COLLEGE STUDENTS

Students' Philosophical and Theological Thought

To document accurately the philosophical framework in which the typical Chinese person of the eighties operates is a major undertaking; for it presents a complex picture with a mixture of old and new thoughts, along with a mixture of Chinese and foreign thoughts.

The modern Chinese could probably be described as syncretistic in their approach to life. The center of syncretistic thinking tends either to be deistic or pantheistic. The former emphasizes the transcendence of God and is rationalistic and moralistic. The latter emphasizes the eminence of God and the mystical identity of man with the cosmos. While claiming to champion religious tolerance, syncretistic thinking is generally intolerant of all systems not in accord with its own principles.

The term *three ways to one goal* is a key in an historical approach to the Chinese philosophy of life. To elaborate, these three ways, or three religions are:

1. Confucianism, with its emphasis on sociopolitical morals, ceremonies, and the active life;

2. Taoism, with its concern for idyllic idealism, mystical life and superstitious geomancy (divination by means of a figure made by a handful of earth thrown down at random; or by figures or lines formed by a number of dots made at random).

3. Buddhism, with its affirmation of reincarnation, ritual, and the philosophical life.

Still another term that expresses a basic, modern Chinese philosophy is the Three Principles of the People. Dr. Sun, as a result of his studies in the West, patterned this *San min ju yi* after Lincoln's Gettysburg Address: "... government of the people, for the people, and by the people."

Married to a strong political platform of nationalism is the belief in *militarism*—a term, if properly applied, that is used only when war is regarded by any group, society, or nation as a primary ethical or political value. Among the Taiwan-Chinese this mindset is by no means limited to fighting forces, for many in the civilian population evidence this point of view. External pressures or threats to internal security may have brought the nation to regard military force as the only hope of continuance and development.

A third segment of modern Chinese philosophical thought in Taiwan may be identified as a pattern that revolves around the country's economic development program.

Taiwan's people have all to some degree been exposed to these thought forms. In general terms, the oldest generation has been greatly influenced by the three traditional religions: Confucianism, Taoism, and Buddhism. The middle-aged portion of Taiwan's society has been influenced most by the Three Principles of the People. The youngest generation is now caught up in the drive for modernization and its accompanying thought forms. However, all the people have been partially influenced by the several patterns of thought already mentioned; so it is unrealistic to literally stratify society according to adherence to prevailing philosophies.

Philosophical Challenge to Christianity

The enormous task confronting Christianity is to find a suitable thought form for conveying Christ as the one who redeems souls, and thereby correct erroneous Chinese thought forms. Several other challenges have emerged for the proclamation of the Christian message to the student population:

1. Christianity is monotheistic, not polytheistic, as Taiwan's religions are.

2. Christianity clearly teaches absolute concepts of life and death. On the other hand, Buddhism teaches that life is a continuous process through reincarnation.

3. Christianity's ultimate good and absolute value is God himself, not an abstract concept or simply a tangible reward.

4. Christianity's salvation from personal sin is attainable only

by God's grace through faith. In other religions salvation is never attainable.

5. Christianity has an absolute value system, not negotiable on a day-to-day basis, as a dialectic system offers.

6. Christianity does not reduce life to a formula, but offers to the world's peoples a personal, loving relationship with the living God.

State of the Church in Taiwan

Commenting in her book, *Protestantism in Changing Taiwan*, Dorothy Raber states that during the ten-year period of 1964-74, Protestant churches reached levels of no growth. Since that time they have lost further ground by their inability to keep up with population growth. Bold plans and unprecedented development must take place in the years immediately ahead if the church is to catch up.

So how can we saturate Taiwan with the gospel and build a strong, growing church? There are sufficient numbers of books and studies to indicate why church growth in Taiwan has stagnated and how to turn the situation around. A few comments are appropriate for statement here:

Allen Swanson writes that the mainline churches of Taiwan must free themselves from static, nonproductive, obviously Western methods and seek to establish truly indigenous Chinese congregations. Nationals and missionaries must together convince every Taiwanese Christian of the obligation, privilege, and dignity of self-support.

David Liao has said that we must recognize the urgency of the possibilities today, while people are experiencing a measure of cultural vacuum, especially in connection with the Hakka Chinese people. Liao also suggests that a more positive approach to the tradition of ancestor worship be taken and that the possibility of using functional substitutes to replace its demonic components be sought.

Robert Bolten's studies suggest that a move be made toward an urban strategy based on proven principles. His suggestions are worthy of consideration for sake of their application to a strategy for evangelizing students.

Barriers to the Gospel among Students

Three major barriers can be identified as hindrances to sharing the gospel with college-age young people. These issues may be described briefly as:

1. *Cultural barrier.* Christianity is thought of as an American, or, at least a Western religion. Chinese parents strongly resist their children's forsaking the traditional religions of the family. Nothing is more important for a family than to assure that the ancestral tablets are taken care of, worshiped, and passed on to succeeding generations. Christianity is known to oppose the worship of ancestors. In the West, Christianity is seen as a matter of individual concern. This approach in the Orient is often opposed as being foreign.

2. *Social Barriers.* These hindrances to Christianity are major issues to many Chinese who feel that becoming a church member, a pastor, or a Christian worker is demeaning. The value placed on affluence and sophistication hurts the spread of the gospel. For it is seen as a religion for the lowly and unsuccessful in a society that gives high priority to achieving an education, influence, and wealth.

Another social barrier to the gospel, is the urbanization that offers a materialistic, sensual life-style with strong, big-city attractions for young adults.

A third social barrier that can prove to be a problem is language differences. This is evident when a student enters a church service or other Christian gathering to find that his or her mother tongue is not being used.

3. *Lack of church's outreach.* The obvious failure of the Chinese church itself to reach out is a third barrier that reflects an uncaring exclusivism that contradicts the heart of the gospel message. Without a burden for evangelization, the Chinese churches leave the youth to suffer.

In some cases the youth are a threat to the church because of their educational achievement and the pastor's lack of education. The members with money generally rule the church. The youth, who usually have little money, are therefore not included as contributors to the functioning of the church.

Building Bridges to the Gospel

The problems previously described are but some of the barriers college-age youth face in considering Christianity. But all is not negative for there are bridges being built to reach the youth of Taiwan with the gospel.

Some vital college student ministries are now reaching out to students that the church cannot reach. However, there are some churches that are open for Saturday night youth meetings, with the host church having only a loose and unofficial connection.

English teaching by foreign missionaries is probably one of the most widespread bridges being built at the present. The amount of gospel witness and Bible study included in the language study varies from group to group.

The Chung Tai English Radio program reports annual statistics that indicate when the vast majority of listeners are asked if they want someone to talk with them further about Christianity, few respond. In the churches, when asked why they came to the radio-sponsored service, a large percentage indicated "brought by friends."

These various bridges mentioned here have already proven effective in reaching out to Chinese young people and sowing the seed in Taiwan. But herein lies a problem: these bridges are basically outside the church. When the outside groups try to bring young people into the church, the members have trouble accepting and involving them in the work and worship of the church. Consequently, young people are not entering the life of the organized church in any significant numbers. And this factor points again to the need for the church to develop and activate a sound strategy for reaching out as well as bringing these young people into the church

A STRATEGY FOR EVANGELIZING TAIWAN-CHINESE COLLEGE STUDENTS

A young missionary going home on furlough for the second time cogently expressed his frustration when he stated, "You can't build the future of the Taiwanese church on college students!" He had spent his first term working with college students, and his second term working with families in southern Taiwan. His second term was substantially more rewarding than his first, for the fruits of his first term seemed to be racked with the five-year turnover syndrome and the failure to integrate the young people into the churches.

College-age young people make decisions for Christ, but five years later they are caught up in making money and following traditions. Even young women who make excellent progress in their walk with Christ during their college years were crushed by their parents' plans committing them to marry non-Christians.

Analyzing the Problems

To address the problems of this ministry and fulfill the goals of the gospel, the inherent problems first must be analyzed. Over the years Taiwan has experienced the full spectrum of mission and church organizations—some traditional, some charismatic, some classical, and some human-relations oriented. Campus ministries have experienced a similar pattern. In each of these programs some common areas of difficulty have emerged, in spite of a wide variety of methods and procedures.

Each organization and ministry has had its strengths and weaknesses, but seldom have they been eclectic in their outreach plans. It seems as if each organization is attempting to carve its own chunk out of the student body. Subsequently, churches, Young Life, Campus Crusade, Navigators, Bible-study groups, and the campus chapel are all competing for the same students. And in this same context, many collegians have become involved in a dynamic Christian campus program only to find that it becomes nonexistent after the leader has left the island or the funds have been spent.

A second problem is that students on campuses have been exposed only to experience oriented Christian programs. Over the past ten years, there has been a tremendous growth in the popularity of small Bible study, support, sharing, and discussion group methods. Students have found Christ in small Bible-study groups where they have had an opportunity to share, discuss, pray, and worship together informally. However, students in these situations often lack exposure to an overview of the Scriptures and Christian doctrine. Seldom do these students have opportunities, for instance, to survey the logical writing of C. S. Lewis or Francis Schaeffer, to provide opportunity for crystalizing and conceptualizing their faith.

The problems of young college graduates trying to fit into a traditional, classically oriented church structure presents a third major difficulty. As students they have been groomed in experience oriented Christianity and training. Then, to become integrated into the Christian church, they must switch to fit into a totally different social pattern, organizational plan, and structured expression of worship.

Determining the Focus

In light of these problems, a strategy must be designed beginning with goal statements which determine the thrusts of the ministries to and with college students. This goal-setting (input stage) of the plan is a critical time for determining the major directions of the program; second, for identifying the specific target populations of students who might be receptive to the gospel; and third, designing and constructing programs that will meet needs of these students.

Many kinds of programs and services for Christian students are initiated, but few are focused on assisting them to examine their faith or on finding students who are open and receptive to the gospel. In some instances, attention is centered on a few, and other students waiting, looking and listening in the background are forgotten. Another tendency of campus ministries is to initiate programs that fit the goals of the church or of the educational institution, but fail to meet the needs of the students.

Many times a program is designed and activated with no thought given to the disastrous effects it is having on the total system. For instance, the decision is made to set up small Bible-study groups for evangelizing students, but the plan fails to include something for the students who already have made a commitment to Christ and need to grow in knowledge and understanding of him. Or, the plan for evangelization fails to include follow-up methods that will help students develop an enduring and growing relationship in fellowship with Christ and with his people. These outgrowth functions need to be thoughtfully considered and worked through prior to the initiation of a specific program, no matter how worthy it may be in itself.

Setting the Goals

What, then, should be the major thrust or goals of a student evangelism program? First, it should use all its resources to bring students to an understanding of Christ and a commitment to him. The programs, methods, and techniques that assist in achieving this goal are many and varied. Youth groups, Bible teaching in English, mandatory or elective courses (Bible, doctrine, Christian living, etc.) in the curriculum, counseling with students, chapel services, Bible-study fellowship groups, vocational planning, assistance, and whatever other means may be selected should all help provide individual students with an experience of what it means for Christ to become an integral part of his or her life.

A second goal is also mandatory—that of providing vehicles whereby students can develop and synthesize their Christian faith. Courses in philosophy or apologetics and small discussion groups of current Christian writers' works in Asia and the Western world could be useful in helping students conceptually and culturally wrestle with God, nature, and themselves.

A third imperative is to aid students to become integrated into the body of Christ and into the community of the fellowship of believers—the church. All possible efforts should be employed to help the pastors and the lay people accept and involve college students into the life of the church. This may be achieved, for example, by raising the educational level of pastors so they are not threatened by the more advanced educational status of the students; also, by providing church leaders with in-service coworkers selected from college and postcollege young people.

In practical terms, outreach programs to students should be part of the church. Christian youth should be involved in the church's operations and functioning as teachers, group leaders, and in other areas of appropriate service. Churches and seminaries need to emphasize and improve the Sunday school, catechism instruction and building the home into a strong Christian education center and laboratory for daily Christian living.

Outside the organized church, student ministry personnel should serve as a bridge between the para-church groups and the local churches. Efforts should be made to assist students leaving school to find appropriate church homes. Student ministry personnel should also incorporate church people into their student-oriented programs, and thereby expand the horizons of students to see the role and function of continued fellowship in the body of believers.

Finally, efforts must be directed toward assisting students as they live in their families and work in community vocations. Records of personal data could be kept on other Christians who live in the same communities and work for the same companies so young Christian adults might be encouraged by a "spiritual mentor" and friend in Christ. Students need help in sorting out areas of potential conflict with parents and in coming up with viable options.

In summary, the goals of student evangelism and outreach must include the assistance of students to integrate their Christian faith into their culture. Obviously, the listing of these goals stated in the preceding paragraphs are not intended to be either sequential or weighted in their presentation. Rather, these goals should be worked out simultaneously, and they should be supportive of one another.

Given the previously stated goals, personnel involved in student ministries must identify the students they will assist from all the students who need to be reached; and to select the student populations that are receptive to the gospel. Friends of Christian students, campus student leaders, groping and intellectually oriented students, students with low self-esteem—these are just some of many possible groupings that would make good target populations. Then, using classroom discussions, surveys, papers, opinion questionnaires, discussions about other young people, Christian students could be guided to focus on other students as potential contacts. Response and question cards and the raising of hands in chapel services are methods for discovering students who are open to outreach and follow-up evangelism.

Programming to Meet Student Needs

Having determined goals and identified the target group(s), leaders need to delineate various program options based on the needs of the population selected. To initiate programs that do not match needs, interests, and aptitudes of the constituency being served is obviously folly. To begin, include a broad outline of program possibilities to give direction and stimulate the thought of program personnel working in the initiation and operational stages. During these first stages, all the elements are continually being programmed in order to meet previously identified needs and goals. Goals, resource materials, and methods form a continuing cycle of evaluation if the programming is to stay on target and to achieve the determined goals.

IN SUMMARY

The preceding overview has but briefly described a systematic, inductive method for examining student ministries and evangelism on the university and college campuses of Taiwan. The process, with each of its procedures, requires timely and thorough study before adoption as a model for evangelism among the student/youth adult population.

To expect that a plan for meeting student needs effectively can be developed hurriedly is unrealistic. And to assume that programs which have been successful on Western campuses will also be appropriate to Taiwan is unreasonable in light of the facts.

Societal dynamics, cultural norms and value systems, religious traditions and philosophies combine in formulating the unique needs of the student population in Taiwan. Integrating those who respond to evangelism and outreach programs into the existing church presents great challenges. These must be thoughtfully met by leaders of para-church student ministries in close cooperation with leaders of the churches. A new thrust of evangelism and resulting harvest will, by God's Spirit, be the evident response to effective planning and operation of campus and church strategies in Taiwan.

Dr. Jack Rae serves with the Friends Mission in Taiwan. **Cliff Good** is with OMS International, serving as a teacher in Taichung, Taiwan. **Samuel Chao** is the librarian at Chung Yuan Christian University in Chung Li, Taiwan. **David Wyma** teaches at Chung Fhan Medical School and Tung Hsi University in Taiwan.

NOTES TO PART 2

1. A tribal agricultural practice of cutting and clearing the trees; then, burning the underbrush. This is followed by dry farming until the soil is depleted. At this point the farmers move to another site and repeat the process, leaving formerly planted areas unusable for future agriculture or for return of the land to its natural growth. (from *The Philippines* by Esther Maring. Metuchen, N.J.: Scarecrow Press, 1973, pp. 101, 102).

Part 3
The Task Remaining

The Task Remaining

by Ralph Winter

The overall picture given on these pages is an attempt to describe the major proportions of the different aspects of the missionary challenge. Since this table (figure 1) and its accompanying chart (figure 2) first appeared in 1977, practically every number has changed. This means we can't go on forever quoting numbers like the "2.4 billion" or the "2.5 billion." The numbers should actually change every hour of every day, but we need to adjust them to the latest estimates on at least a yearly basis. They will never be exact or accurate. But they do help us put the task of world evangelization in proper perspective.

The changes from last year to this year are not necessarily the result of actual growth because of evangelism or even biological growth from the expansion of Christian families. Some of the major changes are simply revisions of previous estimates. This time, for example, the number of Christians in Africa has been greatly increased due to more precise estimates by Dr. David Barrett.

However, the most drastic revision this year is the introduction of the new category of *Tribals*. It is not as though we omitted the tribal peoples in previous counts; they were included in the Other

WORLD STATISTICS, MID-1980 IN MISSIONARY PERSPECTIVE[1]
(population given in millions)

	CHRISTIAN		NON-CHRISTIAN		POP.[2] TOTALS	N.A. FOREIGN MISSIONARIES		DIVERSITY IN COLUMN 4	HIDDEN PEOPLE GROUPS
	1 ACTIVE	2 INACTIVE E-0	3 CULTURALLY NEAR E-1,	4 CULTURALLY DISTANT E-2, E-3[3]	5	6 WORKING WITH 1, 2, 3	7 WORKING WITH 4	8 LAN-GUAGES	9
Western									
USA, Canada	69.75	147.75	16.5	12	246	—	100	40	300
Other Western	64.5	723.5	185	104	1,077	—	200	30	200
Sub Total	134	871	202	116	1,323	15,000	300	70	500
Non-Western									
Chinese	5	1	140	757	903	1,700	100	50	2,000
Hindus	8	12	50	504	574	950	50	200	3,000
Muslims, Asian	.150	.050	25	497	522.2	100	50	300	3,500
Muslims, African	.030	.010	400	181	181.44	50	50	280	500
Tribals	24.75	34.75	29.5	186	275	5,000	2,400	4,200	4,850
Other Asians	43	66	152	198	459	6,000	400	600	1,500
Other Africans	39	106	11	20	176	7,000	100	500	900
Sub Total	120	220	408	2,343	3,091	20,800	3,150	6,130	16,250
Total	245	1,091	610 / 20%	2,459 / 80%	4,414	35,800 / 91%	3,450 / 9%	6,200	16,750
Combined Totals	1,345 / 30.5%		3,069 / 69.5%			39,250			

[1] E-0, E-1, and E-2 represent degrees of difference from the evangelist's culture, which in shorthand is called an E-1 culture. E-1, or "monocultural evangelism," is contrasted to "cross-cultural evangelism," for which the symbols E-2 and E-3 stand.

[2] Population Reference Bureau, Washington, D.C.
[3] Hidden Peoples

U.S. Center for World Mission
Box 9, Pasadena, CA 91109

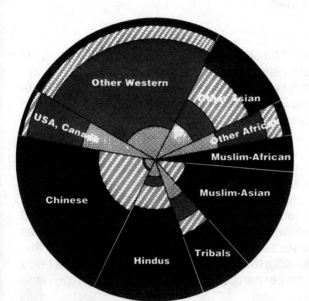

The pie chart contains the following labels:
- Other Western
- USA, Canada
- Chinese
- Hindus
- Tribals
- ...sian
- ...ther Afric...
- Muslim-African
- Muslim-Asian

The World in Missionary Perspective

Active Christians (COLUMN 1)

These people definitely possess a genuine personal faith and are capable of winning others to that faith. They do need Christian nurture, and many missionaries are involved in this task.

Inactive Christians (COLUMN 2)

These people are culturally within the Christian tradition but hardly qualify as committed Christians. They need "renewal." Most evangelism and mission effort (in India one report has it 98%) is focused on this group.

Culturally-near Non-Christians (COLUMN 3)

These are those whose cultural tradition and social sphere have already been penetrated by the Christian faith. For these people there now already exists, *culturally* near at hand, some Christian congregation or denomination where they can readily fit in linguistically and socially. National Christians are evangelizing these people.

Culturally-distant Non-Christians (COLUMN 4)

These are the "Hidden People" — individuals and groups who, whether geographically near or far from Christian outreach, are sufficiently different linguistically, socially, economically, or culturally so that they are simply not realistic candidates for membership in existing Christian churches. They are thus people that are "hidden" from Christian witness. In the Book of Acts the "devout persons" were Greeks and did not fit well into the Jewish synagogues Paul visited. The church as we know it was not truly born until Greeks and other Romans were able to run their own churches.

FIGURE 2

Asian and Other African categories. Some of them were also in the two Western categories, USA-Canada and Other Western.

With the exception of column 5, which comes from the Population Reference Bureau, we need to emphasize that we have no reliable justification for the breakdowns of column 5 into columns 1, 2, 3, and 4. These estimates are based upon categories significant mainly to missionaries and evangelists, and are not the subject of widespread discussion or investigation. In this sense, all of the data given is really only an approximation of reality, and, in effect, a plea for help! If you don't think that a given number is correct, your judgment may be as good as ours, and we would appreciate hearing from you about it. These estimates are in many cases very rough estimates, but we know well that any estimate is better than no data at all, especially when it helps put the total in proper perspective. And so, we have simply done our best.

Although the writer is principally responsible and principally to blame for any incorrect or unfair estimates, I am glad this year to acknowledge the additional help of Dr. Samuel Wilson, the new director of MARC, World Vision, and also Boyd Johnson, Research Associate of MARC, who has accompanied me in this task. In previous years I have had the help of another former World Vision staff person, David Fraser. In the area of the Hindus, we have gone to Dr. McGavran, of the Fuller School of World Mission. In the case of the Chinese, the data was supplied by our own people who do research in that area here at the U.S. Center for World Mission. For the Muslim area we have drawn upon the insights of the Samuel Zwemer Institute. But in no case should the final conclusions be blamed on others. They have only given us advice. We must take the responsibility for our interpretations. Once more, this presentation is more a plea for help than a pronouncement which we are bold to justify.

There are some comments that have merely to do with the construction of the categories. The category of *Chinese,* for example, does not refer to the people who live in China, but rather to the Han Chinese people, whether they live in China or anyplace else. This means that quite a few people in China are not counted, while quite a few people outside of China are included. The same is true with the Hindus and the Muslims, although the Muslims are at least broken down into two geographical divisions. As in previous tabulations, we have excluded Muslims who are in residence in the Western world on the grounds that the longer they stay, it may be more meaningful to approach them on the basis of some category other than their Muslim faith. On the other hand, we have brought into the non-Western category tribal peoples who live in the Western world, on the grounds that tribal people are more isolated (than the Muslims living in the Western world) and are thus probably more reasonably approached in terms of their non-Western cultural tradition. The number of total missionaries from North America has gone up, but we don't know how much it should go up until the next edition of the MARC *Mission Handbook* comes out, which should be fairly soon. Next year we will record that additional amount, and, if possible, will include missionaries from every part of the world as that data becomes available.

For those who may not have seen previous editions of this chart, you need to understand the significance of the North American missionary data. Note that 91 percent of the North American missionaries are estimated to be involved in E-0 or E-1 evangelism while only 9 percent are attempting to reach those among whom there is no, or only minimal, Christian witness. We hope that in coming years we will see an impressive shift in these numbers.

Dramatic new insights come from this year's rearrangement of the circle diagram to allow for an additional piece of the pie for the tribal category. The upper portion of the large circle still portrays the Western, Other Asian or Other African categories as being those sectors within which the least amount of missiological effort is still necessary. The bottom portion shows the "still needing mission" sectors. But the tribal piece of the pie is by far the largest single task remaining, even though the total number of tribal peoples, by whatever definition, is nowhere near as large as the other major pieces of the pie in the bottom half.

There are many interesting things about this data which are

not actually calculated and written down. For example, you can add the subtotals for non-Western Christians (committed and nominal) and get 340 million, which constitutes 11 percent of the 3091 million non-Western peoples. Compared with last year's data, this 11 percent figure is in fact 2 percent higher than last year. This is a happy increase, even though in great part it is the result of David Barrett's discovery of more Christians rather than the results of evangelism!

Also note that the percentage of Christians in the entire world is shown as 30.5 percent. Quite a few of these, of course, are Christians who don't count for very much in terms of assisting with the task of world evangelization. (They are part of the problem, not part of the solution.) Thus, it is likely that this number will remain very nearly stationary for a few years simply because the rapid growth rate of the population in the non-Western world is not sufficient to counterbalance the near-zero growth rate of population in general in the Western world, where the highest proportion of Christians is to be found.

From time to time we are asked how we derive the data on "committed" and "nominal" Christians. First, let us remember that those two figures include all Christian traditions, Protestant, Roman Catholic, and Orthodox. Of the over 700 million Roman Catholics, the official position of the Roman church is that the vast majority are not practicing Catholics and need to be evangelized. Our estimates attempt to reflect not only our own opinions about who is committed to spreading the gospel, but the estimates of the churches themselves.

Nevertheless, it is more important to note that in no one country of the world is it true that the percentage of Christians is getting smaller. Everywhere in the world where there are Christians, and surely where there are vital Christians, their percentage of the general population is definitely increasing. Let no one say (on the basis of statistics) that the gospel has lost its power, or that the Christian movement is not growing. The key point is not how many Christians or new non-Christians there are per year, but what the relative proportion of Christians is per year in each area of the world. For almost one-third of the world's population to claim to be Christian is still of some significance, especially in view of the fact that another sixth of the world's population (being Muslim) knows at least something about this Christ. This allows us to say that over half of the world's population has some very distant knowledge about Jesus Christ.

While not necessarily a glowing achievement, this is certainly not a depressing fact at a time when many are thinking that the Christian movement is losing touch with the world. Furthermore, the other half of the world's population, the "non-Christian" half, has been penetrated to a great extent by some awareness of who Jesus Christ is, even though the people in that second half of the world do not name Christ as the principal religious figure in their own lives.

The most important reason for this chart is the ninth column, which stresses the number of *hidden people groups* rather than simply the masses of individuals that must yet be contacted. Once the gospel penetrates these groups, then it can grow by evangelistic processes within. Thus the key distinction in this chart is the distinction between column 3 and column 4. For some peoples of the world there has not yet been any missiological breakthrough into their culture. Our estimate for this group, the hidden peoples, is 16,750. For others, equally unsaved, there has at least been a breakthrough so that the remaining task to reach them is one of evangelism, not missions. Column 4 constitutes the hidden peoples of the world, those peoples within whose cultural tradition there is not yet an indigenous church able to evangelize its own people. This is the group referred to in the phrase "A church for every people by the year 2000." Such peoples are a particular variety of unreached peoples. They are the ones for whom a missiological breakthrough is still necessary—something comparable to Paul's establishment of the church within the gentile world.

Ralph D. Winter is founder and director of the United States Center for World Mission. This agency seeks to focus mission strategy and resources on non-Christians presently bypassed by Christian outreach.

THE TASK REMAINING

Dr. Winter received a Ph.D. in structural linguistics from Cornell University and the B.D. from Princeton Theological Seminary. He served for ten years as a missionary to the Mayan Indians of Guatemala. While there, he helped to found the theological education-by-extension movement.

He has contributed regularly to several Christian periodicals and his publications include *The 25 Unbelievable Years, 1945-1969, Theological Education by Extension,* and *Penetrating New Frontiers.*

Part 4
Unreached Peoples — Expanded Descriptions

The following section contains descriptions of seventy Asian people groups in alphabetical order. Each group has a data table printed above the written description, containing information based on questionnaires completed by persons in the same country or otherwise knowledgeable about the people group. (Please see Appendix A for a sample of this questionnaire.)

In the data table, the most common name of the people group is given first, followed by the name of the country in which the group is located. Stars in front of the name indicate receptivity to the gospel; ★★★ = very receptive, ★★ = receptive and ★ = indifferent.

The following is a summary of the remaining data categories:

Alternate names: Any alternate names or spellings for the people group.

Size of group: Latest population estimate of the group.

EXPANDED DESCRIPTIONS

MARC ID: An identification number by which information on that particular group is filed. Any correspondence sent to MARC dealing with a group, sending corrections, updates, additions, or requests for further information should refer to that number.

Distinctives: Distinctives that unify this group. Many different things may make a group distinctive or cause them to consider themselves a people. Often several factors give them some kind of affinity toward one another, or make them different from other groups. Respondents to the Unreached Peoples questionnaire were asked to indicate the relative importance of various factors in making the group distinctive. Those factors were: speaking the same language, common political loyalty, similar occupation, racial or ethnic similarity, shared religious customs, common kinship ties, strong sense of unity, similar education level, common residential area, similar social class or caste, similar economic status, shared hobby or special interest, discrimination from other groups, unique health situation, distinctive legal status, similar age, common significant problems, and "other(s)."

Social change: This represents an estimate of the overall rate that cultural and social change is taking place in the group—very rapid, rapid, moderate, slow, and very slow.

Languages: Primary languages. Multilingual communities often use different languages in different situations. They may learn one language in school, another in the market, and yet another in religious ceremonies. Respondents were asked to indicate the major languages used by the group as well as the place or function of each language. These functions are indicated by the following codes:

V—vernacular or common language

T—trade language or lingua franca

S—language used for instruction in schools

W—the language used for any current or past Christian witness

G—the language most suitable for presentation of the gospel

P—the language used in any non-Christian ceremonies

The percentage listed next to the headings *speak* and *read* indicate respectively the percentage of the total group that speak and read the language listed.

Scripture: Indicates the availability of various forms of biblical literature in the languages of the group.

Christian literacy: This indicates the percentage of Christians among the people (if any) over 15 years of age who can and do read in any language.

Religion: This indicates the primary religion(s) found among members of the group. The percentage shown next to adherents estimates the percentage of the group who would say that they follow the religion(s) listed. The percentage next to practicing indicates the number who actively practice the religion(s) listed (in the opinion of the researcher or reporter). The determination of the percentage of those adhering to a certain religion versus the percentage that practice their faith is admittedly a subjective judgment. This figure is important, however, when considering Christian populations, because the definition of "unreached" used here is a group that is less than 20 percent *practicing* Christian. −1 percent means less than one percent practicing, and is used when the Christian population is extremely small and difficult to estimate.

Churches and missions: This indicates the primary Christian churches or missions, national or foreign, that are active in the area where the people group is concentrated. The figure under membership is the approximate number of full members of this church or mission denomination from the people group. The figure under community is the approximate number of adherents (including children) to the denomination or mission from the people group. These are not *all* the churches and missions among this group—only the ones that have been reported.

Openness to religious change: This is an estimate of how open the group is to religious change of any kind. Categories are: very open, somewhat open, indifferent, somewhat closed and very closed.

Receptivity to Christianity: This is an estimate of the openness of the group to Christianity in particular. Categories are: very receptive, receptive, indifferent, reluctant and very reluctant.

Evangelism profile: People tend to come to Christ in more or less well-defined steps. This scale (based on a scale developed by Dr. James Engel of the Wheaton Graduate School) indicates the approximate percentage of the group who are at various levels of awareness of the gospel. The scale ranges from people with no awareness of Christianity to those who are active propagators of the gospel. A further explanation of this useful tool may be found in Edward Dayton's article, "To Reach the Unreached" in *Unreached Peoples '79.*

Not Reported (nr): Whenever this appears in any category, it indicates that the information has not yet been received by the MARC computers. In future volumes of this series, information will be added as it becomes available.

Validity Code: An estimate of the accuracy and completeness of the data on a scale from one to nine. The code is:

1. The only information available at this point is the group name, country, language, population and primary religion. The percentage listed under practicing Christians is at best a rough estimate.

2. There has been more data collected than the "baseline" information in 1, but it is scanty and/or of poor quality.

3. About one-half of the information on the unreached peoples questionnaire (Appendix A) has been collected, and information on the Christian community, if any, is missing or probably inaccurate.

4. Almost all the data on the unreached peoples questionnaire has been collected *or* the source document has supplied most of the necessary information.

5. Information has been supplied by a completed unreached peoples questionnaire and at least one other document.

6. In addition to 5, there is enough detailed information about the people group to write an accurate, up-to-date description.

7. There exists an extensive description of the people group in secular or Christian literature.

8. There has been a major research study (thesis or dissertation quality) done on the group which includes detailed information on the Christian community.

9. In addition to 8, the study includes a thorough exploration of evangelism strategy for the particular group, based on firsthand experience.

Following the data table with the basic information about the people group are several paragraphs further detailing the characteristics of the group.

A complete listing of all unreached people groups currently identified in the MARC files can be found in Part 5. For many of these groups there is more information available. To obtain the data on a particular group, just send in the reply page located in the back of this book.

INDEX OF PEOPLE GROUPS WITH DESCRIPTIONS
IN *Unreached Peoples '81*

EXPANDED DESCRIPTIONS

Alor, Kolana (Indonesia)

ALTERNATE NAMES: not reported

SIZE OF GROUP: 90,000   MARC ID: 2858

DISTINCTIVES: language; ethnicity; kinship

SOCIAL CHANGE: slow

LANGUAGES: Alor, Kolana

SCRIPTURE: none

CHRISTIAN LITERACY: not reported

RELIGION: Animism; Christianity (-1% practicing)

CHURCHES AND MISSIONS: not reported

OPENNESS TO RELIGIOUS CHANGE: not reported

RECEPTIVITY TO CHRISTIANITY: not reported

GROWTH RATE OF CHRISTIAN COMMUNITY: not reported

EVANGELISM PROFILE: not reported

VALIDITY: 5

An elaborate exchange system characterizes the life of the Kolana Alor. Along with other Alor mountain groups, they trade pigs, gongs, and metal kettledrums in a complex reciprocal pattern that determines wealth and prestige. This system links groups together through means of profit, interest, credit and reciprocity. It also provides a creative outlet for the men as well as a valuable means of maintaining intergroup relationships.

Men join this trade system also to raise the bride-price that is needed to obtain a wife. Kettledrums are considered particularly valuable and are used to "purchase" a woman. The greater a man's wealth (and hence his prestige) the greater are his chances of obtaining the bride he wants. Wealth to a large degree depends on how well someone can manipulate the system to his own advantage - amassing large debts from others. An important social aspect of the process are the displays of pigs, gongs and kettledrums and the public arguments between debtors and creditors. Generally these disputes are only for show; however in the past they occasionally led to small scale warfare between families.

Another reason for wanting to accumulate wealth is the fear of illness. Every man is required to give goods for the death feasts of his relatives and failure to do this is believed to anger the departed spirits. These spirits are just a few of the many village, lineage and local spirits that dominate Kolana Alor religious life. They also believe in "Good Beings" who live in the sky and will one day return to earth. This has led in the past to the occasional emergence of "Cargo Cults", where a prophet will convince his followers that this return is soon and will be accompanied by material prosperity.

In the 1940s Protestant missions organized schools in this area but taught in Malay. Few understood the language and it had limited impact on the lives of this mountain people.

EXPANDED DESCRIPTIONS

Ami (Taiwan)

ALTERNATE NAMES: Pangtsah

SIZE OF GROUP: 99,000   MARC ID: 7032

DISTINCTIVES: language; ethnicity; religion; kinship; political loyalty; occupation; discrimination

SOCIAL CHANGE: moderate

LANGUAGES: Ami (100% speak; V, G); Mandarin (70% speak; T, S, P)

SCRIPTURE: New Testament

CHRISTIAN LITERACY: not reported

RELIGION: Animism; Christianity (7% adherents/2% practicing); Buddhism; Buddhist-Animist

CHURCHES AND MISSIONS	BEGAN	MEMBERSHIP	COMMUNITY
Evangelical Alliance Mission	nr	nr	nr
Presbyterian Church	1877	nr	nr
Oriental Msny. Society	nr	nr	nr

OPENNESS TO RELIGIOUS CHANGE: somewhat closed

RECEPTIVITY TO CHRISTIANITY: indifferent

GROWTH RATE OF CHRISTIAN COMMUNITY: not reported

EVANGELISM PROFILE:
     5% No awareness of Christianity
    40% Aware that Christianity exists
    15% Some knowledge of the gospel
    15% Understand the message of the gospel
    18% Personally challenged to receive Christ
     2% Decision to accept Christ
     3% Incorporated into a fellowship of Christians
     2% Active propagators of the gospel

VALIDITY: 5

One of Taiwan's indigenous tribes is the Ami, who live on the east coast between Hualien and Taitung. The Ami view themselves as a distinct group and identify most strongly with their local villages, which are located mainly along the Hiralien, Siukuluan, and Peinan Rivers. They are the largest of Taiwan's aboriginal groups with the highest rate of growth as well - from 52,000 in 1939 to almost 100,000 today.

The origin of the Ami is somewhat of a mystery. This is further confused by widespread migration during the last century. They are unique in that many villages have a matrilineal clan system, with the eldest woman acting as head of the household (men, however, are the political leaders at the village level.) Most individuals choose partners for marriage from outside their clan but from within their village. Some of the larger lineages within villages have a geneology expert who can trace several generations back through history.

A number of Ami are nominal Christians, mixing their traditional beliefs in a syncretistic fashion. They have a well-developed animistic faith which has proven to be a large obstacle to their acceptance of the gospel of Christ. Village shamans play an important role in the continuance of this religious system.

Baguio Area Miners (Philippines)

ALTERNATE NAMES: not reported

SIZE OF GROUP: 40,000   MARC ID: 7004

DISTINCTIVES: occupation; education; social class; health
    situation; significant problems

SOCIAL CHANGE: moderate

LANGUAGES: Ilocano (V); English (T)

SCRIPTURE: Bible

CHRISTIAN LITERACY: not reported

RELIGION: Roman Catholic (60% adherents/10% practicing);
    Protestant (10% adherents/5% practicing); Animism (15%
    adherents); Christian Cultic (15% adherents)

CHURCHES AND MISSIONS	BEGAN	MEMBERSHIP	COMMUNITY
Roman Catholic Church	nr	nr	nr
Episcopal Church	nr	nr	nr

OPENNESS TO RELIGIOUS CHANGE: somewhat open

RECEPTIVITY TO CHRISTIANITY: not reported

GROWTH RATE OF CHRISTIAN COMMUNITY: not reported

EVANGELISM PROFILE: not reported

VALIDITY: 5

Miners in any region share a common occupation, economic
status, and particular health hazards. This establishes an
identity among them that helps them to feel like a group. They
feel an affinity or bond because of the common situation they
share.

The miners of the Baguio area in the Philippines are no
exception. They generally work in difficult circumstances,
mining gold, silver, and copper. Their wages are low; the
average worker receives about 14 pesos (US $2) per day and works
six days a week. Even though the mining companies often provide
housing for the miners and their families this salary isn't
enough to provide for the basic necessities of life.

The Episcopal Church in the Philippines began mission work
in this area in the late 1930s, two years after the mining began.
This work was pioneered by American missionaries. Today there
are four Filipino clergy, with five organized missions, three
outstations, and one church school. Roman Catholics are also
active in the area, having begun after World War II. They have
schools in eight of the mines.

In addition, Iglesia ni Christo and Jehovah's Witnesses are
widespread, attempting to win converts whenever possible. Many
of the miners have only a nominal Christian faith and are
basically animistic in their beliefs and world view. There is a
definite lack of teaching and instruction in the faith within the
Christian churches of this region.

Because of the difficult working and living conditions,
miners do not stay here long. After earning sufficient funds
they generally return to the mountain provinces where they came
from. Women and children are more open to the gospel - the men,
even when they are open, have little free time. Alcoholism is
also a major problem. The most effective means of evangelism
seems to be home visitation programs.

EXPANDED DESCRIPTIONS

Bidayuh of Sarawak (Malaysia)

ALTERNATE NAMES: Dayak, Land

SIZE OF GROUP: 110,000   MARC ID: 2123

DISTINCTIVES: language; ethnicity

SOCIAL CHANGE: moderate

LANGUAGES: Jagoi (45% speak/10% read; V); Bakau (31% speak/10% read; V); Biatah (24% speak/30% read; V, G, W); Malay (20% speak/15% read; T)

SCRIPTURE: New Testament

CHRISTIAN LITERACY: not reported

RELIGION: Christo-Paganism (65% adherents); Animism (34% adherents); Christianity (-1% practicing)

CHURCHES AND MISSIONS	BEGAN	MEMBERSHIP	COMMUNITY
Roman Catholic Church	1885	nr	nr
Anglican Church	1870	nr	66,000
Evangelical Church	1977	nr	600
Seventh-day Adventist Church	1960	nr	6,000

OPENNESS TO RELIGIOUS CHANGE: somewhat closed

RECEPTIVITY TO CHRISTIANITY: receptive

GROWTH RATE OF CHRISTIAN COMMUNITY: not reported

EVANGELISM PROFILE: not reported

VALIDITY: 5

The Bidayuh have been commonly called "Land Dayak" to distinguish them from Iban (formerly called Sea Dayak). The word Dayak is rather loosely used in Sarawak and Kalimantan to designate "up-river people". Although Bidayuh embraces at least three language groupings, a remarkable solidarity has appeared during recent political elections when one would hear terms like "we Bidayuh" and "the Bidayuh vote."

The Bidayuh are mainly subsistence farmers but many individuals have distinguished themselves in professions. Even where education and Christian customs have had long influence there persists old cultural beliefs and practices.

It appears that the Bidayuh are ready to respond to the gospel if it is presented in a way they can understand. English has been the medium of education in Government schools until 1975. Now the change to Malay means that more people have been able to comprehend the gospel as it has been heard on the radio both in English and Malay. There are remarkable examples of individuals being converted to Christ, but no examples of evangelical church life taking root in a Bidayuh community.

It will be necessary for the gospel to be communicated in the language of the people, but Malay could serve to initiate contact for those engaging in cross-cultural evangelism. One factor in planning evangelism of the Bidayuh people would be the coordination of the Bidayuh individuals who have been converted to Christ. Most of them have comprehended the gospel in English. With the appropriate advice and direction they could be a vital force in developing a strategy for evangelism and implementing it.

Bisaya (Malaysia)

ALTERNATE NAMES: Bisayah

SIZE OF GROUP: 2,800   MARC ID: 7022

DISTINCTIVES: language; kinship; religion; ethnicity

SOCIAL CHANGE: slow

LANGUAGES: Bisaya (V)

SCRIPTURE: portions

CHRISTIAN LITERACY: not reported

RELIGION: Animism (97% adherents); Christianity (3% adherents)

CHURCHES AND MISSIONS	BEGAN	MEMBERSHIP	COMMUNITY
Borneo Evangelical Mission	1928	nr	nr
Bisaya Church	nr	nr	nr

OPENNESS TO RELIGIOUS CHANGE: not reported

RECEPTIVITY TO CHRISTIANITY: not reported

GROWTH RATE OF CHRISTIAN COMMUNITY: not reported

EVANGELISM PROFILE: not reported

VALIDITY: 6

The Bisaya inhabit the river areas in northern Sarawak and
western Sabah, especially along the banks of the Limbang River.
They refer to themselves rather as the "people of the middle."
Despite a strong sense of being a unique group they have
incorporated many customs from other groups.
The Bisaya live in small long houses that are built on piles
10 to 15 feet above the ground. Approximately four families will
live together in each of these long houses with three or more
families together in a village. Their staple food is rice, and
they also grow a wide variety of vegetables and fruit. Fishing
is sometimes engaged in but hunting tends to be somewhat more
important as a source of food. They are quite skilled in
carpentry and woodcarving.
The kinship system among the Bisaya is very important for it
establishes and validates land rights. An individual, however,
may claim affiliation with one or many descent lines and
manipulate them to achieve higher status within the community.
Kinship ties are used to initiate cooperative labor groups, to
provide support in large disputes, and also are used to gain help
in providing food for competitive feast.
The first Christian work among the Bisaya was begun in 1928
by Borneo Evangelical Mission (BEM). Only one family responded
at that time and BEM had to withdraw in 1942. At the present
time there are about 70 known Christians among the group, and one
Bisaya student is in Bible school. The gospel of Mark and The
Way of Salvation have been translated along with some tracts.
The religion of most of the group is essentially animistic with
Islamic elements. Formerly shamanism and spirit mediumship were
practiced. Their major functions in the past, as today, were in
the realm of healing, and this is a great felt need of the Bisaya
people. Medical work combined with a strong gospel outreach
would most likely be very effective in this area.

EXPANDED DESCRIPTIONS

Bontoc, Central (Philippines)

ALTERNATE NAMES: not reported

SIZE OF GROUP: 20,000   MARC ID: 632

DISTINCTIVES: language; ethnicity

SOCIAL CHANGE: slow

LANGUAGES: Bontoc, Central (100% speak; V); Ilocano (50% speak); English (30% speak); Tagalog (10% speak)

SCRIPTURE: portions

CHRISTIAN LITERACY: not reported

RELIGION: Christianity (1% adherents/1% practicing); Animism (90% adherents); Unknown (9% adherents)

CHURCHES AND MISSIONS	BEGAN	MEMBERSHIP	COMMUNITY
Roman Catholic Church	1930	nr	nr
Episcopal Church	1905	nr	nr
Baptist Church	1955	nr	nr
United Church of Christ	nr	nr	nr
Seventh-day Adventist Church	nr	nr	nr

OPENNESS TO RELIGIOUS CHANGE: very open

RECEPTIVITY TO CHRISTIANITY: receptive

GROWTH RATE OF CHRISTIAN COMMUNITY: slow growth

EVANGELISM PROFILE: not reported

VALIDITY: 5

A group that used to be known for its headhunting practices is the Central Bontoc. Living in the Cordillera Mountains along the Chico River, the Bontoc now are a peaceful agricultural people who have retained most of their traditional culture despite frequent contacts with other groups.

Though many of the Bontoc have joined the Church (primarily Angelican and Catholic), they still actively practice their animistic religion. Their belief system centers around a hierarchy of spirits, the highest being a supreme deity called "Lumawig." Probably an ancient culture hero, Lumawig "personifies the forces of nature and is the legendary creator, friend, and teacher of the Bontoc" (Lebar 1975: 85). A hereditary class of priests hold various monthly ceremonies for this deity for their crops, the weather, and for healing. In addition the Bontoc believe in the "anito" - spirits of the dead who must be consulted before anything important is done. Ancestral anitos are invited to family feasts when a death occurs to ensure the well-being of the deceased's soul.

The Bontoc social structure is centered around village wards ("ato"), containing about 14 to 50 homes. Traditionally, young men and women lived in dormitories and ate meals with their families. This is gradually changing as they have more contact with lowland populations. In general, however, it can be said that all Bontoc are very aware of their own way of life and are not overly eager to change.

Though several churches and missions have been active in this area, animistic beliefs are still very strong. Of those who have joined the church, nominalism is a major problem.

Buwid (Philippines)

ALTERNATE NAMES: Tau-Buwid

SIZE OF GROUP: 6,000   MARC ID: 4161

DISTINCTIVES: language; ethnicity; religion; sense of unity

SOCIAL CHANGE: slow

LANGUAGES: Buwid (V)

SCRIPTURE: portions

CHRISTIAN LITERACY: not reported

RELIGION: Animism

CHURCHES AND MISSIONS	BEGAN	MEMBERSHIP	COMMUNITY
Overseas Missionary Fellowship	nr	nr	nr

OPENNESS TO RELIGIOUS CHANGE: not reported

RECEPTIVITY TO CHRISTIANITY: not reported

GROWTH RATE OF CHRISTIAN COMMUNITY: not reported

EVANGELISM PROFILE: not reported

VALIDITY: 5

The Buwid are a mountain dwelling sub-group of the Hanunuo, one of the ethnic groups on the Island of Mindoro in the Philippines. Despite the government's efforts to stress the importance of the members of the ethnic communities in the Philippines, the mountain people are looked down on by the ethnic majority. While the abuse of their women has been minimized, exploitation hasn't been eradicated. To the uneducated Buwid the best employment available is to become a cattle keeper for a pastureland lease holder. As such he is paid starvation-level wages by his employer.

While attempts to bring the gospel to the Hanunuo have been going on for several years, it appears that the approaches haven't been culturally sensitive. There is still no Buwid church to speak of. Church workers sent to this group should have enough knowledge in basic cultural anthropology to be able to relate to the people and then to reinterpret the gospel in terms of their culture.

In general, the ethnic groups in Mindoro are among the most backward in the Philippines. While there are educated members among the other groups in the country, the Buwid have none. Literacy is a great need here.

Concerned Christians should pray that God will raise evangelists who will be willing to invest their lives working among these people. Workers with technical knowledge should combine evangelism and development activities in their ministries. Workers are needed who are willing to undergo deprivation in order to live out God's concern in and among these people in the mountains of Mindoro.

EXPANDED DESCRIPTIONS

Central Thailand Farmers (Thailand)

ALTERNATE NAMES: Central Area Farmers; Peasant Farmers

SIZE OF GROUP: 5,000,000   MARC ID: 645

DISTINCTIVES: sense of unity; occupation; residence

SOCIAL CHANGE: not reported

LANGUAGES: Thai (100% speak; V); Lao (10% speak); Chinese
     (Teochu) (5% speak)

SCRIPTURE: Bible

CHRISTIAN LITERACY: 80%

RELIGION: Buddhist-Animist (99% adherents); Christianity (1%
     adherents/1% practicing)

CHURCHES AND MISSIONS	BEGAN	MEMBERSHIP	COMMUNITY
Church in Central Thailand	1952	nr	700

OPENNESS TO RELIGIOUS CHANGE: somewhat open

RECEPTIVITY TO CHRISTIANITY: indifferent

GROWTH RATE OF CHRISTIAN COMMUNITY: not reported

EVANGELISM PROFILE: not reported

VALIDITY: 5

It is said that throughout Thailand 80% of the population is
rural, and the large majority are farmers. Central Thailand,
being the large alluvial plain north of Bangkok, is a rich rice
growing area and the rural farmer is by far the most common
person within this population group. Although irrigation has
improved, especially along the area adjacent to the main river,
the farmers are still by and large dependant on the rainfall for
their crops of rice and corn.

Their life style is very different from urban dwellers.
From May to August the farmer is very busy ploughing and planting
with little time for interests outside of his occupation.
September to November he is moderately busy caring for the
growing crop, but can be found at home and is often very
interested in some diversion. December into January is harvest
time and once again he is extremely busy. February through early
May he rests and will sit and talk for hours about any subject
including religion. Films, plays, music and visitation teams are
all effective in reaching the farmer in these times of rest from
work.

Buddhism, however, is very firmly entrenched in the lives of
rural farmers. Centuries of Buddhist teaching and lifestyle take
a long time to be challenged and even longer to be removed and
replaced by Christian teaching and lifestyle. Thus the pattern
of conversion is usually slow and new Christians require a lot of
pastoral care and encouragement. Efforts must be made to win
these people to Christ in groups at the family level first, and
then at the village level, for it is extremely difficult for them
to stand out alone against the presence of the old religion. The
strength of the church will depend on the number of complete
Christian families in that church.

Chakmas of Mizoram (India)

ALTERNATE NAMES: Takam

SIZE OF GROUP: 20,000   MARC ID: 2011

DISTINCTIVES: language; ethnicity

SOCIAL CHANGE: not reported

LANGUAGES: Chakma (100% speak; V); Bengali (T, S)

SCRIPTURE: New Testament

CHRISTIAN LITERACY: 4%

RELIGION: Buddhist-Animist; Christianity (-1% practicing)

CHURCHES AND MISSIONS	BEGAN	MEMBERSHIP	COMMUNITY
Baptist Church of Mizoram	1965	25	nr

OPENNESS TO RELIGIOUS CHANGE: somewhat closed

RECEPTIVITY TO CHRISTIANITY: indifferent

GROWTH RATE OF CHRISTIAN COMMUNITY: not reported

EVANGELISM PROFILE: not reported

VALIDITY: 5

    The original home of the Chakmas is thought to have been somewhere in Malacca, somewhat similiar to the Malays. Living a semi-nomadic life, they settled in the Arakans (Burma) and eventually migrated into Mizoram in northeast India.
    During the British rule the Chakmas occassionally came into conflict with the English. This resulted in payment of heavy revenues to the British raj and also a further migration into India. They were not allowed to enter the Lushai Hills (Mizoram) during the Imperial rule, but a few Mizo chiefs kept them secretly along the western borders and employed them as laborers. When political disturbances shook the state of Mizoram in 1966, the Chakmas were officially numbered for the first time since their migration after India's independence. Many more came into Mizoram after the Indo-Pakistan wars, in which the Chakmas suffered severely.
    The Himayana Buddhism of the Chakmas is mixed with animism. This religion does not have any caste system, but their society consists of more than 33 class groups (Goya). Muslim converts have to leave the society but Christians have been sheltered by their families. The Chakmas have their own script but it is known only to a few Buddhist priests. Bengali script is dominant.
    Although attempts to reach the Chakmas were not officially made in the past by the churches in India (or by the missions in Bangladesh), the Baptist Church of Mizoram sent missionaries in 1965. A Mizo missionary was martyred and two pastors have died since then. At present there are no Chakma pastors even though there are two fellowship groups that meet regularly.

EXPANDED DESCRIPTIONS

Chang-Pa of Kashmir (India)

ALTERNATE NAMES: not reported

SIZE OF GROUP: 7,000   MARC ID: 7011

DISTINCTIVES: language; ethnicity; kinship; religion; sense
    of unity; social class; hobby or interest

SOCIAL CHANGE: slow

LANGUAGES: Tibetan Dialect (100% speak; V); Tibetan (100%
    speak; T); Urdu (T)

SCRIPTURE: Bible

CHRISTIAN LITERACY: not reported

RELIGION: Buddhist-Animist

CHURCHES AND MISSIONS: not reported

OPENNESS TO RELIGIOUS CHANGE: indifferent

RECEPTIVITY TO CHRISTIANITY: indifferent

GROWTH RATE OF CHRISTIAN COMMUNITY: not reported

EVANGELISM PROFILE: not reported

VALIDITY: 5

The Chang-Pa are the people of "Chang-Thang", or the
northern Upland valleys of the Indus River. The mean height of
these plains is over 13,000 feet--the highest plateaus in the
world. Tough and hardy, the Chang-Pa can withstand heights and
extreme cold, but cannot tolerate heat.

Because the plains are so elevated there is no significant
cultivation. The Chang-Pa raise livestock such as sheep, goats,
yaks, and horses on vast areas totaling about 20,000 sq.
kilometers. Only a dozen or so villages cultivate some barley
and peas. They eat mutton and yak (fresh or dry), but do not
consume fish or fowl.

Nomad tent villages are few and far between, the houses are
occupied only during the winter when the temperature may drop to
-30 C. with gale-force winds. In the summer most of these houses
lie vacant while the people live in yak-hair tents. The women
spin and weave thick woolen cloth while the men spin yak or goat
hair for their tents and rugs. Many of the men play dice and
drink the local brew called "chang." In the evenings they sing
and dance or recite "Kesar" epics and stories. They are great
star-gazers, changing their grazing grounds according to astral
calendars. They are highly superstitious too, believing in evil
spirits known as the "Nagas" (subterranean spirits).

Most of the male members of the group are literate in
Tibetan. Indian schools have been opened in some of the larger
semi-nomadic villages. They trade by bartering their wool
(better known in this area as "Pashmina"), lake salt, and borax
for things like cotton cloth, rice, wheat flour, tea, spices,
felt hats, and other necessities. They sometimes use silver
coins but do not accept paper currency.

There have been only two known converts to Christianity
among the Chang-Pa. Missionaries to them would have to be
physically strong, have a good fluency in Tibetan, and be able to
present a contextualized interpretation of the gospel.

Chinese Businessmen (Hong Kong)

ALTERNATE NAMES: Wealthy Business Class

SIZE OF GROUP: 10,000   MARC ID: 2111

DISTINCTIVES: language; political loyalty; occupation;
     kinship; social class; economic status

SOCIAL CHANGE: rapid

LANGUAGES: Cantonese (100% speak/100% read; V, G, W); English
     (80% speak/100% read; T, S)

SCRIPTURE: Bible

CHRISTIAN LITERACY: 100%

RELIGION: Roman Catholic (3% adherents/3% practicing);
     Protestant (5% adherents/5% practicing); Traditional
     Chinese (80% adherents/40% practicing); Secularism (12%
     adherents)

CHURCHES AND MISSIONS: not reported

OPENNESS TO RELIGIOUS CHANGE: not reported

RECEPTIVITY TO CHRISTIANITY: not reported

GROWTH RATE OF CHRISTIAN COMMUNITY: not reported

EVANGELISM PROFILE:
     0% No awareness of Christianity
     45% Aware that Christianity exists
     30% Some knowledge of the gospel
     7% Understand the message of the gospel
     8% Personally challenged to receive Christ
     2% Decision to accept Christ
     7% Incorporated into a fellowship of Christians
     1% Active propagators of the gospel

VALIDITY: 5

Chinese businessmen feel a unity and social pride in being
Chinese, but this is an ethnic rather than a geographical
identification. They feel some affinity for other groups from
the same ethnic stock but the wealth of the businessmen contrasts
with others' poverty. Past prejudices against non-Cantonese is
dying out through education in Cantonese schools.
Evangelistic attempts have been fairly successful. Most
youth attend church oriented schools where there is usually some
evangelism. Conversion may be costly as the businesses are very
tightly organized. A young Christian executive may feel a
conflict between his values and some business ethics. In
general, Christian ideas are not considered harmful, but baptism
is recognized making a religious break with tradition in a way
which some regard as being unfaithful to the family.
Businessmen usually do not take pastors seriously unless
they are exceptionally well educated. Pastors are generally not
considered to be of the "profesional class", and thus other
businessmen are more likely to be able to reach their colleagues.
Evangelistic meetings should be held in Chinese, not English.
Since homes are usually crowded, a restaurant, hotel room, or
small hall could be rented. Speakers should be educated,
informed, and well-spoken, able to command the respect of the
audience. It must also be remembered how important "face" is to
the businessmen.

EXPANDED DESCRIPTIONS

Chinese Muslims (Taiwan)

ALTERNATE NAMES: Hui

SIZE OF GROUP: 45,000   MARC ID: 7019

DISTINCTIVES: religion; ethnicity; language

SOCIAL CHANGE: slow

LANGUAGES: Mandarin (V)

SCRIPTURE: Bible

CHRISTIAN LITERACY: not reported

RELIGION: Islam; Christianity (-1% practicing)

CHURCHES AND MISSIONS: not reported

OPENNESS TO RELIGIOUS CHANGE: not reported

RECEPTIVITY TO CHRISTIANITY: not reported

GROWTH RATE OF CHRISTIAN COMMUNITY: not reported

EVANGELISM PROFILE: not reported

VALIDITY: 5

The Chinese Muslims in Taiwan are descendants of two Hui migrations from the mainland of China. The first wave of about 25,000 people came in the mid 1600s. Many who came then settled in coastal cities and became almost completely assimilated into the Taiwanese culture. Only about 5 - 6,000 of their descendants remain today. The second big wave came to Taiwan in 1949 and settled in the major cities, with the largest concentration in Taipei. Most Hui run special non-pork restaurants, while others are in the military, civil service, or have small businesses.

Like the Hui on the mainland, the primary distinctions between the Hui and other Chinese in Taiwan are their religious beliefs, their abstinence from eating pork, and the desire to marry only among themselves. Other than these distinctions they are virtually indistinguishable from other Chinese in appearance, language, and dress.

The government of Taiwan is very cooperative in dealing with them as a distinct people and encourages their faith in many ways. The government has helped to finance pilgrimages of individual Chinese Muslims to Mecca each year and has given scholarships to college-age students to study at universities in Saudi Arabia and Libya. For political as well as cultural reasons, Taiwan also has been very cooperative in establishing mosques in four major cities (Taipei, Kaohsiung, Taichung and Lungkang). The Taiwan government has provided the land for these mosques, while Saudi Arabia provided the money for the buildings.

To date there have been no church planting efforts specifically designed for this distinct Hui culture. There have been occasional converts from this group but life becomes very difficult for them. The converts' families object in particular to the cultural practice of pork eating among Christians. Some converts have endured these pressures from their families but it would be much better if the Hui converts could have their own fellowship groups instead of making them join churches that deny their cultural background.

Chinese Refugees in Macau (Macau)

ALTERNATE NAMES: not reported

SIZE OF GROUP: 100,000   MARC ID: 129

DISTINCTIVES: significant problems; legal status; health
    situation; kinship; ethnicity; religion; language

SOCIAL CHANGE: not reported

LANGUAGES: Cantonese (99% speak; T); English (5% speak)

SCRIPTURE: Bible

CHRISTIAN LITERACY: 85%

RELIGION: Traditional Chinese (90% adherents); Secularism (9%
    adherents); Christianity (1% adherents/1% practicing)

CHURCHES AND MISSIONS	BEGAN	MEMBERSHIP	COMMUNITY
Macao Baptist Association	nr	nr	20
Roman Catholic Church	nr	nr	10
Ye Lung Hau Baptist Church	nr	nr	nr

OPENNESS TO RELIGIOUS CHANGE: somewhat closed

RECEPTIVITY TO CHRISTIANITY: indifferent

GROWTH RATE OF CHRISTIAN COMMUNITY: not reported

EVANGELISM PROFILE: not reported

VALIDITY: 5

In 1979, the influx of some 100,000 immigrants from China
boosted the population of Macau by 37 percent. These new
residents constitute a significant segment which is expected to
expand as the Chinese government allows more of her people to
leave the country.

Most of these refugees were from villages, towns and cities
of the province of Guangdong (Kwangtung), the nearest neighbor of
Macau. They speak Cantonese and use the simplified Chinese
script as their written language. As they move from a Communist
country to a democratic society the adjustment is far from easy.
The one major problem they share in common is that of survival.
Jobs, housing, getting children into schools, etc. have become
their major concerns. Some have met tremendous difficulties in
these areas and have returned to China or left for Hong Kong.

Thirty years under a Communist government has not completely
eradicated the influence of Chinese culture from the mind of
those above the age of 40. There is a definite inclination
towards traditional Chinese folk religion. The younger
generation under the age of 40 was brought up under Mao's
thought. They are atheists not because they choose to be so but
because that is the only philosophy they have been exposed to.
Among this group very few are followers of Maoism. Christianity
to most of them is totally foreign, although a handful have been
active in house churches in China. These are strong in their
faith.

There are presently at least two churches who work with
these immigrants from China. However, the work demands a lot of
time for it involves spiritual ministry as well as helping the
refugees to find jobs and housing and meet other physical needs.

EXPANDED DESCRIPTIONS

Chuang (China)

ALTERNATE NAMES: T'u

SIZE OF GROUP: 12,000,000   MARC ID: 7014

DISTINCTIVES: language; ethnicity; religion

SOCIAL CHANGE: rapid

LANGUAGES: Chuang (V)

SCRIPTURE: none

CHRISTIAN LITERACY: not reported

RELIGION: Animism

CHURCHES AND MISSIONS: not reported

OPENNESS TO RELIGIOUS CHANGE: not reported

RECEPTIVITY TO CHRISTIANITY: not reported

GROWTH RATE OF CHRISTIAN COMMUNITY: not reported

EVANGELISM PROFILE: not reported

VALIDITY: 5

The largest ethnic group in the Peoples Republic of China is the Chuang. They are concentrated in the southern province of Guangxi Province (renamed Guangxi Zhuang Autonomous Region in 1958), and are also found in parts of Guangdong (Kwangtung), Guizhou (Kweichow), and Yunnan provinces.

Also known as the T'u or "people of the soil", the Chuang are primarily plains dwellers who carry out wet-rice agriculture. Where land is scarce they'll also grow rice and other crops on terraced hillsides.

The social structure of the Chuang is not particularly well developed, and so they have historically assimilated cultural traits from Chinese and Vietnamese sources. This is also evidenced by their more recent open mingling and intermarriage with the Han Chinese, reducing their ethnic differences even more. Most Chuang people now speak Chinese in addition to their own tongue, a northern Thai dialect. Early attempts to write the Chuang language with Chinese characters have had limited usage. In 1956 a romanized script was designed and promoted in schools with the encouragement of the government, but acceptance was also very poor.

The Chuang make cotton cloth and have a well-developed art and handicraft style which includes batiks. Other traits include tatooing, betel chewing, pile dwellings, and (traditionally) polygny, all of which suggests links to Thai culture.

The Chuang are basically animistic and have been cool to the literate Buddhist traditions of the Thai groups to their south and west. As far as can be determined at this time, Christianity has had minimal (if any) impact among them.

Dog-Pa of Ladakh (India)

ALTERNATE NAMES: Srin; Shrin; Brog-Pa

SIZE OF GROUP: 2,000   MARC ID: 7005

DISTINCTIVES: language; ethnicity; religion

SOCIAL CHANGE: slow

LANGUAGES: Shrina (V); Tibetan Dialects (T); Urdu (S)

SCRIPTURE: none

CHRISTIAN LITERACY: not reported

RELIGION: Animism; Buddhist-Animist

CHURCHES AND MISSIONS: not reported

OPENNESS TO RELIGIOUS CHANGE: indifferent

RECEPTIVITY TO CHRISTIANITY: indifferent

GROWTH RATE OF CHRISTIAN COMMUNITY: not reported

EVANGELISM PROFILE:
        35% No awareness of Christianity
        65% Aware that Christianity exists
         0% Some knowledge of the gospel
         0% Understand the message of the gospel
         0% Personally challenged to receive Christ
         0% Decision to accept Christ
         0% Incorporated into a fellowship of Christians
         0% Active propagators of the gospel

VALIDITY: 6

        The Dog-pa people are somewhat unique by the standards set
by their neighbors in the northern Indian state of Jammu and
Kashmir. The Tibetans living in Ladakh (the ones who originally
called them Dog-pa) are unsure about their religious practices.
The Dog-pas are moving toward a Tibetan Buddhism (or Lamaism) but
retain much of their old animistic beliefs. They have blended
the two religious systems into a mixture that is to their own
liking and that reflects their particular culture.
        The Dog-pa also are unique in that they do not have any sort
of a king or a tribal chief. Instead, the society is run by
"democratic" principles (called "Jir-gak"). In addition, the
Dog-pa are without caste though there is, of course, status
ranking in the group. A great amount of respect in particular is
given to the maternal uncle. Though they are typically
close-knit, it is reported that they carry this to the point of
having unrestricted sexual relations during a harvest festival
every three or four years.
        Rather than cows the Dog-pa keep goats, which they use for
meat, milk, skin and sacrifices. Cultivable land is very scarce
since it is occupied by the Balti people and so they concentrate
on herding for their livelihood. Some of the men are employed as
army laborers and this has added to their income, but in general
a good deal of development work needs to be done. Primary
schools are run by the government of Jammu and Kashmir. Missions
could help with income generation projects and work to raise the
generally poor standards of hygiene in the community.

EXPANDED DESCRIPTIONS

Dumagat, Casiguran (Philippines)

ALTERNATE NAMES: Agta; Negrito

SIZE OF GROUP: 1,000   MARC ID: 2

DISTINCTIVES: language; ethnicity; kinship

SOCIAL CHANGE: not reported

LANGUAGES: Dumagat (100% speak; V); Casiguranin (85% speak/1% read; T); Tagalog (60% speak/10% read)

SCRIPTURE: portions

CHRISTIAN LITERACY: not reported

RELIGION: Animism (97% adherents); Christianity (5% adherents/3% practicing)

CHURCHES AND MISSIONS	BEGAN	MEMBERSHIP	COMMUNITY
New Tribes Mission	nr	nr	nr
Roman Catholic Church	nr	nr	nr
Wycliffe Bible Translators	1962	nr	nr

OPENNESS TO RELIGIOUS CHANGE: somewhat closed

RECEPTIVITY TO CHRISTIANITY: indifferent

GROWTH RATE OF CHRISTIAN COMMUNITY: not reported

EVANGELISM PROFILE: not reported

VALIDITY: 6

The Casiguran Dumagat people live in a remote part of Aurora Province in Luzon, 12 hours up the coast from the end of the government road at Baler, Quezon. Their villages are widely dispersed in the foothills of the jungle surrounding the Casiguran valley. Approximately 1000 Dumagats have been subdivided into 35 settlements, ranging from three to five households in each settlement.

The Dumagats are traditional hunters and gatherers with some farming. The men mainly fish or hunt with bows and arrows, and the women fish, plant small gardens, and gather uncultivated jungle roots and fruits. Many now work as unskilled laborers for lowland Filipinos in payment for rice.

The Dumagats have suffered a population decline of 60% since 1936 because of a very high death rate: 19% of adults die of tuberculosis, 15% of adult women die in childbirth, 8% of adults die of homicide, 6.5% die of alcoholism. The child death rate is 48%.

Non-believers are not interested in the Bible or the gospel, and are even less interested in literacy. In spite of repeated efforts to teach literacy classes, there are a total of only 23 literates, 12 of whom are under age 20. There are 15 public elementary schools in the Casiguran valley, but few Dumagat children attend.

Breaking away from the prevalent animistic practices, 30 adults and about 20 children and teenagers have put their faith in Christ. Wycliffe Bible Translators first arrived in April of 1962, and hopefully some New Tribes missionaries will be allocated there soon. There is currently one Dumagat congregation in the area.

Dusun (Malaysia)

ALTERNATE NAMES: Kadazan

SIZE OF GROUP: 160,000   MARC ID: 7023

DISTINCTIVES: language; kinship; ethnicity

SOCIAL CHANGE: slow

LANGUAGES: Kadazan (V); Malay (T)

SCRIPTURE: New Testament; portions

CHRISTIAN LITERACY: not reported

RELIGION: Animism; Islam-Animist; Christianity

CHURCHES AND MISSIONS	BEGAN	MEMBERSHIP	COMMUNITY
Dusun Church	nr	nr	nr

OPENNESS TO RELIGIOUS CHANGE: not reported

RECEPTIVITY TO CHRISTIANITY: not reported

GROWTH RATE OF CHRISTIAN COMMUNITY: not reported

EVANGELISM PROFILE: not reported

VALIDITY: 6

The Dusun live in central and northern Sabah in a mountainous region that has only recently been opened up to bus service and aircraft links to the coast. The origins of this group are unclear but a widespread origin legend describes a flood and the movement of the Dusun people from their original homeland in the highlands. Formerly they were headhunters, but there is an emerging sense of ethnic awareness and pride and the stirrings of a nationalist movement. The main unit of society is the family, who live in small houses perched on steep hillsides. Originally they lived in long houses like many of the groups around them. Wet-rice farming is a rather recent development and hunting is done only occasionally.

Traditionally the Dusun believed in a pantheon of gods as well as a large number of lesser spirits that cause disease, fertility, etc. Female "priestesses" or spirit mediums carried out healing ceremonies that recalled lost souls. Often a spirit language was used during which a spirit would speak through the priestess. Rituals still include ceremonial feasts at which great amounts of rice beer and food are consumed.

Before World War II there was little contact with Christian missionaries. After the War there were a number of conversions from the traditional animistic practices through the evangelism efforts of some local Dusun Christians. Older churches from Sarawak have contributed to the growth of the church in this area as well. Short-term adult schools organized by the Dusun Church have been largely responsible for a sharp rise in literacy in the villages. The children also are attending primary schools. Final checking of the New Testament in Dusun is now completed and printing of the manuscript by the Bible Society is expected soon. Many New Testament portions have already been distributed.

The church among the Dusun appears to be strong. One of its most outstanding features is an intense program of month-long schooling for discipleship led by teams of pastors with occasional help from missionaries. There is a need for the Church to have a renewed vision of reaching the remainder of the unevangelized Dusun people.

EXPANDED DESCRIPTIONS

Ewenkis (China)

ALTERNATE NAMES: Owenke

SIZE OF GROUP: 10,000   MARC ID: 7020

DISTINCTIVES: language; ethnicity; kinship

SOCIAL CHANGE: moderate

LANGUAGES: Altaic (V); Mandarin (T)

SCRIPTURE: not reported

CHRISTIAN LITERACY: not reported

RELIGION: Animism

CHURCHES AND MISSIONS: not reported

OPENNESS TO RELIGIOUS CHANGE: not reported

RECEPTIVITY TO CHRISTIANITY: not reported

GROWTH RATE OF CHRISTIAN COMMUNITY: not reported

EVANGELISM PROFILE: not reported

VALIDITY: 5

The Ewenkis are one of the smallest minority groups within China, located within the grasslands of Heilongjiang (Heilungkiang) Province and the Xinjiang Uygur Autonomous Region. They number some 10,000 individuals. Formerly called Solons Tunguses or Yakuts the name Ewenkis is the one that they have always used for themselves.

The Ewenkis are herders who used to move a dozen or more times a year to accommodate to the dramatic climatic changes in this region. They now move three times a year. They live in a winter camp with warehouses, animal sheds and power operated wells. In the spring they move to another area for the lambing season, and again in summer to find grazing lands for their herds. They still live in their tents which are built with wood poles and beams with local reed thatching. It is reported that 99% of the school age children attend school and there is a cooperative medical care center in their communities which the communists have organized. Cooperatives for livestock breeding and production brigades have been formed. The government's goal is to build mechanized ranches where the Ewenkis can live and work.

In the past the Ewenkis had to work for herd owners and were extremely poor. Since 1948 the Chinese government has abolished feudal privileges and opened up the pastures to all herdsmen. Recently mutual aid teams have been formed as well as cooperatives for livestock breeding, etc. The government reports that they now have the services of "a bank, a post and telecommunication office, a supply and marketing co-op, a clinic, a vetenary station, a cultural center, a weather station, a film production team, and middle and primary schools."

Traditionally the Ewenkis practiced various forms of witchcraft and depended on shamans for healing and other animistic practices. Before the communists gained control of the area, there were reported to be some Christians among the Ewenkis, but the current situation is unclear.

Gujars of Kashmir (India)

ALTERNATE NAMES: not reported

SIZE OF GROUP: 150,000   MARC ID: 7012

DISTINCTIVES: kinship; language; occupation; ethnicity;
    religion; social class; discrimination

SOCIAL CHANGE: moderate

LANGUAGES: Gujari (100% speak/2% read; V, G); Urdu (T, W, S)

SCRIPTURE: New Testament

CHRISTIAN LITERACY: not reported

RELIGION: Islam-Animist (7% adherents)

CHURCHES AND MISSIONS	BEGAN	MEMBERSHIP	COMMUNITY
Kashmir Evang. Fellowship	1974	nr	nr

OPENNESS TO RELIGIOUS CHANGE: somewhat closed

RECEPTIVITY TO CHRISTIANITY: reluctant

GROWTH RATE OF CHRISTIAN COMMUNITY: not reported

EVANGELISM PROFILE: not reported

VALIDITY: 5

The Gujars are a unique group, living on the fringes of the
mountains of Kashmir. This semi-nomadic tribal people are
distributed all over northwest India and north Pakistan (formerly
known as the Northwest Frontier Province).
    The Gujars make clearings in the forest and build
flat-topped houses, in contrast to the angular roofs of typical
Kashmiri houses. These houses tend to have one to three rooms
which are often dark and smokey from the cooking fires within.
    The Gujars rarely mix with or intermarry other Kashmiris,
though like the Kashmiris they also are Muslims. Kashmiris often
look down on the Gujars because they are often cheated in
business transactions. The Gujars tend to be inoffensive, simple
people, though they are sometimes reported to be thieves. They
can be very generous; very often giving whey (highly valued in
Kashmir) to weary mountain travelers free of cost and also giving
away milk on Friday.
    The Gujar language (called Parimu, Hindki, or simply Gujari)
is wholly different from Kashmiri languages. The origin of this
people group is still debated, but it is thought that they have
some connection with the Huns of Central Asia. Like the Huns,
the Gujar ancestors were probably once sun worshippers, but all
traces of this practice have vanished. Some may have acquired a
little knowledge of Christianity either from their neighbors in
Central Asia or from their connection with Christians among the
Huns. Generally they are quite conservative in their attitude
toward religious change. At the present time a Muslim holy man
has an itinerant ministry, going from one settlement ("deh-ra")
to another, performing the necessary cultic activities. He is a
very respected man. This could possibly be a pattern for
Christian evangelists to take also. For the evangelism of the
Gujars there should be specialized Christian workers who know
their language very well.

EXPANDED DESCRIPTIONS

Hotel Workers in Manila (Philippines)

ALTERNATE NAMES: not reported

SIZE OF GROUP: 11,000   MARC ID: 7036

DISTINCTIVES: occupation; social class; age; education;
    significant problems; language

SOCIAL CHANGE: not reported

LANGUAGES: Pilipino (V); English (T, S)

SCRIPTURE: Bible

CHRISTIAN LITERACY: 100%

RELIGION: Roman Catholic (85% adherents/10% practicing);
    Protestant (5% adherents/3% practicing); Other (5%
    adherents); Secularism (5% adherents)

CHURCHES AND MISSIONS	BEGAN	MEMBERSHIP	COMMUNITY
Roman Catholic Church	nr	nr	nr

OPENNESS TO RELIGIOUS CHANGE: somewhat open

RECEPTIVITY TO CHRISTIANITY: receptive

GROWTH RATE OF CHRISTIAN COMMUNITY: not reported

EVANGELISM PROFILE:
    0% No awareness of Christianity
    10% Aware that Christianity exists
    67% Some knowledge of the gospel
    10% Understand the message of the gospel
    0% Personally challenged to receive Christ
    6% Decision to accept Christ
    7% Incorporated into a fellowship of Christians
    0% Active propagators of the gospel

VALIDITY: 5

Metro Manila has over 11,000 "rank-and-file" hotel workers
who are employed by the 2-star to 5-star establishments in the
area. These hotels serve the business visitors and tourists who
bring vast sums of money into the Philippines every year. The
importance of this industry is emphasized by the government's
efforts to attract more revenue as well as creating a more
favorable image to the outside world.

Metro Manila is expanding with new modern office buildings
and hotels, but little of this wealth reaches the hotel workers.
They receive very low salaries and are often exploited by the
management which sometimes denies them their legitimate
percentage of the service charges.

The average age of hotel workers is 29 and more than half
are married. Most come from the provinces of Luzon and as a
group they are well-educated; virtually all are high school
graduates and many have been to college as well. This makes them
a highly literate group that would probably respond well to
printed materials as a means of "preparing the soil" for
evangelism.

Little or no organized efforts have been made to reach this
group, though they are reported to have a somewhat receptive
attitude towards Christianity. Some factors that should be
considered in evangelism would be their different working hours
(including Sundays), their Roman Catholic background, and the
impact that exposure to others' wealth has had on their values.

Iban (Malaysia)

ALTERNATE NAMES: Sea Dayak

SIZE OF GROUP: 30,000   MARC ID: 7024

DISTINCTIVES: language; kinship; ethnicity

SOCIAL CHANGE: slow

LANGUAGES: Iban (V)

SCRIPTURE: New Testament

CHRISTIAN LITERACY: not reported

RELIGION: Animism; Christianity

CHURCHES AND MISSIONS	BEGAN	MEMBERSHIP	COMMUNITY
Methodist Church	nr	nr	nr
Angelican Church	nr	nr	nr
Roman Catholic Church	nr	nr	nr
Borneo Evangelical Mission	nr	nr	nr

OPENNESS TO RELIGIOUS CHANGE: somewhat open

RECEPTIVITY TO CHRISTIANITY: receptive

GROWTH RATE OF CHRISTIAN COMMUNITY: not reported

EVANGELISM PROFILE: not reported

VALIDITY: 6

The Iban live primarily in the hills behind the coast of Sarawak. They are certainly one of the best known of all the people groups of this region, having engaged in piracy in the last century. This activity led Europeans to call them "Sea Dayaks". They are generally a clever people who show a great deal of initiative in all their activities. Though some of the sub-groups differ in small respects, the Iban "have in common a homogenous language and complex of religious belief and ritual that make them essentially one people" (Lebar, 1972: 181).

The Iban subsist primarily by growing hill rice. This is considered as a distinctive part of their life. Their agricultural practices are sanctified in their myths and surrounded with ritual. Each family is an economic unit and farms its own fields, though there is a great deal of cooperation among related families during clearing and harvest.

Once known as fierce headhunters, at the present time there is a sharp decline in the power of animism among this group. Though mission work was carried out from 1928 to 1938 by Borneo Evangelical Mission there was not any significant response until the 1960's. At this time some members of a group of Iban in the Julau River area turned to Christ following initial contacts by upriver Kenya Christians accompanied by a missionary. A center was set up at Pakan in 1961 and other Iban in this area have turned to the Lord. Small churches have been established in other areas and another center was set up 1965 at Batu Niah.

The entire New Testament has been available for some years but is now in need of revision. Currently, the Old Testament is being translated by a combined team from the Methodist, Anglican, and Roman Catholic churches. Some elementary correspondence courses are being used as well as a booklet explaining the Christian life. There is currently a considerable interest in the gospel reported among the Iban and this openess should be seen as a great opportunity for many more to be led to the Lord.

EXPANDED DESCRIPTIONS

Industrial Workers (Taiwan)

ALTERNATE NAMES: not reported

SIZE OF GROUP: 500,000   MARC ID: 4121

DISTINCTIVES: occupation; residence; social class; economic
    status; age; significant problems

SOCIAL CHANGE: very rapid

LANGUAGES: Taiwanese (Hoklo) (90% speak; V, G); Mandarin (100%
    speak; T, S)

SCRIPTURE: Bible

CHRISTIAN LITERACY: 100%

RELIGION: Secularism (78% adherents); Protestant (1%
    adherents/1% practicing); Roman Catholic (1% adherents/1%
    practicing); Animism (20% adherents)

CHURCHES AND MISSIONS	BEGAN	MEMBERSHIP	COMMUNITY
Overseas Missionary Fellowship	1974	200	100
So. Taiwan Ecum. Mission	1970	nr	nr
Christian Reformed Church	1973	nr	nr
Little Flock	nr	nr	nr
True Jesus Church	nr	nr	nr

OPENNESS TO RELIGIOUS CHANGE: indifferent

RECEPTIVITY TO CHRISTIANITY: indifferent

GROWTH RATE OF CHRISTIAN COMMUNITY: stable

EVANGELISM PROFILE:
    5% No awareness of Christianity
    75% Aware that Christianity exists
    10% Some knowledge of the gospel
    5% Understand the message of the gospel
    2% Personally challenged to receive Christ
    1% Decision to accept Christ
    1% Incorporated into a fellowship of Christians
    1% Active propagators of the gospel

VALIDITY: 5

The explosive growth of the industrial community has been a
distinctive mark of Taiwan since 1970. Most industrial workers
come from small towns and approximately ten percent of the
300,000 mountain people have also moved in looking for work.
Employment is virtually assured, but job turnover is high due to
boredom and job dissatisfaction.

Although up to 50% of the mountain people and 2% of the
rural people are Christian by background the vast majority break
ties (or lose them) with the church when migrating into the city.
Overseas Missionary Fellowship (OMF) now employs some
missionaries who have small group meetings and some service
projects. Almost no other missionaries work with this group who
now comprise over 5% of the total population. Hostels,
counseling and activity centers, "mediators", and workers
knowledgeable in industrial problems are needed, missionaries
included.

Jeepney Drivers in Manila (Philippines)

ALTERNATE NAMES: not reported

SIZE OF GROUP: 20,000   MARC ID: 7018

DISTINCTIVES: occupation; religion; social class; economic
    status; significant problems

SOCIAL CHANGE: moderate

LANGUAGES: Pilipino (V); Tagalog (T)

SCRIPTURE: Bible

CHRISTIAN LITERACY: not reported

RELIGION: Roman Catholic; Christo-Paganism; Christianity

CHURCHES AND MISSIONS: not reported

OPENNESS TO RELIGIOUS CHANGE: indifferent

RECEPTIVITY TO CHRISTIANITY: indifferent

GROWTH RATE OF CHRISTIAN COMMUNITY: not reported

EVANGELISM PROFILE:
    0% No awareness of Christianity
    89% Aware that Christianity exists
    10% Some knowledge of the gospel
    0% Understand the message of the gospel
    0% Personally challenged to receive Christ
    0% Decision to accept Christ
    1% Incorporated into a fellowship of Christians
    0% Active propagators of the gospel

VALIDITY: 5

Every major city of the world has its taxi drivers.
Generally, they are marginal to other social groupings since
their lifestyle and working hours differ from those of other city
residents. Not trusted by tourists and locals alike, these
drivers are usually considered (often unfairly) to be dishonest,
rude, and only interested in money.
    The situation in Manila is no different. Here
transportation is provided by "Jeepneys" - small trucks
colorfully decorated to reflect their owner's personal taste.
Most Jeepney drivers are from the provinces of the Philippines,
coming to Manila primarily for economic reasons. Many have
commonlaw wives in the city, having left their families back
home. Though some originally desired to return to their homes,
they usually end up staying in Manila.
    Boredom is a problem. Most fill their free hours reading
comic books and Tagalog newspapers or attending Tagalog movies.
Movies are especially popular with this group because films offer
an escape from their problems. They also enjoy playing Tagalog
pop songs on the radio at an extremely high volume, shattering
the eardrums of passengers and pedestrians as well. The Jeepney
drivers seem to have a superficial religious nature. This is
manifested by their intense superstition--for example, they will
make the sign of the cross whenever passing by Catholic churches.
Publicly they ridicule Christianity, which they are usually
ignorant of. Most are very nominal in their Catholic faith and
have a deep spiritual hunger for meaning and truth in their
lives.

EXPANDED DESCRIPTIONS

Jinuos (China)

ALTERNATE NAMES: Youles

SIZE OF GROUP: 10,000   MARC ID: 7021

DISTINCTIVES: language; ethnicity; kinship

SOCIAL CHANGE: moderate

LANGUAGES: Tibeto-Burman (V); Mandarin (T)

SCRIPTURE: none

CHRISTIAN LITERACY: not reported

RELIGION: Animism

CHURCHES AND MISSIONS: not reported

OPENNESS TO RELIGIOUS CHANGE: not reported

RECEPTIVITY TO CHRISTIANITY: not reported

GROWTH RATE OF CHRISTIAN COMMUNITY: not reported

EVANGELISM PROFILE: not reported

VALIDITY: 5

The Jinuo people are the latest "nationality" to be recognized by the Chinese government. This was approved in June of 1979 making them China's 56th nationality. This was a decision based on the fact that they have a separate language, customs, economic structure, and psychology unique to their own group.

The Jinuos (sometimes known as the Youles) are concentrated in the Yunnan Province. They live in approximately 1,300 family groups in 40 villages. Formerly they lived in a clan structure with each village headed by the two oldest men. The borders of each village were strictly maintained, and if a dispute arose the villagers would gather together and pray for help in solving the problem. Spring ceremonies with animal sacrifices mark the beginning of the agriculture cycle. The Jinuos farm by the slash-and-burn method, rotating their crops on different pieces of land. Since grain production was only adequate for four months the rest of the year the men would hunt.

Customs among the Jinuos included earlobe decoration, teeth painting, and the wearing of pointed bonnets. Marriage between brothers and sisters was allowed and today marriage between cousins is still the custom. Monogamy is the rule today. When people die they are buried in hollowed-out trees and a small bamboo house is built over the grave where the family gives daily offerings of food for two to three years. After several years the body is removed and the coffin is used to bury someone else in the same spot.

The origins of the Jinous is unknown but several legends are quite interesting. According to one legend a brother and sister survived a great flood and are later married. From a god who guides them, they received 10 calabash seeds which eventually sprout and produce the ancestors of neighboring people groups.

The Jinous have no written language but an increasing number of individuals are receiving education in Mandarin. The status of Christianity among these people is unknown at this time.

Kalinga, Northern (Philippines)

ALTERNATE NAMES: Linimos

SIZE OF GROUP: 20,000   MARC ID: 1146

DISTINCTIVES: language; ethnicity

SOCIAL CHANGE: not reported

LANGUAGES: Kalinga (100% speak; V); Ilocano (T); English

SCRIPTURE: none

CHRISTIAN LITERACY: not reported

RELIGION: Roman Catholic (5% adherents/3% practicing);
    Christo-Paganism (95% adherents)

CHURCHES AND MISSIONS	BEGAN	MEMBERSHIP	COMMUNITY
Roman Catholic Church	nr	nr	nr

OPENNESS TO RELIGIOUS CHANGE: not reported

RECEPTIVITY TO CHRISTIANITY: receptive

GROWTH RATE OF CHRISTIAN COMMUNITY: not reported

EVANGELISM PROFILE: not reported

VALIDITY: 5

The name "Kalinga" means "enemy" in the language of some of the Kalinga neighbors. This reflects traditional disputes (usually over land) among the groups that inhabit the drainage areas of the middle Chico River in Luzon. The Kalinga are noted for their strong sense of tribal awareness and the peace pacts they have made among themselves.

These peace pacts ("bodong") began around the turn of the century and probably emerged from the trading partnerships that the Kalinga maintained. The pacts are usually developed between two individuals from different regions. In time they become binding on their kinship networks and eventually the whole region. The final details of the pacts are based on a detailed body of custom law and are worked out at large meetings. Regional leaders who are skilled in public speaking lead these meetings and use these occasions to gain prestige.

Northern Kalinga society is very kinship oriented and relatives are held responsible for avenging any injury to a member. Disputes are usually settled by the regional leaders, who listen to all sides and then impose fines on the guilty party. These are not formal council meetings but carry a good deal of authority.

Almost all of the Northern Kalinga are "christo-pagans", practicing a blend of animistic and pseudo-Christian religion. Kalinga mediums make offerings to ancestral spirits and other spirits that they believe cause illnesses. Witchcraft and sorcery are sometimes practiced and most people are afraid of poisoning. Though they believe in a creator-god, he is seldom called upon. There is a great need for these people to be freed from their spiritual darkness and to learn about the Creator who cares for them and who can be approached through His son, Jesus Christ.

EXPANDED DESCRIPTIONS

Kazakhs (China)

ALTERNATE NAMES: not reported

SIZE OF GROUP: 700,000   MARC ID: 7013

DISTINCTIVES: ethnicity; sense of unity; kinship

SOCIAL CHANGE: moderate

LANGUAGES: Kazakh (V)

SCRIPTURE: New Testament

CHRISTIAN LITERACY: not reported

RELIGION: Islam-Animist

CHURCHES AND MISSIONS: not reported

OPENNESS TO RELIGIOUS CHANGE: not reported

RECEPTIVITY TO CHRISTIANITY: not reported

GROWTH RATE OF CHRISTIAN COMMUNITY: not reported

EVANGELISM PROFILE: not reported

VALIDITY: 6

The Kazakhs are one of the Muslim people groups living in China's Xinjiang (Sinkiang) Province. They are but one of the world's many minority people divided by political boundaries. While China has 700,000 Kazakhs, Iran has 3,000 (see Unreached Peoples '80, p. 161), and another 5.3 million live across the border in the Soviet Republic of Kazakhstan. The Chinese authorities are concerned about the Kazakhs because they are a nomadic people and it would be easy for them to cross the border. They are also easily aroused to battle, and if the Chinese allow the Kazakhs to be swayed by the Soviets, they could find themselves facing a conflict with Russia.

The Kazakhs have been resistant to assimilation into the Chinese way of life. The Chinese government is attempting to set up communes according to kin groups, since the Kazakhs do not accept anyone except relatives to be part of their group.

Many Kazakhs do not speak Chinese. The Kazakh language was originally written as an Arabic script, but in the 1950's the Chinese government adopted the Cyrillic script for them. In 1964 this was abandoned and a Latin script may have been adopted to give greater distance between the Soviet and Chinese Kazakhs.

Kazakhs are thought to be the least Islamic of the Central Asian Turks. Their religion is a combination of Islam and folk practices, and they continue to acknowledge local demons and spirits. Mullahs (holy men) are also shamans. While earlier attempts by groups like the Swedish Missionary Society saw limited results before 1949, Islamic persecution all but obliterated the infant church leaving only the fruits of translation.

It is also possible that Little Flock efforts at immigration evangelism (moving of Christian Chinese families into the area) may have resulted in some planting of Christian groups among the Kazakhs of Xinjiang. Post-1949 government policies of forced resettlement of ethnic Chinese in border areas may also have included some Christians.

Kelabit (Malaysia)

ALTERNATE NAMES: Kalabit

SIZE OF GROUP: 17,000   MARC ID: 7025

DISTINCTIVES: language; kinship; ethnicity; religion

SOCIAL CHANGE: not reported

LANGUAGES: Kelabit (V); Lun Bawang (T)

SCRIPTURE: portions

CHRISTIAN LITERACY: not reported

RELIGION: Animism; Christianity

CHURCHES AND MISSIONS	BEGAN	MEMBERSHIP	COMMUNITY
Kelabit Church	nr	nr	nr

OPENNESS TO RELIGIOUS CHANGE: not reported

RECEPTIVITY TO CHRISTIANITY: not reported

GROWTH RATE OF CHRISTIAN COMMUNITY: not reported

EVANGELISM PROFILE: not reported

VALIDITY: 6

Famous for their colorful bead work, hospitality, blacksmithing, and sword dancing, the Kelabit live in eastern Sarawak on the Kelabit Plateau bordering Indonesia. Kelabit villages average about 400 people and are located along rivers or streams. Usually village residents live together in long houses that are up to 250 ft. in length. Long house residents tend to be exogamous, that is, marrying outside their immediate group. Populations are divided into those who are "good" (aristocratic) and "bad" (lower class). This status depends primarily on inherited wealth and though class differences are rarely openly expressed in everyday life, in times of crises the head aristocrat has final say.

The Kelabit indigenous religion was structured to maintain the well-being of the long house members. Health and well-being were associated with ideas of "hot" and "cold", and concepts of death are still associated with beliefs about this dichotomy. Any major problems are considered to be signs that the long house is becoming "cold", that is, spiritually imbalanced. Various deities and spirits are appeased in order to regain this spiritual balance. These beliefs are beginning to fade under the impact of Christianity.

Funerals are considered to be important events, especially the burial of an aristocrat. Usually they are buried in a boat-shaped wooden coffin which is kept at the long house for a year, after which the bones are removed and a secondary burial takes place in a jar or stone vat. At the time of this secondary burial an elaborate feast is held and this marks the end of the mourning period for the close relatives. These funerals are social events and often are used by aristocratic families to compete with each other.

Recently there has been a work of the Spirit among the churches on the Kelabit Plateau. Twelve churches have been established so far and there are hopes for several more. Many Kelabit are serving in the police and field security forces, while others can be a witness in their new settings as well.

EXPANDED DESCRIPTIONS

Koreans in Manchuria (China)

ALTERNATE NAMES: not reported

SIZE OF GROUP: 3,000,000   MARC ID: 7007

DISTINCTIVES: language; political loyalty; occupation;
    discrimination

SOCIAL CHANGE: slow

LANGUAGES: Korean (V); Mandarin (T)

SCRIPTURE: none

CHRISTIAN LITERACY: not reported

RELIGION: Buddhism; Christianity; Animism

CHURCHES AND MISSIONS	BEGAN	MEMBERSHIP	COMMUNITY
House Churches	nr	3,000	nr

OPENNESS TO RELIGIOUS CHANGE: not reported

RECEPTIVITY TO CHRISTIANITY: not reported

GROWTH RATE OF CHRISTIAN COMMUNITY: not reported

EVANGELISM PROFILE: not reported

VALIDITY: 5

The Korean minority in northeast China (Manchuria) is
estimated at three million -- three times the official figure.
Koreans have been living in Manchuria since the early part of
this century. They are a completely unassimilated people who
speak and write their native language, operate schools (including
a university at Yen-chi), and maintain the society and culture of
their homeland. Most are rural residents living on
state-organized communes, although many are now in the labor
force of industrialized Manchuria.

Since the 1978 normalization of US-China relations, letters
have been received by FEBC Korea from Christians among the
Koreans in northeast China. One letter talks of over 200
believers scattered all over Manchuria.

Korean Christians are excited about this news and have plans
to reach their fellows in China. However, their outreach is
limited by the political barriers between China and South Korea.
Koreans overseas who have foreign passports (i.e., US, Canadian,
Japanese, etc.) are needed at this time to penetrate into
Manchuria. The region is open for tourism by the Chinese, who
will readily accept any foreign passport holder.

Radio ministry is also profitable, as indicated above. The
potential of these Christian Koreans is great as they seek to
reach out to the Chinese around them. It is known that there are
many Chinese believers in the northeast as many were sent there
as prisoners exiled for their faith. Prayer is needed that the
two groups, Chinese and Korean, would overcome their mutual
prejudices in the Lord, support and encourage one another, and
reach out in witness to the unsaved in both their communities.

In 1908 revival swept through Korea and into Manchuria,
including the Korean villages there. Under communism, though,
all religions have been suppressed. Presently there are reports
of 120 Korean house churches in Manchuria with an estimated total
of 3,000 believers. Worship in these churches is in Korean.
Five cities in Manchuria have opened up state churches and these
worship services are conducted in Mandarin.

Kubu (Indonesia)

ALTERNATE NAMES: not reported

SIZE OF GROUP: 25,000   MARC ID: 7026

DISTINCTIVES: language; ethnicity; religion; kinship

SOCIAL CHANGE: moderate

LANGUAGES: Kubu (V)

SCRIPTURE: not reported

CHRISTIAN LITERACY: not reported

RELIGION: Islam-Animist; Animism; Islam; Christianity

CHURCHES AND MISSIONS	BEGAN	MEMBERSHIP	COMMUNITY
Gereja Kristen Protestan	nr	nr	nr

OPENNESS TO RELIGIOUS CHANGE: not reported

RECEPTIVITY TO CHRISTIANITY: not reported

GROWTH RATE OF CHRISTIAN COMMUNITY: not reported

EVANGELISM PROFILE: not reported

VALIDITY: 6

The Kubu people live in central Sumatra, primarily in the Province of Jambi. Their name probably comes from the word "Ngubu" ("elusive"). This name has been given to them by others and has a negative connotation of being "backwoods" or "primitive." Population estimates are very difficult to obtain because the Kubu people are being assimilated into other surrounding groups. Most likely they number over 25,000. This pattern of assimilation is common for many of the other people groups in this area, with most of them living as marginal populations near Malay villages and towns. Despite these circumstances the Kubu have a distinct culture that makes them a unique people group.

Most of the Kubu are settled agriculturalists who grow yams, maize, rice, plantain, and sugarcane. As farmers they are generally indifferent and their fields are rather poorly kept. They also practice hunting, fishing, and gathering to obtain additional food.

The Kubu are considered to be nominal Muslims, though their traditional animistic practices, such as curing rites, are still carried on. They have a traditional concept of a great protector or original ancestor though there are no ancestor cults to speak of. There have been several efforts by Christians to evangelize the Kubu people and in one of the larger villages two evangelists are working full-time among them. Children are enrolled in a school run by the evangelists and it is hoped that this will be a motivation for the parents to gain an interest in the gospel. The evangelists are also trying to introduce mixed farming and have started a cooperative so that the Kubu won't be treated unfairly by those that they trade with.

One of the great problems for evangelism in this area is the hostility of the local Muslims. Even many of the Christians have been influenced by Islamic teaching. There is a great need for more teaching and a deeper understanding of the Christian faith to be able to stand up to this persecution. Medical and agricultural help would probably be a vital part of any effective ministry to the Kubu people.

EXPANDED DESCRIPTIONS

Kuluis in Himachal Pradesh (India)

ALTERNATE NAMES: Paharis

SIZE OF GROUP: 200,000   MARC ID: 2015

DISTINCTIVES: ethnicity; religion

SOCIAL CHANGE: slow

LANGUAGES: Kului (80% speak/10% read; V, T, G); Hindi (60%
     speak/10% read; S, G, W)

SCRIPTURE: portions

CHRISTIAN LITERACY: 25%

RELIGION: Protestant (1% adherents/1% practicing); Hinduism
     (70% adherents/50% practicing); Animism (20% adherents/10%
     practicing); Unknown (9% adherents)

CHURCHES AND MISSIONS   BEGAN MEMBERSHIP   COMMUNITY
     Indian Evangelical Mission   1968   16   35

OPENNESS TO RELIGIOUS CHANGE: somewhat open

RECEPTIVITY TO CHRISTIANITY: receptive

GROWTH RATE OF CHRISTIAN COMMUNITY: not reported

EVANGELISM PROFILE:
     50% No awareness of Christianity
     30% Aware that Christianity exists
     10% Some knowledge of the gospel
     5% Understand the message of the gospel
     4% Personally challenged to receive Christ
     1% Decision to accept Christ
     0% Incorporated into a fellowship of Christians
     0% Active propagators of the gospel

VALIDITY: 5

     The Kulu Valley in Aimachal Pradesh is known as the "valley
of gods." Well over 300 deities are worshipped here. Once a year
the gold, silver, and brass idols are carried to an October
festival where for seven days rituals are carried out to appease
the gods and ward off evil spirits. Folk dances are accompanied
by the blowing of trumpets and the beating of drums. Homage is
paid especially to the chief god Raghunathji. In the midst of
this spiritual darkness live the Kului people.
     Evangelists have visited the Kului to distribute Christian
literature during the October festival, and some medical missions
work was done in the Manali area. In 1968 a systematic
long-range work was begun by Indian Evangelical Mission in
cooperation with these medical workers. There were no Kului
believers at that time, but by 1970 five persons were baptised.
Three of these five reverted to their old beliefs due to
persecution, and others were prevented from converting by
pressure from their chiefs. In 1976, however, fifteen more were
baptised and today there are about fifty believers.
     The Kului peple are reported to be increasingly responsive
to the gospel. Because they're generally friendly and sociable,
personal evangelism which displays genuine friendship will be
successful. So far literature, gospel records and cassettes,
radio, visual aids, adult literacy classes, and medical work have
been used to reach the Kului.

Kurichiya in Kerala (India)

ALTERNATE NAMES: not reported

SIZE OF GROUP: 12,130   MARC ID: 2716

DISTINCTIVES: language; ethnicity

SOCIAL CHANGE: not reported

LANGUAGES: Kurichiya

SCRIPTURE: none

CHRISTIAN LITERACY: not reported

RELIGION: Hindu-Animist; Christianity (-1% practicing)

CHURCHES AND MISSIONS: not reported

OPENNESS TO RELIGIOUS CHANGE: not reported

RECEPTIVITY TO CHRISTIANITY: not reported

GROWTH RATE OF CHRISTIAN COMMUNITY: not reported

EVANGELISM PROFILE: not reported

VALIDITY: 5

Status and ranking are extremely important to the majority of people in India. Thus it is surprising to discover a group that consider themselves higher than the Brahmin caste. The Kurichiyas are so concerned with keeping themseles "pure" that they will burn their huts touched by others. They also will not eat with any other groups and even refuse to drink water from a pot that has come into contact with anyone who isn't a Kurichiya.

It is said that this people group derived its name from the sandelwood mark ("Kuri") they put on their forehead and chest. The Kurichiyas are found in the forest areas near Calicut, Tellichery, and Wynad, and were one of the first to cultivate this area. Although they are primarily farmers they are also expert archers, and eat meat in addition to the crops they grow. A number of families own their own land and cultivate pepper. Some work on land provided by the government while others make their living by cutting wood in the forest.

The Kurichiyas are Hindi-animists, worshipping a variety of gods and demons. One of the most powerful individuals in the group is the sorcerer. Their headman is elected during a ritual performed before their idols, when one of the group will go into a trance and do a frenzied dance. This is accepted as a sign that the gods have chosen this individual to be their leader. He then assumes responsibility by wearing on his waist the silver-handled knife worn by his predecessor.

Because of their superior status the conversion of the Kurichiyas would probably be influential in winning the people groups around them as well. One of the most effective ways of evangelizing this group is by prayer for the sick. Though they once considered this to be chanting like that of their socerer, they realize now that praying is something different. A strategy for reaching the Kurichiyas should include a Christ-centered prayer group that could develop into an evangelistic Bible study.

EXPANDED DESCRIPTIONS

Lahu (Thailand)

ALTERNATE NAMES: not reported

SIZE OF GROUP: 22,500   MARC ID: 2088

DISTINCTIVES: language; ethnicity; religion; sense of unity

SOCIAL CHANGE: slow

LANGUAGES: Lahu (100% speak; V, G, W); Thai (50% speak; T, S)

SCRIPTURE: New Testament

CHRISTIAN LITERACY: not reported

RELIGION: Christianity (19% adherents/7% practicing); Animism
(81% adherents)

CHURCHES AND MISSIONS	BEGAN	MEMBERSHIP	COMMUNITY
American Baptists	nr	2,500	4,500

OPENNESS TO RELIGIOUS CHANGE: somewhat open

RECEPTIVITY TO CHRISTIANITY: indifferent

GROWTH RATE OF CHRISTIAN COMMUNITY: not reported

EVANGELISM PROFILE: not reported

VALIDITY: 5

The Lahu of Taiwan "are a proud people, inclined to be
quarrelsome if they feel that they have been insulted" (Lebar
1964: 30). This fighting spirit has given them a reputation
throughout this region for fierceness and independence. They
live by strict rules of behavior with harsh punishments for
offenders, and until recently occasionally executed those who
broke the tribal codes. As might be expected, the Lahu are
excellent hunters. This provides not only a good part of their
diet but also income from the selling of dried meat. The men are
especially keen on receiving the title "Supreme hunter." In
addition to this pursuit, the Lahu engage in slash-and-burn
agriculture to produce dry rice, maize, and other vegetables.
They usually avoid plains people except to trade dried meat and
peppers for salt. It's not clear whether their former practice
of growing opium as a cash crop has been continued.
    Several of the more remote Lahu villages have limited
contact with the Thai government. It's reported that they don't
like the Chinese at all, and while contacts with other groups
occur, they refuse to intermarry. A village chief handles
disputes and decides punishments. Difficult cases are sometimes
still decided by ordeal or by divination. Strong village
solidarity exists, and individuals are very reluctant to do
anything without the consent of the leaders.
    Conversions to Christianity thus have tended to be in people
movements - that is, entire villages will decide together to
adopt the faith if the chief is in favor of it. To date only
about seven percent of the Lahu are practicing Christians, while
another 12 percent have a nominal faith. The vast majority
maintain their animistic beliefs and there is great pressure on
the Christians to return to their former practices.
    Lahu traditional religion is a blend of many features and is
more sophisticated than that of neighboring tribes. It is
speculated that the Lahu may once have been Buddhists or were
greatly influenced by Buddhism: to this day they're attracted to
quasi-religious sects and other religious movements.

Lambadi in Andhra Pradesh (India)

ALTERNATE NAMES: Banjara; Sugalis

SIZE OF GROUP: 1,300,000   MARC ID: 2018

DISTINCTIVES: kinship; sense of unity

SOCIAL CHANGE: not reported

LANGUAGES: Lambadi (100% speak; V, G); Telugu (T, W)

SCRIPTURE: portions

CHRISTIAN LITERACY: not reported

RELIGION: Animism; Christianity

CHURCHES AND MISSIONS: not reported

OPENNESS TO RELIGIOUS CHANGE: somewhat open

RECEPTIVITY TO CHRISTIANITY: receptive

GROWTH RATE OF CHRISTIAN COMMUNITY: not reported

EVANGELISM PROFILE: not reported

VALIDITY: 5

Originating in the state of Rajasthan, the Lambadi are now concentrated in the state of Andhra Pradesh. Legend has it that they were once in the army of a Raja, but when this king was defeated the Lambadi were scattered into the jungles of northwest India. They lived a nomadic existence for hundreds of years, keeping cattle and trading salt. Eventually they settled into organized communities.

The basic unit of Lambadi society is the "Thanda" which is led by the "Naik." This leader settles disputes and administers punishment. Guilty parties are usually fined and the money is used by the Thanda for drinking and eating. If the case is not settled at this level it will eventually go to the government court.

The Lambadi, like so many other people groups in India, are very reluctant to become Christians because they view conversion as a break with their caste. There is a fear that if they leave their idol worshipping, the gods will bring down calamity on their families and community. Past evangelism efforts have also been hindered because of an ignorance of the Lambadi language. This is changing slowly as a few Lambadi Christians have witnessed among their own people; when the gospel is presented in a way they understand a great deal of interest is shown.

Since the Lambadi love singing and dancing, future evangelism should incorporate these favored cultural practices. Lambadi evangelists report that an audience is easily formed when music (especially in their own language) is played. Because of the poverty among this group, it's also felt that evangelism should be linked with meeting basic human needs through medical, agricultural, and educational assistance. It is hoped that these kinds of expressions of the love of Christ, combined with a thorough presentation of the gospel, will further to open the hearts of the Lambadi to the Living God.

EXPANDED DESCRIPTIONS

Lawa, Eastern (Thailand)

ALTERNATE NAMES: not reported

SIZE OF GROUP: 2,500   MARC ID: 7039

DISTINCTIVES: language; ethnicity; religion; kinship

SOCIAL CHANGE: not reported

LANGUAGES: Tibeto-Burman Dialect (V); Thai (T)

SCRIPTURE: none

CHRISTIAN LITERACY: not reported

RELIGION: Buddhist-Animist; Christianity (-1% practicing)

CHURCHES AND MISSIONS: not reported

OPENNESS TO RELIGIOUS CHANGE: indifferent

RECEPTIVITY TO CHRISTIANITY: reluctant

GROWTH RATE OF CHRISTIAN COMMUNITY: not reported

EVANGELISM PROFILE: not reported

VALIDITY: 5

The Eastern Lawa are a Mon-Khmar speaking group located in the highlands of Central Thailand on the borders of the Petchaboon and Chaiyapoom provinces. They are mostly highland farmers who cultivate wet-rice crops and occasionally engage in slash-and-burn agriculture. Some of them work for Thai settlers in this area as day laborers.

The Lawa (along with the Kui) are thought to be of an older culture than that of contemporary Thai people. Contact with the larger Thai society has been extensive, and most of the Lawa live in permanent villages like their Thai neighbors. A small number of villages still cultivate rice and maize in hill clearings.

The religion of the Lawa used to be a mixture of several types of animistic practices but now includes elements of the Buddhist faith as well. Though there has been a Christian witness among the Lawa, the number of believers is still relatively small. The group is reported to be somewhat opposed to Christianity. As cultural change increases it is hoped that their receptivity to the gospel will increase as well. A growing percentage of the Lawa, particularly the younger people, now speak Thai, and more Christian materials are available in this language.

Lepers of Central Thailand (Thailand)

ALTERNATE NAMES: not reported

SIZE OF GROUP: 20,000　　　　　　MARC ID: 7003

DISTINCTIVES: social class; economic status; discrimination; health situation; significant problems

SOCIAL CHANGE: slow

LANGUAGES: Thai (V)

SCRIPTURE: Bible

CHRISTIAN LITERACY: not reported

RELIGION: Buddhist-Animist (98% adherents/30% practicing); Protestant (2% adherents/1% practicing)

CHURCHES AND MISSIONS	BEGAN	MEMBERSHIP	COMMUNITY
Overseas Missionary Fellowship	1952	nr	nr
Leprosy Mission	nr	nr	nr

OPENNESS TO RELIGIOUS CHANGE: indifferent

RECEPTIVITY TO CHRISTIANITY: receptive

GROWTH RATE OF CHRISTIAN COMMUNITY: slow growth

EVANGELISM PROFILE: not reported

VALIDITY: 6

Throughout Thailand it is estimated that there are over 200,000 people with leprosy. It is thought that they are fairly evenly distributed throughout the 70 provinces of Thailand, but as yet there are no reliable statistics available that would confirm this. In Central Thailand, a region of 8 provinces, we can estimate a number of 20,000.

Leprosy is a disease that often leads to disfigurement. This immediately makes it a social disease and because of this the leprosy patient has always been set apart in society. From the teachings of Buddhism it follows that such disfigurement and disease must be a result of sin in a previous life. Thus the leprosy patient is at the very bottom of the social scale. For centuries this pattern has meant that the leprosy patients themselves have given up all hope of improvement in this life and so they are a group of people with no desire for betterment.

The advent of modern drugs has given hope to this group of people. The Christian medic has spearheaded the treatment of leprosy in Thailand. Quite a large number of these people have responded to the Christian gospel message of love, for they have seen that love in action as doctors and nurses care for them. Today government programs are also reaching the leprosy patient and bold attempts are being made to integrate these people back into general society, but progress is slow because of the centuries of separation. The cross-cultural missionary and the Christian Church, if it is established locally, can continue to be a leader in this area of reintegration and the breaking down of false barriers often caused by fears and misunderstandings. There is still the need for Christian medical work among these people as well as direct evangelism and Bible teaching.

EXPANDED DESCRIPTIONS

Lisu (China)

ALTERNATE NAMES: Li-Hsaw

SIZE OF GROUP: 470,000   MARC ID: 7009

DISTINCTIVES: language; ethnicity; religion

SOCIAL CHANGE: moderate

LANGUAGES: Tibeto-Burman (V); Mandarin (T)

SCRIPTURE: not reported

CHRISTIAN LITERACY: not reported

RELIGION: Animism

CHURCHES AND MISSIONS: not reported

OPENNESS TO RELIGIOUS CHANGE: not reported

RECEPTIVITY TO CHRISTIANITY: not reported

GROWTH RATE OF CHRISTIAN COMMUNITY: not reported

EVANGELISM PROFILE: not reported

VALIDITY: 5

The Lisu are a good example of a people group that
transcends political boundaries and yet retains a unique culture.
Though found in Burma and Thailand, this description will focus
on the Lisu of China, who live primarily in western Yunnan.

The Lisu language is of Tibeto-Burman origin, closely
related to Lahu and Akha. Although the Lisu have no indigenous
writing, there have been reports in the past of a
hieroglyphic-type writing used by their medicine men. At one
point there also was a missionary-devised script.

Contact with other groups is fairly common, and the Lisu
have adapted many Chinese cultural practices. Intermarriage is
accepted. Writers have called the Lisu a "fine people - robust,
and independent of spirit. . . ." They have adapted to the varied
geographies they live in, using a variety of agricultural styles
to grow food.

Traditionally the Lisu were animists with an emphasis on
ancestor worship and exorcism. There are very few Buddhist
elements in their religious practices despite their contact with
other groups, though some parts of their rituals are similar to
those of Chinese Taoism. The Lisu year centers around an annual
spring festival that lasts for four to six days. One day in
particular is reserved for honoring the ancestors by visiting
graves and sometimes making sacrifices of pigs. If there is a
serious illness individuals will contribute to a sacrifice
ceremony and feast for the village (guardian) spirit.

This belief in spirits permeates Lisu society. They believe
that a village "sorcerer" must be the intermediary between
spirits and humans to assure the success of their appeals for
help. Amulets and cotton threads on which he has breathed are
sometimes worn to ward off illness or bad luck.

Before the communist takeover it was reported that
Christianity played an important part in Lisu life. Since that
time the situation is unclear.

Loinang (Indonesia)

ALTERNATE NAMES: not reported

SIZE OF GROUP: 100,000   MARC ID: 2969

DISTINCTIVES: language; ethnicity; religion; kinship

SOCIAL CHANGE: not reported

LANGUAGES: Loinang

SCRIPTURE: none

CHRISTIAN LITERACY: not reported

RELIGION: Islam; Animism; Christianity

CHURCHES AND MISSIONS: not reported

OPENNESS TO RELIGIOUS CHANGE: not reported

RECEPTIVITY TO CHRISTIANITY: not reported

GROWTH RATE OF CHRISTIAN COMMUNITY: not reported

EVANGELISM PROFILE: not reported

VALIDITY: 5

At one time ruled by the Sultan of Banggai, the Loinang came under the authority of the Dutch around 1900. Today they are a farming group living in the interior region of the eastern peninsula of Sulawesi. Each individual considers himself to be a kinsman of the others who live in his village, which may have from 50 to 700 members. Subtribal units called "bosanjo" are formed by grouping several villages together who share a common territory and ancestors. The chief of this larger group is chosen from a family that has a direct relationship to a founding ancestor of the bosanjo. He is paid a "tribute" by the villagers that usually consists of beeswax, rice, and other goods. Each Loinang village is a unit for religious ritual as well as social interaction and thus members have a strong loyalty to their own village. Formerly wars were fought because of boundary disputes.

Most Loinang marriages take place within the bosanjo. Individuals are allowed to choose their partners but their families make most of the arrangements. Bride-price is made up of two parts – the actual payment and then gifts to compensate the bride's family for her loss (especially the loss of her working hands!). Monogamy is the standard marriage pattern. Parallel cousins (children of the father's brother or mother's sister) are the preferred partners.

Islam and Christianity both made some inroads into Loinang society around the turn of the century. Animist beliefs still predominate, however, and spirits are appeased through various rituals. Ancestor spirits are especially important. Illness caused by evil forces are cured by priests who "recapture" the sick person's life force while in a possessed state. Sacrifices and divination are also performed.

EXPANDED DESCRIPTIONS

Lolo (China)

ALTERNATE NAMES: Yi

SIZE OF GROUP: 4,800,000   MARC ID: 7006

DISTINCTIVES: language; sense of unity

SOCIAL CHANGE: moderate

LANGUAGES: Yi (V)

SCRIPTURE: not reported

CHRISTIAN LITERACY: not reported

RELIGION: Animism

CHURCHES AND MISSIONS: not reported

OPENNESS TO RELIGIOUS CHANGE: not reported

RECEPTIVITY TO CHRISTIANITY: not reported

GROWTH RATE OF CHRISTIAN COMMUNITY: not reported

EVANGELISM PROFILE: not reported

VALIDITY: 5

The Lolo are a people group united by a common culture and heritage. They don't share a common ethnic background. In fact, the group is made up of individuals from different racial stocks. However, there is a unity because of a shared way of life and a shared world view.

The origin of the Lolo is a mystery with clues leading in several different directions. Their language, Yi, points to Tibet, while their generally Caucasoid features seem to put their origin further west. They have several cultural traits in common with the Mongols in the north, including the use of felt, herding, and the lack of pottery, while some older features, such as the use of poison arrows, links them to people in the south.

The homeland of the Lolo has been consistent, however, for at least several hundred years. They live throughout the mountains of Yunnan and even into southwestern Sichuan (Szechwan), western Guizhou (Kweichow), and northern Indochina. They are concentrated in the Taliang Shan (cold mountains) of Sichuan, and fascinated western travelers around the turn of the century as a "blood-proud caste of nobility. . . who fought, rode, herded horses, and ruled. . . a stratum of underlings and slaves." This traditional social structure of hereditary nobles, serfs, and slaves has almost completely broken down since the 1950s. Communes have been organized as in other parts of China. Many are accultured and have adopted Chinese dress, observe Chinese religious festivals, and take on Chinese surnames. The traditional pictographic script, which was used by religious practitioners, has now been replaced by a romanized script that is used in schools and offices.

Before the communist takeover missionary work was attempted on the fringes of the Lolo people by the Roman Catholics. This had minimal results and the current status of Christianity among this people is not known.

Loven (Laos)

ALTERNATE NAMES: Boloven

SIZE OF GROUP: 25,000   MARC ID: 107

DISTINCTIVES: language; ethnicity

SOCIAL CHANGE: not reported

LANGUAGES: Loven (100% speak; V); Lao (T)

SCRIPTURE: not reported

CHRISTIAN LITERACY: not reported

RELIGION: Buddhist-Animist (99% adherents); Christianity (1% adherents/1% practicing)

CHURCHES AND MISSIONS: not reported

OPENNESS TO RELIGIOUS CHANGE: somewhat closed

RECEPTIVITY TO CHRISTIANITY: not reported

GROWTH RATE OF CHRISTIAN COMMUNITY: not reported

EVANGELISM PROFILE: not reported

VALIDITY: 5

   One would not usually associate Irish potatoes with a tribal group in Laos, but in the case of the Loven this is an accurate association. Potatoes were introduced by the French when Laos was part of French Indochina and developed into an important cash crop along with coffee. Other tribal groups work for the Loven and the produce is sold to Chinese merchants, making this system an interesting case of cross-cultural adaptation and interaction.
   Loven villages, located in Southern Laos, generally are small. Houses are rectangular and built on piles. Dry rice is the principle crop grown for consumption along with maize, red peppers, cardamom, yams and other vegetables. The Loven are skilled woodworkers, though unlike other people groups in this area they don't weave or work with metal.
   The Loven are also somewhat unique in their marriage customs. The couple have more say than most in the process, and their consent (along with their parents'), is necessary for the wedding to take place. In addition no bride price, bride service, or dowry is required if it is a first marriage. If it is a second marriage a bride price is given to the second wife's parents. Village headmen perform the weddings and provide a written document to make the ceremony official.
   Though most Loven believe in animistic spirits, large numbers are turning to Buddhism and some of the young men are even becoming monks. Only one percent are practicing Christians at this point.

EXPANDED DESCRIPTIONS

Lubang Islanders (Philippines)

ALTERNATE NAMES: not reported

SIZE OF GROUP: 18,000   MARC ID: 7016

DISTINCTIVES: religion; ethnicity; education; kinship

SOCIAL CHANGE: moderate

LANGUAGES: Pilipino (V)

SCRIPTURE: Bible

CHRISTIAN LITERACY: not reported

RELIGION: Christo-Paganism

CHURCHES AND MISSIONS	BEGAN	MEMBERSHIP	COMMUNITY
Caloocan Bible Church	1977	nr	nr
I.V. Student Medical Mission	1977	nr	nr
Assoc. Bible Churches Philipp.	1978	nr	nr

OPENNESS TO RELIGIOUS CHANGE: somewhat closed

RECEPTIVITY TO CHRISTIANITY: reluctant

GROWTH RATE OF CHRISTIAN COMMUNITY: not reported

EVANGELISM PROFILE: not reported

VALIDITY: 5

It is said that the people of Lubang Island were originally migrants from mainland Mindoro and Batangas Provinces. Linked by very strong kinship ties every family feels a close affinity to others on the island. This close kinship link is the primary element in the Lubang Islander's identity. a distinct people group.

Attempts have been made in the past by missionaries to preach the gospel but they have generally not been successful. Overseas Missionary Fellowship has won a few converts and in the early 1950s a small number of believers formed a church. The number of believers didn't exceed 10 until 1978 when the work was turned over to the Association of Bible Churches of the Philippines.

The population of Lubang Island adheres very strictly to a syncretistic blend of Roman Catholicism and animistic beliefs. Most people are very superstitious and conservative. Other religions and cults in addition to Christianity have had difficulty penetrating the Island. Persecution is still very strong against believers and ostracism is an effective tool for maintaining the status quo.

The Inter-Varsity Student Medical Mission has attempted to win converts through medical assistance programs. They have carried out this work for six summers but failed to achieve their goal because no one was able to nuture any of the converts once they left the Island. The Caloocan Bible Church youth group has also started a summer mission work which began in 1977. Their vision is to build a library and recreation center to indirectly proclaim the message of salvation. The chances of success for this program look very good.

It is reported that almost 95 percent of the youth are attending or have graduated from high school. A large number are also college graduates who have attended school in Manila. With such a highly education population, literature evangelism seems to be a very appropriate way of presentating the Gospel.

198

Malakkaras of Kerela (India)

ALTERNATE NAMES: Mala Muthas; Malamuthas

SIZE OF GROUP: 1,000   MARC ID: 2019

DISTINCTIVES: language; ethnicity; religion; kinship;
     residence; social class; discrimination

SOCIAL CHANGE: very slow

LANGUAGES: Malamutha (100% speak; V, G); Malayalam (60%
     speak/5% read; T, S, G)

SCRIPTURE: Bible

CHRISTIAN LITERACY: 5%

RELIGION: Hindu-Animist (100% adherents/40% practicing)

CHURCHES AND MISSIONS: not reported

OPENNESS TO RELIGIOUS CHANGE: very closed

RECEPTIVITY TO CHRISTIANITY: very reluctant

GROWTH RATE OF CHRISTIAN COMMUNITY: not reported

EVANGELISM PROFILE:
     98% No awareness of Christianity
      2% Aware that Christianity exists
      0% Some knowledge of the gospel
      0% Understand the message of the gospel
      0% Personally challenged to receive Christ
      0% Decision to accept Christ
      0% Incorporated into a fellowship of Christians
      0% Active propagators of the gospel

VALIDITY: 5

The Malakkaras are a tribal people in Kerala, South India.
Their name means "mighty people of the forests" and they live in
the jungle, generally avoiding outsiders. They are very proud of
their group identity, and even will not walk through a field
ploughed by a member of a lower social class.
    The Malakkaras are gradually becoming Hindus, though
elements of their old animist religion remains. They used to
worship various trees and animals; to this day they still show
reverence by kneeling down before "holy trees", rocks, and
mountains. They believe in a life after death when the righteous
will be rewarded with another human life while the evil will be
condemned to live as animals. Though they even go so far as to
give their children Hindu names, the animist themes in their
daily religion run very deep.
    It is estimated that 98% of the Malakkaras have no awareness
of the gospel. No real efforts have been made to reach them.
Their isolation and their racial pride are barriers that have
made them unreached. Their deep-seated belief that all other
religions are socially inferior to their own makes them strongly
opposed to any type of religious change. Any contact with people
from other groups is unlawful and can result in expulsion.
    Some young people in this people group are challenging these
attitudes and are seeking help from outsiders. They can function
as a link with the larger group. Though most of the Malakkara
people are illiterate, 60% of the group can speak Malayalam, and
their language contains many Malayalam and Tamil words. Tamil
speakers can be useful as missionaries to these people.

EXPANDED DESCRIPTIONS

Mamanua (Philippines)

ALTERNATE NAMES: Amamanua; Mamanwa

SIZE OF GROUP: 1,000   MARC ID: 628

DISTINCTIVES: language; ethnicity; kinship

SOCIAL CHANGE: not reported

LANGUAGES: Minamanwa (100% speak/5% read; V); Surigueno (T);
    Cebuano (85% speak); Agusan Manobo (Northern) (35% speak)

SCRIPTURE: portions

CHRISTIAN LITERACY: 75%

RELIGION: Christo-Paganism (97% adherents); Protestant (3%
    adherents/3% practicing)

CHURCHES AND MISSIONS	BEGAN	MEMBERSHIP	COMMUNITY
Philippine Missionary Fellshp.	1959	nr	nr
Santiago Pentecostal Church	1967	nr	nr
Summer Institute Linguistics	1956	nr	nr

OPENNESS TO RELIGIOUS CHANGE: not reported

RECEPTIVITY TO CHRISTIANITY: receptive

GROWTH RATE OF CHRISTIAN COMMUNITY: not reported

EVANGELISM PROFILE: not reported

VALIDITY: 6

The Mamanua make their home in the Diuata Mountains of
northeastern Mindanao. Although they've had extensive exposure
to Christianity it's estimated that 97 percent are
"christo-pagans"; that is, they've mixed the external rituals of
Christianity with pagan practices to produce a distorted
religious hybrid. They have a totally inadequate understanding
of the gospel and view Christianity more as a form of magic than
a relationship with the living God.

The Mamanua are now in a changing situation, switching from
a former nomadic hunting and gathering economy to a more settled
farming lifestyle. Sometimes they even plant coconuts as a cash
crop. They still move occasionally when a better environment can
be found, arranging their homes in a circle. The Mamanua grow
sweet potatoes, maize, taro, yams and rice, and supplement their
diet with wild pig, deer, pythons and monkeys. Recently fishing
has become important as well. They work as loggers and hunting
guides to earn money for goods that they can't produce.

The Mamanua have a belief in a supreme deity named
Magbabaya, who created the world. The group shamans have many
functions, including curing seances where they go into a trance.
During the full moon a ceremony is held where spirits are asked
to heal the sick and purify those who attend. Prayers at this
ceremony are mixed with dancing and the beating of gongs. Other
rituals are held to assure good crops and for thanksgiving.

The key individuals in the maintenance of this system are
the shamans. Often they are the child of a former shaman, or
they may be called in a dream. Evangelists should consider
focusing on these leaders in order to win the hearts of the
Mamanua people.

Manchu (China)

ALTERNATE NAMES: not reported

SIZE OF GROUP: 200,000   MARC ID: 2832

DISTINCTIVES: kinship; ethnicity

SOCIAL CHANGE: not reported

LANGUAGES: Manchu (V); Mandarin (T)

SCRIPTURE: New Testament

CHRISTIAN LITERACY: not reported

RELIGION: Christianity (-1% practicing); Traditional Chinese

CHURCHES AND MISSIONS	BEGAN	MEMBERSHIP	COMMUNITY
State Churches	nr	nr	nr

OPENNESS TO RELIGIOUS CHANGE: not reported

RECEPTIVITY TO CHRISTIANITY: not reported

GROWTH RATE OF CHRISTIAN COMMUNITY: not reported

EVANGELISM PROFILE: not reported

VALIDITY: 5

 The Manchus are considered one of the larger minority groups within the Peoples Republic of China, yet they have been largely assimilated into the Chinese culture. In the past they played an important part in China's history. The Manchus were the Qing Dynasty, the Imperial House of China, which ruled from 1644 to 1911. In the Revolution of 1912 they lost power. Now even their language is considered a dead language and most speak Mandarin. They are located in northeast China (Manchuria), but they have no separate autonomous areas as other minorities do. In Heilongjiang (Heilungkiang) Province they are the largest minority group. Farming is the typical way of life for most Manchus. They are so accepted by the Chinese that intermarriage between Chinese and Manchus occurs frequently.
 In earlier days, Manchuria saw much Christian work both by Catholics and Protestants. At the turn of the century village after village was requesting evangelists. In 1908, revival had swept through Manchuria and by 1910 some churches were even reported to be supporting their own pastors. Manchuria, though, was the area occupied by the Japanese in the war between the Japanese and the Chinese. It was later occupied by the communists. At this time there are reported to be underground churches in Manchuria, but no one knows for sure how many Christians are involved. There are also newly opened state churches in the area.

EXPANDED DESCRIPTIONS

Manggarai Muslims (Indonesia)

ALTERNATE NAMES: not reported

SIZE OF GROUP: 25,000   MARC ID: 7029

DISTINCTIVES: religion; language; kinship

SOCIAL CHANGE: not reported

LANGUAGES: Manggarai (V)

SCRIPTURE: none

CHRISTIAN LITERACY: not reported

RELIGION: Islam; Islam-Animist

CHURCHES AND MISSIONS: not reported

OPENNESS TO RELIGIOUS CHANGE: not reported

RECEPTIVITY TO CHRISTIANITY: not reported

GROWTH RATE OF CHRISTIAN COMMUNITY: not reported

EVANGELISM PROFILE: not reported

VALIDITY: 5

The Manggarai Muslims are part of a larger group of Manggarai that live on western Flores Island, Indonesia. Though they share most of the culture of this larger group, the Manggarai Muslims are a distinct people because of their religious beliefs and their world view.

Villages are organized around a single clan. Traditionally, the Manggarai lived together in large cone-shaped huts that can hold up to 200 people, though today extended (and even nuclear) families live mainly in rectangular housing. Most agricultural activities are centered around the cultivation of maize and rice. Members of extended families will cooperate in harvesting these crops. Buffalos are kept for prestige, bride-price, and also for ceremonial purposes.

Manggarai Muslim descent takes place through the paternal line. Kinship is very important, and terms are sometimes used to denote major lineages five to six generations back. Among more orthodox families marriages may be arranged, though many young couples elope in order to avoid the bride-price. Formerly, the culture had three social classes: a dominant group, the middle class, and slaves. Slavery has been abolished by the Dutch, but individuals are still aware of the stigma of slave descent.

The Manggarai Muslims profess Islam but are influenced by the animist orientation in their cultural background. Indigenous Manggarai religious beliefs are significant in the way that this group has fit Islam into their overall world view. Virtually all Manggarai believe in ancestral and nature spirits, and delight in telling ghost stories. An important part of their indigenous religion is the belief in the supreme being who created the world and man and controls the environment. Most stories picture him as a stern ruler who punishes those who violate his laws. The Manggarai believe that after death the soul becomes a spirit and goes to where the supreme being is, and then acts as intermediary with ancestors on earth.

There is a great need for the Manggarai Muslims to learn about the One true Mediator between God and man. Thus far, evangelism efforts have had limited success.

Miao (China)

ALTERNATE NAMES: Meo

SIZE OF GROUP: 2,800,000   MARC ID: 7000

DISTINCTIVES: language; occupation; ethnicity; religion; kinship; sense of unity

SOCIAL CHANGE: moderate

LANGUAGES: Miao (100% speak; V); Mandarin (T)

SCRIPTURE: New Testament

CHRISTIAN LITERACY: not reported

RELIGION: Animism (99% adherents); Christianity (-1% practicing)

CHURCHES AND MISSIONS: not reported

OPENNESS TO RELIGIOUS CHANGE: indifferent

RECEPTIVITY TO CHRISTIANITY: not reported

GROWTH RATE OF CHRISTIAN COMMUNITY: not reported

EVANGELISM PROFILE: not reported

VALIDITY: 5

The Miao are a vigorous, strongly clan-oriented people living in the southwest provinces of China. Most live in the mountainous regions but some are rice farmers living along the river valleys. Two thirds are in the province of Guizhou (Kweichow) where they share two autonomous regions with other ethnic groups.

Agriculture is the chief means of subsistence for all the Miao who grow corn and rice in dry fields or paddy fields. In religion, most of the Miao venerate demons and various spirits including those of their ancestors. They have village shamans who exorcise malevolent spirits and perform ceremonial functions, often calling for animal sacrifice.

Prior to 1950, active Christian witness resulted in many strong churches among several of the Miao sub-groups. Leadership was trained in their own Bible School and the New Testament was available in their own language. Almost no news has been received of the state of the church from that time to the present. In recent years, with highways penetrating deep into remote hills and valleys, the Miao have had more opportunity to communicate with other groups and to enjoy better living conditions and education. Many have begun to adopt the lifestyle of the Chinese. It is presumed that there are still Christians among the Miao, though a very small minority. Any evangelism among them could likely be done using Mandarin.

Over the past century, large numbers of Miao have migrated into the mountain areas of North Vietnam, Laos, North Thailand and Burma. In these areas they are called Meo but they much prefer to be known as Hmong, their name for themselves (sometimes seen as Hmung or Hmu) and by which they are now most often referred to in the Western press. In recent years, numbers of these same people have come from Laos as refugees to the United States, France, and a few to other countries.

EXPANDED DESCRIPTIONS

Mien (China)

ALTERNATE NAMES: Yao

SIZE OF GROUP: 740,000   MARC ID: 7001

DISTINCTIVES: language; occupation; ethnicity; religion; kinship; significant problems

SOCIAL CHANGE: slow

LANGUAGES: Mien (100% speak; V); Mandarin (T)

SCRIPTURE: New Testament

CHRISTIAN LITERACY: not reported

RELIGION: Animism; Taoism; Christianity (-1% practicing)

CHURCHES AND MISSIONS: not reported

OPENNESS TO RELIGIOUS CHANGE: somewhat closed

RECEPTIVITY TO CHRISTIANITY: not reported

GROWTH RATE OF CHRISTIAN COMMUNITY: not reported

EVANGELISM PROFILE: not reported

VALIDITY: 6

    The Mien, first recorded by Chinese historians in central China about 500 B.C., moved because of political pressure to Nanking. From there they continued down the China coast to Canton, then inland to Kweicho, Kwangsi, and Yunnan, and then back towards the coast to Hainan Island, Vietnam, Laos and Thailand. Recent refugee movements have carried well over 1000 of them to the USA (mainly on the west coast), France, and Canada.

    The Mien are animists, worshipping both the spirits of their ancestors and the spirits of the woods and fields. Shamans are the religious leaders. The Mien living in remote areas have traditionally been strongly resistant to change, especially religious change. They feel their ancestor's spirits are too strong to be challenged. As political change has forced them from their opium fields and separated them from their herds of pigs (so necessary for spirit worship), they have opened up somewhat to change.

    One useful point of contact has been the many similarities between Jewish and Mien culture and religion. Mien Christian leaders are capitalizing on this in evangelism. Now turning back to God, they say, is turning back to real Mien tradition. It is reported that the P.R.C. has given each of her minority groups orthographies and allowed them to use these in their schools. Linguistic studies would be necessary to determine if existing materials could be adapted for evangelistic use among the Mien the strong ethnic unity of the clan system stimulates real excitement among the Mien of the possibility of reaching their own people with the gospel.

    Cross-cultural missionaries would have a very marginal part in such a thrust, but would be needed for encouragement and counseling. Prayer could open the doors of the P. R. C. for the necessary work to be done.

Mon (Burma)

ALTERNATE NAMES: not reported

SIZE OF GROUP: 350,000   MARC ID: 2583

DISTINCTIVES: language; ethnicity; religion; kinship

SOCIAL CHANGE: not reported

LANGUAGES: Mon (V); Burmese (T)

SCRIPTURE: Bible

CHRISTIAN LITERACY: not reported

RELIGION: Buddhist-Animist; Christianity (-1% practicing)

CHURCHES AND MISSIONS	BEGAN	MEMBERSHIP	COMMUNITY
American Bap. Msny. Union	nr	nr	nr
Church of Christ	nr	nr	nr

OPENNESS TO RELIGIOUS CHANGE: not reported

RECEPTIVITY TO CHRISTIANITY: not reported

GROWTH RATE OF CHRISTIAN COMMUNITY: not reported

EVANGELISM PROFILE: not reported

VALIDITY: 5

The Mon are an ancient people of Burma. Independent until 1757, they now make up one of the larger indigenous groups in this country. The majority are bilingual in Burmese, having been influenced by the surrounding Burmese culture, but they still remain uniquely "Mon."

As peasant agriculturalists, the Mon grow a variety of crops for consumption and for sale. Buffalo or oxen are used to plow irrigated rice fields. Several crafts are well-developed, including carpentry, metal work, pottery, weaving and basketry. The nuclear family comprises the basic unit of their society.

Each lineage has a house spirit that is thought to reside in the southeast corner of the eldest male's home. A basket is hung there with clothes and other goods for the spirit's use. This belief is blended with a Hindu-influenced concept of nature deities and a well-developed tradition of Theravada (Hinayana) Buddhism. Most Mon villages contain a pagoda and an image house with images of Buddha. Monasteries are also quite common and function as schools. Monks have limited ceremonial duties but often act as intermediaries with supernatural beings, giving offerings particularly in times of sickness. They're also consulted for advice on important matters, both public and private. Village shamans are also widespread. Their most important role is in leading spirit dances, dressing up in the clothes of the family spirit to cure an illness or fulfill a vow. In some cases an astrologer is consulted as well, since it's believed that each person has a ruling planet that occasionally may cause difficulties and need to be propitiated.

Christian missions are working in this area but have had a limited response from the Mon people.

EXPANDED DESCRIPTIONS

Mongondow (Indonesia)

ALTERNATE NAMES: not reported

SIZE OF GROUP: 400,000   MARC ID: 2997

DISTINCTIVES: language; ethnicity; kinship

SOCIAL CHANGE: not reported

LANGUAGES: Mongondow (V)

SCRIPTURE: portions

CHRISTIAN LITERACY: not reported

RELIGION: Animism; Islam-Animist; Christianity (-1% practicing)

CHURCHES AND MISSIONS: not reported

OPENNESS TO RELIGIOUS CHANGE: not reported

RECEPTIVITY TO CHRISTIANITY: not reported

GROWTH RATE OF CHRISTIAN COMMUNITY: not reported

EVANGELISM PROFILE: not reported

VALIDITY: 5

    The Mongondow live on the northern peninsula of Sulawesi in Indonesia, primarily on the upland plateaus of this region. In the past they engaged in some gold mining but today they are agriculturalists who grow irrigated rice, sago, maize, yams and cassava. Cash crops include coconuts, coffee and rice. Land is owned by the villages, with farming rights given to individuals. Cooperative work groups help each other in clearing, planting and harvesting crops, and sharecropping of fields has been reported.
    Traditionally the Mongondow were divided into three broad categories: nobles, commoners and slaves. Each of these were also broken down into many subdivisions that were created in part by interclass marriages. Feuding between villages occured often, as well as warfare with traditional enemies (particularly the Minahasans). The Mongondow were occasional headhunters in order to honor their dead chiefs.
    Individuals in Mongondow society are free to choose their spouses but their families are involved in negotiating the bride-price. Monogamy is the usual marriage pattern, with occasional polygamy when the husband can afford the expense. Couples generally live with both sets of parents and then eventually establish a house of their own.
    Mongondow indigenous religion was a type of ancestor cult. Various offerings were also made to nature spirits and illness is thought to be caused by ancestral and evil spirits. Islam was begun in 1830 and has continued to be a major part of Mongondow society, influencing everything from incest taboos to funeral rites. Christian missions have had some impact but the percentage of active believers is still extremely small.

Mori (Indonesia)

ALTERNATE NAMES: not reported

SIZE OF GROUP: 200,000   MARC ID: 3000

DISTINCTIVES: language; ethnicity; religion; kinship

SOCIAL CHANGE: not reported

LANGUAGES: Mori

SCRIPTURE: New Testament

CHRISTIAN LITERACY: not reported

RELIGION: Animism; Islam

CHURCHES AND MISSIONS: not reported

OPENNESS TO RELIGIOUS CHANGE: not reported

RECEPTIVITY TO CHRISTIANITY: not reported

GROWTH RATE OF CHRISTIAN COMMUNITY: not reported

EVANGELISM PROFILE: not reported

VALIDITY: 5

The Mori live in central Sulawesi next to the Eastern Toraja. Their physical features are similar to the Toraja, but they've been heavily influenced (espcially in their political structure) by other groups in Indonesia and possibly even the Philippines.

Mori villages are built on an east-west axis with the village temple in the center. In the past dry rice was cultivated but this has been largely replaced by wet-rice farming. Other crops are maize, taro and tobacco, while coffee is grown for sale. Some Mori are blacksmiths and are particularly skilled in making swords.

The members of each Mori village are very aware of their relationships to each other and to their village. They also have a loyalty to their "tribe", which is made up of several villages that have a common "mother village." These tribal members protect each others' villages and go to each others' death feasts. Aristocratic rulers head up the political hierarchy, with elders leading local kin groups. The rulers were once thought to be divine but this belief has faded. Traditionally the Mori went on headhunting raids against hereditary enemies when their kin group chief died. Heads were also required for general village welfare and for the building of a new temple. The Dutch outlawed this practice in 1905.

Islam is the primary religion today among the Mori, though belief in ancestral and nature spirits is still very strong. Some of the more important deities are associated with smallpox, rice, air and fate. Priestesses with spirit familiars are the main practitioners of traditional ceremonies. The most significant of these ceremonies is the "woke" - the rewrapping and burial of bones every three to five years in honor of the ancestors. Bones are cleaned and put in caves at the "tewusa" or death feast, when an important person dies.

EXPANDED DESCRIPTIONS

Pai (China)

ALTERNATE NAMES: Minchia

SIZE OF GROUP: 1,000,000   MARC ID: 7008

DISTINCTIVES: language; kinship; residence

SOCIAL CHANGE: slow

LANGUAGES: Yi (V); Mandarin (T)

SCRIPTURE: none

CHRISTIAN LITERACY: not reported

RELIGION: Buddhist-Animist; Animism; Christianity (-1%
    practicing)

CHURCHES AND MISSIONS: not reported

OPENNESS TO RELIGIOUS CHANGE: not reported

RECEPTIVITY TO CHRISTIANITY: not reported

GROWTH RATE OF CHRISTIAN COMMUNITY: not reported

EVANGELISM PROFILE: not reported

VALIDITY: 5

The Pai people (also known as the Minchia) are one of the
many minority groups in Yunnan in the south of the Peoples
Republic of China. They are related to the Yi people and share
the same language.

In social organization and kinship the Pai are largely
indigenous. The village is the important social unit above the
extended family. Regardless of their surname, individuals in a
village honor a common ancestor who is believed to have founded
the village. Most are agriculturalists who cultivate wet-rice
fields. Though most land is by tradition privately owned, the
government is now establishing communes in this area.

The Pai have limited contact with other outside groups
because their population centers are surrounded by hills. They
don't consider themselves to be oppressed and haven't felt a
strong need to distinguish themselves from the Chinese. There
has been little culture change, and poverty is widespread since
the local opium trade was banned in the 1930s.

Local deities and ancestors are worshipped by these people
along with Buddhist and Taoist gods. During sickness the
Buddhist priests are sometimes called, but generally spiritual
matters are handled by the head of the family. Ceremonies
honoring the family ancestors were once common, as were
hereditary exorcists, but the extent of these practices today are
unknown. The Pai generally believe in the Buddhist view of the
afterlife.

It is reported that there were some Christians among the
Pai, but now that the area is under communist rule it is unknown
what the current religious situation is. Anthropologists have
stated that the primary influence of former western missionaries
was to set the standard of living for the small rich class. This
class has now, of course, disappeared, and there is a need for a
Christian witness that speaks to the hearts of all the Pai
people.

Pala'wan (Philippines)

ALTERNATE NAMES: not reported

SIZE OF GROUP: 50,000   MARC ID: 4162

DISTINCTIVES: language; ethnicity; kinship; sense of unity

SOCIAL CHANGE: slow

LANGUAGES: Pala'wan (V)

SCRIPTURE: New Testament

CHRISTIAN LITERACY: not reported

RELIGION: Animism; Islam; Christianity (-1% practicing)

CHURCHES AND MISSIONS	BEGAN	MEMBERSHIP	COMMUNITY
Pala'wan Church	nr	nr	nr

OPENNESS TO RELIGIOUS CHANGE: indifferent

RECEPTIVITY TO CHRISTIANITY: indifferent

GROWTH RATE OF CHRISTIAN COMMUNITY: not reported

EVANGELISM PROFILE: not reported

VALIDITY: 5

The Pala'wan inhabit the mountains of the southern portion of the Island of Pala'wan, Philippines. They are one of the two largest ethnic groups on the island, the other being the Tagbanua. While those along the coast have embraced Islam and a few further inland have heard the gospel through New Tribes Missions workers, there are still thousands to be reached in the interiors.

Since the Pala'wan have had minimal exposure to lowland ways, they are usually easy prey for manipulation. Slowly they are losing their lands to lowlanders and are being driven further into the interior. Very soon they will have nowhere to go because they are being hemmed in by speculators on all sides.

To the Pala'wan, Ampo (literally, owner) made everything, and he is the keeper of his creation. Aside from this term, the Pala'wan god has no name simply because he never told his name even to their forbears. Ampo is worshipped through thanksgiving offerings during harvest. His will for the people is made known through the "balian" (religious practitioner) who in a trance can get in touch with Ampo. The sick are healed through the ministration of the balian and guidance is given for a more bountiful harvest.

Evangelism among the Pala'wan could be facilitated through the balian to whom the gospel must be explained. The moment the balian accepts the faith, he will be instrumental in making it easier for the others to follow suit. This was observed in one group in Ransang, a barrio in Quezon, Pala'wan. The church worker was a former balian who now pastors a chapel among his people.

Cross-cultural missionaries can train Pala'wan believers to become church leaders among their own people. Upon gaining fluency in the language, they could also translate the Scriptures into Pala'wan. A Pala'wan version of the New Testament exists, but there is a need to check the translation.

EXPANDED DESCRIPTIONS

Paniyan of Kerela (India)

ALTERNATE NAMES: not reported

SIZE OF GROUP: 6,330   MARC ID: 2772

DISTINCTIVES: language; kinship; ethnicity; religion; sense
of unity

SOCIAL CHANGE: not reported

LANGUAGES: Paniyan

SCRIPTURE: none

CHRISTIAN LITERACY: not reported

RELIGION: Christianity (-1% practicing); Hindu-Animist;
Animism

CHURCHES AND MISSIONS	BEGAN	MEMBERSHIP	COMMUNITY
Tribal Mission	1978	nr	nr

OPENNESS TO RELIGIOUS CHANGE: not reported

RECEPTIVITY TO CHRISTIANITY: receptive

GROWTH RATE OF CHRISTIAN COMMUNITY: not reported

EVANGELISM PROFILE: not reported

VALIDITY: 5

At present, a life of exploitation is all the Paniyan of
Kerela expect. As agricultural laborers who work for landlords
in the Calicut, Malappuram, and Cannannoore districts, their name
means "those who always work" and this is a good summary of their
lifestyle. The Paniyans were sold as slaves long ago; today
they live in temporary huts on plantations and are essentially
bond servants to the landlords.
Traditionally the Paniyan people worshipped a tribal
goddess. To this day they believe that any contract made in the
presence of the goddess cannot be broken. Since many of their
labor contracts are made in this fashion, they continue to work
even in bad situations. The landlords take advantage of this
situation and exploit their fear of the goddess.
The Paniyans rarely visit Hindu temples, but worship a
variety of ghosts, demons, and animals. They believe that the
dead turn into ghosts and then inhabit trees. When someone dies,
the family members must mourn and not work for sixteen days.
However, if the death occurs during a busy time, they'll store
the deceased's spirit in an enclosed vessel and continue the
rituals at a later, more convenient date.
Since 1978, missionaries from the Tribal Mission have been
working among the Paniyans. Because of their belief in spirits
the Paniyan are especially interested in the resurrection of
Jesus, but most are held back from making a commitment due to the
fear of their goddess. There are signs of a responsiveness to
the gospel in the group, however. Some young people are
interested in attending Bible study groups and enjoy learning
choruses. Income generating projects could begin to free them
from their economic bondage and build their dignity - this might
be a way of increasing their openness to a new life with the
Living God.

Parsees (India)

ALTERNATE NAMES: Parsis

SIZE OF GROUP: 120,000   MARC ID: 2121

DISTINCTIVES: language; ethnicity; religion; sense of unity;
    residence

SOCIAL CHANGE: moderate

LANGUAGES: Gujarati (100% speak/100% read; V, T, S); English
    (80% speak/80% read; T, S, G, W)

SCRIPTURE: Bible

CHRISTIAN LITERACY: 100%

RELIGION: Zoroastrianism (39% adherents); Secularism (60%
    adherents); Christianity (-1% practicing)

CHURCHES AND MISSIONS: not reported

OPENNESS TO RELIGIOUS CHANGE: very closed

RECEPTIVITY TO CHRISTIANITY: indifferent

GROWTH RATE OF CHRISTIAN COMMUNITY: not reported

EVANGELISM PROFILE:
    89% No awareness of Christianity
    8% Aware that Christianity exists
    1% Some knowledge of the gospel
    1% Understand the message of the gospel
    0% Personally challenged to receive Christ
    0% Decision to accept Christ
    1% Incorporated into a fellowship of Christians
    0% Active propagators of the gospel

VALIDITY: 5

The Parsees are the Persians who left their nation because
of persecution many centuries ago. They fled to India and
settled on the west coast. Today, most of the Parsees in India
are found in Gujarat and Bombay.

Other groups in the country admire this people because they
have contributed much to the progress of India. They are also
not active proselytizers. In fact, their main interest centers
on their own community, and they have set up charitable trusts
mainly to cater to Parsee needs. Through their businesses,
however, they have helped the nation. India as a whole does not
feel threatened by them, but rather regards them as a valuable
community.

Very few attempts have been made to reach the Parsees with
the gospel. Although some have become Christians, they are a
very small minority.

An opportunity for evangelization now exists because many of
the Parsees have stopped practising their religion. About 60%
are now secular and a major change is occurring. Parsees are
particularly amenable to western culture, and thus it might be
possible that English-speaking men and women could have a vital
role to play as cross-cultural missionaries. Because so many
Parsees are involved in business and management professions, it
is also probable that Christian businessmen/managers and
professionals would have the best access to the Parsee community.

EXPANDED DESCRIPTIONS

Penan, Western (Malaysia)

ALTERNATE NAMES: not reported

SIZE OF GROUP: 2,600   MARC ID: 7027

DISTINCTIVES: language; occupation; ethnicity; religion; kinship; discrimination

SOCIAL CHANGE: slow

LANGUAGES: Penan (V)

SCRIPTURE: portions

CHRISTIAN LITERACY: not reported

RELIGION: Animism; Islam-Animist; Christianity

CHURCHES AND MISSIONS	BEGAN	MEMBERSHIP	COMMUNITY
Roman Catholic Church	nr	nr	nr
Penan Church	nr	nr	nr

OPENNESS TO RELIGIOUS CHANGE: not reported

RECEPTIVITY TO CHRISTIANITY: not reported

GROWTH RATE OF CHRISTIAN COMMUNITY: not reported

EVANGELISM PROFILE: not reported

VALIDITY: 6

The Western Penan are an indigenous forest-dwelling group. Culturally and linguistically they are distinct from the Eastern Penan, who live on the other side of the Baram River in Sarawak. Though formerly a nomadic people, the Western Penan now live mainly in settled villages and travel by dugout canoe. The dialects of the two groups are unintelligible, with the Western Penan dialect being very similar to Sebup. The Western Penan are reported to be timid, especially in the presence of other groups, though they need to trade with them in order to obtain various necessities. Formerly they had blood pacts with patrons of these other groups in order to secure protection, but now the government has abolished this practice.

The Western Penan still maintain their traditional animistic beliefs which are rather vague and undeveloped. They believe in a supreme creator-divinity named Peselong, who cares little about human affairs. They also believe in a number of spirits who are thought to cause daily events, both good and bad. Shamans summon spirits in order to cure various diseases. Their initial contacts with Christianity were begun by Kelabit Christians and later by Christians from other groups. During the 1950s several missionaries who were engaged in other tribal work had intermittent contact with the Western Penan. Currently Christians from the Eastern Penan group are attempting to evangelize the Western Penan. Individuals and couples have spent a number of months among the group and are having an effective ministry. So far the Book of Acts has been translated and printed by the Bible Society. Several portions of the Bible are now available while others are still being worked on.

Purig-Pa of Kashmir (India)

ALTERNATE NAMES: not reported

SIZE OF GROUP: not reported   MARC ID: 7010

DISTINCTIVES: language; ethnicity; religion; kinship; sense
     of unity; social class

SOCIAL CHANGE: very slow

LANGUAGES: Purig-Skad (100% speak/20% read; V); Tibetan Purig
     Dialects (100% speak/20% read; T); Urdu (50% speak/25%
     read; T)

SCRIPTURE: none

CHRISTIAN LITERACY: not reported

RELIGION: Islam (99% adherents); Christianity (-1% practicing)

CHURCHES AND MISSIONS: not reported

OPENNESS TO RELIGIOUS CHANGE: somewhat closed

RECEPTIVITY TO CHRISTIANITY: reluctant

GROWTH RATE OF CHRISTIAN COMMUNITY: not reported

EVANGELISM PROFILE: not reported

VALIDITY: 5

　　　The name Purig-Pa is given by the people of Ladakh and
Baltistan to the inhabitants of the Kargil area in Jammu and
Kashmir. Purig-Pa means "Of Tibetan Origin." Their language,
Purig-Skad, is a hybrid of Ladakh Tibetan and the Balti language.
But since the conversion of the people to Islam, their language
has been influenced by the Balti. All the religious sermons,
hymns (Qasidas), and cultic mourning (Natam) are sung in Balti or
Persian.
　　　Before their conversion to Islam, Buddhism was the main
religion of the Purig-Pa people. Food and fodder were plentiful
because a check on population was kept through such practices as
polyandry, primogeniture and sending boys and girls to the
monastery. With the introduction of Islam, the people started
practising polygamy, Muta (temporary concubinage) and division of
the land among the children. As a result there has been a big
increase in the population. With the exception of half a dozen
villages, all the population is Muslim of the Shia sect, very
orthodox and fanatical in their religious attitude. This has
been enhanced due to a sizeable group of Sheikhs who have
returned from Iraq and Iran after their religious education.
　　　Pioneer work in this area was done by the Central Asian
Mission based in England. Besides running an orphanage (at
present there are 3 converts through that work, two of them in
Ladakh), a Balti grammar and a few simple books were published.
Gospel messages and songs have been made by Gospel Recordings.
With the closure of the mission station in the mid-1950s, people
joined other mission agencies working in Kashmir. Christian work
among this people is not easy. They are 'somewhat' to 'strongly
opposed' to Christianity and great care is needed in the
presentation of the gospel.

EXPANDED DESCRIPTIONS

Puyuma (Taiwan)

ALTERNATE NAMES: Pyuma

SIZE OF GROUP: 7,300   MARC ID: 7033

DISTINCTIVES: language; ethnicity; kinship

SOCIAL CHANGE: moderate

LANGUAGES: Puyuma (V)

SCRIPTURE: none

CHRISTIAN LITERACY: not reported

RELIGION: Christo-Paganism; Folk Religion; Secularism; Roman
  Catholic; Protestant

CHURCHES AND MISSIONS	BEGAN	MEMBERSHIP	COMMUNITY
Evangelical Alliance Mission	nr	nr	nr
Roman Catholic Church	nr	nr	nr

OPENNESS TO RELIGIOUS CHANGE: very open

RECEPTIVITY TO CHRISTIANITY: receptive

GROWTH RATE OF CHRISTIAN COMMUNITY: not reported

EVANGELISM PROFILE: not reported

VALIDITY: 5

The Puyuma of east Taiwan have been heavily influenced by
various external forces but have managed to retain their culture
and sense of being a people group. How long they will remain
truly Puyuma is impossible to say, especially in light of the way
in which their young people have adopted the language and some of
the culture of the donimant Chinese society around them. They
are an adaptable group, however, and their future cannot be
predicted with any certainty.

Historically, the Puyuma most likely migrated from the coast
inland. They were skilled in warfare and at one time dominated a
large part of southeastern Taiwan. An age-grade system which
rigorously trained young men both militarily and spiritually was
discontinued in the late 1950s. Today they are an agricultural
people, growing rice and various vegetables in addition to some
cash crops such as sugarcane, pineapples, and peanuts.

Bride-price generally can't be avoided even though the cost
in most cases is very high. The majority of couples live at
first with the bride's family and then establish their own home.
Divorce and remarriage are reported to be very common. Within
villages political control is exercised by the heads of chiefly
families, with one headman who is choosen by the sons of the
former headman.

The goal of traditional Puyuma religions ritual was to
attain the "good and happy life", both in this world and the
next. This life consisted of four elements - physical and
spiritual vigor, wealth, rank, and prestige - which only a good
man could achieve. This continues to be a goal, but most people
have abandoned the old religion in favor of Chinese folk
religions, secularism, or a syncretistic blend of tribal beliefs
and some kind of Christianity. A great need exists for a
uncompromised proclamation of the gospel and an explanation of
how Christ fulfills humanity's deepest longings.

Saisiat (Taiwan)

ALTERNATE NAMES: Saiset

SIZE OF GROUP: 2,900   MARC ID: 7034

DISTINCTIVES: language; ethnicity; religion; kinship

SOCIAL CHANGE: not reported

LANGUAGES: Saisiat (V)

SCRIPTURE: none

CHRISTIAN LITERACY: not reported

RELIGION: Animism; Christianity

CHURCHES AND MISSIONS	BEGAN	MEMBERSHIP	COMMUNITY
Saisiat Churches	nr	nr	nr

OPENNESS TO RELIGIOUS CHANGE: not reported

RECEPTIVITY TO CHRISTIANITY: not reported

GROWTH RATE OF CHRISTIAN COMMUNITY: not reported

EVANGELISM PROFILE: not reported

VALIDITY: 5

    The Saisiat are a small people group who reside in the foothills of northwestern Taiwan. Living in a few large villages, they are dependent on trade and other economic links with the coastal plains peasant economy.

    Formerly the Saisiat lived in fairly unstructured hamlets. The present system of organized village settlements and village headmen seems to be a response to pressure from the government and an exposure to other groups. Land is now owned privately, whereby once it was regulated by localized clan segments. Marriage customs have continued virtually unaltered, with a young man often having to work for a girl's parents before their wedding.

    Millet and glutinous rice are sacred foods, and domesticated bees are kept for honey. Bees are prominant symbolically in Saisiat folklore and indigenous religious ritual, which seems to be unique to this group. Animistic beliefs are the norm, with a well-developed pantheon of deities and spirits. The most significant ceremony is the "pasta'ai", a village renewal held every two years to honor the ancestor spirits. The pasta'ai also is held to appease the "ta'ai", a mythical tribe of dwarfs who were killed by the Saisiat ancestors.

    There are five churches reported among the Saisiat, but the status of Christianity is unclear. Traditional beliefs, including shamanistic healing, have no doubt been influenced by contact with other groups and the larger Chinese population. The desire or capacity of the Saisiat Christians to reach their own people for Christ is also unclear at this point.

EXPANDED DESCRIPTIONS

Senoi (Malaysia)

ALTERNATE NAMES: Orang Asli

SIZE OF GROUP: 337,400   MARC ID: 1009

DISTINCTIVES: language; ethnicity; religion; economic status; discrimination

SOCIAL CHANGE: very slow

LANGUAGES: Native Senoi (100% speak; V, P); Malay (80% speak/10% read; T, G, W)

SCRIPTURE: portions

CHRISTIAN LITERACY: 10%

RELIGION: Protestant (2% adherents/2% practicing); Animism (95% adherents/95% practicing); Islam (3% adherents/3% practicing)

CHURCHES AND MISSIONS	BEGAN	MEMBERSHIP	COMMUNITY
Lutheran Church	1970	2,000	2,000
Methodist Church	1965	4,000	4,000

OPENNESS TO RELIGIOUS CHANGE: very open

RECEPTIVITY TO CHRISTIANITY: receptive

GROWTH RATE OF CHRISTIAN COMMUNITY: not reported

EVANGELISM PROFILE:
        95% No awareness of Christianity
        3% Aware that Christianity exists
        0% Some knowledge of the gospel
        0% Understand the message of the gospel
        0% Personally challenged to receive Christ
        0% Decision to accept Christ
        2% Incorporated into a fellowship of Christians
        0% Active propagators of the gospel

VALIDITY: 5

Two features characterize Senoi culture: a great fear of violence and a strong belief in each individual's personal freedom. These characteristics permeate every part of the society and influence most acts. The Senoi view man as free but also alone in the world and thus continually exposed to danger.
Their fear of violence has led the Senoi to be pacifists. As such, they've been exploited by other groups and driven into inhospitable highland areas. The Senoi especially resent the Malays because of their treatment during the communist rebellion in the late 1940s and 1950s. Relocated by the government, the Senoi suffered great cultural upset as well as a loss of property and a very high death rate. The Malaysian Department of Aborigines now oversees the welfare of the Senoi along with other minority groups.
Senoi leaders are selected because of their ability to settle matters peacefully, not because of their power or wealth. Leaders tend to be good speakers who never use violence to persuade their followers.
Senoi religion has been described as "formless animism" due to their belief in a vague spirit world made up of ghosts and "disease spirits." Some aspects of Islamic religion have been incorporated into this system, but in general the Senoi adhere to their traditional beliefs.

Serawai (Indonesia)

ALTERNATE NAMES: not reported

SIZE OF GROUP: 60,000   MARC ID: 1091

DISTINCTIVES: language; occupation; ethnicity

SOCIAL CHANGE: not reported

LANGUAGES: Serawai (Pasemah) (100% speak/30% read; V);
    Indonesian (40% speak; T)

SCRIPTURE: none

CHRISTIAN LITERACY: not reported

RELIGION: Islam-Animist (95% adherents/50% practicing);
    Protestant (5% adherents/1% practicing)

CHURCHES AND MISSIONS	BEGAN	MEMBERSHIP	COMMUNITY
Gekisus	1974	2,500	nr
GKII	1968	1,000	nr

OPENNESS TO RELIGIOUS CHANGE: very open

RECEPTIVITY TO CHRISTIANITY: receptive

GROWTH RATE OF CHRISTIAN COMMUNITY: not reported

EVANGELISM PROFILE: not reported

VALIDITY: 5

The Serawi people live in the coastal area of southwest Sumatra. Their area borders the Indian Ocean and stretches about 250 kilometers from the provincial town of Benqkulu to the province of Lampung. Though some live in the mountains, the majority are farmers, growing rice (their primary crop), coffee, cloves, and various fruits.

Though they call themselves Muslim, the Serawi practice an animistic religion inherited from their ancestors. They are afraid, however, to violate Islamic dietary restrictions. Conversions are extremely difficult because the group strongly opposes anyone changing his or her religion.

Despite this group opposition, a small movement to Christianity began in 1964 in the Manna area. Some Serawi who became dissatisfied with the communist movement formed the nucleus of a church. The church now has three clinics which treat hundreds of patients everyday. The outreach of these clinics is effective too because many people are bound by witchcraft and need to have the power of Jesus Christ demonstrated in their lives. A number have begun to trust in the Lord but haven't joined any Christian fellowship because of fear.

About 30,000 pieces of Christian literature are distributed each year but the impact is unknown. A cassette ministry has been started as well. It is hoped that these efforts, combined with personal witnessing and the medical work of the clinics, will lead many more to Christ. There is an openness to the gospel among the Serawi people, but few are prepared to be baptised because of group pressure. Despite this, some who haven't joined a fellowship are witnessing and winning others to the Lord.

Workers are needed to follow-up on the many contacts in scattered villages. There are new opportunities in the jungles where people are setting up new farms. They're happy to be visited and are open to change.

EXPANDED DESCRIPTIONS

So (Thailand)

ALTERNATE NAMES: not reported

SIZE OF GROUP: 8,000   MARC ID: 2091

DISTINCTIVES: language; ethnicity

SOCIAL CHANGE: slow

LANGUAGES: So (V, G); Thai (T)

SCRIPTURE: none

CHRISTIAN LITERACY: not reported

RELIGION: Buddhist-Animist; Animism; Christianity (-1%
    practicing)

CHURCHES AND MISSIONS	BEGAN	MEMBERSHIP	COMMUNITY
New Tribes Mission	nr	nr	nr

OPENNESS TO RELIGIOUS CHANGE: indifferent

RECEPTIVITY TO CHRISTIANITY: indifferent

GROWTH RATE OF CHRISTIAN COMMUNITY: not reported

EVANGELISM PROFILE: not reported

VALIDITY: 5

Settled along both sides of the Mekong River in Thailand and
Laos, the So are a small group that have adapted cultural traits
freely from those around them. They have frequent contact with
the Thai for bartering goods such as meat and vegetables for
clothing and salt. They intermarry with the Sek and use the same
agricultural methods as the Lao. Their flexibility has made them
"successful" from an adaptive point of view but unfortunately
hasn't yet given them an openness to the Christian faith.

The So cultivate a wide variety of crops for both
consumption and trade. Fishing, and to a lesser degree hunting,
are important activities. Men clear fields for planting, fish,
hunt, and build the houses; women weed the fields, help with the
harvest, and carry out most of the trading. The So also make
their own baskets, weave cloth, and do occasional blacksmithing.

The village is the significant political unit of So society.
Each is independent of the others, with a village headman who
decides important issues. The nuclear family, headed by the
father, is an important part of the culture as well.

Though some of the So are Theravada Buddhists, the majority
adhere to their traditional animistic beliefs. Ancestor worship
is common and most families have a small ancestral spirit house
near their home. These ancestral spirits are thought to cause
illness and have to be appeased through offerings. It's believed
that each village has a guardian spirit in addition to various
spirits who are linked to the forces of nature.

Solorese Muslims (Indonesia)

ALTERNATE NAMES: not reported

SIZE OF GROUP: 131,000   MARC ID: 3049

DISTINCTIVES: religion; language; kinship

SOCIAL CHANGE: not reported

LANGUAGES: Solor (V)

SCRIPTURE: none

CHRISTIAN LITERACY: not reported

RELIGION: Islam; Islam-Animist

CHURCHES AND MISSIONS: not reported

OPENNESS TO RELIGIOUS CHANGE: not reported

RECEPTIVITY TO CHRISTIANITY: reluctant

GROWTH RATE OF CHRISTIAN COMMUNITY: not reported

EVANGELISM PROFILE: not reported

VALIDITY: 5

    Islam reached the island of Solor in Indonesia several hundred years ago. The exact date is unknown, but records from the sixteenth century already reported the presence of Muslims along the coast. Portuguese missionaries arrived around this time but this long contact with Christianity has failed to influence the Solorese Muslims. Most associate Islam with their culture, and to embrace a different faith appears to be a rejection of their identity.

    The Solonese Muslims follow a similar life style to their neighbors, growing maize, rice, yams, beans and various fruits. Usually a field is worked for two years and then is let to lie fallow for six or seven years. Land is generally owned by large clans rather than individuals, while household goods are owned by families. Permission to farm any new land must come from the village head, who is the head of the largest clan in a village. These landowning clans are usually rich and have great influence, their members numbering sometimes in the hundreds in a single village.

    Though the Solorese Muslims practice Islam, the faith of many is mixed with indigenous elements. These include belief in a High God, lesser spirits, nature spirits and a lower world. Bad events are thought to be caused by evil spirits who may be dealt with by possessed individuals. Various religious ceremonies are held in clan ritual houses. It is believed that after death people are reborn on lower levels of the world and will complete a cycle of these levels after several lives.

    It's unclear what the attitude of the Solorese Muslims might be to a Christianity that doesn't separate them from most of their culture. Certainly parts of their animistic beliefs are unacceptable, but there is much of their culture that could be retained. The gospel should be proclaimed in a way that helps them to see this.

EXPANDED DESCRIPTIONS

T'boli (Philippines)

ALTERNATE NAMES: Tagabili

SIZE OF GROUP: 150,000   MARC ID: 624

DISTINCTIVES: language; ethnicity

SOCIAL CHANGE: not reported

LANGUAGES: Tboli (100% speak/12% read; V); Ilongo (5% speak);
Bilaan (20% speak)

SCRIPTURE: not reported

CHRISTIAN LITERACY: 10%

RELIGION: Animism (80% adherents); Christianity (3%
adherents/3% practicing); Unknown (17% adherents)

CHURCHES AND MISSIONS	BEGAN	MEMBERSHIP	COMMUNITY
Independent Church	nr	nr	nr
Christian & Msny. Alliance	1940	nr	nr
Roman Catholic Church	1960	nr	nr
Summer Institute Linguistics	1953	nr	nr

OPENNESS TO RELIGIOUS CHANGE: not reported

RECEPTIVITY TO CHRISTIANITY: receptive

GROWTH RATE OF CHRISTIAN COMMUNITY: not reported

EVANGELISM PROFILE: not reported

VALIDITY: 5

The T'boli (or Tagabili as the lowlanders call them) live in
the mountains of South Cotabato on the Island of Mindanao. In
addition to their language, the T'boli are distinct from other
Philippine ethnic groups because of their clothing and adornment.
The T'boli share their pantheon of gods with other tribal
neighbors. They believe that their highest deities, Kadaw la
Sambad and Bulon la Mogow, gave birth to the lesser gods who
either bestow benefits to people or afflict them with ailments.
The earth came from the body of Sifindit, a lesser deity, and
thus the traditionally-oriented T'boli will not use iron to till
the land because it will desecrate the soil. The T'boli believe
that their gods have given them their rules of conduct and
provide guidance in their day-to-day activities.
The Santa Cruz mission in Lake Sebu, manned by Roman
Catholic missionaries, has pioneered trying to relate the
Christian message to the T'boli culture. The Summer Institute of
Linguistics has also started a mission in the T'boli area.
However there is still much to be done. Even those who have
become Christians among the T'boli are treated as low class
people by the church people in South Cotabato.
While ethnocentrism cannot be entirely erased from Christian
workers, those assigned among the T'boli should be willing to
accept this group as God's people when they accept the faith.
The missionary must be willing to live among the T'boli, be
identified with them, and then, making use of the T'boli cultural
categories, strive to relate the gospel to them. This will
require a deep understanding of the T'boli way of life.

T'in (Thailand)

ALTERNATE NAMES: Lua'; P'ai; Mal

SIZE OF GROUP: 25,000   MARC ID: 81

DISTINCTIVES: language; ethnicity

SOCIAL CHANGE: not reported

LANGUAGES: T'in (100% speak; V); Northern Thai (99% speak/1% read; T)

SCRIPTURE: not reported

CHRISTIAN LITERACY: not reported

RELIGION: Animism; Buddhist-Animist; Christianity (-1% practicing)

CHURCHES AND MISSIONS	BEGAN	MEMBERSHIP	COMMUNITY
Ban Nam Sot	1972	nr	2
Churches of Christ	nr	nr	nr
Presbyterian Mission Churches	nr	nr	nr

OPENNESS TO RELIGIOUS CHANGE: somewhat open

RECEPTIVITY TO CHRISTIANITY: reluctant

GROWTH RATE OF CHRISTIAN COMMUNITY: not reported

EVANGELISM PROFILE: not reported

VALIDITY: 5

A marginal lifestyle has characterized the T'in people of northern Thailand since they migrated from Laos in the early part of this century. Their crops are usually poor and they often have to work for Meo and Yao landowners in order to subsist. Some T'in also produce pickled tea for sale or work as domestics for Thai government officials or Chinese businessmen. Their lives are difficult and it's reported that they have a generally dejected appearance.

The T'in live in villages of approximately 600 to 1000 people in mountainous regions around 3000 ft. Their houses are permanent structures built on piles. They spend most of their time doing swidden agriculture: burning underbrush and then planting seeds by hand. Four or five households work together clearing the fields and harvesting the crops. Usually after one year the soil is depleted and it's left fallow for ten years, a practice that forces smaller villages to keep moving in search of new land.

Since most T'in want to marry someone from within their villages, first-cousin marriages are common. Couples usually live with the bride's family until several children are born, then they move to their own home. Property is inherited by the youngest daughter.

The T'in are virtually all animists. Their sorcerers are very well known among neighboring groups - which may explain in part why they have so little contact with the T'in. Some have adopted aspects of Buddhism and there are five villages that are reported to have Buddhist temples. Though there is some Christian work among the T'in, missions have not yet had much of a response.

EXPANDED DESCRIPTIONS

Tagal (Malaysia)

ALTERNATE NAMES: Murut

SIZE OF GROUP: 19,000   MARC ID: 7028

DISTINCTIVES: language; ethnicity; religion; kinship

SOCIAL CHANGE: moderate

LANGUAGES: Tagal (V)

SCRIPTURE: portions

CHRISTIAN LITERACY: not reported

RELIGION: Animism; Christianity

CHURCHES AND MISSIONS	BEGAN	MEMBERSHIP	COMMUNITY
Tagal Church	nr	nr	nr

OPENNESS TO RELIGIOUS CHANGE: not reported

RECEPTIVITY TO CHRISTIANITY: not reported

GROWTH RATE OF CHRISTIAN COMMUNITY: not reported

EVANGELISM PROFILE: not reported

VALIDITY: 6

  The mountain areas of Sabah contain a number of tribal
groups. In the southwestern region live the Tagal. Called the
"Murut" by the Sabah government, the Tagal are unrelated to the
Sarawak Lun Bawang who were formerly also called the "Murut."
Identifying groups in this area is difficult because of the
problem of overlapping names and vast numbers of sub-groups.
  The Tagal live in long houses that have a square common area
in the center. A section of the plank flooring in this area is
sunk about one foot lower than the regular floor level and is
supported on saplings attached to the underside of the house.
This flooring then springs up and down and is used for religious
singing and dancing as well as for jumping contests. Usually
festivals accompany these events, and "Tapai" (a beer made from
rice or cassava) is drunk. Tapai drinking is an important part
of all Tagal ceremonies including funerals, weddings, planting,
harvesting, house building, arrival of guests, etc. The Tagal
are primarily animist in their beliefs, and their religious
system centers around a belief in three kinds of supernatural
beings: spirits who were originally human beings, human-like
spirits living in the sky, and non-human spirits who are
dangerous. Some women are spirit mediums and this vocation is
often passed on to their daughters. The Tagal believe that after
death people's souls have to be ferried over a large river while
a second soul remains on earth.
  The first strong Christian contacts with the Tagal people
took place in the 1950s. At that time two Tagals entered Bible
school. One third of the New Testament in Tagal is now being
circulated in a bound volume. The rest of it is still in draft
form. Approximately 35 churches have been formed, primarily
through the witness of lay members. Nominalism and the false
teaching of certain sects are threatening the Tagal church.
There is a great felt need for a complete translation of the
Bible.

Thai University Students (Thailand)

ALTERNATE NAMES: not reported

SIZE OF GROUP: not reported   MARC ID: 7015

DISTINCTIVES: education; social class; age

SOCIAL CHANGE: moderate

LANGUAGES: Thai (V)

SCRIPTURE: Bible

CHRISTIAN LITERACY: 100%

RELIGION: Buddhism; Secularism; Christianity

CHURCHES AND MISSIONS: not reported

OPENNESS TO RELIGIOUS CHANGE: somewhat open

RECEPTIVITY TO CHRISTIANITY: indifferent

GROWTH RATE OF CHRISTIAN COMMUNITY: slow growth

EVANGELISM PROFILE: not reported

VALIDITY: 5

University students in Thailand are the "chosen ones" of their generation. Graduates are influential in all aspects of Thai society. Because of this, ambitious parents make every effort to get their children into the universities especially into the medical, engineering, and accounting programs. The pictures of the graduation ceremonies, which show their sons and daughters receiving diplomas from the King, are treasured family possessions.

The majority of the Thai university students come from a Buddhist background. Though they go through the motions of practicing this faith, most of them feel that the superstitious aspects are backward and out of date. Many are open to what they consider to be a more "modern" way of thinking, which is essentially materialistic and secular. Though most of them are highly intelligent they don't have any real concept of God. Buddhists and Muslims are active on the university campuses and all kinds of religions are respected and tolerated.

Around 1970 some missionaries began Christian work on the university campuses. This work became more firmly established when students themselves got a vision and a burden for evangelism of their fellow students. Cell-group activities and training camps provided the background many students needed to be able to witness. This work seems to have a good future potential if student leaders are raised up.

Though their numbers are still quite small a handful of graduates are going into full-time Christian ministries. These graduates are able to witness quite effectively to university students as well as other influential members of Thai society. Their educational background is stimulating a higher level of theological education in general for pastors, church leaders, and other Christian leaders. Missionaries are needed to participate in this training and to encourage a wider vision for the Thai workers. There is a need for national staff workers, students, and missionaries to work together in the evangelization and nuture of university students. It is hoped that the students who commit their lives to Christ will have a major impact in the overall evangelization of Thailand.

EXPANDED DESCRIPTIONS

Tibetans in Bhutan (Bhutan)

ALTERNATE NAMES: not reported

SIZE OF GROUP: 5,000   MARC ID: 7017

DISTINCTIVES: language; political loyalty; ethnicity;
    religion; kinship; sense of unity; discrimination

SOCIAL CHANGE: not reported

LANGUAGES: Tibetan (V)

SCRIPTURE: Bible

CHRISTIAN LITERACY: not reported

RELIGION: Buddhism; Secularism; Christianity (-1% practicing)

CHURCHES AND MISSIONS	BEGAN	MEMBERSHIP	COMMUNITY
Moravian Institute	nr	nr	nr
Evangelical Alliance Mission	nr	nr	nr
Tibetan Christian Fellowship	nr	nr	nr

OPENNESS TO RELIGIOUS CHANGE: somewhat closed

RECEPTIVITY TO CHRISTIANITY: reluctant

GROWTH RATE OF CHRISTIAN COMMUNITY: not reported

EVANGELISM PROFILE: not reported

VALIDITY: 5

    Tibetans fall into two groups: those still living in their homeland of Tibet (approximately 3 million), and those in exile (approximately 120,0000). The latter are found chiefly in India and Nepal, with small colonies in Switzerland, Norway, Taiwan and the United States. There are approximately 5,000 in Bhutan.
    Six or seven small congregations of Christians have been formed among Tibetans outside of Tibet, stretching from Kashmir in the west to Bhutan in the east. The strongest work is located in Rajpur, Uttar Pradesh, where a Moravian Institute trains children and young people, and where the Evangelical Alliance Mission also works. Several young Tibetan evangelists have just completed training or are in training. The Tibetan Christian Fellowship maintains regular prayer for Tibetan churches and holds an annual meeting from church to church.
    Radio broadcasting is a major key to evangelization of this group. Listeners have written to FEBC from several countries. Most of the younger generation can understand Chinese, which considerably broadens the gospel witness they can receive. The Moravians, working with Tibetan converts, have produced a Tibetan translation of the whole Bible, and the New Testament has recently been revised and published in India.
    Traditionally, Tibetan Buddhism has been the strong unifying force which has given Tibetans everywhere a shared faith, a common language, and a cohesive social structure. In general, the Tibetans in Bhutan think of Christianity as belonging to another culture, and thus changing religion involves more than an individual decision.
    Permission for foreigners to enter Bhutan is given only at the request of the government of Bhutan or by personal invitation from the Royal family. At the present time doctors, nurses, engineers and teachers are employed, but it is expected that more tourists will be welcome in the near future.

Toraja, Southern (Indonesia)

ALTERNATE NAMES: Sa'dan Toraja; Sa'dan Toradja

SIZE OF GROUP: 250,000   MARC ID: 3074

DISTINCTIVES: language; ethnicity; religion; kinship

SOCIAL CHANGE: not reported

LANGUAGES: Toradja; Tae' (V)

SCRIPTURE: Bible

CHRISTIAN LITERACY: not reported

RELIGION: Animism; Christianity

CHURCHES AND MISSIONS: not reported

OPENNESS TO RELIGIOUS CHANGE: not reported

RECEPTIVITY TO CHRISTIANITY: not reported

GROWTH RATE OF CHRISTIAN COMMUNITY: not reported

EVANGELISM PROFILE: not reported

VALIDITY: 5

The Toraja of Sulawesi can be divided into three broad groups: Eastern, Western and Southern. Each is culturally distinct and lives in a particular region. There is little on-going contact between the groups.

The Southern Toraja live in the mountainous southwestern region of Sulawesi near the Sa'dan River. In their traditional stories their ancestors came in eight canoes from a mythical island named Pongko'. It's likely that they came from the southwest and have been living in this part of Sulawesi over 500 years. A good deal of cultural change occured with the Dutch occupation in 1905, including the establishing of mission schools.

Traditionally Southern Toraja villages were built on hill tops, which were considered to be sacred. The Dutch made them move to the plains, where they're surrounded by bamboo, sugar palms, coconuts and bananas. The villages are usally divided into halfs, each of which is a ceremonial unit. Rice, the staple food, is thought to have sacred origins and is grown on terraced, irrigated fields. Buffalos are kept for prestige, ceremonies and for their milk (which is considered to be medicinal).

The Southern Toraja believe that the universe is divided into three parts: The Upper World, the World of Men and the Underworld. Balance between these worlds is achieved through rituals and the maintenance of various taboos established by their ancestors. Each of the worlds has its own god, and men are throught to have been created by the most important god from the Upper World, Puang Matua. Ancestor worship is a significant element of the indigenous religion and is carried out by a variety of practitioners.

Though mission schools have been responsible for nominally converting a number of the Southern Toraja, only a small percentage are practicing Christians today.

EXPANDED DESCRIPTIONS

Tsou (Taiwan)

ALTERNATE NAMES: Tsu'u

SIZE OF GROUP: 4,100   MARC ID: 7035

DISTINCTIVES: language; ethnicity; religion; kinship; sense of unity

SOCIAL CHANGE: not reported

LANGUAGES: Tsou (V)

SCRIPTURE: none

CHRISTIAN LITERACY: not reported

RELIGION: Animism; Christianity (-1% practicing)

CHURCHES AND MISSIONS	BEGAN	MEMBERSHIP	COMMUNITY
Tsou Churches	nr	nr	nr

OPENNESS TO RELIGIOUS CHANGE: not reported

RECEPTIVITY TO CHRISTIANITY: not reported

GROWTH RATE OF CHRISTIAN COMMUNITY: not reported

EVANGELISM PROFILE: not reported

VALIDITY: 5

The Tsou are a farming hill tribe in the west central mountains of Taiwan. Some of their culture traits (such as traditional leather clothing and bark containers) suggest links with northern Asia, while other aspects of their language and culture point to Indonesia and other areas to the south and east. Whatever their origins, they are considered to be different in many basic respects from the other indigenous groups of Taiwan.

In the late 1930s the government moved the Tsou into lower altitude villages and encouraged them to grow irrigated rice. Originally dry farmers, they still grow sweet potatoes as their primary staple food, along with dry rice, taro, maize, beans, pumpkins, garlic, bananas, and peanuts. Since the 30s contacts with other groups have impacted the Tsou culture also. Extended family households are now giving way to nuclear family organization, and traditional oval-shaped houses are beginning to change also. Land was once owned and regulated by clans, but the practice of private ownership is increasing.

Tsou marriages usually take place during annual agricultural festivals. The couple are fed sacred millet by their new father-in-laws to represent the unity of their kin groups. The bride becomes part of her husband's clan, and receives gifts from the men of the clan to assure the well-being of her children. Generally bride service is still required - with the prospective groom working for the girl's parents for a set period of time before the wedding.

Tsou traditional religion is unique for this area in that it attributes humanity's origin to an act of deliberate creation instead of some other cause. Also, there are no rituals associated with ancestor spirits, though they do believe in a pantheon of named deities who live in a kind of "heaven" and are friendly to mankind. Offerings are made to these gods and various ceremonies are held. There are some Tsou Christians, and churches have been established, though most Tsou still follow the traditional animistic religion.

Tung-Chia (China)

ALTERNATE NAMES: Tung

SIZE OF GROUP: 1,100,000   MARC ID: 7031

DISTINCTIVES: language; ethnicity; kinship

SOCIAL CHANGE: rapid

LANGUAGES: Tung (V); Mandarin (T)

SCRIPTURE: not reported

CHRISTIAN LITERACY: not reported

RELIGION: Animism

CHURCHES AND MISSIONS: not reported

OPENNESS TO RELIGIOUS CHANGE: not reported

RECEPTIVITY TO CHRISTIANITY: not reported

GROWTH RATE OF CHRISTIAN COMMUNITY: not reported

EVANGELISM PROFILE: not reported

VALIDITY: 5

The Tung-Chia people of Guangxi (Kwangsi) Province have experienced a great deal of change since the communists gained control of China. Up to that time they lived in a stable social structure based on feudal chiefdoms. Villages today are now farming communes. Instead of using pine torches for light, electricity is available, while trucks and railroads have replaced donkeys for bringing in supplies.

The Tung-Chia have reached a high level of cultural achievement and are especially well-known for their wood carvings. Music plays an important part in their lives, whether at weddings, various celebrations, or just while working in the fields. Songs are usually accompained by a "pipa" (a Mandolin-like instrument), other string instruments, or a special flute played with the nose. Ballad singers are highly respected.

Livng mainly in valleys, the Tung-Chia cultivate irrigated glutinous rice as well as cotton. They are excellent bird hunters and fish breeders. A special part of their culture are occasional water buffalo fights. These fights used to carry religious meaning, in that it was thought they guaranteed good crops, but they've evolved into events that now are just for entertainment. Neighboring villages compete against each other and group solidarity is reinforced. Usually a bazaar and a feast are held as well, often with several thousand people attending.

Little is known of Tung-Chia religious beliefs. It is also unknown whether the gospel has ever penetrated this people group or the area they live in.

EXPANDED DESCRIPTIONS

Zemi Naga of Assam (India)

ALTERNATE NAMES: Zeliang

SIZE OF GROUP: 16,000   MARC ID: 7002

DISTINCTIVES: ethnicity; religion; language; occupation

SOCIAL CHANGE: slow

LANGUAGES: Jeme (100% speak/5% read; V, P)

SCRIPTURE: New Testament

CHRISTIAN LITERACY: 55%

RELIGION: Animism (90% adherents); Roman Catholic (3% adherents); Protestant (2% adherents); Other (5% adherents)

CHURCHES AND MISSIONS	BEGAN	MEMBERSHIP	COMMUNITY
Zemi Presbyterian Church	1960	nr	nr
Anglican Church	nr	nr	nr
Roman Catholic Church	nr	nr	nr

OPENNESS TO RELIGIOUS CHANGE: very closed

RECEPTIVITY TO CHRISTIANITY: very reluctant

GROWTH RATE OF CHRISTIAN COMMUNITY: not reported

EVANGELISM PROFILE:
    20% No awareness of Christianity
    40% Aware that Christianity exists
    30% Some knowledge of the gospel
    5% Understand the message of the gospel
    1% Personally challenged to receive Christ
    1% Decision to accept Christ
    2% Incorporated into a fellowship of Christians
    1% Active propagators of the gospel

VALIDITY: 6

The Zemi Nagas of north Cachar Hills in Assam probably migrated from Burma along with their distant cousins, the Nagas of Nagaland.

The Zemes were head-hunters until a few decades ago; a practice closely associated with their animistic beliefs. The influence of the British in India had little impact and the irradication of head-hunting came only after India's independence. The government has safe-guarded their religion from any further changes to preserve their identity. This protection has limited evangelism efforts. The Jeme language has been put into Roman script, and the literacy rate among Christians is 55 percent. This language is quite distinct from the Zeliangs, although the Zemi Nagas are categorized under the Zeliang group linguistically.

The Zemi Nagas live in areas under the jurisdiction of the Presbyterians of northeast India and the Anglican Church. The Zemi Presbyterian Church, with its six presbyteries, was established in 1960. This church has 20 workers and a theological student but no pastor as yet.

Persecution of Christians still continues. In the past the only form of evangelism was preaching. The concern today is uplifting the economy, education, and introducing better methods of agriculture. Cassette and radio evangelism would also be quite effective in bringing the gospel message to this people.

Part 5
Registry
of
the
Unreached

The information on the 2914 unreached peoples in the registry is presented in five different lists. Each list organizes the information differently. Only the first list, which indexes the peoples alphabetically by group name, includes the estimated percentage of those that practice Christianity and a code that indicates the overall accuracy of the data.

Groups are also listed by receptivity, principal professed religion, language, and country. All five lists indicate those groups reported to be very receptive (***), receptive (**), or indifferent (*). There is also another code (79, 80, or 81) attached to the group name to indicate that a description has been written about this people group in *Unreached Peoples '79* (79), *Unreached Peoples '80* (80), or *Unreached Peoples '81* (81).

A comparison with the indices in *Unreached Peoples '79* and *Unreached Peoples '80* will show that some early data has been changed. In a few cases the group has been removed because of more accurate information. This reflects the on-going nature of this data collection and research.

A more detailed explanation of the information contained in each of the following lists may be found at the beginning of the appropriate sections.

Index by
Group
Name

INDEX BY GROUP NAME

This is the basic listing of people groups in this registry. Peoples are listed by their primary **name,** and effort has been made to standardize names and use the most commonly accepted English spelling. This listing includes the **country** for which the information was provided, principal vernacular **language** used by the group, population estimate of the **group size** in the country listed and principal professed religion **(primary religion),** which in some cases is less than 50 percent of the total group membership.

In addition, this index includes the estimated percentage of the group that practices Christianity in any recognized tradition **(Practicing Christian).** Included in this percentage are Protestant, Roman Catholic, Orthodox, African Independent, and other Christian groups. Excluded in this percentage were Christo-pagans and Christian cultic groups. It is important to note that this figure is the estimated percentage of *practicing* Christians within the group. If the group was listed in *Unreached Peoples '80,* the figure recorded here will most likely be different, because that volume recorded the percentage of professing Christians (or adherents), which most often will be a higher number. Thus these figures should not be compared or used as a time series, since the changes indicate a different kind of data. Differences might also be due to a new and better data source or revised data, as we are continually updating our files.

The index also lists a validity code **(Valid)** which estimates the accuracy and completeness of the data on a scale from 1 to 9. The code is:

1 — The only information available at this point is the group name, country, language, population, and primary religion. The percentage listed under practicing Christians is, at best, a rough estimate.

2 — There has been more data collected than the "baseline" information in 1, but it is scanty and/or of poor quality.

3 — About one-half of the information on the unreached peoples questionnaire (Appendix B) has been collected, and information on the Christian community, if any, is missing or probably inaccurate.

4 — Almost all the data on the unreached peoples questionnaire has been collected *or* the source document has supplied most of the necessary information.

5 — Information has been supplied by a completed unreached peoples questionnaire and at least one other document.

6 — In addition to 5, there is enough detailed information about the people group to write an accurate, up-to-date description.

7 — There exists an extensive description of the people group in secular or Christian literature.

8 — There has been a major research study (thesis or

dissertation quality) done on the group which includes detailed information on the Christian community.

9 — In addition to 8, the study includes a thorough exploration of evangelism strategy for the particular group, based on firsthand experience.

The final column in this section indicates the year of the volume **(Year Described)** of *Unreached Peoples* in which a description of the group appeared.

NAME	COUNTRY	LANGUAGE	GROUP SIZE	PRIMARY RELIGION	% CHR	V	VOL U.P.
"Au"ei	Botswana	"Au"ei	5,000	Animism	0%	1	
Abaknon	Philippines	Abaknon	10,000	Christo-Paganism	1%	1	
Abanyom	Nigeria	Abanyom	3,850	Animism	1%	1	
Abau	Indonesia	Abau	3,390	Animism	0%	1	
Abazin	Soviet Russia	Abazin	25,000	Islam	0%	1	
Abe	Ivory Coast	Abe	28,500	Islam-Animist	1%	1	
Abialang	Sudan	Abialang	7,200	Islam-Animist	0%	1	
Abidji	Ivory Coast	Adidji	23,000	Islam-Animist	1%	1	
Abkhaz	Soviet Russia	Abkhaz	83,000	Unknown	1%	1	
	Turkey	Abkhaz	12,400	Islam	1%	1	
Abong	Nigeria	Abong	1,000	Islam	1%	1	
Abou Charib	Chad	Abou Charib	25,000	Islam-Animist	1%	1	
Abu Leila	Sudan	Abu Leila	4,100	Islam	0%	1	
Abua	Nigeria	Abua	24,000	Animism	1%	1	
Abujmaria in M.P.	India	Abujmaria	11,000	Hindu-Animism	1%	1	
Abure	Ivory Coast	Abure	25,000	Islam-Animist	1%	1	
Ach'ang	China	Ach'ang	10,000	Traditional Chinese	1%	1	
Achagua	Colombia	Achagua	100	Animism	1%	6	80
Achehnese	Indonesia	Achehnese	2,200,000	Islam	1%	1	
Acheron	Sudan	Acheron	1,300	Islam	0%	1	
Achi, Cubulco	Guatemala	Achi, Cubulco	15,000	Animism	1%	1	
Achi, Rabinal	Guatemala	Achi, Rabinal	21,000	Animism	1%	1	
Achipa	Nigeria	Achipa	3,600	Islam	1%	1	
Achode	Ghana	Achode	4,890	Islam-Animist	1%	1	
Acholi	Uganda	Acholi	nr	Animism	1%	1	
Achual	Peru	Achual	5,000	Animism	1%	1	
Adamawa	Cameroon	Fulani	380,000	Islam-Animist	1%	5	
Adele	Togo	Adele	3,000	Islam-Animist	0%	1	
Adhola	Uganda	Adhola	200,000	Animism	0%	1	
***Adi	India	Adi	80,000	Animism	2%	4	
Adiyan in Kerala	India	Adiyan	2,500	Hinduism	1%	1	
**Adja	Benin	Ge	250,000	Animism	5%	4	
Adygei	Soviet Russia	Adygei	100,000	Islam-Animist	0%	1	
Adyukru	Ivory Coast	Adyukru	50,450	Islam-Animist	1%	1	
Aeta	Philippines	Aeta	500	Christo-Paganism	1%	6	79
Afar	Ethiopia	Afar	300,000	Islam-Animist	1%	6	80
*Afawa	Nigeria	Afanci	10,000	Animism	1%	1	
Afitti	Sudan	Afitti	3,600	Islam	1%	6	80
**Afo	Nigeria	Eloyi	25,000	Animism	1%	4	
**African Students in Cairo	Egypt	Various dialects	700	Islam	9%	4	
Afshars	Iran	Afshari	290,000	Islam	0%	1	
Agajanis	Iran	Agajanis	1,100	Islam	0%	3	
Agariya in Bihar	India	Agariya	11,790	Hinduism	1%	1	

239

NAME	COUNTRY	LANGUAGE	GROUP SIZE	PRIMARY RELIGION	% CHR	V	VOL U.P.
Age	Cameroon	Age	5,000	Animism	0%	1	
Aghem	Cameroon	Aghem	7,000	Animism	0%	1	
Aghu	Indonesia	Aghu	3,000	Animism	-1%	1	
Agoi	Nigeria	Agoi	3,650	Animism	-1%	1	
Aguacateco	Guatemala	Aguacateco	22,000	Animism	-1%	1	
Aguaruna	Peru	Aguaruna	8,800	Islam	-1%	1	
Agul	Soviet Russia	Agul	7,000	Islam-Animist	-1%	1	
Agutaynon	Philippines	Agutaynon	20,000	Animism	-1%	1	
Agwagwune	Nigeria	Agwagwune	132,520	Islam	-1%	1	
**Ahir in Maharashtra	India	Ahir	500,000	Islam	0%	6	79
**Ahl-i-Haqq in Iran	Iran	Kurdish dialects	2,900	Islam-Animist	0%	1	
Ahlo	Togo	Ahlo	150	Animism	-1%	1	
Aibondeni	Indonesia	Aibondeni	400	Animism	-1%	1	
Aikwakai	Indonesia	Aikwakai	110	Hindu-Animist	-1%	1	
Aimol in Assam	India	Aimol	2,000	Animism	-1%	1	
Airo-Sumaghaghe	Indonesia	Airo-Sumaghaghe	350	Animism	-1%	1	
Airoran	Indonesia	Airoran	1,000	Islam	0%	1	
Aja	Sudan	Aja	580	Hindu-Animist	-1%	1	
Ajmeri in Rajasthan	India	Ajmeri	2,257	Animism	-1%	3	
Aka	India	Aka	50,000	Islam-Animist	-1%	1	
Akan, Brong	Ivory Coast	Akan, Brong	3,000	Christo-Paganism	-1%	1	
Akawaio	Guyana	Akawaio	300	Animism	-1%	1	
Ake	Nigeria	Ake	9,916	Ancestor Worship	1%	6	79
**Akha	Thailand	Akha	5,000	Unknown	0%	4	
Akhavakh	Soviet Russia	Akhavakh	nr	Islam-Animist	-1%	1	
***Akhdam	Yemen, Arab Republic	Arabic	15,000	Animism	0%	1	
Akpa-Yache	Nigeria	Akpa-Yache	8,300	Islam-Animist	0%	1	
Akpafu	Ghana	Akpafu	50,000	Islam	3%	4	
Alaba	Ethiopia	Alaban	14,770	Islam-Animist	2%	5	
Aladian	Ivory Coast	Aladian	35,500	Animism	1%	5	
Alago	Nigeria	Alago	8,000	Animism	-1%	5	
Alak	Laos	Alak	6,000	Christo-Paganism	-1%	4	
Alangan	Philippines	Alangan	400	Folk Religion	0%	5	
*Alars	India	Allar	30,000	Islam-Animist	0%	6	79
Alas	Indonesia	Gayo	600,000	Islam	0%	6	80
*Alawites	Syria	Arabic	1,700,000	Islam	-1%	5	
*Albanian Muslims	Albania	Albanian Tosk	1,500,000	Islam	0%	1	
*Albanians in Yugoslavia	Yugoslavia	Albanian (Gheg)	1,200	Animism	-1%	6	80
Alege	Nigeria	Alege	8,000,000	Islam	0%	3	
Algerian (Arabs)	Algeria	Arabic	804,000	Islam	-18	5	81
Algerian Arabs in France	France	Arabic	96,000	Animism	-18	5	81
Alor, Kolana	Indonesia	Alor, Kolana	19,000	Animism	0%	1	
Alur	Zaire	Alur					

240

Name	Country	Language	Population	Religion	%	Code
Alutor	Soviet Russia	Alutor	2,000	Unknown	0%	1
Amahuaca	Peru	Amahuaca	1,500	Animism	-1%	1
Amanab	Indonesia	Amanab	2,800	Animism	-1%	1
Amar	Ethiopia	Amar	22,500	Animism	-1%	1
Amarakaeri	Peru	Amarakaeri	500	Animism	-1%	1
Amasi	Cameroon	Amasi	10,000	Animism	0%	1
Ambai	Indonesia	Ambai	6,000	Animism	-1%	1
Amber	Indonesia	Amber	300	Animism	-1%	1
Amberbaken	Indonesia	Amberbaken	5,000	Animism	-1%	1
Ambo	Zambia	Ambo	1,000	Animism	0%	1
Ambonese	Indonesia	Ambonese	80,000	Animism	-1%	1
Ambonese	Netherlands	Ambonese	30,000	Animism	-1%	1
*Americans in Geneva	Switzerland	English	45,000	Secularism	2%	4
*Ami	Taiwan	Ami	99,000	Buddhist-Animist	2%	5 81
*Amo	Nigeria	Amo	3,550	Animism	2%	4
**Ampeeli	Papua New Guinea	Ampale	1,000	Christo-Paganism	-1%	4
Amsterdam Boat Dwellers	Netherlands	Dutch	7,500	Secularism	0%	3
Amuesha	Peru	Amuesha	5,000	Animism	-1%	1
Amuzgo, Guerrero	Mexico	Amuzgo, Guerrero	20,000	Christo-Paganism	-1%	1
Amuzgo, Oaxaca	Mexico	Amuzgo, Oaxaca	5,000	Christo-Paganism	0%	1
Ana	Togo	Ana	36,000	Islam-Animist	-1%	1
Anaang	Nigeria	Anaang	246,000	Animism	-1%	1
Anal in Manipur	India	Anal	6,590	Animism	-1%	1
Andha in Andhra Pradesh	India	Andha	64,650	Animism	-1%	1
Andi	Soviet Russia	Andi	9,000	Animism	0%	1
Andoque	Colombia	Andoque	100	Unknown	-1%	1
Anga in Bihar	India	Anga	423,500	Hinduism	-1%	1
Angas	Nigeria	Angas	100,000	Animism	-1%	4
Animere	Togo	Animere	10,250	Islam-Animist	0%	1
Ankwe	Nigeria	Ankwai	10,000	Animism	-1%	4
Ansus	Indonesia	Ansus	3,000	Animism	-1%	5
Anuak	Ethiopia	Anuak	52,000	Animism	-1%	1
Anuak	Sudan	Anuak	30,000	Animism	0%	1
Anyanga	Togo	Anyanga	3,000	Islam-Animist	-1%	4
Apalai	Brazil	Apalai	100	Animism	11%	4
**Apartment Residents-Seoul	Korea, Republic of	Korean	87,000	Folk Religion	-1%	4
**Apatani in Assam	India	Apartani	11,000	Animism	9%	6
*Apayao	Philippines	Isneg	12,000	Christo-Paganism	-1%	1
Apinaye	Brazil	Apinaye	210	Animism	-1%	1
Apurina	Brazil	Apurina	1,000	Animism	0%	3
Ara	Indonesia	Ara	75,000	Islam	0%	3
Arab-Jabbari (Kamesh)	Iran	Arabic	13,000	Islam	0%	3
Arab-Shaibani (Kamesh)	Iran	Arabic	16,000	Islam	0%	3

NAME	COUNTRY	LANGUAGE	GROUP SIZE	PRIMARY RELIGION	% CHR	V	VOL U.P.
Arabela	Peru	Arabela	200	Animism	-1%	1	
Arabs in Morocco	Morocco	Arabic dialect	5,250,000	Islam	1%	5	
Arabs of Khuzestan	Iran	Arabic	520,000	Islam	-1%	4	
Aranadan in Tamil Nadu	India	Aranadan	600	Hindu-Animist	-1%	1	
Arandai	Indonesia	Arandai	2,000	Animism	-1%	1	
Arapaco	Brazil	Tucanoan	310	Animism	-1%	4	
Arawa	Nigeria	Hausa	200,000	Islam	-1%	1	
Arawak	Guyana	Arawak	5,000	Christo-Paganism	-1%	1	
Arbore	Ethiopia	Arbore	2,000	Animism	-1%	1	
Archin	Soviet Russia	Archin	900	Unknown	0%	1	
Arecuna	Venezuela	Arecuna	14,000	Animism	-1%	1	
Argobba	Ethiopia	Argobba	3,000	Animism	0%	1	
Arguni	Indonesia	Arguni	200	Animism	-1%	1	
*Arnatas	India	Aranatan	700	Animism	-1%	4	
Arusha	Tanzania	Arusha	110,000	Animism	8%	5	
Arutani	Venezuela	Spanish	100	Animism	0%	1	
Arya in Andhra Pradesh	India	Arya	2,590	Hinduism	-1%	1	
*Asienara	Indonesia	Asienara	700	Animism	7%	6	79
Asmat	Indonesia	Asmat	30,000	Animism	-1%	1	
Assamese	Bangladesh	Assamese	10,000,000	Islam	-1%	1	
Assumbo	Cameroon	Assumbo	10,000	Animism	-1%	1	
Asu	Tanzania	Asu	110,000	Animism	0%	1	
Asuri in Bihar	India	Asuri	4,540	Animism	4%	4	
*Ata of Davao	Philippines	Manobo	10,000	Animism	-1%	1	
Aten	Nigeria	Aten	4,000	Islam	-1%	1	
Ati	Philippines	Ati	1,500	Christo-Paganism	0%	1	
Atoc	Sudan	Atoc	5,200	Islam	-1%	1	
Atruahi	Brazil	Atruahi	500	Animism	0%	1	
*Atta	Philippines	Atta	1,000	Animism	-1%	5	
Attie	Ivory Coast	Attie	160,000	Islam-Animist	-1%	1	
Atuot	Sudan	Atuot	8,000	Islam	0%	1	
*Atye	Ivory Coast	Atye	210,000	Animism	9%	4	
Avatime	Ghana	Avatime	10,400	Islam-Animist	-1%	1	
Avikam	Ivory Coast	Avikam	7,940	Islam-Animist	-1%	1	
Avukaya	Sudan	Avukaya	5,200	Islam	0%	1	
Awngi	Ethiopia	Awngi	50,000	Islam	-1%	1	
Awutu	Ghana	Awutu	85,000	Islam-Animist	0%	1	
Awyi	Indonesia	Awyi	400	Animism	-1%	1	
Awyu	Indonesia	Awyu	18,000	Animism	-1%	1	
Ayana	Kenya	Ayana	5,000	Islam-Animist	-1%	3	
*Aymara, Carangas	Bolivia	Aymara	850,000	Animism	7%	5	
Aymara, Carangas	Chile	Aymara, Carangas	20,000	Christo-Paganism	0%	1	
Ayoreo	Paraguay	Ayoreo	700	Animism	-1%	1	

Name	Language	Country	Population	Religion				
Ayu	Ayu	Nigeria	4,000	Islam	-1	0	1	
*Azerbaijani	Azerbaijani	Afghanistan	5,000	Islam	-1	0	1	80
*Azerbaijani Turks	Azerbaijani Turkish	Iran	6,000,000	Islam	2	6	79	
***Azteca	Nahuatl, Hidalgo	Mexico	250,000	Christo-Paganism	2	6	1	
Baali	Baali	Zaire	38,000	Animism	0	0	1	
Babajou	Babajou	Cameroon	500	Animism	0	0	1	
Babri	Babri	India	9,700	Hinduism	-1	1	1	
**Babur Thali	Bura (Babur)	Nigeria	75,000	Hinduism	3	6	80	
Baburiwa	Baburiwa	Indonesia	160	Animism	-1	0	1	
Bachama	Bachama	Nigeria	20,000	Islam	-1	0	1	
Bada	Bada	Nigeria	10,000	Animism	-1	0	1	
Badagu in Nilgiri	Badagu	India	104,920	Animism	-1	0	1	
Bade	Bade	Nigeria	100,000	Islam	-1	0	1	
Badyara	Badyara	Guinea-Bissau	10,000	Islam	0	0	1	
Bafut	Bafut	Cameroon	25,000	Animism	-1	0	1	
Bagelkhandi in M.P.	Bagelkhandi	India	231,230	Hindu-Animist	-1	0	1	
Baghati in H.P.	Baghati	India	3,980	Animism	-1	0	1	
Bagirmi	Bagirmi	Chad	40,000	Islam-Animist	-1	0	1	
***Bagobo	Bagobo	Philippines	35,000	Christo-Paganism	14	5	4	
Bagri	Bagri	Pakistan	20,000	Hinduism	1	0	1	
Baguio Area Miners	Ilocano	Philippines	40,000	Nominal Christian	15	5	81	
Baharlu (Kamesh)	Baham	Indonesia	500	Animism	1	0	1	
Bahawalpuri in M.P.	Turkish	Iran	7,500	Islam	-0	0	3	
Bai	Bahawalpuri	India	640	Animism	-1	0	1	
Baiga in Bihar	Bai	Sudan	2,500	Islam	-1	0	1	
Bajania	Baiga	India	11,110	Animism	-1	6	79	
Bajau, Indonesian	Gujarati Dialect	Pakistan	50,000	Hinduism	-1	0	1	
Bajau, Land	Bajau, Indonesian	Indonesia	90,000	Islam-Animist	0	0	2	
Baka	Bajaus	Malaysia	15,000	Animism	-1	0	1	
Bakairi	Baka	Cameroon	2,600	Animism	-0	0	1	
Bakhtiaris	Bakairi	Brazil	300	Animism	-1	0	1	
**Bakuba	Bakhtiaris	Iran	590,000	Islam	-1	0	5	80
Bakwe	Tshiluba	Zaire	75,000	Animism	14	5	1	
Bakwele	Bakwele	Ivory Coast	5,060	Islam-Animist	-1	0	1	
**Balangao	Bakwele	Congo	8,000	Animism	0	0	1	
Balangaw	Balangao	Philippines	4,500	Christo-Paganism	3	0	4	
Balanta	Balangaw	Philippines	5,000	Animism	-1	0	1	
Balantak	Balanta	Senegal	49,200	not reported	nr		3	
Balante	Balantak	Indonesia	125,000	Islam-Animist	-7	8	4	
Bali	Balanta	Guinea-Bissau	100,000	Animism	-7	0	1	
Balinese	Bali	Nigeria	1,000	Islam-Animist	-1	0	1	
	Balinese	Indonesia	2,000,000	Hindu-Animist	-1	0	5	

NAME	COUNTRY	LANGUAGE	GROUP SIZE	PRIMARY RELIGION	% CHR	VOL V	U.P.
Balkars	Soviet Russia	Balkar	60,000	Islam	0%	1	
Balmiki	Pakistan	Hindustani	20,000	Hinduism	1%	5	
Balong	Cameroon	Duala	4,500	Animism	-1%	1	
Balti in Jammu	India	Balti	40,140	Animism	-1%	1	
Baluchi	Iran	Baluchi	1,100,000	Islam	0%	6	80
Bambara	Ivory Coast	Bambara	1,000,000	Islam-Animist	-1%	1	
	Mali	Bambara	1,000,000	Islam	-1%	5	
Bambuka	Nigeria	Bambuka	10,000	Islam	0%	1	
Bamougoun-Bamenjou	Cameroon	Bamougoun-Bamenjou	31,000	Animism	0%	1	
Bamum	Cameroon	Bamum	75,000	not reported	nr	1	
***Banai	Bangladesh	Bengali	2,000	Buddhist-Animist	1%	4	
Banaro	Papua New Guinea	Banaro	2,500	Animism	5%	4	
Bandawa-Minda	Nigeria	Bandawa-Minda	10,000	Islam	-1%	1	
Bandi	Liberia	Bandi	32,000	Animism	6%	4	
Bandjoun	Cameroon	Bandjoun	60,000	Animism	0%	1	
Banen	Cameroon	Banen	28,000	Animism	0%	1	
Banga	Nigeria	Banga	8,000	Islam	-1%	1	
Bangangte	Cameroon	Local Dialects	8,000	Unknown	-1%	1	
Bangaru in Punjab	India	Bangri	475,000	Hindu-Animist	-1%	1	
Bangba	Zaire	Bangba	29,000	Animism	0%	1	
Banggai	Indonesia	Banggai	200,000	Islam	-1%	1	
Baniwa	Brazil	Baniwa	2,448	Animism	-1%	1	
Bantuanon	Philippines	Bantuanon	50,000	Christo-Paganism	6%	5	
***Banyarwanda	Rwanda	Kinyarwanda	4,000,000	Animism	0%	1	
Banyum	Senegal	Banyum	9,000	Islam-Animist	0%	1	
Banyun	Guinea-Bissau	Banyun	15,000	Animism	6%	4	
***Baoule	Ivory Coast	Baule	1,200,000	Animism	9%	4	
Barabaig	Tanzania	Tatoga	49,000	Animism	2%	5	79
Barambu	Sudan	Barambu	46,000	Islam	0%	1	
Barasano	Colombia	Barasano	400	Animism	-1%	1	
Barasano, Northern	Colombia	Barasano, Northern	450	Animism	3%	5	
Barasano, Southern	Colombia	Janena	400	Animism	2%	4	
Barau	Indonesia	Barau	150	Animism	-1%	1	
Bare'e	Indonesia	Bare'e	325,000	Animism	-1%	1	
Bareli in Madhya Pradesh	India	Bareli	230,030	Hinduism	-1%	1	
Bari	Sudan	Bari	340,000	Islam	0%	1	
*Bariba	Benin	Bariba	400,000	Animism	4%	6	80
Bariba	Nigeria	Bariba	55,000	Islam-Animist	-1%	1	
Basa	Cameroon	Basaa	170,000	Unknown	0%	1	
Basakomo	Nigeria	not reported	60,000	Animism	12%	4	
Basari	Guinea	Basari	3,500	Animism	0%	4	
Basari	Senegal	Gasari	8,000	Animism	0%	3	
Basari	Senegal	Basari	8,000	Animism	0%	1	

Bashar	Togo	Basari	100,000	Animism	10%	5	
Bashgali	Nigeria	Bashar	20,000	Animism	-1%	1	
Bashkir	Afghanistan	Bashgali	10,000	Islam	-1%	1	
Basila	Soviet Russia	Tatar	1,200,000	Islam	0%	5	80
Basketo	Togo	Basila	4,750	Islam-Animist	-1%	1	
***Basotho, Mountain	Ethiopia	Basketo	9,000	Animism	-1%	1	
*Bassa	Lesotho	Southern Sesotho	70,000	Animism	8%	6	79
**Bassa	Liberia	Bassa	200,000	Animism	11%	5	
Bata	Nigeria	Bassa	100,000	Animism	8%	5	
*Batak, Angkola	Nigeria	Bata	26,400	Islam-Animist	-1%	1	
Batak, Karo	Indonesia	Batak, Angkola	nr	Islam	0%	6	80
Batak, Palawan	Indonesia	Batak, Karo	400,000	Animism	-1%	1	
Batak, Simalungun	Philippines	Batak, Palawan	390	Christo-Paganism	-1%	1	
Batak, Toba	Indonesia	Batak, Simalungun	800,000	Animism	-1%	1	
Batanga-Ngolo	Indonesia	Batak, Toba	1,600,000	Animism	-1%	1	
**Batangeno	Cameroon	Batanga-Ngolo	9,000	Animism	7%	4	
Bateg	Philippines	Tagalog	nr	Nominal Christian	0%	2	
Bathudi in Bihar	Malaysia	Bateg	400	Animism	-1%	1	
Batsi	India	Bathudi	73,890	Hinduism	0%	1	
Batu	Soviet Russia	Batsi	3,000	Unknown	-1%	1	
Baushi	Nigeria	Batu	25,000	Islam	-1%	1	
Bawm	Nigeria	Baushi	2,650	Islam	-1%	1	
Bayats	Bangladesh	Bawm	7,000	Islam	0%	3	
Bayot	Iran	Bayat	nr	Islam	-1%	1	
	Gambia	Bayot	4,000	Islam-Animist	-1%	1	
	Guinea-Bissau	Bayot	3,000	Islam-Animist	0%	1	
	Senegal	Bayot	4,000	Islam-Animist	-1%	1	
Bazigar in Gujarat	India	Bazigar	100	Animism	-1%	1	
Bediya in Bihar	India	Bediya	32,200	Animism	-1%	1	
Bedoanas	Indonesia	Bedoanas	250	Animism	-1%	1	
Beja	Ethiopia	Beja	39,000	Islam	-1%	1	
	Sudan	Beja	91,000	Islam	-1%	1	
Bekwarra	Nigeria	Bekwarra	34,000	Animism	-1%	1	
Bembe	Zaire	Bembe	50,000	Animism	0%	1	
Bena	Tanzania	Bena	150,000	Animism	0%	1	
Bencho	Ethiopia	Bencho	5,000	Animism	-1%	1	
Bende	Tanzania	Bende	9,000	Animism	0%	1	
Bene	Cameroon	Bene	60,000	Animism	0%	1	
Benga	Gabon	Benga	nr	Animism	-1%	6	80
Bengali	Bangladesh	Bengali	80,000,000	Islam	0%	1	
Berba	Benin	Berba	44,000	Animism	0%	1	
Berik	Indonesia	Berik	800	Animism	-1%	1	
Berom	Nigeria	Berom	116,000	Animism	-1%	1	

NAME	COUNTRY	LANGUAGE	GROUP SIZE	PRIMARY RELIGION	% CHR	V	VOL U.P.
Besisi	Malaysia	Besisi	7,000	Animism	0%	2	
Bete	India	Bete	2,960	Animism	-1%	1	
*Bete	Ivory Coast	Bete	300,000	Animism	1%	5	
Bethen	Cameroon	Bethen	10,000	Animism	0%	1	
Betsinga	Cameroon	Betsinga	10,000	Animism	0%	1	
Bette-Bende	Nigeria	Bette-Bende	36,000	Animism	-1%	1	
Bhakta	India	Bhakta	55,150	Hindu-Animist	-1%	1	
Bharia in Madhya Pradesh	India	Bharia	5,380	Animism	-1%	1	
Bhatneri	India	Bhatneri	190	Islam	-1%	1	
Bhattri	India	Bhattri	103,770	Hindu-Animist	-1%	1	
**Bhil	Pakistan	Marwari	800,000	Hinduism	1%	6	
Bhilala	India	Bhilala	246,720	Hindu-Animist	1%	6	
**Bhils	India	Dangi	800,000	Animism	-1%	1	
*Bhojpuri	Nepal	Bhojpuri	806,480	Hinduism	1%	6	79
Bhoyari in Maharashtra	India	Bhoyari	5,390	Hindu-Animist	-1%	1	
Bhuiya in Bihar	India	Bhuiya	4,430	Animism	-1%	1	
Bhunji in Assam	India	Bhumij	48,240	Hindu-Animist	-1%	1	
Bhunjia in Madhya Pradesh	India	Bhunjia	5,240	Hindu-Animist	-1%	1	
Bhutias	Bhutan	Sharchagpakha	780,000	Buddhism	1%	6	
Biafada	Guinea-Bissau	Biafada	15,000	Animism	6%	4	
Biak	Indonesia	Biak	40,000	Animism	-1%	1	
**Bidayuh of Sarawak	Malaysia	Biatah	110,000	Christo-Paganism	1%	5	81
Biduanda	Malaysia	Biduanda	4,000	Animism	0%	2	
Bidyogo	Guinea-Bissau	Bidyogo	10,000	Islam-Animist	-1%	1	
**Bijogo	Guinea-Bissau	Bidyogo	25,000	Animism	8%	4	
Bijori in Bihar	India	Bijori	2,390	Hindu-Animist	-1%	1	
Biksi	Indonesia	Biksi	200	Animism	-1%	1	
Bilala	Chad	Bilala	42,000	Islam-Animist	-1%	1	
**Bilan	Philippines	Bilaan	75,000	Animism	1%	5	
Bile	Nigeria	Bile	1,000	Islam-Animist	-1%	1	
Bilen	Ethiopia	Bilen	32,000	Islam	-1%	1	
Bimanese	Indonesia	Bima	300,000	Islam	1%	5	
Bimoba	Ghana	Bimoba	49,800	Islam-Animist	-1%	1	
	Togo	Bimoba	70,000	Islam-Animist	-1%	1	
Binawa	Nigeria	Binawa	2,000	Islam	-1%	1	
Binga	Sudan	Binga	1,000	Islam	0%	1	
Bingkokak	Indonesia	Bingkokak	150,000	Islam	-1%	1	
Binjhwari in Bihar	India	Binjhwari	48,800	Hindu-Animist	-1%	1	
Binji	Zaire	Binji	64,000	Animism	0%	1	
***Bipim	Indonesia	Bipim	450	Christo-Paganism	5%	4	
Bira	Zaire	Bira	75,000	Islam-Animist	-1%	1	
Birhor in Bihar	India	Birhor	35,000	Animism	-1%	1	
	India	Birhor	590	Hindu-Animist	-1%	1	

Index	Name	Country	Population	Religion	Code
Birifor	Birifor	Ghana	40,000	Animism	-18 5
	Birifor	Upper Volta	50,000	Islam-Animist	-18 1
Bisa	Bisa	Zambia	83,000	Animism	nr 6 81
Bisaya	Bisaya	Malaysia	2,800	Animism	08 1
Bitare	Bitare	Cameroon	50,000	Islam-Animist	-18 1
	Bitare	Nigeria	3,000	Islam-Animist	08 1
Biti	Biti	Sudan	280	Islam	-18 1
**Black Caribs, Belize	Moreno	Belize	10,000	Christo-Paganism	18 6 79
**Black Caribs, Guatemala	Moreno	Guatemala	1,500	Christo-Paganism	18 6
**Black Caribs, Honduras	Moreno	Honduras	20,000	Christo-Paganism	18 5
Bobe	Bobe	Cameroon	600	Animism	08 1
Bobo Fing	Bobo Fing	Mali	3,000	Animism	-18 1
Bobo Wule	Bobo Wule	Mali	366,000	Animism	-18 1
Bodo in Assam	Bodo	India	509,010	Animism	-18 1
**Bodo Kachari	Bodo	India	610,000	Hindu-Animist	28 4
Boghom	Boghom	Nigeria	50,000	Animism	-18 1
**boko	Boko (Busa)	Benin	40,000	Animism	28 4
Bokyi	Bokyi	Nigeria	87,000	Animism	-18 1
Bole	Bole	Nigeria	87,000	Animism	-18 1
***Bolinao	Bolinao	Philippines	32,000	Islam	198 4
Bolon	Bolon	Upper Volta	26,000	Nominal Christian	-18 1
Bolondo	Bolondo	Zaire	4,000	Islam-Animist	08 1
Boma	Boma	Zaire	1,000	Animism	-18 1
Bomboko	Bomboko	Cameroon	15,000	Animism	08 1
Bomou	Bomou	Chad	2,500	Animism	-18 1
Bondei	Bondei	Tanzania	15,000	Islam-Animist	08 1
Bondo in Orissa	Bondo	India	30,000	Islam	-18 1
Bonerif	Bonerif	Indonesia	2,370	Hinduism	-18 1
Bonggo	Bonggo	Indonesia	100	Animism	-18 1
Bongili	Bongili	Congo	430	Animism	08 1
Bongo	Bongo	Sudan	4,000	Animism	08 1
Bonkeng-Pendia	Bonkeng-Pendia	Cameroon	2,400	Animism	08 1
**Bontoc, Central	Bontoc, Central	Philippines	1,500	Animism	08 1
**Bontoc, Southern	Southern Bontoc	Philippines	20,000	Animism	18 5 81
Bor Gok	Bor Gok	Sudan	12,000	Christo-Paganism	48 5
Bora	Bora	Colombia	5,800	Islam	08 1
Borai	Borai	Indonesia	400	Animism	-18 1
Boran	Boran	Ethiopia	1,000	Animism	-18 1
**Boran	Boran	Kenya	132,000	Islam-Animist	-18 1
*Boran	Boran	Kenya	37,000	Islam-Animist	38 5
	Boran	Kenya	40,000	Islam-Animist	08 3
*Bororo	Bororo	Brazil	500	Animism	-18 6
*Bosnian	Serbo-Croation	Yugoslavia	1,740,000	Islam	-18 6 80

NAME	LANGUAGE	COUNTRY	GROUP SIZE	PRIMARY RELIGION	% CHR	V	VOL U.P.
Botlikh	Botlikh	Soviet Russia	3,500	Unknown	0%	1	
Bousansi	Bisa	Upper Volta	140,000	Islam-Animist	0%	1	
Bovir-Ahmadi	Lori	Iran	110,000	Islam	-1%	1	
Bowili	Bowili	Togo	3,300	Islam-Animist	0%	4	
Boya	Boya	Sudan	15,000	Animism	-1%	4	
Bozo	Bozo	Mali	nr	Animism	0%	1	
Brahui	Brahui	Pakistan	745,000	Islam	-1%	5	
Braj in Uttar Pradesh	Braj	India	6,000,000	Animism	-1%	1	
Brao	Brao	Laos	18,000	Animism	-1%	6	79
Brat	Brat	Indonesia	20,000	Animism	-1%	2	
Bruneis	Bruneis	Malaysia	25,000	Animism	0%	1	
Bua	Bua	Chad	20,000	Animism	0%	3	
Bual	Bual	Indonesia	150,000	Islam	-1%	1	
Bube	Bube	Equatorial Guinea	20,000	Animism	0%	1	
Budu	Budu	Zaire	83,000	Animism	0%	1	
Budug	Budug	Soviet Russia	2,000	Unknown	0%	1	
Budugum	Masa	Cameroon	10,000	Animism	-1%	4	
Buduma	Buduma	Nigeria	80,000	Islam	-1%	1	
Bugis	Bugis	Indonesia	3,500,000	Islam-Animist	-1%	6	80
Buglere	Buglere	Panama	2,000	Christo-Paganism	-1%	1	
Bugombe	Bugombe	Zaire	12,000	Animism	0%	1	
Buhid	Buhid	Philippines	6,000	Christo-Paganism	0%	1	
Builsa	Buli	Ghana	97,000	Animism	-1%	4	
Buja	Buja	Zaire	200,000	Animism	0%	1	
Buka-khwe	Local dialects	Botswana	9,000	Animism	0%	1	
**Bukidnon	Manobo, Binukid	Philippines	100,000	Animism	158%	5	
Buli	Buli	Upper Volta	1,000	Islam-Animist	-1%	1	
Bulia	Bulia	Zaire	60,000	Islam-Animist	0%	1	
Bullom, Northern	Bullom, Northern	Sierra Leone	45,000	Animism	0%	1	
Bullom, Southern	Bullom, Southern	Sierra Leone	167,000	Islam-Animist	-1%	1	
Bunak	Bunak	Indonesia	40,000	Islam-Animist	-1%	1	
Bunann in Kashmir	Bunan	India	50,000	Animism	-1%	1	
Bungku	Bungku	Indonesia	2,000	Animism	-1%	1	
Bunu	Bunu	Nigeria	180,000	Animism	-1%	4	
Bura	Bura	Cameroon	150,000	Animism	-1%	1	
Burak	Burak	Nigeria	100,000	Animism	-1%	1	
Buraka-Gbanziri	Buraka-Gbanziri	Congo	2,000	Islam	0%	1	
Buriat	Buriat	China	26,500	Traditional Chinese	-1%	1	
	Buriat	Soviet Russia	315,000	Buddhist-Animist	-1%	1	
Burig	Buriq	China	148,000	Traditional Chinese	-1%	1	
Burig in Kashmir	Burig	India	132,200	Animism	-1%	1	
Burji	Burji	Ethiopia	20,000	Animism	-1%	1	

Name	Country	Group	Population	Religion	%		
Buru	Indonesia	Buru	6,000	Animism	-1%	1	
Burun	Sudan	Burun	5,000	Islam	0%	1	
Burungi	Tanzania	Burungi	20,000	Animism	7%	4	
**Bus Drivers, South Korea	Korea, Republic of	Korean	26,000	Unknown	8%	4	
Busa	Nigeria	Busa (Bokobarn Akiba)	50,000	Islam	1%	6	80
Busami	Indonesia	Busami	350	Animism	-1%	1	
**Busanse	Ghana	Bisa (Busanga)	50,000	Animism	2%	5	
Bushmen (Heikum)	Namibia	Heikum	16,000	Animism	6%	4	
*Bushmen (Hiechware)	Rhodesia	Kwe-Etshari	1,600	Animism	6%	5	
*Bushmen (Kung)	Namibia	Xu	30,000	Animism	6%	6	79
Bushmen in Botswana	Botswana	Buka-khwe	100,000	Animism	7%	4	
Bushoong	Zaire	Bushoong	30,000	Animism	-1%	1	
Bussa	Ethiopia	Bussa	1,000	Animism	-1%	1	
Butawa	Nigeria	Buta	20,000	Islam	0%	5	
Butung	Indonesia	Butung	200,000	Islam-Animist	-1%	1	
Buwid	Philippines	Buwid	6,000	Animism	0%	5	
Bviri	Sudan	Bviri	16,000	Islam	0%	1	
Bwa	Upper Volta	Buamu (Bobo Wule)	140,000	Animism	9%	6	80
Bwisi	Zaire	Bwa	35,000	Animism	-1%	1	
Cacua	Zaire	Bwisi	6,000	Animism	0%	1	
Caiwa	Colombia	Cacua	150	Animism	-1%	1	
Cakchiquel, Central	Brazil	Caiwa	7,000	Animism	-1%	1	
Caluyanhon	Guatemala	Cakchiquel, Central	300,000	Animism	-1%	1	
*Cambodians	Philippines	Caluyanhon	30,000	Christo-Paganism	-1%	5	
Campa	Thailand	Northern Kamer	1,000,000	Buddhist-Animist	-1%	5	
Camsa	Peru	Campa	5,000	Animism	-1%	1	
Candoshi	Colombia	Camsa	2,000	Animism	-1%	1	
Canela	Peru	Candoshi	3,000	Animism	-1%	1	
Capanahua	Brazil	Canela	1,400	Animism	-1%	1	
Carapana	Peru	Capanahua	500	Animism	-1%	1	
Cashibo	Colombia	Carapana	200	Animism	-1%	1	
*Casiguranin	Peru	Cashibo	1,500	Animism	-1%	1	
Cayapa	Philippines	Casiguranin	10,000	Nominal Christian	17%	4	
***Cebu, Middle-Class	Ecuador	Cayapa	3,000	Animism	-1%	1	
*Central Thailand Farmers	Philippines	Cebuano	500,000	Christo-Paganism	12%	4	
Cewa	Thailand	Thai	5,000,000	Buddhist-Animist	18%	5	81
Ch'iang	Zambia	Cewa	200,000	Animism	0%	1	
***Ch'ol Sabanilla	China	Ch'iang	77,000	Traditional Chinese	-1%	1	
Ch'ol Tila	Mexico	Ch'ol	20,000	Christo-Paganism	5%	4	
Chacobo	Mexico	Tila Chol	38,000	Animism	1%	5	
Chagga	Bolivia	Chacobo	250	Animism	-1%	1	
Chaghatai	Tanzania	Chagga	800,000	Animism	0%	1	
	Afghanistan	Chaghatai	300,000	Islam	-1%	1	

NAME	COUNTRY	LANGUAGE	GROUP SIZE	PRIMARY RELIGION	% CHR	V	VOL U.P.
Chakfem-Mushere	Nigeria	Chakfem-Mushere	5,000	Animism	-1%	1	
*Chakmas of Mizoram	India	Chakma	20,000	Buddhist-Animist	-1%	5	81
Chakossi in Ghana	Ghana	Chakossi	31,000	Animism	1%	5	
Chakossi in Togo	Togo	Chakossi	20,000	Animism	3%	4	
Chala	Ghana	Chala	1,000	Islam-Animist	0%	1	
*Cham (Western)	Viet Nam	Cham	45,000	Hindu-Animist	1%	5	
	Kampuchea, Democratic	Cham	90,000	Islam	0%	6	80
Chamacoco, Bahia Negra	Paraguay	Chamacoco, Bahia Negra	1,000	Animism	-1%	1	
Chamalin	Soviet Russia	Chamalin	5,320	Unknown	0%	1	
Chamari in Madhya Pradesh	India	Chamari	5,320	Hindu-Animist	-1%	1	
Chamba Daka	Nigeria	Chamba Daka	66,000	Islam-Animist	-1%	1	
Chamba Leko	Nigeria	Chamba Leko	30,000	Islam-Animist	-1%	1	
Chameali in H.P.	India	Chameali	52,970	Hindu-Animist	-1%	1	
Chami	Colombia	Chami	3,000	Animism	-1%	1	
Chamicuro	Peru	Chamicuro	150	Animism	-1%	1	
Chamula	Mexico	Tzotzil (Chamula)	15,000	Christo-Paganism	10%	4	
*Chang-Pa of Kashmir	India	Tibetan Dialect	50,000	Christo-Paganism	0%	5	79
Chara	Ethiopia	Chara	7,000	Buddhist-Animist	0%	5	81
Chatino, Nopala	Mexico	Chatino, Nopala	1,000	Animism	-1%	1	
Chatino, Panixtlahuaca	Mexico	Chatino, Panixtlahuaca	7,500	Christo-Paganism	-1%	1	
Chatino, Tataltepec	Mexico	Chatino, Tataltepec	4,500	Christo-Paganism	0%	1	
Chatino, Yaitepec	Mexico	Spanish	2,000	Christo-Paganism	-1%	1	
Chatino, Zacatepec	Mexico	Chatino, Zacatepec	2,000	Christo-Paganism	-1%	1	
Chatino, Zenzontepec	Mexico	Chatino, Zenzontepec	500	Christo-Paganism	0%	1	
Chaungtha	Burma	Chaungtha	4,600	Buddhist-Animist	0%	1	
Chawai	Nigeria	Chawai	34,600	Animism	-1%	1	
**Chayahuita	Peru	Chayawita	6,000	Christo-Paganism	11%	4	
Chenchu in Andhra Pradesh	India	Chenchu	17,610	Hindu-Animist	-1%	1	
Cherkess	Soviet Russia	Cherkes	40,000	Islam	0%	1	
Chero in Bihar	India	Chero	28,370	Animism	-1%	1	
Chiga	Uganda	Chiga	272,000	Animism	0%	1	
Chik-Barik in Bihar	India	Chik-Barik	30,040	Animism	-1%	1	
Chin, Asho	China	Traditional Chinese	95,500	Traditional Chinese	-1%	1	
Chin, Asho	Burma	Chin, Asho	11,000	Buddhist-Animist	-1%	1	
Chin, Falam	Burma	Chin, Falam	92,000	Buddhist-Animist	-1%	1	
Chin, Haka	Burma	Chin, Haka	85,000	Buddhist-Animist	-1%	1	
Chin, Khumi	Burma	Chin, Khumi	30,000	Buddhist-Animist	-1%	1	
Chin, Ngawn	Burma	Chin, Ngawn	5,000	Buddhist-Animist	-1%	1	
Chin, Tiddim	Burma	Chin, Tiddim	38,000	Buddhist-Animist	-1%	1	
Chinanteco, Tepinapa	Mexico	Chinanteco, Tepinapa	3,000	Christo-Paganism	0%	1	
Chinanteco, Ayotzintepec	Mexico	Chinanteco, Ayotzintepec	2,000	Christo-Paganism	0%	1	
Chinanteco, Chiltepec	Mexico	Chinanteco, Chiltepec	3,000	Christo-Paganism	0%	1	

NAME	COUNTRY	LANGUAGE	GROUP SIZE	PRIMARY RELIGION	% CHR	V	VOL U.P.
*Chinese of W. Malaysia	Malaysia	Cantonese	3,500,000	Traditional Chinese	4%	4	
*Chinese Refugees in Macau	Macau	Cantonese	100,000	Traditional Chinese	1%	5	81
**Chinese Refugees, France	France	Tien-Chiu	100,000	Traditional Chinese	2%	4	79
**Chinese Restaurant Wkrs.	France	Won Chow	50,000	Traditional Chinese	2%	4	
**Chinese Stud., Australia	Australia	Chinese Dialects	5,500	Secularism	5%	4	
**Chinese Students Glasgow	United Kingdom	Mandarin	1,000	Traditional Chinese	15%	4	
Chinese Villagers	Hong Kong	Cantonese	500,000	Traditional Chinese	1%	3	
Chinga	Cameroon	Chinga	12,600	Animism	0%	1	
	Cameroon	Chinga	12,600	Animism	0%	1	
Chingp'o	China	Chingp'o	101,850	Traditional Chinese	-1%	1	
Chip	Nigeria	Chip	6,000	Animism	-1%	1	
Chipaya	Bolivia	Chipaya	850	Animism	-1%	1	
Chiquitano	Bolivia	Chiquitano	20,000	Animism	8%	5	
**Chiriguano	Argentina	Guarani (Bolivian)	15,000	Animism	8%	5	79
Chitralis	Pakistan	Khuwar	120,000	Islam	0%	1	
Chocho	Mexico	Spanish	2,500	Christo-Paganism	0%	1	
Chodhari in Gujarat	India	Chodhari	138,980	Hindu-Animist	-1%	1	
Chokobo	Nigeria	Chokobo	425	Animism	-1%	1	
Chokwe (Lunda)	Zambia	Chokwe	25,000	Animism	0%	1	
	Angola	Chokwe	400,000	Animism	0%	1	
Chola Naickans	India	Canarese	100	Animism	9%	5	
Chopi	Mozambique	Chopi	400,000	Animism	0%	1	
Chorote	Argentina	Chorote	500	Animism	-1%	3	
	Paraguay	Chorote	nr	Animism	-1%	1	
Chorti	Guatemala	Chorti	25,000	Animism	-1%	1	
**Chrau	Viet Nam	Jro	15,000	Animism	14%	4	
Chuabo	Mozambique	Chwabo	250,000	Animism	9%	4	81
Chuang	China	Chuang	12,000,000	Animism	0%	5	
Chuj	Guatemala	Chuj	15,000	Animism	-1%	1	
Chuj of San Mateo Ixtatan	Guatemala	Chuj, San Mateo Ixtatan	17,000	Animism	12%	5	
Chuj, San Mateo Ixtatan	Mexico	Chuj, San Mateo Ixtatan	3,000	Animism	-1%	1	
Chukot	Soviet Russia	Chukot	14,000	Unknown	0%	1	
Chulupe	Paraguay	Chulupe	5,000	Christo-Paganism	-1%	1	
Chungchia	China	Chungchia	1,500,000	Traditional Chinese	0%	1	
Churahi in H.P.	India	Churahi	34,670	Hindu-Animist	-1%	1	
Chwang	China	Chwang	7,785,410	Traditional Chinese	-1%	1	
Cinta Larga	Brazil	Cinta Larga	500	Animism	-1%	1	
Circassian	Turkey	Circassian	113,370	Islam	-1%	1	
Cirebon	Indonesia	Javanese, Tjirebon	2,500,000	Islam-Animist	1%	5	
***Citak	Indonesia	Citak (Asmat)	6,500	Animism	-1%	1	
Citak	Indonesia	Citak	6,000	Animism	-1%	5	
Cocama	Peru	Cocama	18,000	Animism	-1%	1	
Cocopa	Mexico	Cocopa	900	Christo-Paganism	0%	1	

Name	Country	Language/Name	Population	Religion			
Cofan	Colombia	Cofan	250	Animism	-1%	1	
Cogui	Colombia	Cogui	4,000	Animism	-1%	1	
*Comorians	Comoros	Comorian (Shingazidja)	300,000	Islam	1%	6	79
***Copacabana Apt. Dwellers	Brazil	Portuguese	400,000	Nominal Christian	1%	4	
Cora	Mexico	Cora	8,000	Christo-Paganism	-1%	4	
**Coreguaje	Colombia	Coreguaje	500	Animism	-1%	1	
Coreguaje	Colombia	Coreguaje	500	Animism	-1%	1	
Cubeo	Colombia	Cubeo	2,000	Animism	-1%	1	
Cuiba	Colombia	Cuiba	2,000	Animism	-1%	1	
Cuicateco, Tepeuxila	Mexico	Cuicateco, Tepeuxila	10,000	Christo-Paganism	-1%	1	
Cuicateco, Teutila	Mexico	Cuicateco, Teutila	6,000	Christo-Paganism	-1%	1	
Cujareno	Peru	Cujareno	100	Animism	-1%	1	
Culina	Brazil	Culina	800	Animism	-1%	1	
*Cuna	Colombia	Cuna	600	Animism	-1%	1	
Cuna	Colombia	Cuna	600	Animism	7%	5	79
Curipaco	Colombia	Curipaco	2,500	Animism	-1%	1	
Cuyonon	Philippines	Cuyonon	49,000	Christo-Paganism	-1%	1	
Daba	Cameroon	Daba	31,000	Animism	-1%	1	
	Cameroon	Daba	31,000	Animism	-1%	1	
Dabra	Indonesia	Dabra	100	Animism	-1%	1	
Dadiya	Nigeria	Dadiya	2,300	Islam	-1%	1	
Dagada	Indonesia	Dagada	30,000	Animism	-1%	1	
Dagari	Ghana	Dagari	200,000	Animism	-1%	4	
**Dagomba	Upper Volta	Dagbani	150,000	Islam-Animist	-1%	4	
Dagur	Ghana	Dagur	350,000	Islam-Animist	-1%	1	
Dai	China	Dai	22,600	Traditional Chinese	-1%	1	
Dair	Burma	Dair	10,000	Buddhist-Animist	0%	1	
Daju of Dar Dadju	Sudan	Daju of Dar Dadju	225	Islam	-1%	1	
Daju of Dar Fur	Chad	Daju of Dar Sila	27,000	Islam-Animist	0%	1	
Daju of Dar Sila	Sudan	Daju	12,000	Animism	-1%	1	
Daju of West Kordofan	Chad	Dakanci	33,000	Islam-Animist	-1%	1	
*Daka	Sudan	Dan	6,000	Islam	3%	4	
Dan	Nigeria	Dan	10,000	Animism	2%	5	
***Dan	Ivory Coast	Dangaleat	270,000	Animism	-1%	1	
Dangaleat	Liberia	Dani, Grand Valley	94,000	Islam-Animist	3%	6	79
*Dani, Baliem	Chad	Burmese	20,000	Islam-Animist	3%	2	
Danu	Indonesia	Dargin	50,000	Animism	0%	1	
Dargin	Burma	Dass	70,000	Buddhism	0%	1	
Dass	Soviet Russia	Dathanik	231,000	Islam	-1%	1	
Dathanik	Nigeria	Davaweno	8,830	Islam-Animist	-1%	1	
Davaweno	Ethiopia	Gujarati	18,000	Animism	-1%	1	
Dawoodi Muslims	Philippines		13,000	Christo-Paganism	-1%	1	
	India		225,000	Islam	0%	4	

NAME	LANGUAGE	COUNTRY	GROUP SIZE	PRIMARY RELIGION	% CHR	V	VOL U.P.
Day	Day	Central African Empire	1,600	Animism	<1%	1	
Daza	Dzaga	Chad	159,000	Islam	<1%	5	
Deccani Muslims	Dakhni (Urdu)	India	nr	Islam	<1%	5	
Degema	Degeme	Nigeria	10,000	Animism	<1%	1	
Dem	Dem	Indonesia	2,000	Animism	<1%	1	
Demta	Demta	Indonesia	840	Animism	<1%	1	
Dendi	Dendi	Benin	40,000	Islam	0%	3	
Dengese	Dengese	Zaire	4,000	Animism	<1%	1	
Deno	Deno	Nigeria	10,000	Islam	<1%	1	
Deori in Assam	Deori	India	14,940	Animism	<1%	1	
Dera	Dera	Nigeria	20,000	Islam	<1%	1	
Desano	Desano	Brazil	1,040	Animism	<1%	1	
*Dewein	De	Liberia	5,000	Islam	1%	4	
Dghwede	Dghwede	Cameroon	13,000	Animism	<1%	1	
*Dghwede	Dghwede	Cameroon	13,000	Animism	<1%	5	
	Zighvana(Dghwede)	Nigeria	13,000	Animism	<1%	1	
Dhaiso	Dhaiso	Tanzania	12,000	Animism	<1%	5	
Dhanka in Gujarat	Dhanka	India	10,230	Animism	<1%	1	
Dhanwar in Madhya Pradesh	Dhanwar	India	21,140	Animism	<1%	1	
**Dhodias	Dhodia Dialects	India	300,000	Hindu-Animist	1%	4	
**Dhurwa	Parji	India	20,000	Hindu-Animist	0%	1	
Dida	Dida	Ivory Coast	115,000	Islam-Animist	<1%	1	
**Dida	Dida	Ivory Coast	120,000	African Independent	7%	4	
Didinga	Didinga	Sudan	30,000	Animism	<1%	1	
	Didinga	Sudan	3,000	Islam	0%	1	
Didoi	Didoi	Soviet Russia	7,000	Unknown	<1%	1	
Digo	Digo	Kenya	168,000	Islam	0%	1	
	Digo	Tanzania	30,000	Animism	<1%	1	
Dimasa in Cachar	Dimasa	India	37,900	Animism	<1%	4	
Dime	Dime	Ethiopia	2,000	Animism	<1%	1	
Dinka	Dinka	Sudan	1,944,000	Animism	4%	5	
Dinka, Agar	Dinka, Agar	Sudan	16,000	Islam	0%	1	
Diola	Diola	Guinea-Bissau	15,000	Islam	3%	5	80
	Diola	Senegal	266,000	Islam-Animist	1%	5	
	Diola	Nigeria	11,000	Islam-Animist	<1%	1	
Dirim	Dirim	Nigeria	3,750	Islam	<1%	1	
Dirya	Dirya	Nigeria			<1%	1	
Divehi	Divehi	Maldives		Islam	0%	6	80
Djuka	Djuka	Surinam	120,000	Christo-Paganism	<1%	1	
Doe	Doe	Tanzania	8,000	Animism	<1%	1	
*Dog-Pa of Ladakh	Shrina	India	2,000	Animism	<1%	1	
Doghosie	Doghosie	Upper Volta	7,900	Islam-Animist	0%	6	81
*Dogon	Dogon	Mali	312,000	Animism	10%	6	79
Dolgans	Dolgan	Soviet Russia	4,900	Unknown	0%	1	

Dompago	Benin	Dompago	19,000	Animism	7% 4
Dongjoi	Sudan	Dongjoi	9,000	Islam	0% 1
Dongo	Sudan	Dongo	100	Islam	0% 1
	Zaire	Dongo	5,000	Animism	0% 1
**Doohwaayo	Cameroon	Doohyaayo	15,000	Animism	12% 5
Dorlin in Andhra Pradesh	India	Dorli	24,320	Hindu-Animist	-1% 1
Dorobo	Kenya	Nandi	22,000	Animism	1% 5
	Tanzania	Hadza	3,000	Animism	1% 4
Dorze	Ethiopia	Dorze	3,000	Animism	-1% 1
Druzes	Israel	Arabic	33,000	Folk Religion	0% 6 79
**Dubla	India	Gujarati	202,218	Hindu-Animist	4% 4
Dubu	Indonesia	Dubu	130	Animism	-1% 1
Duguir	Nigeria	Duquri	12,000	Islam	-1% 1
Duguza	Nigeria	Duguza	2,000	Islam	-1% 1
**Duka	Nigeria	Dukanci	10,000	Animism	1% 5
Duma	Gabon	Duma	10,000	Animism	0% 1
*Dumagat , Casiguran	Philippines	Dumagat	1,000	Animism	3% 6 81
Dungan	Soviet Russia	Dungan	39,000	Islam	0% 1
Duru	Cameroon	Duru	20,000	Animism	-1% 4
Dusun	Malaysia	Kadazan	160,000	Animism	nr 6 81
Duvele	Indonesia	Duvele	500	Animism	-1% 1
Dyan	Upper Volta	Dyan	8,000	Islam-Animist	0% 1
Dyerma	Niger	Dyerma	1,000,000	Islam-Animist	1% 6 80
	Nigeria	Dyerma	50,000	Islam	-1% 1
Dyola	Gambia	Dyola	216,000	Islam-Animist	-1% 1
	Guinea-Bissau	Dyola	nr	Islam-Animist	-1% 1
	Senegal	Dyola	nr	Islam-Animist	0% 1
Ebira	Nigeria	Ebira	325,000	Islam-Animist	-1% 1
Ebrie	Ivory Coast	Ebrie	50,000	Islam-Animist	-1% 1
Edo	Nigeria	Edo	430,000	Animism	-1% 1
Efik	Nigeria	Efik	26,300	Animism	-1% 1
Efutop	Nigeria	Efutop	10,000	Animism	-1% 1
Eggon	Nigeria	Eggon	80,000	Animism	12% 5
Ejagham	Nigeria	Ejagham	100,000	Animism	-1% 1
Ekagi	Indonesia	Ekagi	100,000	Animism	-1% 1
Ekajuk	Nigeria	Ekajuk	15,000	Animism	-1% 1
Eket	Nigeria	Eket	22,000	Animism	-1% 1
Ekpeye	Nigeria	Ekpeye	30,000	Animism	-1% 1
El Molo	Kenya	Samburu	1,000	Animism	3% 4
Eleme	Nigeria	Eleme	16,000	Animism	-1% 1
Emai-Iuleha-Ora	Nigeria	Emai-Iuleha-Ora	48,000	Animism	-1% 1
Embera, Northern	Colombia	Embera	2,000	Animism	-1% 1
Emumu	Indonesia	Emumu	1,100	Animism	-1% 1

NAME	COUNTRY	LANGUAGE	GROUP SIZE	PRIMARY RELIGION	% CHR	V	VOL U.P.
Engenni	Nigeria	Engenni	10,000	Animism	-1%		1
Enya	Zaire	Enya	7,000	Animism	-1%		1
Eotile	Ivory Coast	Eotile	4,000	Islam-Animist	-1%		1
Epie	Nigeria	Epie	12,000	Animism	-1%		1
Erokwanas	Indonesia	Erokwanas	250	Animism	-1%		1
Esan	Nigeria	Esan	200,000	Animism	-1%		1
Eton	Cameroon	Eton	112,000	Animism	0%		1
Eton	Cameroon	Eton	112,000	Animism	0%		1
Etulo	Nigeria	Etulo	2,900	Animism	-1%		1
Evant	Nigeria	Evant	5,000	Animism	0%		1
Evenki	China	Evenki	7,200	Traditional Chinese	-1%		1
Evenks	Soviet Russia	Evenk	25,000	Buddhist-Animist	0%	5	81
Ewenkis	China	Altaic	10,000	Animism	0%	5	
Fa D'Ambu	Equatorial Guinea	Fa D'Ambu	2,000	Animism	0%	6	
*Factory Workers	Hong Kong	Cantonese	40,000	Unknown	5%		
**Fakai	Nigeria	Faka	15,000	Animism	1%	5	
**Falasha	Ethiopia	Agau	30,000	Judaism	7%	7	79
Fali	Cameroon	Fali	50,000	Islam	7%	7	
Fali	Cameroon	Fali	50,000	Islam	0%		1
**Fali	Nigeria	Fali	25,000	Animism	2%	5	
Farmers of Japan	Japan	Japanese	24,988,740	Traditional Japanese	1%	4	
Fipa	Tanzania	Fipa	78,000	Animism	1%	4	
Fishing Village People	Taiwan	Amoy	150,000	Traditional Chinese	2%	4	
Foau	Indonesia	Foau	230	Animism	-1%		1
Fordat	Indonesia	Fordat	9,770	Animism	-1%		1
Fra-Fra	Ghana	Fra-Fra	230,000	Animism	-1%		1
Fula	Guinea	Fula	1,500,000	Islam	1%	4	
Fula	Sierra Leone	Fula	250,000	Islam	0%	5	
Fula, Cunda	Upper Volta	Fula	250,000	Islam-Animist	-1%		1
Fula, Macina	Gambia	Fula, Macina	70,200	Islam-Animist	-1%		1
Fula, Peuhala	Mali	Fula, Peuhala	450,000	Animism	0%		1
Fulah	Upper Volta	Fulani	300,000	Islam	1%	5	
*Fulani	Benin	Fulani	70,000	Islam-Animist	1%	4	79
*Fulani	Cameroon	Fulani	250,000	Islam-Animist	1%	5	
*Fulbe	Ghana	Fulani	5,500	Islam-Animist	0%	5	
Fuliro	Zaire	Fuliro	56,000	Animism	-1%		1
Fulnio	Brazil	Fulnio	1,500	Animism	0%		1
Fungom, Northern	Cameroon	Fungom, Northern	15,000	Animism	0%		1
	Cameroon	Fungom, Northern	15,000	Animism	-1%		1
Fungor	Sudan	Fungor	4,500	Islam	0%		1
Furu	Zaire	Furu	5,000	Animism	0%		1
Fyam	Nigeria	Fyam	14,000	Animism	-1%		1

Name	Country	Name	Population	Religion		
Fyer	Nigeria	Fyer	3,000	Animism	-10	1
Ga-Dang	Philippines	Ga-Dang	5,500	Animism	10	5
*Gabbra	Ethiopia	Gabrinja	nr	Folk Religion	10	4
Gabbra	Kenya	Galla	12,000	Folk Religion	10	4
Gabri	Chad	Gabri	20,000	Islam-Animist	-10	1
Gadaban in Andhra Pradesh	India	Gadaba	20,410	Hindu-Animist	10	1
Gaddi in Himachal Pradesh	India	Gaddi	70,220	Hindu-Animist	10	4
Gade	Nigeria	Gade	25,000	Animism	10	4
Gagauzes	Soviet Russia	Gaguaz	157,000	Christo-Paganism	10	1
**Gagre	Pakistan	Punjabi	40,000	Animism	10	4
Gagu	Ivory Coast	Gagou	25,000	Animism	10	4
Galambi	Nigeria	Galambi	1,000	Islam	-10	1
Galeshis	Iran	Galeshi	2,000	Islam	00	3
*Galla (Bale)	Ethiopia	Galla	750,000	Islam-Animist	70	5
Galla of Bucho	Ethiopia	Gallinya (Oromo)	1,500	Christo-Paganism	10	3
Galla, Harar	Ethiopia	Gallinya	1,305,400	Islam	10	5
Galler	Laos	Galler	50,000	Animism	10	4
Galong in Assam	India	Galong	36,860	Hindu-Animist	-10	1
Gambai	Chad	Gambai	200,000	Islam-Animist	-10	1
Gamti in Gujarat	India	Gamti	136,210	Hindu-Animist	-10	1
Gan	Upper Volta	Gan	4,000	Islam-Animist	-10	1
Gane	Indonesia	Gane	1,500	Animism	-10	1
Gangam	Togo	Gangam	16,000	Islam-Animist	00	1
Gangte in Assam	India	Gangte	6,030	Hindu-Animist	-10	1
Gawar-Bati	Afghanistan	Gawar-Bati	21,100	Hindu-Animist	-10	1
Gawari in Andhra Pradesh	India	Gawari	4,000	Animism	-10	1
Gawwada	Ethiopia	Gawwada	200,000	Islam-Animist	00	4	80
Gayo	Indonesia	Gayo	66,000	Animism	30	4
Gbande	Guinea	Bandi	500,000	Animism	20	6	80
Gbari	Nigeria	Gbari	350,000	Islam	-10	1
Gbaya	Nigeria	Gbaya	1,800	Islam	00	3
Gbaya-Ndogo	Sudan	Gbaya-Ndogo	9,000	Islam	00	1
Gbazantche	Benin	Gbazantche	600	Islam	00	1
Gberi	Sudan	Gberi	250,000	Animism	-10	1
Gedeo	Ethiopia	Gedeo	2,650	Islam	-10	1
Geji	Nigeria	Geji	13,300	Islam	-10	1
Gera	Nigeria	Gera	4,700	Islam	-10	1
Geruma	Nigeria	Geruma	200	Animism	-10	1
Gesa	Indonesia	Gesa	4,000	Buddhist-Animist	-10	1
Gheko	Burma	Gheko	50,000	Animism	40	5
**Ghimeera	Ethiopia	Ginira	2,000	Islam	00	1
Ghol	Sudan	Ghol	9,000	Animism	-10	1
Ghotuo	Nigeria	Ghotuo				

NAME	COUNTRY	LANGUAGE	GROUP SIZE	PRIMARY RELIGION	% CHR	VOL V U.P.
Ghulfan	Sudan	Ghulfan	3,300	Islam	0%	1
Gidar	Cameroon	Gidar	50,000	Animism	-1%	1
	Cameroon	Gidar	50,000	Animism	-1%	1
	Chad	Gidar	50,000	Islam-Animist	-1%	1
Gidicho	Ethiopia	Gidicho	500	Animism	-1%	4
Gilakis	Iran	Gilaki	1,950,000	Islam	1%	1
Gilyak	Soviet Russia	Gilyak	4,400	Unknown	0%	1
Gio	Liberia	Dan (Yacouba)	92,000	Animism	5%	5
Giryama	Kenya	Giryama	335,900	Animism	9%	4
Gisei	Cameroon	Masa	10,000	Animism	-1%	1
Gisiga	Cameroon	Gisiga	30,000	Animism	11%	4
*Glavda	Nigeria	Glavda	19,000	Animism	4%	5
Gobato	Ethiopia	Gobato	1,000	Animism	-1%	1
Gobeze	Ethiopia	Gobeze	22,000	Animism	-1%	1
***Godie	Ivory Coast	Godie	20,000	Animism	12%	4
Goemai	Nigeria	Goemai	80,000	Animism	-1%	1
Gogo	Tanzania	Gogo	280,000	Animism	0%	1
Gokana	Nigeria	Gokana	54,000	Animism	-1%	1
Gola	Sierra Leone	Gola	47,000	Islam-Animist	-1%	1
	Liberia	Mende	1,400	Islam-Animist	-1%	1
Golo	Chad	Golo	3,400	Islam-Animist	-1%	5
*Gonds	India	Gondi	4,000,000	Animism	-1%	5
Gonja	Ghana	Gonja	100,000	Islam-Animist	2%	5
*Gorkha	India	Napali	180,000	Hinduism	0%	4
Goroa	Tanzania	Goroa	180,000	Animism	0%	1
Gorontalo	Indonesia	Gorontalo	500,000	Islam	-1%	1
Gosha	Kenya	Gosha	3,000	Islam-Animist	0%	3
Goudari	Iran	Goudari	2,000	Islam	0%	3
Gouin-Turka	Upper Volta	Gouin-Turka	25,000	Islam-Animist	-1%	1
Goulai	Chad	Goulai	30,000	Islam-Animist	-1%	1
Gourency	Upper Volta	Gourendi	300,000	Animism	5%	4
**Gouro	Ivory Coast	Gouro	200,000	Animism	4%	4
Gouwar	Cameroon	Gouwar	5,000	Animism	0%	1
	Cameroon	Gouwar	5,000	Animism	0%	1
Government officials	Thailand	Thai	100,000	Buddhism	0%	3
Grasia in Gujarat	India	Grasia	27,160	Hindu-Animist	-1%	1
**Grebo	Liberia	Grebo Dialects	65,000	Animism	8%	4
Grunshi	Ghana	not reported	200,000	Animism	-1%	4
Gu	Benin	Gu	173,000	Animism	0%	1
Guaiagui	Paraguay	Guaiagui	350	Animism	-1%	1
Guajajara	Brazil	Guajajara	5,000	Animism	-1%	1
Guajibo	Colombia	Guajibo	15,000	Animism	-1%	1
*Guajiro	Colombia	Guajiro	60,000	Animism	12%	5

258

Name	Language	Country	Population	Religion	
Guambiano	Guambiano	Colombia	9,000	Animism	-1% 1
Guana	Guana	Paraguay	3,000	Animism	0% 1
*Guanano	Guanano	Colombia	800	Christo-Paganism	1% 4 79
**Guarani	Guarani	Bolivia	15,000	Animism	10% 6 79
Guarayu	Guarayu	Bolivia	5,000	Christo-Paganism	1% 5
Guarojio	Guarojio	Mexico	5,000	Christo-Paganism	-1% 1
Guayabero	Guayabero	Colombia	700	Animism	-1% 1
Guayabevo	Guayabero	Colombia	600	Animism	8% 5
Gude	Gude	Cameroon	100,000	Animism	-1% 4
Gudu	Gudu	Nigeria	40,000	Animism	-1% 1
Guduf	Guduf	Nigeria	1,200	Animism	-1% 1
Guere	Guere	Ivory Coast	21,300	Animism	-1% 1
Gugu-Yalanji	Gugu-yalanji	Australia	117,870	Islam-Animist	-1% 4
Gujarati	Gujarati	United Kingdom	5,400	Animism	-1% 1
Gujarati	Gujarati	India	300,000	Hinduism	1% 6
Gujars of Kashmir	Gujari	India	150,000	Islam-Animist	0% 5 81
Gujuri	Gujuri	Afghanistan	10,000	Islam	-1% 1
Gula	Gula	Chad	2,500	Islam-Animist	0% 1
Gulfe	Gulfe	Cameroon	36,000	Animism	0% 1
Gulfe	Gulfe	Cameroon	36,000	Animism	-1% 1
Gumuz	Gumuz	Ethiopia	53,000	Animism	0% 1
Gumuz	Gumuz	Sudan	40,000	Islam	0% 1
Gurage	Gurage Dialects	Ethiopia	750,000	Islam-Animist	3% 6 80
Gure-Kahugu	Gure-Kahugu	Nigeria	5,000	Islam	-1% 1
Gurensi	Gurenne	Ghana	250,000	Animism	-1% 4
Gurma	Gurma	Upper Volta	250,000	Islam-Animist	0% 1
Gurung	Gurung	Nepal	172,000	Hinduism	0% 5
Guruntum-Mbaaru	Guruntum-Mbaaru	Nigeria	8,300	Islam	-1% 1
Gwa	Gwa	Ivory Coast	10,000	Islam-Animist	-1% 5
Gwandara	Gwandara	Nigeria	25,000	Islam	-1% 1
Gwari Matai	Gwari Matai	Nigeria	200,000	Animism	-1% 1
Gwere	Gwere	Uganda	162,000	Islam	-1% 3
	not reported	Soviet Russia	175,000	Christo-Paganism	0% 1
*Gypsies in Spain	Rom (Serbian Kaldnash)	Spain	200,000	Islam	0% 1
*Gypsies in Yugoslavia	Romany (Serbian Kaldnash)	Yugoslavia	800,000	Folk Religion	3% 6 79
Ha	Ha	Tanzania	286,000	Islam	17% 4
**Hadiyya	Hadiyya	Ethiopia	700,000	Animism	-1% 1
**Hadrami	Arabic	Yemen, Democratic	151,000	Islam	0% 3
**Hajong	Bengali	Bangladesh	17,000	Hindu-Animist	1% 5
***Halam in Tripura	Tribal dialects	India	20,000	Animism	1% 5
Halbi in Madhya Pradesh	Halbi	India	349,260	Hindu-Animist	3% 5
Hallam	Hallam	Burma	11,000	Buddhist-Animist	-1% 1

NAME	COUNTRY	LANGUAGE	GROUP SIZE	PRIMARY RELIGION	% CHR	V	VOL U.P.
Hangaza	Tanzania	Hangaza	54,000	Animism	0%	1	
Hani	China	Hani	138,000	Traditional Chinese	<1%	1	
Hanonoo	Philippines	Hanonoo	6,000	Christo-paganism	<1%	1	
Harari	Ethiopia	Harari	13,380	Islam	<1%	1	
Harauti in Rajasthan	India	Harauti	334,380	Hindu-Animist	<1%	1	
Hatsa	Tanzania	Hatsa	2,000	Animism	<1%	1	
*Havasupai	United States of America	English	300	Unknown	3%	4	
Havu	Zaire	Havu	262,000	Animism	0%	4	
Havunese	Indonesia	Havunese)	40,000	Animism	0%	1	
Haya	Tanzania	Haya	276,000	Animism	0%	1	
Hehe	Tanzania	Hehe	192,000	Animism	0%	1	
Heiban	Sudan	Heiban	25,000	Islam	<1%	1	
Helong	Indonesia	Helong	10,000	Animism	0%	1	
Herero	Botswana	Herero	5,000	Animism	<1%	1	
	Namibia	Dhimba	40,000	Animism	<1%	1	
Heso	Zaire	Heso	6,000	Animism	0%	1	
**Hewa	Papua New Guinea	Hewa	1,500	Animism	5%	6	79
Hezareh	Iran	Hezara'i	nr	Islam	5%	3	
***High School Students	Hong Kong	Cantonese	453,000	Traditional Chinese	7%	4	
***Higi	Nigeria	Higi	150,000	Animism	7%	5	
Hixkaryana	Brazil	Hixkaryana	150	Animism	<1%	1	
Hkun	Burma	Shan	20,000	Buddhism	0%	2	
Ho in Bihar	India	Ho	749,800	Hindu-Animist	<1%	1	
Hohodene	Brazil	Hohodene	1,000	Animism	<1%	1	
Holiya in Madhya Pradesh	India	Holiya	3,090	Hindu-Animist	<1%	1	
Holoholo	Tanzania	Holoholo	5,000	Animism	0%	1	
Holu	Angola	Holu	12,000	Animism	4%	5	
Hopi	United States of America	Hopi	11,000	Animism	13%	5	81
**Hotel Workers in Manila	Philippines	Pilipino	8,500	Nominal Christian	<1%	1	
Hrangkhol	Burma	Hrangkhol	215	Buddhist-Animist	<1%	1	
Huachipaire	Peru	Huachipaire	5,000	Animism	<1%	1	
Huambisa	Peru	Huambisa		Animism	<1%	1	
Huasteco	Mexico	Huasteco	80,000	Christo-Paganism	5%	5	
**Huave	Mexico	Huave	18,000	Christo-Paganism	0%	6	80
Hui	China	Hui-hui-yu	5,200,000	Islam	<1%	1	
Huichol	Mexico	Huichol	8,000	Christo-Paganism	0%	5	
**Huila	Angola	Huila	200,000	Animism	1%	4	
Huitoto, Meneca	Colombia	Huitoto, Meneca	600	Animism	<1%	1	
Huitoto, Murui	Peru	Huitoto, Murui	800	Animism	<1%	1	
Hukwe	Angola	Hukwe	9,000	Animism	3%	4	
Hunde	Zaire	Hunde	33,500	Animism	0%	1	
**Hunzakut	Pakistan	Burushaski	10,000	Islam	0%	6	79
Hupda Maku	Colombia	Hupda Maku	150	Animism	<1%	1	

Name	Alternate Name	Country	Population	Religion	%	Code	Yr
Hwana	Hwana	Nigeria	20,000	Islam	-1%	1	
Hwela-Numu	Hwela-Numu	Ivory Coast	50,000	Islam-Animist	-1%	1	
Hyam	Hyam	Nigeria	60,000	Islam	-1%	1	
Ibaji	Ibaji	Nigeria	30,000	Animism	-1%	4	
**Iban	Iban	Malaysia			nr	6	81
Ibanag	Ibanag	Philippines	319	Animism	-1%	1	
*Ibataan	Ibataan	Philippines	500	Christo-Paganism	0%	4	
Ibibio	Ibibio	Nigeria	2,000,000	Animism	-1%	1	
Ica	Ica	Colombia	3,000	Animism	-1%	1	
Icen	Icen	Nigeria	7,000	Islam-Animist	2%	5	
Idoma	Idoma	Nigeria	300,000	Animism	-1%	1	
Idoma, North	Idoma, North	Nigeria	56,000	Animism	-1%	1	
Ifugao, Antipolo	Keley-i	Philippines	5,000	Animism	6%	5	
*Ifugao (Kalangoya)	Ifugao	Philippines	95,000	Animism	6%	5	
**Ifugao (Kalangoya)	Kalangoya	Philippines	35,000	Animism	5%	4	
Ifugao in Cababuyan	Ifugao	Philippines	4,000	Animism	14%	4	
Ifugao, Ambanad	Ifugao, Ambanad	Philippines	15,000	Animism	-1%	1	
Ifugao, Kiangan	Ifugao, Kiangan	Philippines	25,000	Animism	-1%	1	
Ifumu	Ifumu	Congo	200	Animism	0%	1	
Igala	Igala	Nigeria	350,000	Animism	-1%	1	
Igbirra	Igbirra	Nigeria	400,000	Islam-Animist	14%	6	80
Igede	Igede	Nigeria	70,000	Animism	-1%	1	
Ignaciano	Ignaciano	Bolivia	5,000	Animism	-1%	1	
Igorot	Igorot	Philippines	20,000	Animism	-1%	1	
Iha	Iha	Indonesia	5,500	Animism	-1%	1	
Ihceve	Icheve	Nigeria	5,000	Animism	-1%	1	
Ijo, Central-Western	Ijo	Nigeria	338,700	Animism	-1%	1	
Ijo, Northeast	Ijo	Nigeria	395,300	Animism	-1%	1	
Ijo, Northeast Central	Ijo	Nigeria			-1%	1	
Ikalahan	Ikalahan	Philippines	8,400	Animism	nr	6	
Ikizu	Swahili	Tanzania	40,000	Animism	0%	1	
Ikulu	Ikulu	Nigeria	9,000	Animism	-1%	1	
Ikwere	Ikwere	Nigeria	6,000	Islam	-1%	1	
Ila	Ila	Zambia	200,000	Animism	0%	1	
Ilongot	Ilongot	Philippines	39,000	Animism	-1%	1	
Inallu	Afshari	Iran	5,000	Islam	0%	3	
Inanwatan	Hindustani	Indonesia	1,100	Animism	-1%	1	
Indians in Fiji	Hindustani	Fiji	265,000	Hinduism	2%	6	79
**Indians, East	Gujarati	Rhodesia	9,600	Hinduism	9%	4	
**Indians In Rhodesia	English with Hindi	Trinidad and Tobago	400,000	Hinduism	5%	6	79
*Indust.Workers Yongdungpo	Korean	Korea, Republic of	140,000	Folk Religion	6%	4	
*Industrial Workers	Taiwanese (Hoklo)	Taiwan	500,000	Secularism	2%	5	81
*Industry Laborers-Japan	Japanese	Japan	21,000,000	Traditional Japanese	1%	4	

NAME	COUNTRY	LANGUAGE	GROUP SIZE	PRIMARY RELIGION	% CHR	VOL V	U.P.
Inga	Colombia	Inga	6,000	Christo-Paganism	-1%		1
Ingassana	Sudan	Tabi	35,000	Animism	0%	5	
Ingushes	Soviet Russia	Ingush	158,000	Islam	0%		1
*Inland Sea Island Peoples	Japan	Japanese	1,000,000	Traditional Japanese	1%	4	
Insinai	Philippines	Insinai	10,000	Animism	-1%		1
*Int'l Stud., Los Banos	Philippines	Vietnamese	nr	Islam	2%	4	
Intha	Burma	Intha	80,000	Buddhist-Animist	-1%		1
Iquito	Peru	Spanish	150	Animism	-1%		1
Irahutu	Indonesia	Irahutu	4,000	Animism	-1%		1
Iraqw	Tanzania	Iraqw	218,000	Animism	1%	4	
	Tanzania	Iraqw	103,000	Animism	0%		1
Iravas in Kerala	India	English	3,700,000	Hinduism	1%	4	
Iraya	Philippines	Iraya	6,000	Christo-Paganism	-1%		1
Iresim	Indonesia	Iresim	100	Animism	-1%		1
Iria	Indonesia	Iria	850	Animism	-1%		1
Irigwe	Nigeria	Irigwe	15,000	Animism	-1%		1
***Irulas in Kerala	India	Irula	10,000	Hinduism	0%	4	
Isanzu	Tanzania	Isanzu	12,000	Animism	0%		1
Isekiri	Nigeria	Isekiri	33,000	Animism	-1%		1
**Ishans	Nigeria	Esan	25,000	Nominal Christian	16%	5	
Isneg, Dibagat-Kabugao	Philippines	Isneg, Dibagat-Kabugao	10,000	Animism	-1%		1
Isneg, Karagawan	Philippines	Isneg, Karagawan	8,000	Animism	-1%		1
Isoko	Nigeria	Isoko	20,000	Animism	-1%		1
Itawit	Philippines	Itawit	15,000	Christo-Paganism	-1%		1
Itelmen	Soviet Russia	Itelmen	1,300	Animism	0%		1
Itik	Indonesia	Itik	100	Unknown	-1%		1
Itneg, Adasen	Philippines	Itneg, Adasen	4,000	Christo-Paganism	-1%		1
Itneg, Binongan	Philippines	Itneg, Binongan	7,000	Christo-Paganism	-1%		1
Itneg, Masadiit	Philippines	Itneg, Masadiit	7,500	Christo-Paganism	-1%		1
Itonama	Bolivia	Itonama	110	Animism	-1%		1
Ivbie North-Okpela-Atte	Nigeria	Ivbie North-Okpela-Atte	20,000	Animism	-1%		1
Iwa	Zambia	Iwa	15,000	Animism	-1%		1
*Iwaidja	Austria	Iwaidja	150	Animism	0%		1
Iwur	Indonesia	Iwur	1,000	Animism	-1%		1
Ixil	Guatemala	Cuyolbal	45,000	Christo-Paganism	1%	4	
Iyon	Cameroon	Iyon	4,000	Animism	0%		1
	Cameroon	Iyon	4,000	Animism	0%		1
	Nigeria	Iyon	2,000	Animism	0%		1
Izarek	Nigeria	Izarek	30,000	Animism	-1%		1
Izhor	Soviet Russia	Izhor	1,100	Unknown	0%		1
**Izi	Nigeria	Izi	200,000	Animism	11%	4	
Jaba	Nigeria	Jaba	60,000	Animism	-1%		4
Jacalteco	Guatemala	Jacalteco	12,000	Animism	-1%		1

Group	Country	Language	Population	Religion			
Jagannathi in A.P.	India	Jagannathi	1,310	Hindu-Animist	-1%	1	
Jains	India	Hindi	2,000,000	Jain	-1%	1	
Jama Mapun	Philippines	Cagayan	15,000	Islam-Animist	-1%	5	80
**Jamaican Elite	Jamaica	Jamaican Patois	800,000	Secularism	0%	4	
Jamamadi	Brazil	Jamamadi	1,200	Animism	-1%	1	
Jambi	Indonesia	Indonesian	850,000	Islam-Animist	0%	3	
Jamden	Indonesia	Jamden	14,330	Animism	-1%	1	
Jamshidis	Iran	Jamshidi	1,000	Islam	0%	3	
Janjero	Ethiopia	Janjero	1,000	Animism	-1%	1	
Janjo	Nigeria	Janjo	6,100	Animism	-1%	1	
Japanese in Brazil	Brazil	Japanese	750,000	Buddhism	8%	8	79
**Japanese in Korea	Korea, Republic of	Japanese	5,000	Traditional Japanese	1%	3	
**Japanese Students In USA	United States of America	Japanese	nr	Secularism	1%	4	
Jaqaru	Peru	Jaqaru	2,000	Animism	-1%	1	
**Jarawa	Nigeria	Jara	40,000	Islam	-1%	5	
Jaranchi	Nigeria	Jaranchi	150,000	Animism	-6%	5	
Jatapu in Andhra Pradesh	India	Jatapu	36,450	Hindu-Animist	-1%	1	
Jati	Afghanistan	Jati	1,000	Islam	-1%	1	
Jaunsari in Uttar Pradesh	India	Jaunsari	56,560	Hindu-Animist	-1%	1	
**Javanese (rural)	Indonesia	Javanese	60,000,000	Islam-Animist	2%	6	79
**Javanese of Central Java	Indonesia	Javanese	20,000,000	Islam-Animist	5%	5	
**Javanese of Pejompongan	Indonesia	Bahasa Jawa	5,000	Islam	7%	4	
Jebero	Peru	Spanish	3,000	Animism	-1%	1	
*Jeepney Drivers in Manila	Philippines	Pilipino	20,000	Nominal Christian	nr	5	81
	Philippines	Pilipino	20,000	Nominal Christian	nr	5	81
Jemez Pueblo	United States of America	Tewa (Jemez)	1,800	Christo-Paganism	5%	4	
Jeng	Laos	Jeng	500	Animism	-1%	1	
Jera	Nigeria	Jera	23,000	Islam	-1%	4	
Jerawa	Nigeria	not reported	70,000	Animism	0%	3	
*Jewish Imgrnts.-American	Israel	Hebrew	25,797	Judaism	0%	3	
*Jewish Imgrnts.-Argentine	Israel	Hebrew	17,686	Judaism	0%	3	
*Jewish Imgrnts.-Australia	Israel	Hebrew	1,257	Judaism	0%	3	
*Jewish Imgrnts.-Brazilian	Israel	Hebrew	4,005	Judaism	0%	3	
*Jewish Imgrnts.-Mexican	Israel	Hebrew	1,065	Judaism	0%	3	
*Jewish Imgrnts.-Uruguayan	Israel	Hebrew	2,720	Judaism	0%	3	
*Jewish Immigrants, Other	Israel	Hebrew	5,520	Judaism	0%	3	
Jews of Iran	Iran	Farsi	93,000	Judaism	1%	4	
Jews of Montreal	Canada	English	120,000	Judaism	1%	5	
Jews, Sephardic	Canada	French	26,000	Judaism	1%	3	
Jharia in Orissa	India	Jharia	2,060	Hinduism	-1%	5	
*Jibu	Nigeria	Jibu, Jibanci	20,000	Animism	1%	5	
Jiji	Tanzania	Jiji	3,000	Animism	0%	1	
Jimbin	Nigeria	Jimbin	1,500	Islam	-1%	1	

NAME	COUNTRY	LANGUAGE	GROUP SIZE	PRIMARY RELIGION	% CHR	V	VOL U.P.
*Jimini	Ivory Coast	Jimini	42,000	Islam	14%	5	
Jinja	Tanzania	Jinja	66,000	Animism	0%	5	
Jinuos	China	Tibeto-Burman	10,000	Animism	0%	5	81
Jita	Tanzania	Jita	71,000	Animism	0%	4	
*Jivaro (Achuara)	Venezuela	Jivaro	20,000	Christo-Paganism	6%	4	
*Jiye	Sudan	Jiye (Karamojong)	7,000	Animism	0%	5	
	Uganda	Jiye	34,000	Animism	-1%	5	
Jongor	Chad	Jongor	16,000	Islam-Animist	-1%	1	
Juang in Orissa	India	Juang	12,170	Hinduism	0%	2	
Juhai	Malaysia	Juhai	400	Animism	-1%	4	
Jukun	Nigeria	not reported	20,000	Animism	-1%	5	
Jyarung	China	Jyarung	70,000	Traditional Chinese	10%	5	
**K'anjobal of San Miguel	Guatemala	K'anjobal	18,000	Ancestor Worship	2%	3	
Ka'mis	Papua New Guinea	Waffa Dialect	50	Christo-Paganism	0%	1	
Kaagan	Philippines	Kaagan	20,000	Christo-Paganism	0%	1	
Kaalong	Cameroon	Kaalong	50,000	Animism	0%	1	
	Cameroon	Kaalong	50,000	Animism	0%	1	
Kaba	Central African Empire	Kaba	11,000	Animism	0%	1	
Kaba Dunjo	Central African Empire	Kaba Dunjo	17,000	Animism	0%	1	
Kabixi	Brazil	Kabixi	100	Animism	-1%	1	
Kabre	Benin	Kabre	35,000	Animism	-1%	1	
	Togo	Kabre	273,000	Animism	9%	5	
Kabyle	Algeria	Kabyle	1,000,000	Islam	1%	6	79
Kachama	Ethiopia	Kachama	500	Animism	-1%	1	
Kachchi in Andhra Pradesh	India	Kachchi	470,990	Hinduism	-1%	1	
Kachin in Shan State	Burma	Burmese	80,000	Buddhism	0%	2	
Kadaklan-Barlig Bontoc	Philippines	Kadaklan-Barlig Bontoc	4,000	Animism	-1%	1	
Kadar in Andhra Pradesh	India	Kadar	800	Hindu-Animist	-1%	1	
Kadara	Nigeria	Kadara	40,000	Animism	9%	5	
Kadazans	Malaysia	Kadazans	110,000	Animism	-1%	2	
Kadiweu	Brazil	Kadiweu	550	Animism	-1%	1	
Kadugli	Sudan	Kadugli	19,000	Islam	0%	1	
Kaeti	Indonesia	Kaeti	4,000	Animism	-1%	1	
*Kaffa	Ethiopia	Kaffenya (Kefa)	320,000	Christo-Paganism	2%	6	80
**Kafirs	Pakistan	Kafiristani (Bashgali)	3,000	Animism	-1%	6	79
Kagoma	Nigeria	Kagoma	6,250	Islam	-1%	1	
Kagoro	Mali	Logoro (Bambara)	30,000	Animism	-1%	4	
Kaqulu	Tanzania	Kaqulu	59,000	Animism	0%	1	
Kahluri in Andamans	India	Kahluri	66,190	Hindu-Animist	-1%	1	
Kaibu	Nigeria	Kaibu	650	Islam	-1%	1	
Kaikadi in Maharashtra	India	Kaikadi	11,850	Hindu-Animist	-1%	1	
Kaili	Indonesia	Kaili	300,000	Animism	-1%	1	
Kaingang	Brazil	Kaingang	7,000	Christo-Paganism	-1%	1	

NAME	COUNTRY	LANGUAGE	GROUP SIZE	PRIMARY RELIGION	% CHR	V	VOL. U.P.
**Kankanay, Central	Philippines	Kankanay	40,000	Animism	2%	5	
**Kankanay, Northern	Philippines	Northern Kankanay	40,000	Animism	2%	5	
Kanu	Zaire	Kanu	3,500	Animism	0%	1	
Kanum	Indonesia	Kanum	320	Animism	-1%	1	
Kanuri	Nigeria	Kanuri Dialects	3,000,000	Islam	-1%	6	80
Kao	Ethiopia	Karo	600	Animism	-1%	1	
Kaonde	Zaire	Kaonde	20,000	Animism	-1%	1	
	Zambia	Kaonde	116,000	Animism	-1%	1	
Kapori	Indonesia	Kapori	60	Animism	-1%	1	
Kapuchin	Soviet Russia	Kapuchin	2,500	Unknown	0%	1	
Kara	Tanzania	Kara	32,000	Animism	0%	1	
*Karaboro	Upper Volta	Karaboro	40,000	Animism	1%	4	
Karachay	Soviet Russia	Karachay-Balkan	173,000	Islam-Animist	0%	5	
Karagas	Soviet Russia	Karagas	600	Unknown	0%	1	
Karaim	Soviet Russia	Karaim	1,000	Unknown	0%	1	
Karakalpak	Soviet Russia	Karakalpak	277,000	Islam	0%	6	80
	Soviet Russia	Karakalpak	236,000	Unknown	0%	1	
Karanga	Chad	Karanga	57,000	Islam-Animist	-1%	1	
Karas	Indonesia	Karas	200	Animism	0%	1	
Karatin	Soviet Russia	Karatin	6,000	Unknown	0%	1	
**Karbis	India	Mikir	300,000	Hindu-Animist	5%	5	
Karekare	Nigeria	Karekare	39,000	Islam	-1%	1	
Karen	Thailand	Sgaw Karen	80,000	Animism	1%	6	79
Karen, Pwo	Thailand	Pwo Karen	40,000	Animism	1%	5	
Kari	Central African Empire	Kari	40,000	Islam-Animist	-1%	1	
	Chad	Kari	1,000	Animism	0%	1	
Karipuna Creole	Brazil	Karipuna Creole	500	Animism	-1%	1	
Karipuna Do Guapore	Brazil	Karipuna Do Guapore	150	Animism	-1%	1	
Kariya	Nigeria	Kariya	2,200	Islam	-1%	1	
Karko	Sudan	Karko	2,200	Islam	-1%	1	
Karmali in Dihar	India	Karmali	69,620	Hindu-Animist	-1%	1	
Karon Dori	Indonesia	Karon Dori	5,000	Animism	-1%	1	
Karon Pantai	Indonesia	Karon Pantai	2,500	Animism	-1%	1	
Karre	Central African Empire	Karre	40,000	Animism	0%	1	
Kasanga	Guinea-Bissau	Kasanga	420	Islam-Animist	0%	1	
Kasele	Togo	Kasele	20,000	Islam-Animist	0%	1	
Kasem	Upper Volta	Kasem	28,000	Islam-Animist	0%	1	
*Kasena	Ghana	Kasem	70,000	Animism	11%	4	
**Kashmiri Muslims	India	Kashmiri	3,060,000	Islam	1%	6	79
Kasseng	Laos	Kasseng	15,000	Animism	0%	5	
Kasuweri	Indonesia	Kasuweri	1,200	Animism	-1%	1	
Katab	Nigeria	Katab	32,370	Islam	-1%	1	

Name	Country	Population	Religion	Code
Katakari in Gujarat	India	4,950	Hindu-Animist	-18 1
Katcha	Sudan	6,000	Islam	08 1
Kati, Northern	Indonesia	8,000	Animism	-18 1
Kati, Southern	Indonesia	4,000	Animism	-18 1
Katla	Sudan	8,700	Islam	08 1
Katukina, Panoan	Brazil	180	Animism	-18 1
Kaugat	Indonesia	1,000	Animism	-18 3
**Kaur	Indonesia	50,000	Islam-Animist	08 3
Kaure	Indonesia	800	Animism	-18 1
Kavwol	Indonesia	500	Animism	-18 1
Kaw	Burma	30,000	Animism	08 2
Kawar in Madhya Pradesh	India	33,770	Hindu-Animist	08 2
Kawe	Indonesia	300	Animism	-18 1
Kayabi	Brazil	300	Animism	-18 1
Kayagar	Indonesia	9,000	Animism	08 4
Padaung	Burma	18,000	Animism	08 2
Kayan	Malaysia	12,000	Animism	08 3
Kayapo	Brazil	600	Animism	08 4
Kaygir	Indonesia	4,000	Animism	-18 1
Kayupulau	Indonesia	570	Animism	-18 1
Kazakhs	China	700,000	Islam-Animist	08 6 81
Kazakhi	Iran	3,000	Islam	08 5 80
Kebu	Togo	20,000	Islam-Animist	08 1
Kebumtamp	Bhutan	400,000	Buddhist-Animist	-18 1
Kedayanas	Malaysia	25,000	Animism	08 2
Keer in Madhya Pradesh	India	2,890	Hindu-Animist	-18 1
Kei	Indonesia	30,000	Animism	-18 1
Keiga	Sudan	6,000	Islam	08 1
Keiga Jirru	Sudan	1,400	Islam	08 1
**Kekchi	Guatemala	270,000	Christo-Paganism	38 4
Kela	Zaire	100,000	Animism	08 1
Kelabit	Malaysia	17,000	Animism	nr 6 81
Kelao	China	23,000	Traditional Chinese	-18 1
Kele	Gabon	15,000	Animism	-18 1
Kemak	Indonesia	50,000	Animism	08 1
Kembata	Ethiopia	250,000	Animism	08 2
Kemok	Malaysia	400	Animism	-18 1
Kendari	Indonesia	500,000	Islam-Animist	-18 1
Kenga	Chad	25,000	Islam-Animist	08 1
Kenyah	Indonesia	37,500	Animism	-18 1
*Kepas (Kewa)	Papua New Guinea	5,000	Animism	-18 3
Kera	Cameroon	15,000	Animism	-18 1
Kera	Cameroon	15,000	Animism	-18 1

NAME	COUNTRY	LANGUAGE	GROUP SIZE	PRIMARY RELIGION	% CHR	V	VOL U.P.
Kerewe	Chad	Kera	5,000	Islam-Animist	-1%	1	
Kerinchi	Tanzania	Kikerewe	35,000	Animism	-1%	4	
Ket	Indonesia	Kerinchi	170,000	Islam-Animist	-1%	1	
Khakas	Soviet Russia	Ket	1,200	Unknown	0%	1	
Khalaj	Soviet Russia	Khakas	67,000	Unknown	0%	1	
Khalka	Iran	Khalaj	20,000	Islam	0%	1	
Kham	China	Khalka	68,000	Traditional Chinese	-1%	1	
Khamti in Assam	China	Kham	11,400	Traditional Chinese	-1%	1	
*Khamu	India	Khamti	300	Hindu-Buddhist	-1%	1	
Khana	Thailand	Khamu	6,300	Animism	0%	4	
Khandesi	Nigeria	Khana	90,000	Unknown	-1%	5	
Khanti	India	Khandesi	14,700	Hindu-Animist	-1%	1	
Kharia in Bihar	Soviet Russia	Khanti	21,000	Unknown	0%	1	
Khasi in Assam	India	Kharia	88,900	Hindu-Animist	-1%	1	
Khasonke	India	Khasi	384,010	Hinduism	0%	1	
Khinalug	Mali	Khasonke	71,000	Islam	-1%	1	
Khirwar in Madhya Pradesh	Soviet Russia	Khinalug	1,500	Unknown	0%	1	
**Khmer Refugees	India	Khirwar	34,250	Hindu-Animist	-1%	1	
Khojas, Agha Khani	Thailand	Cambodia	15,000	Buddhist-Animist	-1%	4	
Khowar	India	Gujarati	175,000	Islam	0%	4	
Khvarshin	India	Khowar	6,960	Hindu-Animist	0%	1	
Kibet	Soviet Russia	Khvarshin	1,800	Unknown	0%	1	
Kichepo	Chad	Kibet	22,000	Islam-Animist	-1%	1	
Kikapoo	Sudan	Kichepo	16,000	Animism	0%	3	
Kilba	Mexico	Kikapoo	5,001	Christo-Paganism	-1%	1	
Kim	Nigeria	Kilba	80,000	Islam	-1%	1	
	Central African Empire	Kim	5,000	Animism	0%	1	
Kimaghama	Chad	Kim	5,000	Islam-Animist	-1%	1	
Kimbu	Indonesia	Kimaghama	3,000	Animism	-1%	1	
*Kimyal	Tanzania	Kimbu	15,000	Animism	0%	1	
Kinaray-A	Indonesia	Kimyal	7,000	Animism	2%	4	
Kinga	Philippines	Kinaray-A	288,000	Christo-Paganism	-1%	1	
Kirghiz	Tanzania	Kinga	57,000	Animism	0%	1	
Kirgiz	Afghanistan	Kirghiz	45,000	Islam	-1%	1	
	China	Kirgiz	90,000	Islam	0%	5	
	Soviet Russia	Kirgiz	1,700,000	Islam-Animist	0%	6	80
Kirifi	Nigeria	Krifi	14,000	Islam-Animist	-1%	1	
Kisan in Bihar	India	Kisan	73,850	Hindu-Animist	-1%	1	
Kisankasa	Tanzania	Kisankasa	3,600	Animism	0%	1	
Kishanganjia in Bihar	India	Kishanganjia	56,920	Hindu-Animist	0%	1	
Kishtwari in Jammu	India	Kishtwari	12,170	Hindu-Animist	-1%	1	
Kisi	Tanzania	Kisi	3,600	Animism	0%	1	
Kissi	Guinea	Kissi	266,000	Animism	2%	4	

Name	Language / People	Country	Population	Religion	%	Vol
*Kissi	Kissi	Liberia	35,000	Animism	3%	4
Kissi, Southern	Kissi, Southern	Sierra Leone	48,000	Animism	12%	4
	Kissi, Southern	Sierra Leone	58,000	Islam-Animist	-1%	1
Kita	not reported	Mali	150,000	Islam	2%	3
Klaoh	Klaoh	Liberia	81,000	Islam-Animist	-1%	1
Koalib	Koalib (Nuba)	Sudan	320,000	Animism	6%	6 79
Kobiana	Kobiana	Guinea	300	Islam-Animist	0%	1
**Koch	Benqali	Bangladesh	35,000	Hindu-Animist	1%	5
Koda in Bihar	Koda	India	14,140	Hindu-Animist	-1%	1
Kodi	Kodi	Indonesia	25,000	Animism	-1%	1
Koenoem	Koenoem	Nigeria	3,000	Animism	-1%	1
Kofyar	Kofyar	Nigeria	40,000	Animism	-1%	1
**Kohli, Kutchi	Gujarati, Koli	Pakistan	50,000	Hinduism	4%	4
**Kohli, Tharadari	Gujarati, Koli	Pakistan	40,000	Hinduism	1%	5
**Kohli, Wadiara	Gujarati, Koli	Pakistan	40,000	Hindu-Animist	1%	5
**Kohlis, Parkari	Gujarati, Koli	Pakistan	100,000	Hinduism	5%	4
Kohoroxitari	Kohoroxitari	Brazil	620	Animism	-1%	1
Kohumono	Kohumono	Nigeria	11,870	Animism	-1%	1
Kokant	Kokant	Burma	50,000	Buddhist-Animist	0%	2
Koke	Koke	Chad	1,000	Islam-Animist	-1%	1
Kol in Assam	Kol	India	82,900	Hindu-Animist	-1%	1
**Kolam	Kolami	India	60,000	Hindu-Animist	1%	5
Kolbila	Kolbila	Cameroon	1,000	Islam-Animist	1%	5
Kole	Kole	Cameroon	300	Animism	0%	1
	Kole	Cameroon	300	Animism	0%	1
Kom in Manipur	Kom	India	6,970	Hindu-Animist	-1%	1
Koma	Koma	Cameroon	15,000	Animism	0%	1
	Koma	Cameroon	15,000	Animism	0%	1
	Koma	Ghana	1,000	Animism	0%	1
	Koma	Nigeria	15,000	Animism	0%	5
Koma, Central	Koma, Central	Sudan	3,000	Islam	-1%	1
Komering	Komering	Indonesia	400,000	Islam-Animist	0%	3
Komi-Permyat	Komi-Permyat	Soviet Russia	153,000	Christo-Paganism	-1%	1
Komi-Zyrian	Komi-Zyrian	Soviet Russia	322,020	Christo-Paganism	-1%	1
*Komo	Komo	Ethiopia	20,000	Animism	-1%	4
Komono	Komono	Upper Volta	6,000	Islam-Animist	0%	1
Konabem	Konabem	Cameroon	3,000	Animism	0%	1
	Konabem	Cameroon	3,000	Animism	0%	1
***Kond	Kui	India	900,000	Animism	3%	5
Konda-Dora in A.P.	Konda-Dora	India	15,650	Hindu-Animist	-1%	1
Koneraw	Koneraw	Indonesia	300	Animism	-1%	1
Konqo	Kongo	Angola	756,000	Unknown	0%	1
Konkani in Gujarat	Konkani	India	1,522,680	Hindu-Animist	-1%	1

NAME	COUNTRY	LANGUAGE	GROUP SIZE	PRIMARY RELIGION	% CHR	VOL V	U.P.
Konkomba	Ghana	Konkomba	175,000	Animism	9%	5	
*Konkomba	Togo	Kom Komba	25,000	Animism	1%	4	
Kono	Nigeria	Kono	1,550	Islam	1%	5	
**Kono	Sierra Leone	Kono	133,000	Animism	5%	5	
Konongo	Tanzania	Konongo	20,000	Animism	1%	1	
Konso	Ethiopia	Konso	30,000	Animism	1%	5	
Konyagi	Guinea	Konyaqi	85,000	Islam-Animist	-1%	5	
Koraga in Kerala	India	Koraga	1,500	Hindu-Animist	1%	1	
*Koranko	Sierra Leone	Kuranko (Maninka)	103,000	Islam-Animist	1%	5	
Korapun	Indonesia	Korapun	4,000	Animism	1%	1	
**Korean Prisoners	Korea, Republic of	Korean	45,000	Secularism	10%	4	
***Koreans in Germany	German Federal Rep.	Korean	10,000	Unknown	4%	5	
*Koreans in Manchuria	China	Korean	3,000,000	Buddhism	nr	5	81
*Korku in Madhya Pradesh	India	Korku	600,000	Folk Religion	6%	5	
Koro	Nigeria	Koro	250,000	Animism	1%	5	
Koroma	Sudan	Koroma	35,000	Animism	1%	5	
Korop	Cameroon	Korop	30,000	Animism	0%	3	
	Cameroon	Korop	10,000	Animism	0%	1	
	Nigeria	Korop	10,000	Animism	0%	1	
Korwa in Bihar	India	Korwa	14,250	Hindu-Animist	-1%	1	
Koryak	Soviet Russia	Koryak	7,500	Unknown	0%	1	
Kota	Gabon	Kota	nr	Animism	0%	1	
Kota in Tamil Nadu	India	Kota	860	Hindu-Animist	-1%	1	
Kotia in Andhra Pradesh	India	Kotia	15,000	Hindu-Animist	-1%	1	
Kotogut	Indonesia	Kotoqut	1,000	Animism	-1%	1	
Kotoko	Cameroon	Kotoko	31,000	Animism	0%	1	
	Cameroon	Kotoko	31,000	Animism	0%	1	
	Chad	Kotoko	31,000	Islam-Animist	-1%	3	
Kotokoli	Benin	Kotokoli	75,000	Islam	0%	1	
	Togo	Kotokoli	150,000	Islam-Animist	0%	4	
Kotopo	Cameroon	Kotopo	1,200	Animism	0%	5	
Kotta	India	Kota	5,690	Islam-Animist	-1%	1	
Kouya	Ivory Coast	Kouya	7,000	Animism	3%	4	
**Kowaao	Liberia	Kowaao		Islam-Animist	-1%	1	
Koya in Andhra Pradesh	India	Koya	211,880	Hindu-Animist	-1%	4	
	Ethiopia	Koyra	5,000	Animism	-1%	1	
Kpa	Cameroon	Kpa	17,000	Animism	-1%	1	
	Cameroon			Animism	0%	1	
Kpelle	Guinea	Kpelle	250,000	Islam-Animist	-1%	1	
	Liberia	Kpelle	200,000	Islam-Animist	6%	5	
Kposo	Togo	Kposo	45,000	Animism	0%	1	
Krachi	Ghana	Krachi	21,000	Islam-Animist	0%	1	

*Krahn	Ivory Coast	Guere	Ivory Coast	250,000	Animism	3% 4
***Krahn	Liberia	Krahn	Liberia	55,000	Animism	7% 4
Kreen-Akakore	Brazil	Kreen-Akakore	Brazil	90	Animism	1% 1
Krim	Sierra Leone	Mende	Sierra Leone	3,400	Islam-Animist	0% 1
Krio	Gambia	Krio	Gambia	3,400	Islam-Animist	-1% 1
Krobou	Ivory Coast	Krobou	Ivory Coast	121,000	Animism	-1% 1
Krongo	Sudan	Krongo	Sudan	17,000	Animism	1% 4
Krumen	Ivory Coast	Krumen	Ivory Coast	6,000	Unknown	2% 4
Kryz	Soviet Russia	Kryz	Soviet Russia	70	Animism	0% 5
Kuatinema	Brazil	Asurini	Brazil	6,000	Animism	0% 5
Kubu	Indonesia	Local dialects	Indonesia	25,000	Islam-Animist	1% 6 80
Kuda-Chamo	Indonesia	Kuda-Chamo	Indonesia	4,000	Islam	1% 6 81
*Kudisai Vagh Makkal	India	Tamil	India	1,000,000	Hinduism	nr 6 81
Kudiya	India	Kudiya	India	100	Hindu-Animist	2% 3
Kugbo	Nigeria	Kugbo	Nigeria	2,000	Animism	-1% 1
*Kui	Thailand	Kui	Thailand	160,000	Buddhist-Animist	-1% 1
Kuikuro	Brazil	Kuikuro	Brazil	120	Animism	1% 5
Kuka	Chad	Kuka	Chad	38,000	Islam-Animist	-1% 1
Kukele	Nigeria	Kukele	Nigeria	31,700	Animism	-1% 1
*Kuknas	India	Kukni	India	125,000	Hindu-Animist	-1% 4
Kukwa	Congo	Kukwa	Congo	11,000	Animism	0% 1
Kulango	Ivory Coast	Kulango	Ivory Coast	60,000	Animism	3% 4
Kulele	Ivory Coast	Kulele	Ivory Coast	15,000	Islam-Animist	-1% 1
Kulere	Nigeria	Kulere	Nigeria	8,000	Animism	-1% 1
Kullo	Ethiopia	Kullo	Ethiopia	82,000	Islam-Animist	-1% 5
**Kuluis in Himachal Prades	India	Kului	India	200,000	Hinduism	1% 5 81
Kulung	Nigeria	Kulung	Nigeria	15,000	Islam-Animist	-1% 1
Kumam	Uganda	Kumam	Uganda	100,000	Animism	-1% 1
Kumauni in Assam	India	Kumauni	India	1,234,940	Hindu-Animist	0% 1
Kumu	Zaire	Kumu	Zaire	60,000	Animism	-1% 1
Kunama	Ethiopia	Kunama	Ethiopia	70,000	Islam	-1% 1
Kunante	Guinea-Bissau	Kunante	Guinea-Bissau	6,000	Islam-Animist	0% 1
Kunda	Mozambique	Kunda	Mozambique	60,000	Animism	0% 1
		Kunda	Rhodesia	40,000	Animism	0% 1
		Kunda	Zambia	21,000	Animism	0% 1
		Kunda	Zambia	8,000	Animism	0% 1
**Kunimaipa	Papua New Guinea	Kunimaipa	Papua New Guinea	9,000	Christo-Paganism	6% 5
Kupia in Andhra Pradesh	India	Kupia	India	4,000	Hindu-Animist	-1% 1
Kupsabiny	Uganda	Kupsabiny	Uganda	60,000	Animism	0% 1
Kurds in Iran	Iran	Kurdish Dialects	Iran	2,000,000	Islam	1% 6 80
Kurds in Kuwait	Kuwait	Kurdish (Kirmancho)	Kuwait	145,000	Islam	8% 3
*Kurds of Turkey	Turkey	Kurdish	Turkey	1,900,000	Islam	1% 6 79

NAME	COUNTRY	LANGUAGE	GROUP SIZE	PRIMARY RELIGION	% CHR	V	VOL U.P.
Kurfei	Niger	Hausa	50,000	Animism	<1%	4	
Kuria	Tanzania	Kuria	75,000	Animism	0%		
Kurichiya in Kerala	India	Kurichiya	12,130	Hindu-Animist	<1%	5	81
Kuruba in Tamil Nadu	India	Kuruba	7,900	Hindu-Animist	<1%		
Kurudu	Indonesia	Kurudu	1,100	Animism	<1%		
Kurumba	Upper Volta	Kurumba	86,000	Islam-Animist	<1%		
**Kurux in Bihar	India	Kurux	1,244,400	Hindu-Animist	<1%		
Kusaasi	Ghana	Kusaal	150,000	Animism	3%	5	
Kushi	Nigeria	Kushi	4,000	Islam	<1%		
Kusu	Zaire	Kusu	26,000	Animism	0%		
Kuteb	Nigeria	Kuteb	26,000	Islam	<1%		
Kutin	Cameroon	Kutin	400	Animism	0%		
Kutu	Tanzania	Kutu	17,000	Animism	0%		
Kuturmi	Nigeria	Kuturmi	2,950	Islam	<1%		
Kuvi in Orissa	India	Kuvi	190,000	Hindu-Animist	<1%		
Kuwaa	Liberia	Kuwaa	5,500	Islam-Animist	<1%		
Kuzamani	Nigeria	Kuzamani	1,000	Islam	<1%		
Kvanadin	Soviet Russia	Kvanadin	5,500	Unknown	0%		
Kwa	Nigeria	Kwa	1,000	Islam	<1%		
Kwadi	Angola	Kwadi	15,000	Animism	0%		
Kwakum	Cameroon	Kwakum	3,000	Animism	0%		
Kwambi	Namibia	Kwambi	30,000	Animism	0%		
Kwangali	Angola	Kwangali	25,000	Animism	0%		
Kwansu	Indonesia	Kwansu	350	Animism	<1%		
Kwanyama	Angola	Kwanyama	100,000	Animism	<1%		
Kwaya	Namibia	Kwanyama	150,000	Animism	<1%		
Kwe-etshori	Tanzania	Kwaya	35,000	Animism	0%		
Kwe-etshori	Botswana	Kwe-etshori	3,000	Animism	<1%		
Kwe-Etshori	Rhodesia	Kwe-Etshori	1,800	Animism	0%		
Kwerba	Indonesia	Kwerba	2,000	Animism	<1%		
Kwere	Tanzania	Kwere	63,000	Animism	10%	5	
Kwese	Zaire	Kwese	60,000	Animism	<1%		
Kwesten	Indonesia	Kwesten	2,480	Animism	<1%		
Kyibaku	Nigeria	Kyibaku	20,000	Islam	0%		
Laamang	Nigeria	Laamang	40,000	Islam	0%		
Labans	India	Labaang	nr	Hindu-Buddhist	<1%		
Labbai	India	Tamil	nr	Islam	0%		
Labhani in Andhra Pradesh	India	Labhani	1,203,340	Hindu-Buddhist	10%	5	
*Labourers of Jhoparpatti	India	Marathi	1,500	Hinduism	0%		
Lacandon	Mexico	Lacandon	200	Christo-Paganism	10%	4	
Ladakhi in Jammu	India	Ladakhi	56,740	Hindu-Buddhist	<1%		
Ladinos	Lebanon	Ladinos	7,300	Judaism	<1%		
Lafofa	Sudan	Lafofa	2,000	Islam	0%		

Name	Country	Population	Religion	%	
**Lahaulis in Punjab	India	18,000	Buddhism	-1%	4
*Lahu	Burma	40,000	Animism	0%	2
*Lahu	Thailand	22,500	Animism	7%	5	81
Lahul	China	1,600	Traditional Chinese	-1%	1
Laka	Cameroon	10,000	Animism	0%	4
Lakal	Central African Empire	40,000	Animism	-1%	1
Laka	Chad	40,000	Islam-Animist	-1%	1
Lakian	China	6,000	Traditional Chinese	-1%	1
Lakka	Soviet Russia	86,000	Islam	0%	1
Lala	Nigeria	500	Islam	-1%	1
Lalia	Zambia	125,000	Animism	0%	1
Lalung in Assam	Zaire	30,000	Animism	0%	1
Lama	India	10,650	Hindu-Buddhist	-1%	1
Lamba	Burma	3,000	Buddhist-Animist	-1%	1
	Benin	29,000	Animism	0%	1
	Togo	80,000	Animism	3%	4
	Zaire	89,000	Animism	-1%	1
	Zambia		Animism	0%	1
**Lambadi in Andhra Pradesh	India	1,300,000	Animism	nr	5	81
Lambi	Cameroon	1,000	Animism	-1%	1
Lambya	Malawi	18,600	Animism	0%	1
Lambya	Tanzania	7,000	Animism	0%	1
Lame	Nigeria	2,000	Islam	-1%	1
Komering	Indonesia	1,500,000	Islam-Animist	0%	5	80
Landoma	Guinea	4,000	Islam-Animist	0%	1
Landoma	Guinea-Bissau	5,000	Islam-Animist	0%	1
Langi	Tanzania	95,000	Animism	0%	1
*Lango	Ethiopia	8,000	Animism	0%	3
Lango	Uganda	560,000	Animism	0%	3
Lanoh	Malaysia	400	Animism	0%	3
*Lao	Laos	1,900,600	Buddhism	1%	7	79
*Lao Refugees	Thailand	20,000	Buddhist-Animist	-1%	4
Lara	Indonesia	12,000	Animism	-1%	1
Laro	Sudan	3,000	Islam	0%	1
Laru	Nigeria	1,000	Islam	-1%	1
Latdwalam	Indonesia	860	Animism	-1%	1
Lati	China	450	Traditional Chinese	-1%	1
Laudje	Indonesia	125,000	Animism	-1%	1
Tibeto-Burman Dialect	Thailand	2,500	Buddhist-Animist	-1%	5	81
Lawa	Thailand	10,000	Buddhist-Animist	4%	5
Lebgo	Nigeria	30,000	Animism	-1%	1
Redjang-Lebong	Indonesia	nr	Islam	0%	5
Leco	Bolivia	200	Animism	-1%	1

NAME	COUNTRY	LANGUAGE	GROUP SIZE	PRIMARY RELIGION	% CHR	V	VOL U.P.
Lega	Zaire	Lega	150,000	Animism	-1%	1	
Lele	Chad	Lele	30,000	Islam-Animist	-1%	1	
Lele	Upper Volta	Lele	61,000	Islam-Animist	-1%	1	
	Zaire	Lele	26,000	Animism	0%	1	
Lelemi	Ghana	Lelemi	14,900	Islam-Animist	0%	1	
Lendu	Zaire	Lendu	250,000	Animism	0%	1	
Lengua, Northern	Paraguay	Lengua, Northern	95,000	Animism	-1%	1	
Lenje	Zambia	Lenje	79,000	Animism	0%	1	
**Lepcha	Sikkim	Lepcha	18,000	Hindu-Buddhist	10%	3	
**Lepers of Cen. Thailand	Thailand	Thai	20,000	Buddhist-Animist	1%	6	81
**Lepers of N.E. Thailand	Thailand	Northeast Thai	390,000	Buddhism	1%	4	
Lese	Zaire	Lese	20,000	Animism	0%	1	
Letti	Indonesia	Letti	6,000	Animism	0%	1	
Li	China	Li	1,000,000	Traditional Chinese	-1%	1	
Libyans	Libya	Arabic	2,300,000	Islam	0%	3	
Ligbi	Ghana	Ligbi	6,000	Islam	0%	5	
Liguri	Sudan	Liguri	20,000	Islam	-1%	1	
Liko	Zaire	Liko	2,000	Islam-Animist	0%	1	
Lima	Zambia	Lima	26,000	Animism	0%	1	
Limba	Sierra Leone	Limba	12,000	Animism	4%	4	
Lionese	Indonesia	Lio	233,000	Animism	-1%	1	
Lisu	China	Tibeto-Burman	100,000	Christo-Paganism	-1%	5	81
*Lisu	Thailand	Lisu	470,000	Animism	6%	4	
Liv	Soviet Russia	Liv	12,500	Animism	0%	1	
Lo	Nigeria	Lo	1,500	Unknown	-1%	1	
Lobi	Ivory Coast	Lobi	2,000	Animism	0%	1	
Lodhi in Bihar	India	Lodhi	40,000	Animism	-1%	1	
Logba	Ghana	Logba	44,070	Hindu-Animist	-1%	1	
Logo	Zaire	Logo	3,200	Islam-Animist	0%	1	
Lohar	Pakistan	Gujarati Dialect	54,000	Animism	1%	4	
**Loho Loho	Indonesia	Kolaka	nr	Hinduism	1%	3	
Loinang	Indonesia	Loinanq	100,000	Animism	0%	1	
Loko	Guinea	Loko	16,000	Islam-Animist	0%	1	
Loko	Sierra Leone	Loko	80,000	Animism	1%	4	
	Sierra Leone	Loko	60,700	Islam-Animist	-1%	1	
*Lokoro	Sudan	Lokoro	22,000	Christo-Paganism	5%	4	
Lolo	China	Yi	4,800,000	Animism	0%	5	81
Loma	Guinea	Loma	180,000	Animism	3%	4	
	Liberia	Loma	60,000	Animism	12%	4	
Lombi	Zaire	Lombi	8,100	Animism	0%	1	
Lombo	Zaire	Lombo	10,000	Animism	0%	1	
Lomwe	Mozambique	not reported	1,000,000	Animism	9%	4	

Longuda	Nigeria	32,000	Islam	-1% 1	
Lore	Indonesia	140,000	Animism	-1% 1	
Lori	Sudan	1,000	Islam	0% 1	
Lors	Iran	600,000	Islam	0% 5	80
Lotsu-Piri	Nigeria	2,000	Islam	-1% 1	
**Lotuka	Sudan	150,000	Other	6% 5	81
Loven	Laos	25,000	Buddhist-Animist	1% 5	
Lozi	Rhodesia	8,100	Animism	0% 1	
Lozi	Zambia	215,000	Animism	0% 1	
Lu	China	400,000	Buddhist-Animist	-1% 1	
Luac	Sudan	700	Islam	0% 1	
Luano	Zambia	4,000	Animism	0% 1	
Lubang Islanders	Philippines	18,000	Christo-Paganism	0% 5	81
Lubu	Indonesia	1,000,000	Islam	0% 1	
Luchazi	Angola	60,000	Animism	-1% 1	
Luchazi	Zambia	34,000	Animism	-1% 1	
Lue	Cameroon	4,000	Animism	-1% 1	
Lugbara	Uganda	260,000	Unknown	12% 5	
Lugbara	Zaire	350,000	Animism	-1% 1	
Luimbi	Angola	20,000	Animism	-1% 1	
Lumbu	Gabon	12,000	Animism	-1% 1	
Luna	Zaire	50,000	Animism	-1% 1	
Lunda	Angola	50,000	Animism	-1% 1	
Lunda, Ndembu	Zambia	102,000	not reported	nr 1	
Lundu	Cameroon	24,000	Animism	0% 1	
Lungu	Nigeria	10,000	Animism	-1% 4	
Luo	Tanzania	1,522,000	Animism	-1% 1	
Lushai in Assam	India	270,310	Hindu-Animist	-1% 1	
Luwu	Indonesia	500,000	Islam	0% 1	
Luyana	Angola	3,500	Animism	0% 1	
Luyana	Zambia	50,000	Animism	0% 1	
Lwalu	Zaire	21,000	Animism	0% 1	
Lwena	Angola	90,000	Animism	-1% 1	
Lwo	Sudan	20,000	Animism	-1% 1	
Ma	Zaire	4,700	Animism	-1% 1	
Maanyan	Indonesia	15,000	Islam	0% 1	
**Maasai	Kenya	100,000	Animism	-5% 6	79
Maba	Chad	56,000	Islam-Animist	-1% 1	
Maba	Sudan	9,000	Islam	0% 1	
Maban-Jumjum	Sudan	20,000	Islam	-1% 1	
Maca	Paraguay	600	Animism	-1% 1	
Machiguenga	Peru	10,000	Animism	-1% 1	
Macu	Colombia	1,000	Animism	-1% 3	

NAME	COUNTRY	LANGUAGE	GROUP SIZE	PRIMARY RELIGION	% CHR	V	VOL U.P.
Macuna	Colombia	Macuna	300	Animism	-1%	3	
**Macuxi	Brazil	Macuxi	6,000	Animism	5%	3	
Madda	Nigeria	Madda	30,000	Animism	-1%	1	
Madi	Sudan	Madi	6,000	Islam	0%	3	
	Uganda	Madi	114,000	Animism	-1%	1	
Madik	Indonesia	Madik	1,000	Animism	-1%	1	
Madurese	Indonesia	Madurese	7,000,000	Islam	1%	6	79
**Magar	Nepal	Magar	300,000	Hindu-Animist	1%	4	
Maghi	Burma	Maghi	309,000	Buddhist-Animist	-1%	1	
Maguindano	Philippines	Maguindano	700,000	Islam	1%	8	80
***Maguzawa	Nigeria	Hausa	100,000	Islam	1%	6	79
Mahali in Assam	India	Mahali	14,300	Hindu-Animist	-1%	1	
*Mahrah	Yemen, Democratic	Local dialects	50,000	Islam	0%	3	
Mahri	Oman	Mahri	50,000	Animism	-1%	1	
Maiongong	Brazil	Maiongong	86	Animism	1%	3	
Mairasi	Indonesia	Mairasi	1,000	Animism	-1%	3	
Maithili	Nepal	Maithili	1,000,000	Hindu-Animist	-1%	4	
Majhwar in Madhya Pradesh	India	Majhwar	27,960	Hindu-Animist	-1%	1	
Maji	Ethiopia	Maji	15,000	Animism	-1%	4	
Majingai-ngama	Central African Empire	Majingai-ngama	47,000	Islam-Animist	-1%	1	
Majingai-Ngama	Chad	Majingai-Ngama	51,000	Animism	0%	1	
Maka	Cameroon	Maka	70,000	Animism	-1%	1	
Makasai	Indonesia	Makasai	17,500	Animism	-1%	1	
Makere	Uganda	Makere	12,000	Animism	0%	1	
Makian, West	Indonesia	Makiew	120	Animism	-1%	1	
Maklew	Indonesia	Maklew		Animism	-1%	1	
Makonde	Tanzania	not reported	550,000	Islam	6%	5	
Makua	Mozambique	Makua	1,200,000	Islam	10%	5	81
Malamutha	India	Malamutha	1,000	Hindu-Animist	-1%	1	
Malankuravan in Kerala	India	Malankuravan	5,000	Hindu-Animist	-1%	1	
Malapandaram in Kerala	India	Malapandaram	500	Hindu-Animist	-1%	1	
Malappanackers	India	Malappanackan	1,000	Animism	0%	4	
Malaryan in Kerala	India	Malaryan	5,000	Hindu-Animist	-1%	1	
Malavedan in Kerala	India	Malavedan	2,000	Hinduism	-1%	1	
*Malayalars	India	Malayalam	nr	Animism			
Malayo	Colombia	Malayo	1,000	Animism	0%	1	
Malays of Singapore	Singapore	Malay	300,000	Islam	6%	4	
Male	Ethiopia	Male	12,000	Animism	1%	6	79
Mali in Andhra Pradesh	India	Mali	970	Hindu-Animist	-1%	1	
Malila	Tanzania	Malila	175,000	Animism	-1%	1	
Malki in Bihar	India	Malki	88,650	Hindu-Animist	0%	1	
Malpaharia in Assam	India	Maipaharia	9,080	Hindu-Animist	-1%	1	
Malvi in Madhya Pradesh	India	Malvi	644,030	Hindu-Animist	-1%	1	

Group	Country	Listed As	Population	Religion	%		
**Mam Indian	Guatemala	Mam	470,000	Christo-Paganism	7%	5	
Mama	Nigeria	Mama	20,000	Animism	-1%	1	
**Mamanua	Philippines	Minamanwa	1,000	Christo-Paganism	3%	6	81
Mamasani	Iran	Luri	110,000	Islam	-1%	4	
Mambai	Indonesia	Mambai	80,000	Animism	-1%	1	
Mambila	Cameroon	Mambila	40,000	Animism	-1%	1	
Mambwe-Lungu	Tanzania	Mambwe-Lungu	16,000	Animism	0%	1	
	Zambia	Mambwe-Lungu	121,000	Animism	-1%	4	
	Ghana	not reported	80,000	Animism	-1%	1	
Mamprusi	Ghana	Mampruli	90,600	Islam-Animist	0%	1	
Mamvu-Efe	Zaire	Mamvu-Efe	40,000	Animism	-1%	5	81
Mancang	Senegal	Mankanya	35,200	not reported	0%	1	
Manchu	China	Manchu	200,000	Traditional Chinese	-1%	1	
Manda	Tanzania	Manda	10,000	Animism	-1%	1	
Mandar	Indonesia	Mandar	302,000	Islam	-1%	1	
Mandara	Nigeria	Mandara	19,300	Islam	-1%	1	
Mandaya, Mansaka	Philippines	Mandaya, Mansaka	3,000	Animism			
Mander	Indonesia	Mander	35,400	Animism			
	Indonesia		100	Animism			
Manding	Senegal	Malinke, Senegalese	208,400	not reported	nr	3	
Mandingo	Liberia	Mandingo	30,000	Islam	1%	6	79
Mandyak	Gambia	Mandyak	85,000	Islam-Animist	-1%	1	
Manem	Indonesia	Manem	400	Animism	-1%	1	
Mangbai	Chad	Mangbai	2,000	Islam-Animist	0%	1	
Mangbutu	Zaire	Mangbutu	8,000	Animism	-1%	1	
Manggarai Muslims	Indonesia	Manggarai	25,000	Islam	0%	5	81
Mangisa	Cameroon	Mangisa	14,000	Animism	0%	1	
Mangs in Maharashtra	India	Marathi	nr	Hinduism	0%	3	
**Mangyan	Philippines	Various Dialects	60,000	Animism	6%	5	
**Manikion	Indonesia	Sough	8,000	Animism	-1%	5	
Maninka	Sierra Leone	Maninka	65,000	Islam-Animist	0%	1	
	Senegal	Mandyale	64,200	Islam-Animist	0%	1	
Manjack	Guinea-Bissau	Mandyako	44,200	not reported	nr	3	
**Manjaco	Guinea-Bissau	Mankanya	80,000	Animism	7%	4	
Mankanya	Senegal	Mankanya	35,000	Islam-Animist	0%	1	
		Mankanya	16,000	Islam-Animist	0%	1	
Manna-Dora in A.P.	India	Manna-Dora	8,480	Hindu-Animist	-1%	1	
Mannan in Kerala	India	Mannan	4,980	Hindu-Animist	-1%	1	
Mano	Liberia	Mano	65,000	Animism	4%	4	
Manobo, Agusan	Philippines	Manobo, Agusan	15,000	Animism	-1%	1	
Manobo, Ata	Philippines	Manobo, Ata	7,000	Animism	-1%	1	
Manobo, Binokid	Philippines	Manobo, Binokid	40,550	Animism	-1%	1	
**Manobo, Cotabato	Philippines	Cotabato Manobo	10,000	Animism	1%	4	

NAME	LANGUAGE	COUNTRY	GROUP SIZE	PRIMARY RELIGION	% CHR	V	VOL U P.
Manobo, Dibabawon	Manobo, Dibabawon	Philippines	1,790	Animism	-1%	1	
*Manobo, Ilianen	Illanen Manobo	Philippines	5,000	Animism	-3%	5	
Manobo, Obo	Manobo, Obo	Philippines	4,000	Animism	-1%	1	
**Manobo, Salug	Manobo, Tigwa	Philippines	4,000	Animism	4%	5	
Manobo, Sarangani	Manobo, Sarangani	Philippines	15,000	Animism	-1%	1	
Manobo, Tagabawa	Manobo, Tagabawa	Philippines	9,900	Animism	-1%	1	
**Manobo, Tigwa	Manobo, Tigwa	Philippines	4,000	Animism	3%	5	
**Manobo, Western Bukidnon	Manobo, Binokid	Philippines	12,000	Animism	6%	5	
**Manobos, Pulangi	Manobo, Pulangi	Philippines	5,000	Animism	1%	4	
**Mansaka	Mansaka	Philippines	25,000	Christo-Paganism	10%	5	
Mansi	Mansi	Soviet Russia	7,700	Unknown	0%	2	
Mantera	Mantera	Malaysia	4,000	Animism	-1%	1	
Mantion	Mantion	Indonesia	12,000	Animism	-1%	1	
Manu Park Panoan	Manu Park Panoan	Peru	200	Animism	-1%	1	
Manyika	Manyika	Rhodesia	350,000	Animism	-1%	1	
Mao, Northern	Mao, Northern	Ethiopia	13,000	Animism	-1%	1	
Maou	Maou	Ivory Coast	80,000	Islam-Animist	0%	1	
Mapoyo	Mapoyo	Venezuela	200	Animism	-1%	1	
Mappillas	Malayalan	India	4,500,000	Islam	-1%	5	
Mapuche	Mapuche	Chile	300,000	Christo-Paganism	-1%	5	
Maquiritari	Maquiritari	Venezuela	5,000	Animism	-1%	1	
Mara in Assam	Mara	India	11,870	Hindu-Animist	28%	6	79
Maranao	Maranao	Philippines	500,000	Islam	-1%	1	
Maranao, Lanad	Maranao, Lanad	Philippines	500,000	Islam-Animist	-1%	1	
Mararit	Mararit	Chad	42,000	Islam-Animist	-1%	1	
Marau	Marau	Indonesia	1,200	Animism	0%	1	
Marba	Marba	Chad	30,000	Islam-Animist	-1%	5	
Marghi Central	Marghi Central	Nigeria	135,000	Islam	-1%	1	
Mari	Mari	Soviet Russia	599,000	Christo-Paganism	-1%	1	
Maria in Andhra Pradesh	Maria	India	78,500	Hindu-Animist	-1%	1	
Marind	Marind	Indonesia	7,000	Animism	-1%	1	
Marind, Bian	Marind, Bian	Indonesia	900	Islam	-1%	1	
Marka	Marka	Upper Volta	39,000	Islam	0%	1	
Marubo	Marubo	Brazil	400	Animism	-1%	1	
Marwari in Gujarat	Marwari	India	6,807,650	Hindu-Animist	6%	4	
Masa	Masa	Chad	80,000	Animism	-1%	1	
Masaba	Masaba	Uganda	110,000	Animism	0%	1	
Masakin	Masakin	Sudan	16,000	Islam	0%	1	
Masalit	Masalit	Chad	73,500	Islam-Animist	-1%	1	
Masalit in Sudan	Arabic	Sudan	27,000	Islam	-1%	5	
*Masengo	Majanqiir	Ethiopia	7,000	Animism	0%	1	
Masenrempulu	Masenrempulu	Indonesia	250,000	Islam	-1%	1	
Mashi	Mashi	Zambia	21,000	Animism	0%	1	

Name	Alternate Name	Country	Population	Religion		
Massalat	Massalat	Chad	23,000	Islam-Animist	-1%	1
Mataco	Mataco	Argentina	10,000	Animism	-1%	1
Matakam	Matakam	Cameroon	140,000	Animism	2%	4
	Matakam	Nigeria	2,000	Islam	-1%	1
Matawari	Matawari	Surinam	1,000	Animism	0%	1
Matbat	Matbat	Indonesia	550	Animism	-1%	1
Matengo	Matengo	Tanzania	58,000	Animism	2%	5
***Matharis	Teluqu	India	200,000	Hinduism	2%	5
Matipuhy-Nahukua	Matipuhy-Nahukua	Brazil	100	Animism	-1%	1
Matlatzinca, Atzingo	Matlatzinca, Atzingo	Mexico	1,700	Christo-Paganism	0%	1
Matumbi	Matumbi	Tanzania	72,000	Islam-Animist	0%	1
Maure	Maure	Mali	58,000	Islam-Animist	8%	4
Maures	Arabic	Senegal	57,000	Islam	8%	4
Mauri	Hausa	Niger	100,000	Animism	0%	3
Maviha	Maviha	Mozambique	70,000	Animism	-1%	4
**Mawchis	Mawchi	India	300,000	Hindu-Animism	3%	5
Mawes	Mawes	Indonesia	690	Animism	-1%	1
Maxakali	Maxakali	Brazil	400	Animism	-1%	1
Mayo	Mayo	Mexico	30,000	Christo-Paganism	-1%	1
Mayoruna	Mayoruna	Peru	1,000	Animism	-1%	1
**Mazahua	Mazahua	Mexico	150,000	Christo-Paganism	6%	4
Mazandaranis	Mazandarani	Iran	1,620,000	Islam	0%	4
Mba	Mba	Zaire	20,000	Animism	-1%	1
Mbaama	Mbaama	Gabon	12,000	Animism	0%	1
Mbai	Mbai	Central African Empire	73,000	Islam-Animist	-1%	1
	Mbai	Chad	200,000	Animism	0%	1
Mbala	Mbala	Zaire	2,000	Animism	0%	1
Mbangwe	Mbangwe	Zaire	81,000	Animism	0%	1
Mbanja	Mbanja	Zaire	15,000	Animism	0%	1
Mbati	Mbati	Central African Empire	14,300	Animism	0%	1
Mbe	Mbe	Nigeria	45,000	Animism	-1%	1
Mbede	Mbede	Gabon	25,000	Animism	0%	1
Mbembe	Mbembe	Cameroon	2,900	Animism	0%	1
Mbembe (Tigong)	Mbembe	Nigeria	nr	Animism	-1%	1
Mbimu	Mbimu	Cameroon	22,500	Animism	0%	1
Mbo	Mbo	Cameroon	2,000	Animism	-1%	1
	Mbo	Zaire	3,200	Islam	-1%	1
Mboi	Mboi	Nigeria	100,000	Animism	0%	1
Mbole	Mbole	Zaire	8,000	Animism	0%	1
Mbugwe	Mbuqwe	Tanzania	6,000	Animism	8%	1
Mbukushu	Kusso	Angola	7,900	Islam	6%	4
Mbula-Bwazza	Mbula-Bwazza	Nigeria	20,000	Islam-Animist -	-1%	1
Mbum	Mbum	Chad			-1%	1

279

NAME	LANGUAGE	COUNTRY	GROUP SIZE	PRIMARY RELIGION	% CHR	V	VOL U.P.
Mbunda	Mbunda	Angola	59,000	Animism	0%	1	
Mbunga	Mbunga	Tanzania	100,000	Animism	0%	1	
Mbwela	Mbwela	Angola	38,000	Animism	-1%	1	
Me'en	Me'en	Ethiopia	10,000	Animism	-1%	1	
Meax	Meax	Indonesia	10,000	Animism	-1%	4	
Meban	Maban-Jumjum	Sudan	130,000	Animism	-1%	4	
**Meghwar	Marwari	Pakistan	100,000	Hinduism	1%	6	79
**Meitei	Manipuri	India	700,000	Hinduism	1%	6	79
**Mejah	Mejah	India	5,500	Animism	1%	4	
Meje	Meje	Uganda	13,200	Animism	0%	1	
Mekwei	Mekwei	Indonesia	1,200	Animism	-1%	1	
**Melanau of Sarawak	Melanau	Malaysia	61,000	Animism	-1%	6	80
Mende	Mende	Liberia	5,000	Islam-Animist	-1%	1	
Mende	Mende	Sierra Leone	600,000	Animism	13%	5	
Menemo-Mogamo	Menemo-Mogamo	Cameroon	35,000	Animism	-1%	1	
Menka	Menka	Cameroon	10,000	Animism	0%	2	
**Menri	Menri	Malaysia	400	Animism	0%	5	
**Meo	Meo	Thailand	29,173	Animism	9%	5	
Meos of Rajasthan	Rajasthani	India	500,000	Islam	0%	5	80
Mesengo	Mesengo	Ethiopia	28,000	Islam-Animist	-1%	1	
Mesme	Mesme	Chad	28,000	Islam-Animist	-1%	1	
Mesmedje	Mesmedje	Chad	11,000	Islam-Animist	-1%	1	
Miao	Miao	China	2,800,000	Animism	1%	5	81
**Miching	Miching	India	259,551	Hindu-Animist	1%	4	
Midob	Midob	Sudan	1,800	Islam	0%	1	
Mien	Mien	China	740,000	Animism	1%	6	81
Migili	Migili	Nigeria	10,000	Animism	-1%	1	
**Military Personnel	Spanish	Ecuador	80,000	Nominal Christian	15%	3	
Mimi	Mimi	Chad	15,000	Islam-Animist	-1%	1	
*Mimika	Mimika	Indonesia	10,000	Christo-Paganism	3%	5	
Mina in Madhya Pradesh	Mina	India	764,850	Hindu-Animist	-1%	1	
Minangkabau	Minangkabau	Indonesia	5,000,000	Islam	1%	6	80
Minduumo	Minduumo	Gabon	4,000	Animism	0%	1	
Mingat	Mingat	Soviet Russia	4,000	Unknown	0%	4	
Minianka	Suppire	Mali	300,000	Animism	-1%	1	
Mirdha in Orissa	Mirdha	India	5,820	Hindu-Animist	1%	4	
Miri	Miri	Sudan	8,000	Islam	0%	1	
Mirung	Mirung	Bangladesh	12,000	Animism	1%	4	
Mishmi in Assam	Mishmi	India	5,230	Hindu-Animist	-1%	1	
Miskito	Miskito	Nicaragua	20,000	Christo-Paganism	2%	5	
**Mixes	Mixe	Mexico	6,000	Christo-Paganism	0%	1	
Mixteco, Amoltepec	Mixteco, Amoltepec	Mexico	6,000	Christo-Paganism	0%	1	
Mixteco, Apoala	Mixteco, Apoala	Mexico	6,000	Christo-Paganism	-1%	1	

Name	Language	Country	Population	Religion	%	Index
Mixteco, Central Puebla	Spanish	Mexico	3,000	Christo-Paganism	0%	1
Mixteco, Eastern	Mixteco, Eastern	Mexico	15,000	Christo-Paganism	-1%	1
Mixteco, Eastern Putla	Mixteco, Eastern Putla	Mexico	7,000	Christo-Paganism	0%	1
Mixteco, Huajuapan	Mixteco, Huajuapan	Mexico	3,000	Christo-Paganism	0%	1
Mixteco, Silacayoapan	Mixteco, Silacayoapan	Mexico	15,000	Christo-Paganism	-1%	1
Mixteco, Southern Puebla	Mixteco, Southern Puebla	Mexico	12,000	Christo-Paganism	-1%	1
Mixteco, Southern Putla	Mixteco, Southern Putla	Mexico	2,500	Christo-Paganism	0%	1
Mixteco, Tututepec	Mixteco, Tututepec	Mexico	2,000	Christo-Paganism	-1%	1
Mixteco, Yosondua	Mixteco, Yosondua	Mexico	15,000	Christo-Paganism	0%	1
*Mixteco,San Juan Mixtepic	Mixteco	Mexico				
Miya	Miya	Nigeria	5,200	Animism	-1%	4
Mo	Mo (Degha)	Ghana	13,000	Animism	18%	5
	Mo	Ivory Coast	800	Islam-Animism	-1%	1
Moba	Bimoba	Ghana	80,000	Animism	-1%	4
	Bimoba	Togo	70,000	Animism	-8%	4
Mober	Mober	Nigeria	44,800	Islam	-1%	4
***Mocha	Mocha	Ethiopia	170,000	Islam	4%	4
Modo	Modo	Sudan	1,700	Animism	0%	1
Mofu	Mofu	Cameroon	33,000	Animism	-1%	1
Mogholi	Mogholi	Afghanistan	2,000	Islam-Animism	-1%	1
Mogum	Mogum	Chad	6,000	Islam-Animist	-1%	1
Moi	Moi	Indonesia	4,000	Animism	-1%	1
Moken	Moken	Burma	5,000	Animism	-1%	6 79
Moken of Thailand	Local dialects	Thailand	3,000	Animism	-1%	1
*Mokole	Mokole	Benin	7,000	Islam-Animism	0%	3
*Molbog	Molbog	Philippines	5,000	Animism	0%	7
Molof	Molof	Indonesia	200	Animism	-1%	1
Mombum	Mombum	Indonesia	250	Animism	-1%	2
Momoguns	Momoguns	Malaysia	110,000	Buddhist-Animist	-1%	5 81
Mon	Mon	Burma	350,000	Islam-Animist	-1%	1
Mona	Mona	Ivory Coast	5,570	Islam-Animist	-1%	5 81
Mongondow	Mongondow	Indonesia	400,000	Traditional Chinese	-1%	1
Mongour	Mongour	China	50,000	Animism	0%	1
Moni	Moni	Indonesia	20,000	Animism	0%	1
Monjombo	Monjombo	Central African Empire	11,000	Animism	0%	3
Mono	Mono	Zaire	30,000	Animism	0%	3
Monpa	Monpa	India	22,000	Buddhist-Animist	-1%	1
Montol	Montol	Nigeria	20,000	Islam	-1%	6 79
Moor & Malays	Tamil	Sri Lanka	895,322	Islam	0%	5
Moors in Mauritania	Arabic (Hassani)	Mauritania	1,000,000	Islam	0%	1
**Mopan Maya	Mopan Maya	Belize	4,000	Christo-Paganism	15%	5
	Mopan Maya	Guatemala	2,000	Christo-Paganism	15%	5
/Mogadam	Moqadam	Iran	1,000	Islam	0%	3

NAME	COUNTRY	LANGUAGE	GROUP SIZE	PRIMARY RELIGION	% CHR	VOL V	U.P.
Mor	Indonesia	Mor	1,000	Animism	-1%	1	
Moreb	Sudan	Moreb	560	Islam	0%	1	
Mori	Indonesia	Mori	200,000	Islam	0%	5	81
Moru	Ivory Coast	Moru	10,000	Islam-Animist	-1%	1	
Moru	Sudan	Moru	23,000	Islam	0%	1	
Morunahua	Peru	Morunahua	150	Animism	-1%	1	
Morwap	Indonesia	Morwap	300	Animism	-1%	1	
Mossi	Tanzania	Mosi	240,000	Animism	0%	1	
Mossi	Upper Volta	Mole	3,300,000	Animism	7%	6	80
Motilon	Colombia	Motilon	2,000	Animism	-1%	1	
	Venezuela	Motilon	3,000	Animism	-1%	1	
Movima	Bolivia	Movima	1,000	Animism	-1%	1	
Mpoto	Malawi	Mpoto	22,000	Animism	0%	1	
	Tanzania	Mpoto	36,000	Animism	0%	1	
Mru	Bangladesh	Mpoto	50,000	Animism	1%	5	
Mualthuam	India	Mualthuam	2,000	Animism	54%	4	
Mubi	Chad	Mubi	36,900	Islam-Animist	-1%	1	
Muinane	Colombia	Muinane	150	Animism	nr	1	
Mulimba	Cameroon	Mulimba	3,690	Islam-Animist	-1%	1	
Multani in Punjab	India	Multani	15,690	Hindu-Animist	-1%	1	
Mumbake	Nigeria	Mumbake	10,000	Islam	-1%	1	
Mumuye	Nigeria	Mumuye	200,000	Animism	-1%	5	
Mun	Burma	Mun	10,000	Buddhist-Animist	-1%	1	
Muna	Indonesia	Muna	200,000	Islam-Animist	-1%	1	
Mundang	Chad	Mundang	100,000	Islam-Animist	-1%	1	
Mundari in Assam	India	Mundari	770,920	Hindu-Animist	-1%	1	
**Mundas in Bihar	India	Munda	25,000	Animism	0%	4	
	Zaire	Mundu	5,000	Animism	-1%	1	
Munduruku	Brazil	Munduruku	2,000	Animism	-1%	1	
Mungaka	Cameroon	Mungaka	14,000	Animism	-1%	1	
Munggui	Indonesia	Munggui	650	Animism	-1%	1	
Munji-Yidgha	Afghanistan	Munji-Yidgha	14,000	Islam	-1%	1	
Mura-Piraha	Brazil	Mura-Piraha	110	Animism	-1%	1	
Muria in Andhra Pradesh	India	Muria	12,900	Hindu-Animist	-1%	1	
Murle	Sudan	Murle	40,000	Animism	1%	4	
*Murngin (Wulamba)	Australia	Dhuwal	3,500	Animism	1%	4	
Mursi	Ethiopia	Mursi	6,000	Animism	-1%	1	
Murut	Malaysia	Murut	37,500	Animism	0%	3	
Musei	Chad	Musei	60,000	Islam-Animist	-1%	1	
Musgu	Chad	Musgu	75,000	Islam-Animist	-1%	1	
Musi	Indonesia	Indonesian	400,000	Islam-Animist	0%	3	
Muslim Community of Bawku	Ghana	Hausa, Ghana	20,000	Islam	0%	3	
**Muslim Immigrants in U.K.	United Kingdom	not reported	500,000	Islam	-1%	4	

Name	Country	Language	Population / Religion			
Muslim Malays	Malaysia	Bahasa Malaysia	5,500,000 Islam	-1%	6	80
Muslims (West Nile Dist.)	Uganda	Lugbara	45,000 Islam	1%	4	
Muslims in U.A.E.	United Arab Emirates	Arabic	202,000 Islam	1%	6	79
Muslims of Jordan	Jordan	Arabic	1,000,000 Islam	-1%	4	
Muthuvan in A.P.	India	Muthuvan	7,000 Hindu-Animist	-1%	1	
Hutu	Venezuela	Spanish	300 Christo-Paganism	0%	1	
Muwasi in Madhya Pradesh	India	Muwasi	21,120 Hindu-Animist	-1%	1	
Mwanga	Tanzania	Mwanga	27,000 Animism	0%	1	
Mwera	Tanzania	Mwera	110,000 Animism	0%	1	
Myaung-Ze	Burma	Myaung-Ze	7,000 Animism	0%	2	
Nabi	Indonesia	Nabi	550 Animism	-1%	1	
Nadeb Maku	Brazil	Nadeb Maku	200 Animism	-1%	1	
**Nafaara	Ghana	Mafaara	40,000 Animism	15%	6	79
Nafar	Iran	Turkish	3,500 Islam	0%	3	
Nafri	Indonesia	Nafri	1,630 Animism	-1%	1	
Naga, Kalyokengnyu	India	Naga, Kalyokengnyu	14,410 Hindu-Animist	-1%	1	
Naga, Mao	India	Naga, Mao	19,970 Hindu-Buddhist	-1%	1	
Naga, Nruanghmei	India	Naga, Nruanghmei	48,600 Hindu-Buddhist	-1%	1	
Naga, Sangtam	India	Naga, Sangtam	20,000 Hindu-Buddhist	-1%	1	
Naga, Sema	India	Naga, Sema	65,230 Unknown	-1%	1	
Naga, Tangkhul	India	Naga, Tangkhul	58,170 Hindu-Buddhist	-1%	1	
Naga, Wancho	India	Naga, Wancho	28,650 Hindu-Buddhist	-1%	1	
Nagar in Madhya Pradesh	India	Nagar	7,090 Hindu-Animist	-1%	1	
Nahsi	China	Nahsi	155,750 Traditional Chinese	-1%	1	
*Nahua, North Pueblo	Mexico	Nahua	55,000 Christo-Paganism	9%	4	
Naka	Sudan	Naka	3,600 Islam	0%	1	
Naltya	Indonesia	Naltya	7,000 Animism	-1%	1	
Nalu	Guinea	Nalu	10,000 Islam-Animist	0%	1	
Nama	Namibia	Nama	10,000 Animism	-1%	1	
Nama	South Africa	Nama	15,000 Animism	0%	1	
Nambikuara	Brazil	Nambikuara	400 Animism	3%	5	
**Nambya	Rhodesia	Nambya	40,000 Animism	8%	5	
Namshi	Cameroon	Namshi	30,000 Animism	1%	4	
Nanai	China	Nanai	1,000 Traditional Chinese	0%	1	
Nanai	Soviet Russia	Nanai	12,400 Unknown	0%	1	
Nancere	Chad	Nancere	35,000 Islam-Animist	0%	1	
Nandi	Zaire	Nandi	310,000 Animism	-1%	1	
Nandu-Tari	Nigeria	Nandu-Tari	4,000 Islam	-1%	1	
Nao	Ethiopia	Nao	5,000 Animism	-1%	1	
Naoudem	Togo	Naoudem	90,000 Islam-Animist	-1%	1	
Nara	Ethiopia	Nara	25,000 Islam-Animist	-1%	1	
Naraguta	Nigeria	Naraguta	3,000 Animism	-1%	1	
Nata	Tanzania	Nata	9,500 Animism	0%	1	

NAME	COUNTRY	LANGUAGE	GROUP SIZE	PRIMARY RELIGION	% CHR	V	VOL. U.P.
Natemba	Togo	Natemba	17,000	Islam-Animist	0%		1
Natioro	Upper Volta	Natioro	1,100	Islam-Animist	0%		1
Nawuri	Ghana	Nawuri	10,000	Animism	1%		5
Nchimburu	Ghana	Nchumburu	7,000	Animism	7%		5
Nchumbulu	Ghana	Nchumbulu	8,000	Islam-Animist	0%		1
Nchumunu	Ghana	Nchumunu	8,000	Islam-Animist	0%		1
Ndaaka	Zaire	Ndaaka	4,700	Animism	0%		1
Ndali	Tanzania	Ndali	57,000	Animism	0%		1
Ndam	Central African Empire	Ndam	670	Animism	0%		1
Ndamba	Tanzania	Ndamba	19,000	Animism	0%		1
Ndaonese	Indonesia	Ndao	2,160	Animism	-1%		1
Ndau	Rhodesia	Ndau	178,000	Animism	-1%		1
**Nde-Nsele-Nta	Nigeria	Nde-Nsele-Nta	10,000	Animism	-1%		1
**Ndebele	Rhodesia	Sindebele	1,000,000	Animism	7%	6	79
Ndengereko	Tanzania	Ndengereko	53,000	Animism	0%		1
Ndjem	Cameroon	Ndjem	25,000	Animism	0%		1
Ndo	Zaire	Ndo	13,000	Animism	-1%		1
Ndoe	Nigeria	Ndoe	3,000	Animism	-1%		1
Ndogo	Central African Empire	Ndogo	3,500	Animism	0%		1
Ndom	Sudan	Ndom	450	not reported	nr		1
Ndomde	Indonesia	Ndomde	12,000	Animism	-1%		1
Ndoolo	Tanzania	Ndoolo	5,000	Animism	0%		1
Ndop-Bamessing	Zaire	Ndop-Bamessing	17,000	Animism	0%		1
**Ndoro	Cameroon	Ndoro	10,000	Animism	0%		1
Nduga	Cameroon	Nduga	10,000	Animism	6%		5
Ndunga	Nigeria	Ndunga	2,500	Animism	-1%		1
Ndunpa Duupa	Indonesia	Ndunpa Duupa	1,000	Islam-Animist	0%		1
Nentsy	Zaire	Nentsy	29,000	Unknown	1%	4	
**Nepalese in India	Cameroon	Nepali	90,000	Hinduism	12%	4	
*Nepali	Soviet Russia	Nepali	6,060,758	Hinduism	0%	3	
*Newari	India	Newari	500,000	Hindu-Buddhist	0%	3	
Nevo	Nepal	Nevo	5,000	Animism	0%		3
Ngada	Nepal	Ngada	40,000	Christo-Paganism	-1%		1
Ngalik, North	Ivory Coast	Ngalik, North	35,000	Animism	-1%		1
Ngalik, Southern	Indonesia	Ngalik, Southern	5,000	Animism	-1%		1
Ngalum	Indonesia	Ngalum	10,000	Animism	-1%		1
**Ngamo	Indonesia	Ngamo	18,000	Animism	8%	4	
Nganasan	Indonesia	Nganasan	1,000	Unknown	0%		1
Ngando	Nigeria	Ngando	2,000	Animism	0%		1
Ngando	Soviet Russia	Ngando	121,000	Animism	0%		1
Ngasa	Central African Empire	Ngasa	1,000	Animism	0%		1
	Zaire						
	Tanzania						

Name	Country	Name	Population	Religion		
Ngayaba	Cameroon	Ngayaba	1,000	Animism	08	1
Ngbaka	Zaire	Ngbaka	700,000	Animism	-18	1
Ngbaka Ma'bo	Central African Empire	Ngbaka Ma'bo	17,000	Animism	08	1
	Zaire	Ngbaka Ma'bo	17,000	Animism	08	1
Ngbandi	Zaire	Ngbandi	137,000	Animism	08	1
Ngbee	Zaire	Ngbee	30,000	Animism	08	1
Ngemba	Cameroon	Ngemba	33,500	Animism	-18	1
*Ngen	Ivory Coast	Ngen	20,000	Animism	28	4
Ngeq	Laos	Ngeq	50,000	Animism	58	5
Ngere	Ivory Coast	not reported	150,000	Animism	-18	4
Ngi	Cameroon	Ngi	85,000	Animism	08	1
Ngindo	Tanzania	Ngindo	3,800	Islam	08	1
Nginyukwur	Sudan	Nginyukwur	4,200	Islam	08	1
Ngirere	Sudan	Ngirere	6,000	Animism	08	1
Ngiri	Zaire	Ngiri	39,200	Islam	08	1
Ngizim	Nigeria	Ngizim	21,000	Islam	-18	1
Ngok	Sudan	Ngok	5,000	Animism	08	1
**Ngombe	Zaire	Ngombe	85,000	Animism	38	5
Ngoni	Tanzania	Ngoni	257,000	Animism	08	1
	Zambia	Ngoni	476,000	Animism	08	1
Ngulu	Malawi	Ngulu	12,800	Animism	08	1
	Tanzania	Ngulu	10,000	Animism	-18	1
Ngumba	Cameroon	Ngumba	4,000	Animism	08	1
Ngumbi	Equatorial Guinea	Ngumbi	9,000	Islam	08	1
Ngunduna	Sudan	Ngunduna	8,000	Islam	08	1
Nguqwurang	Tanzania	Nguqwurang	11,800	Animism	08	1
Ngurimi	Tanzania	Ngurimi	46,000	Animism	08	1
Nguu	Cameroon	Nguu	10,000	Animism	08	1
Ngwo	Nigeria	Ngwo	1,000	Islam	-18	1
Ngwoi	Botswana	Ngwoi	3,000	Animism	08	1
Nharon	Brazil	Nharon	3,000	Animism	-18	1
Nhengatu	Indonesia	Nhengatu	3,000	Animism	08	1
Nias	Chad	Nias	230,000	Animism	-18	1
Nielim	India	Nielim	2,000	Islam-Animist	-18	1
Nihali in Madhya Pradesh	Tanzania	Nihali	1,170	Hindu-Animist	-18	1
Nilamba	India	Nilamba	210,000	Animism	08	1
Nimadi in Madhya Pradesh	Indonesia	Nimadi	794,250	Hindu-Buddhist	-18	1
Nimboran	Brazil	Nimboran	3,500	Animism	-18	1
Ninam	Papua New Guinea	Ninam	470	Animism	-18	4
*Ningerum	Indonesia	Ningerum	3,000	Animism	-18	1
Ninggrum	Indonesia	Ninggrum	3,500	Animism	-18	1
Ninzam	Nigeria	Ninzam	35,000	Islam	-18	1
Nisa	Indonesia	Nisa	250	Animism	-18	1

NAME	COUNTRY	LANGUAGE	GROUP SIZE	PRIMARY RELIGION	% CHR	V	VOL U.P.
Nivkhi	Soviet Russia	Nivkhi	4,400	Unknown	0%	1	
Njadu	Indonesia	Njadu	9,000	Animism	-1%	1	
Njalgulgule	Sudan	Njalgulgule	900	Islam	0%	1	
Nkem-Nkum	Nigeria	Nkem-Nkum	16,700	Animism	-1%	1	
Nkom	Cameroon	Nkom	30,000	Animism	0%	1	
Nkonya	Ghana	Nkonya	17,000	Islam-Animist	-1%	1	
*Nkoya	Zambia	Shinkoya	nr	Animism	5%	4	
Nkutu	Zaire	Nkutu	40,000	Animism	-1%	1	
***Nocte	India	Nocte	19,400	Animism	0%	3	
Nohu	Cameroon	Nohu	6,500	Animism	0%	1	
Norra	Burma	Norra	10,000	Buddhist-Animist	-1%	1	
North Africans in Belgium	Belgium	Arabic	90,000	Islam	-1%	6	80
Northern Cagayan Negrito	Philippines	Northern Cagayan Negrito	1,200	Christo-Paganism	-1%	1	
Nosu	China	Nosu	556,000	Traditional Chinese	3%	4	
*Nouni	Upper Volta	Nouni	50,000	Animism	-1%	1	
Nsenga	Rhodesia	Nsenga	16,100	Animism	-1%	1	
Nsenga	Zambia	Nsenga	191,000	Animism	-1%	1	
Nso	Cameroon	Nso	100,000	Animism	-1%	1	
Nsongo	Angola	Nsongo	15,000	Animism	-1%	1	
Ntomba	Zaire	Ntomba	50,000	Animism	-1%	1	
Ntrubo	Ghana	Ntrubo	4,600	Animism	-1%	1	
Ntrubo	Togo	Ntrubo	3,000	Islam-Animist	0%	1	
Ntrubs	Ghana	Ntrubo	5,000	Animism	1%	5	
*Nuer	Sudan	Nuer	70,000	Animism	-1%	4	
Numana-Nunku-Gwantu	Nigeria	Numana-Nunku-Gwantu	844,000	Animism	-1%	6	79
Nung	China	Nung	15,000	Islam	-1%	1	
Nungu	Nigeria	Nungu	100,000	Traditional Chinese	-1%	1	
Nunuma	Upper Volta	Nunuma	25,000	Islam-Animist	-1%	1	
**Nupe	Nigeria	Nupe	43,000	Islam-Animist	-1%	1	
Nuristani	Afghanistan	Local dialects	600,000	Islam	2%	5	80
**Nyabwa	Ivory Coast	Nyabwa	67,000	Animism	0%	5	
Nyaheun	Laos	Nyaheun	30,000	Animism	3%	5	
Nyakyusa	Malawi	Nyakyusa	15,000	Animism	2%	4	
Nyakyusa	Tanzania	Nyakyusa	34,000	Animism	-1%	1	
Nyambo	Tanzania	Nyambo	193,000	Animism	0%	1	
Nyamusa	Sudan	Nyamusa	4,000	Animism	0%	1	
Nyamwezi	Tanzania	Nyamwezi	1,200	Islam	0%	1	
Nyaneka	Angola	Nyaneka	590,000	Animism	9%	6	80
Nyang	Cameroon	Nyang	10,000	Animism	0%	1	
Nyanga-Li	Zaire	Nyanga-Li	25,000	Animism	-1%	1	
Nyangbo	Ghana	Nyangbo	3,000	Islam-Animist	0%	1	
Nyanja	Rhodesia	Nyanja	252,000	Animism	0%	1	

Name	Country	Name	Population	Religion	
Nyankole	Uganda	Nyankole	810,000	Animism	-1% 1
*Nyantruku	Benin	Aledjo	4,000	Animism	0% 3
Nyarueng	Sudan	Nyarueng	2,000	Islam	0% 1
Nyemba	Angola	Nyemba	100,000	Animism	-1% 1
Nyiha	Tanzania	Nyiha	64,000	Animism	0% 1
	Zambia	Nyiha	59,000	Animism	0% 1
Nyoro	Uganda	Nyoro	620,000	Animism	0% 1
Nyuli	Uganda	Nyuli	140,000	Animism	0% 1
Nyungwe	Mozambique	Nyungwe	700,000	Animism	-1% 1
Nyzatom	Sudan	Todosa, Donyiro	80,000	Animism	0% 3
Nzakara	Central African Empire	Nzakara	3,000	Animism	0% 1
Nzanyi	Nigeria	Nzanyi	14,000	Islam	-1% 1
Nzebi	Congo	Nzebi	40,000	Animism	0% 1
Nzema	Ghana	Nzema	275,000	Islam-Animist	-1% 1
	Ivory Coast	Nzema	24,080	Islam-Animist	-1% 1
O'ung	Angola	O'ung	5,000	Animism	0% 1
Obanliku	Nigeria	Obanliku	19,800	Animism	-1% 1
Obolo	Nigeria	Obolo	70,000	Animism	-1% 1
Ocaina	Peru	Ocaina	250	Animism	-1% 4
Od	Pakistan	Odki	40,000	Hinduism	-1% 1
Odual	Nigeria	Odual	9,000	Animism	-1% 1
Odut	Nigeria	Odut	700	Animism	-1% 1
Ogan	Indonesia	Indonesian	200,000	Islam-Animist	0% 3
Ogbia	Nigeria	Ogbia	22,000	Animism	-1% 5
Oi	Laos	Oi	10,000	Animism	-1% 1
Oirat	China	Oirat	60,000	Traditional Chinese	-1% 1
Ojhi in Madhya Pradesh	India	Ojhi	1,070	Hindu-Animist	-1% 1
Okobo	Nigeria	Okobo	11,200	Animism	-1% 1
Okpamheri	Nigeria	Okpamheri	30,000	Animism	-1% 1
Oliari in Orissa	India	Ollari	800	Hindu-Animist	-1% 1
Olulumo-Ikom	Nigeria	Olulumo-Ikom	9,250	Animism	-1% 1
Ong in Andamans	India	Onq	200	Hindu-Animist	-1% 1
Onin	Indonesia	Onin	600	Animism	-1% 1
Orang Kanak	Malaysia	Orang Kanak	4,000	Animism	0% 2
Orang Laut	Malaysia	Orang Laut	4,000	Animism	0% 2
Orang Ulu	Malaysia	Orang Ulu	4,000	Animism	-1% 1
Orejon	Peru	Orejon	300	Animism	-1% 1
Oring	Nigeria	Oring	25,000	Animism	-1% 1
Ormu	Indonesia	Ormu	750	Animism	-1% 1
Oroch	Soviet Russia	Oroch	1,100	Unknown	0% 1
Orok	Soviet Russia	Orok	400	Unknown	0% 1
Oron	Nigeria	Oron	48,300	Animism	-1% 1
Oronchon	China	Oronchon	2,400	Traditional Chinese	-1% 1

NAME	LANGUAGE	COUNTRY	GROUP SIZE	PRIMARY RELIGION	% CHR	V	VOL U.P.
Oso	Oso	Cameroon	25,000	Animism	0%	1	
Ot Danum	Ot Danum	Indonesia	70,000	Animism	-1%	1	
Otank	Otank	Nigeria	3,000	Animism	-1%	1	
Otomi, Eastern	Otomi, Eastern	Mexico	20,000	Christo-Paganism	-1%	1	
Otomi, Mezquital	Otomi, Mezquital	Mexico	100,000	Christo-Paganism	-1%	1	
Otomi, Northwestern	Otomi, Northwestern	Mexico	40,000	Christo-Paganism	-1%	1	
Otomi, Southeastern	Otomi, Southeastern	Mexico	1,500	Christo-Paganism	0%	1	
Otomi, State of Mexico	Otomi, Tenango	Mexico	70,000	Christo-Paganism	-1%	1	
Otomi, Tenango	Otomi, Tenango	Mexico	10,000	Christo-Paganism	-1%	1	
Otomi, Texcatepec	Otomi, Texcatepec	Mexico	8,000	Christo-Paganism	0%	1	
Otoro	Otoro	Sudan	28,000	Islam	-1%	1	
Ouaddai	Maba	Chad	320,000	Islam	0%	1	
Oubi	Oubi	Ivory Coast	1,340	Islam-Animist	-1%	4	
Oyampipuku	Oyampipuku	Brazil	100	Animism	-1%	1	
Oyda	Oyda	Ethiopia	3,000	Animism	-1%	1	
Pacu	Tucano	Brazil	120	Animism	-1%	1	
***Paez	Paez	Colombia	40,000	Christo-Paganism	11%	5	81
Pahari Garhwali in U.P.	Pahari Garhwali	India	1,277,150	Hindu-Animist	-1%	1	
Pai	Yi	China	1,000,000	Buddhist-Animist	-1%	5	81
Paipai	Pai	Mexico	2,000	Animism	-1%	1	
	Spanish	Mexico	300	Christo-Paganism	-1%	1	
Paite in Assam	Paite	India	27,520	Hindu-Animist	-1%	1	
Paiute, Northern	Paiute, Northern	United States of America	5,000	Peyote Religion	3%	4	
Pakaasnovos	Pakaasnovos	Brazil	800	Animism	-1%	1	
***Pakabeti of Equator	Pakabeti	Zaire	3,000	Animism	3%	4	
*Pala'wan	Pala'wan	Philippines	50,000	Animism	-1%	5	79
Palara	Palara	Ivory Coast	10,000	Islam-Animist	-1%	1	
Palaung	Palaung	Burma	150,000	Buddhism	-1%	5	79
Palawano	Palawano	Philippines	3,000	Animism	-1%	1	
Palawano, Central	Palawano, Central	Philippines	3,000	Animism	-1%	1	
Palembang	Palembang	Indonesia	500,000	Islam	-1%	1	
Palenquero	Spanish	Colombia	3,000	Animism	-1%	1	
Palikur	Palikur	Brazil	500	Animism	-1%	1	
Paloc	Paloc	Sudan	13,500	Islam	-1%	1	
Pambia	Pambia	Central African Empire	2,500	Animism	0%	1	
Pame, Central Chichimeca	Pame, Central Chichimeca	Mexico	1,200	Christo-Paganism	0%	1	
Pame, Chichimeca-Jonaz	Spanish	Mexico	20,000	Christo-Paganism	-1%	1	
Pame, Northern	Pame, Northern	Mexico	1,200	Christo-Paganism	0%	1	
Pana	Pana	Central African Empire	20,000	Animism	0%	1	
Panare	Panare	Venezuela	1,200	Animism	0%	1	
Pande	Pande	Congo	1,000	Animism	0%	1	
Pangwa	Pangwa	Tanzania	26,000	Animism	0%	1	
Panika	Panika	India	30,690	Hindu-Animist	-1%	1	

Name	Country	Language	Population	Religion	%		
**Paniyan of Kerela	India	Paniyan	6,330	Animism	-1%	5	81
Pankararu	Brazil	Portuguese	2,000	Animism	-1%		
Pankhu	Bangladesh	Pankhu	630	Islam	-1%		
Pantu	Indonesia	Pantu	9,000	Animism	-1%		
Pao	Burma	Pao	100,000	Buddhism	0%	2	
Pao in Madhya Pradesh	India	Pao	15,860	Hindu-Buddhist	-1%		
Paongan	China	Paongan	8,000	Traditional Chinese	-1%		
Pape	Cameroon	Pape	1,000	Animism	0%		
Papel	Guinea-Bissau	Papel	36,300	Islam-Animist	-1%		
Papuma	Indonesia	Papuma	700	Animism	-1%		
Parakanan	Brazil	Parakanan	500	Animism	-1%		
Paranan	Philippines	Paranan	6,000	Christo-Paganism	-1%		
Pardhan in Andhra Pradesh	India	Pardhan	450	Hindu-Animist	-1%		
Pare	Tanzania	Pare	99,000	Animism	0%		
Parengi in Orissa	India	Parengi	3,000	Hindu-Animist	-1%		
Paresi	Brazil	Paresi	350	Animism	-1%		
Parintintin	Brazil	Parintintin	200	Animism	-1%		
*Parsees	India	Gujarati	120,000	Secularism	-1%	5	81
Pashayi	Afghanistan	Pashayi	96,000	Islam-Animist	-1%		
Pashtuns	Iran	Pashtu	3,000	Islam	0%	6	80
Patamona	Guyana	Patamona	1,000	Christo-Paganism	-1%		
Patelia in Gujarat	India	Patelia	23,210	Hindu-Animist	-1%		
Pato Tapuia	Brazil	Pato Tapuia	140	Animism	-1%		
Paumari	Brazil	Paumari	250	Animism	-1%		
Paya	Honduras	Spanish	300	Animism	-1%		
Penan, Western	Malaysia	Penan	2,600	Animism	nr	6	81
Pende	Zaire	Pende	200,000	Animism	0%		
Pengo in Orissa	India	Pengo	1,250	Hindu-Animist	-1%		
Peri	Zaire	Peri	40,000	Animism	0%		
Pero	Nigeria	Pero	20,000	Islam	-1%		
Persians of Iran	Iran	Persian	2,000,000	Islam	-1%	6	80
Phu Thai	Laos	Phu Thai	100,000	Buddhist-Animist	-1%	5	
Piapoco	Colombia	Piapoco	3,000	Animism	-1%		
Piaroa	Venezuela	Piaroa	12,000	Animism	-1%		
**Pila	Benin	Pila-Pila	50,000	Animism	-1%	4	
Pilaga	Argentina	Pilaga	4,000	Animism	-1%		
Pima Bajo	Mexico	Pima Bajo	1,000	Christo-Paganism	0%		
Pimbwe	Tanzania	Pimbwe	13,000	Animism	0%		
Piratapuyo	Brazil	Tucano	800	Animism	-1%		
Piro	Peru	Maniteneri	2,500	Animism	-1%		
Pisa	Indonesia	Pisa	3,500	Animism	-1%		
Pishagchi	Iran	Pishagchi	1,000	Islam	0%	3	
Piti	Nigeria	Piti	1,600	Islam	-1%		

NAME	COUNTRY	LANGUAGE	GROUP SIZE	PRIMARY RELIGION	% CHR	VOL V	U.P.
Pitu Uluna Salu	Indonesia	Pitu Uluna Salu	175,000	Animism	-1%		1
Piya	Nigeria	Piya	2,500	Islam	-1%		1
**Plantation Workers	Papua New Guinea	Local dialects	5,000	Christo-Paganism	6%		5
Pnar in Assam	India	Pnar	82,500	Hindu-Animist	-1%		1
Pocomchi, Eastern	Guatemala	Pocomchi, Eastern	20,000	Christo-Paganism	-1%		1
Pocomchi, Western	Guatemala	Pocomchi, Western	25,000	Christo-Paganism	-1%		1
Podokwo	Cameroon	Podokwo	25,000	Animism	-1%		4
Podzo	Mozambique	Podzo	45,000	Animism	0%		1
Pogolo	Tanzania	Pogolo	65,000	Animism	0%		1
Poke	Zaire	Poke	46,000	Animism	0%		1
Pokot	Uganda	Pokot	170,000	Animism	0%		1
Pol	Congo	Pol	2,000	Animism	0%		1
Polci	Nigeria	Polci	6,150	Islam	-1%		1
Pom	Indonesia	Pom	1,700	Animism	-1%		1
Pongu	Nigeria	Ponqu	3,680	Islam	-1%		1
Poouch in Kashmir	India	Poochi	500,000	Islam	0%		4
Popoloca, Ahuatempan	Mexico	Spanish	6,000	Christo-Paganism	0%		1
Popoloca, Coyotepec	Mexico	Spanish	500	Christo-Paganism	0%		1
Popoloca, Eastern	Mexico	Popoloca, Eastern	2,000	Christo-Paganism	-1%		1
Popoloca, Northern	Mexico	Popoloca, Northern	1,000	Christo-Paganism	-1%		1
Popoloca, Southern	Mexico	Spanish	8,000	Christo-Paganism	-1%		1
Popoloca, Western	Mexico	Popoloca, Western	200	Christo-Paganism	0%		1
Popoloca, Oluta	Mexico	Spanish	200	Christo-Paganism	0%		1
Popoluca, Sayula	Mexico	Popoloca, Sayula	6,000	Christo-Paganism	0%		1
Popoluca, Sierra	Mexico	Popoloca, Sierra	18,000	Christo-Paganism	-1%		1
Popoluca, Texistepec	Mexico	Spanish	2,000	Christo-Paganism	-1%		1
Porohanon	Philippines	Porohanon	23,000	Animism	-1%		1
**Portuguese in France	France	Portuguese	150,000	Secularism	10%		4
Prang	Ghana	Prang	5,000	Islam-Animist	0%		1
***Prasuni	Afghanistan	Prasuni	1,000	Islam	-1%		1
Pu-I	China	Pu-I	1,311,020	Traditional Chinese	-1%		1
Puguli	Upper Volta	Puguli	5,000	Islam-Animist	0%		1
Puku-Geeri-Keri-Wipsi	Nigeria	Puku-Geeri-Keri-Wipsi	15,000	Islam	-1%		1
Pular	Senegal	Fouta Toro	281,900	Islam	nr		3
Punjabis	Pakistan	English	49,000,000	Islam	28%	6	80
Punu	China	Punu	220,000	Traditional Chinese	-1%		1
Punu	Congo	Punu	46,000	Animism	0%		1
Puragi	Indonesia	Puragi	900	Animism	-1%		1
Purig-Pa of Kashmir	India	Purig-Skad	nr	Islam	-1%		5
Purum	Burma	Purum	300	Buddhist-Animist	-1%		1
**Puyuma	Taiwan	Puyuma	7,300	Christo-Paganism	nr		5
Pye	Ivory Coast	Pye	6,120	Islam-Animist	-1%		1
Pygmy (Binga)	Burundi	Local dialects	30,000	Animism	6%		5

Name	Country	Language	Population & Religion	%		
*Pygmy (Mbuti)	Central African Empire	Local dialects	2,000 Animism	0%	4	79
Pyu	Zaire	local languages	40,000 Animism	-1%	5	
Qajars	Indonesia	Pyu	100 Animism	-1%	1	
Qara'i	Iran	Qajar	3,000 Islam	0%	3	
Qaragozlu	Iran	Qara'i	2,000 Islam	0%	3	
Qashqa'i	Iran	Qaragozlu	2,000 Islam	0%	3	
Quaiquer	Iran	Qashqa'i	350,000 Islam	0%	5	80
Quarequena	Colombia	Quaiquer	5,000 Animism	-1%	1	
**Quechua	Brazil	Tucano	340 Animism	-1%	1	
	Bolivia	Quechua	1,000,000 Christo-Paganism	4%	5	
**Quechua, Huanco	Peru	Quechua	3,000,000 Christo-Paganism	2%	5	
**Quiche	Peru	Quechua, Huancayo	275,000 Animism	6%	5	79
**Quichua	Guatemala	Quiche	500,000 Christo-Paganism	5%	6	79
Rabha in Assam	Ecuador	Quichua	2,000,000 Christo-Paganism	6%	5	
Rabinal-Achi	India	Rabha	10,000 Hindu-Animist	3%	4	
**Racetrack Residents	Guatemala	Rabinal Achi	21,000 Christo-Paganism	4%	4	
	United States of America	English	50,000 Secularism	6%	5	79
Rai	Nepal	Rai	232,000 Hindu-Buddhist	0%	3	
*Rai, Danuwar	Nepal	Danuwar Rai	12,000 Hindu-Animist	0%	3	
Rajbansi	Nepal	Rajbansi	15,000 Hindu-Animist	0%	3	
Ralte	Burma	Ralte	17,000 Buddhist-Animist	-1%	1	
*Ramkamhaeng Un. Students	Thailand	Thai	200,000 Buddhism	-1%	4	
Ratahan	Indonesia	Ratahan	150,000 Animism	-1%	1	
Rataning	Chad	Rataning	10,000 Islam-Animist	-1%	1	
*Rava in Assam	India	Rava	45,000 Hindu-Animist	1%	5	
Rawang	China	Rawang	60,000 Traditional Chinese	-1%	6	80
Redjang	Indonesia	Rejang	20,000 Islam	0%	3	
Rendille	Kenya	Rendille	20,000 Islam-Animist	-1%	3	
Reshe	Nigeria	Reshe	30,000 Animism	-1%	1	
Reshiat	Ethiopia	not reported	10,000 Animism	-1%	1	
Reyesano	Bolivia	Reyesano	1,000 Animism	-1%	1	
Riang in Assam	India	Riang	74,930 Hindu-Buddhist	-1%	1	
Riang-Lang	Burma	Riang-Lang	20,000 Buddhist-Animist	-1%	1	
Riantana	Indonesia	Riantana	1,100 Animism	-1%	1	
Rikbaktsa	Brazil	Rikbaktsa	200 Animism	-1%	1	
Romany	Turkey	Romany	200,000 Folk Religion	-1%	1	
Ronga	Mozambique	Ronga	400,000 Animism	0%	1	
	South Africa	Ronga	600,000 Animism	0%	1	
Ruihi	Tanzania	Ruihi	71,000 Animism	0%	1	
Rukuba	Nigeria	not reported	50,000 Islam	-1%	1	
Rumaya	Nigeria	Rumaya	1,800 Islam	-1%	1	
Runga	Central African Empire	Runga	1,000 Animism	0%	1	
	Chad	Runga	13,000 Islam-Animist	-1%	1	

NAME	COUNTRY	LANGUAGE	GROUP SIZE	PRIMARY RELIGION	% CHR	V	U.P.
Rungi	Tanzania	Rungi	95,000	Animism	0%		1
Rungwa	Tanzania	Rungwa	5,000	Animism	0%		1
Ruruma	Nigeria	Ruruma	2,200	Islam	-1%		1
Rusha	Tanzania	Rusha	54,000	Animism	-1%		1
Rut	Sudan	Rut	515	Islam	0%		1
Rutul	Soviet Russia	Rutul	12,000	Islam	0%		1
Rwamba	Uganda	Rwamba	60,000	Islam	0%		1
Rwamba	Zaire	Rwamba	48,000	Animism	0%		1
*Ryukyuan	Japan	Ryukyuan	1,000,000	Traditional Japanese	4%		4
Saamia	Uganda	Saamia	124,000	Animism	0%		1
Saams	Soviet Russia	Saams	1,900	Unknown	0%		1
Sabbra	Kenya	Borai	18,000	Animism	15%		3
Saberi	Indonesia	Saberi	1,500	Animism	-1%		1
Sadan in Andamans	India	Sadan	807,180	Hindu-Animist	-1%		1
Sadang	Indonesia	Sadang	50,000	Animism	-1%		1
Safaliba	Ghana	Safaliba	2,500	Islam-Animist	-1%		1
Safwa	Tanzania	Safwa	102,000	Animism	3%		4
Sagala	Tanzania	Sagala	20,000	Animism	0%		1
*Saguye	Kenya	Galla	30,000	Islam	1%		3
Saija	Colombia	Saija	2,500	Animism	1%		1
Saisiat	Taiwan	Saisiat	2,900	Animism	nr	5	81
*Saiva Vellala	India	Tamil	1,500,000	Hinduism	2%		4
Sakata	Zaire	Sakata	75,000	Animism	-1%		1
Sakuye	Kenya	Sakuye	8,000	Islam-Animist	0%		3
Sala	Zambia	Sala	11,000	Animism	0%		1
Salampasu	Zaire	Salampasu	60,000	Animism	-1%		1
Salar	China	Salar	31,000	Traditional Chinese	-1%		1
Saliba	Colombia	Saliba	900	Animism	-1%		1
Sama Banginqi	Philippines	Sinama Bangini	70,000	Islam-Animist	-1%	6	80
Sama Panqutaran	Philippines	Sama Panqutaran	15,000	Islam	-1%	6	80
Sama, Mapun	Philippines	Sama, Mapun	20,000	Animism	-1%		1
Sama, Siasi	Philippines	Sama, Siasi	100,000	Islam-Animist	-1%		1
Sama, Sibuku	Philippines	Sama, Sibuku	11,000	Islam-Animist	-1%		1
Sama-Badjaw	Philippines	Samal dialects	120,000	Islam-Animist	-1%	5	79
Samarkena	Indonesia	Samarkena	750	Animism	-1%		1
Samburu	Kenya	Masai, Samburu	60,500	Animism	3%		4
Samo, Northern	Mali	Samo, Northern	50,000	Animism	0%		1
Samo, Northern	Upper Volta	Samo, Northern	70,000	Islam-Animist	-1%		1
*Samo-Kubo	Papua New Guinea	Samo	1,500	Animism	1%		4
Samogho	Mali	Samogho	10,000	Animism	0%		1
San	Namibia	San	6,000	Animism	0%		1
Sanapana	Paraguay	Sanapana	4,000	Animism	0%		1
Sandawe	Tanzania	Sandawe	30,000	Animism	0%		1

Name	People Name	Country	Population	% Chr.	V
Sanga	Sanga	Nigeria	5,000	Islam	-1% 1
	Sanga	Zaire	35,000	Islam	0% 1
Sangil	Sangil	Philippines	7,500	Islam	-1% 5
Sangir	Sangir	Indonesia	145,000	Animism	-1% 1
Sangke	Sangke	Indonesia	250	Animism	-1% 1
Sangu	Sangu	Gabon	18,000	Animism	-1% 1
	Sangu	Tanzania	30,000	Animism	0% 1
Santa	Santa	China	155,500	Traditional Chinese	-1% 1
**Santhali	Santhali	Nepal	nr	Animism	3% 4
*Santrokofi	Sele	Ghana	5,000	Islam-Animist	0% 1
*Sanuma	Sanuma	Brazil	326	Animism	1% 3
Sanuma	Sanuma	Venezuela	4,000	Animism	-1% 1
Sanza	Sanza	Zaire	15,000	Animism	0% 1
Sapo	not reported	Liberia	30,000	Animism	12% 4
Sarakole	Soninke	Senegal	67,600	Islam	0% 6 80
Saramaccan	Saramaccan	Surinam	20,000	Christo-Paganism	-1% 1
Sarwa	Sarwa	Chad	400	Islam-Animist	-1% 1
Sasak	Sasak	Indonesia	1,600,000	Islam-Animist	1% 6 80
Sasanis	Sasani	Iran	1,000	Islam	0% 3
Sasaru-Enwan Igwe	Sasaru-Enwan Igwe	Nigeria	3,780	Animism	-1% 1
Satere	Satere	Brazil	3,000	Animism	-1% 1
Satnamis in M.P.	Chhattisqarhi	India	30,000	Animism	2% 4
Sau	Sau	Afghanistan	1,000	Islam	-1% 1
Sause	Sause	Indonesia	500	Animism	-1% 1
**Save	Save (Yoruba)	Benin	15,000	Animism	1% 4
**Sawi	Sawi	Indonesia	2,800	Animism	16% 5
Saya	Saya	Nigeria	50,000	Islam	-1% 1
Sayyids	Arabic	Yemen, Arab Republic	nr	Islam	0% 4
Secoya	Secoya	Ecuador	400	Animism	-1% 1
Sekar	Sekar	Indonesia	450	Animism	-1% 1
Sekayu	Indonesian	Indonesia	200,000	Islam-Animist	0% 3
Seko	Seko	Indonesia	275,000	Animism	-1% 1
Sekpele	Sekoele	Ghana	11,000	Islam-Animist	0% 1
**Selakau of Sarawak	Selkau	Malaysia	5,300	Animism	7% 4
Selkup	Selkup	Soviet Russia	4,300	Unknown	0% 2
Semelai	Semelai	Malaysia	3,000	Animism	-1% 1
Sempan	Sempan	Indonesia	2,000	Animism	0% 1
Sena	Sena	Malawi	115,000	Animism	0% 1
	Sena	Mozambique	85,000	Animism	0% 1
Senggi	Senggi	Indonesia	120	Animism	-1% 1
**Senoi	Native Senoi	Malaysia	337,400	Animism	2% 5 81
Sentani	Sentani	Indonesia	10,000	Animism	-1% 1
Senthang	Senthang	Burma	10,000	Buddhist-Animist	-1% 1

NAME	LANGUAGE	COUNTRY	GROUP SIZE	PRIMARY RELIGION	% CHR	V	VOL U.P.
Senufo	Senari	Ivory Coast	300,000	Animism	2%	6	80
**Serawai	Serawai (Pasemah)	Indonesia	60,000	Islam-Animist	1%	5	81
Sere	Sere	Sudan	3,500	Islam	0%		
Serere	Serere	Senegal	700,000	Animism	9%	6	79
Serere-Non	Serere-Non	Senegal	70,000	Islam-Animist	0%		
Serere-Sine	Serere-Sine	Senegal	315,000	Islam-Animist	-1%	1	
Seri	Seri	Mexico	400	Christo-Paganism	-1%	1	
Serui-Laut	Serui-Laut	Indonesia	1,000	Animism	-1%	1	
Seuci	Tucano	Brazil	400	Animism	-1%	1	
Seychellois	Creole	Seychelles	51,000	Secularism	10%	4	
Sha	Sha	Nigeria	500	Animism	-1%	1	
Shahsavans	Azerbaijani (Shahsavani)	Iran	180,000	Islam	0%	6	80
Shambala	Shambala	Tanzania	152,000	Animism	0%	1	
Shan	Shan	Burma	800,000	Buddhism	0%	2	
Shan Chinese	Shan	Thailand	300,000	Buddhist-Animist	-1%	4	
Shanga	Shan	Burma	20,000	Buddhist-Animist	0%	2	
***Shankilla (Kazza)	Shanga	Nigeria	5,000	Animism	0%	4	
Sharanahua	Shankilla (Kazza)	Ethiopia	20,000	Christo-Paganism	1%	5	
Sharchagpakha	Sharanahua	Peru	1,500	Animism	-1%	1	
Shatt	Sharchagpakha	Bhutan	400,000	Buddhist-Animist	-1%	1	
Shawiya	Shatt	Sudan	9,000	Animism	0%	1	
Sheko	Shawiya	Algeria	150,000	Islam	-1%	1	
*Sherpa	Sheko	Ethiopia	23,000	Animism	-1%	1	
**Shihu	Sherpa	Nepal	20,000	Buddhism	0%	3	
Shilha	Shihu	United Arab Emirates	10,000	Islam	-1%	1	
Shilluk	Shilha	Morocco	3,000,000	Islam-Animist	0%		
Shina	Shilluk	Sudan	110,000	Islam	-1%	1	
Shinasha	Shina	Afghanistan	50,000	Islam-Animist	-1%	1	
Shipibo	Shinasha	Ethiopia	4,000	Animism	-1%	1	
**Shirishana	Shipibo	Peru	15,000	Animism	-1%	1	
**Shluh Berbers	Shirishana	Brazil	240	Animism	-1%	1	
Shor	Tashilhait	Morocco	2,000,000	Islam-Animist	5%	3	
*Shourastra in Tamil Nadu	Shor	Soviet Russia	16,000	Islam-Animist	0%	5	
Shua	Shourastra	India	200,000	Unknown	-1%	4	
Shughni	Shua	Botswana	400	Animism	0%	1	
Shuwa Arabic	Shughni	Afghanistan	3,000	Hinduism	-1%	1	
Shwai	Shuwa Arabic	Nigeria	100,000	Islam	-1%	1	
Siagha-Yenimu	Shwai	Sudan	2,800	Islam	0%	1	
Sibo	Siagha-Yenimu	Indonesia	3,000	Animism	-1%	1	
Sidamo	Sibo	China	21,000	Traditional Chinese	-1%	1	
Sikanese	Sidamo	Ethiopia	857,000	Islam-Animist	-1%	1	
Sikka	Sikka	Indonesia	100,000	Animism	-1%	1	
Sikhule	Sikhule	Indonesia	20,000	Animism	-1%	1	

Index Entry	Group	Country	Population	Religion	Code
Sikkimese	Sikkimese	India	36,580	Hindu-Buddhist	-18 1
Simaa	Simaa	Zambia	40,000	Animism	08 1
*Sindhis of India	Sindhi	India	3,000,000	Hinduism	18 5
Sinhalese	Sinhala	Sri Lanka	9,146,679	Buddhism	68 5
Siona	Siona	Colombia	250	Animism	-18 1
Sira	Sira	Gabon	17,000	Animism	08 1
Siri	Siri	Nigeria	2,000	Islam	-18 1
Siriano	Siriano	Colombia	600	Animism	-18 1
Siriono	Siriono	Bolivia	500	Animism	-18 1
**Sisaala	Isaala	Ghana	60,000	Animism	-18 4
Sisaala	Sisaala	Upper Volta	4,000	Islam-Animist	08 1
Siwu	Siwu	Ghana	4,500	Islam-Animist	-18 1
*Slum Dwellers of Bangkok	Thai	Thailand	45,000	Buddhism	-18 4
So	So	Cameroon	6,000	Animism	08 1
	So	Laos	15,000	Animism	18 5
*So	So	Thailand	8,000	Animism	-18 5 81
*Sobei	Sobei	Indonesia	1,400	Animism	-18 1
Sochi	Sindhi	Pakistan	nr	Hinduism	18 3
Soga	Soqa	Uganda	780,000	Animism	08 1
Soka Gakkai Believers	Japanese	Japan	6,500,000	Buddhism	08 3
Soli	Soli	Zambia	32,000	Animism	08 3
Solorese Muslims	Solor	Indonesia	131,000	Islam	08 5 81
*Somahai	Somaqai	Indonesia	3,000	Animism	08 3
Somahai	Somahai	Indonesia	1,500	Animism	-18 1
	Somali	Ethiopia	1,000,000	Islam	18 5
	Somali	Somalia	2,500,000	Islam	18 6
Somali, Ajuran	Somali (Ajuran)	Kenya	25,374	Islam	18 6 79
Somali, Degodia	Somali	Kenya	68,667	Islam	18 5 79
Somali, Gurreh	Somali	Kenya	54,165	Islam	18 5
Somali, Ogadenya	Somali	Kenya	99,129	Islam	18 5
**Somba	Somba (Detammari)	Benin	67,000	Animism	08 4
Somrai	Somrai	Central African Empire	50,000	Islam-Animist	-18 1
	Somrai	Chad	31,490	Animism	-18 1
Sondwari in M.P.	Sondwari	India	500,000	Hindu-Animism	08 1
Songe	Songe	Zaire	125,100	Animism	-18 1
Songhai	Songhai	Mali	93,000	Islam-Animist	-18 1
	Songhai	Niger	35,000	Islam-Animist	08 1
	Songhai	Upper Volta	40,000	Animism	-18 1
Songomeno	Songomeno	Zaire	1,300	Animism	08 1
Songoora	Songoora	Zaire	10,000	Islam	08 1
Soninke	Soninke	Gambia	283,000	Islam	-18 1
	Soninke	Mali	22,000	Islam	08 1
	Soninke	Mauritania		Islam	08 1

NAME	COUNTRY	LANGUAGE	GROUP SIZE	PRIMARY RELIGION	% CHR	V	VOL U.P.
Sonjo	Tanzania	Sonjo	7,400	Animism	5%	5	
Sopi	Sudan	Sopi	1,600	Islam	0%	1	
Sora in Orissa	India	Sora	221,710	Hinduism	-1%	1	
Soruba	Benin	Soruba	5,000	Animism	0%	3	
Sowanda	Indonesia	Sowanda	1,100	Animism	1%	3	79
Spiritists	Brazil	Portuguese	9,000,000	Folk Religion	1%	3	
Students in Cuiaba	Brazil	Portuguese	20,000	Secularism	1%	3	
Su	Cameroon	Su	500	Animism	1%	1	
Suba	Tanzania	Suba	17,000	Animism	0%	5	
**Subanen (Tuboy)	Philippines	Subanen, Tuboy	20,000	Animism	2%	5	
**Subanen, Sindangan	Philippines	Subanun	80,000	Animism	-2%	6	80
Subanun,Lapuyan	Philippines	Subanun, Lapuyan	25,000	Islam-Animist	-1%	1	
Subi	Tanzania	Subi	74,000	Animism	-1%	1	
**Suena	Papua New Guinea	Suena	2,000	Christo-Paganism	4%	4	
Suga	Cameroon	Suga	10,000	Animism	0%	4	
**Sugut	Malaysia	Dusun	10,000	Animism	0%	4	
Sui	China	Sui	160,310	Traditional Chinese	-1%	1	
Suk	Kenya	not reported	133,200	Animism	8%	5	
Suku	Zaire	Suku	74,000	Animism	0%	1	
Sukur	Nigeria	Sukur	10,000	Islam	-1%	1	
Sulung	India	Sulung	nr	Hindu-Buddhist	-1%	1	
Sumba	Indonesia	Sumba	400,000	Christo-Paganism	-1%	5	
Sumbawa	Indonesia	Sumbawa	114,000	Islam	-1%	1	
Sumbwa	Tanzania	Sumbwa	64,000	Animism	0%	1	
Sumu	Nicaragua	Sumu	2,000	Christo-Paganism	-1%	6	80
**Sundanese	Indonesia	Sundanese	20,000,000	Islam-Animist	-1%	1	
Sungor	Chad	Sungor	39,000	Islam-Animist	-1%	1	
Suppire	Mali	Suppire	300,000	Animism	-1%	1	
Sura	Nigeria	Sura	40,000	Islam	1%	4	
**Suri	Ethiopia	Suri	30,000	Animism	-1%	1	
**Suriguenos	Philippines	Suriqueno	23,000	Secularism	7%	4	
Surubu	Nigeria	Surubu	1,950	Islam	-1%	1	
Surui	Brazil	Surui	1,250	Animism	-1%	1	
Susu	Guinea-Bissau	Susu	2,000	Islam-Animist	-1%	1	
Susu	Sierra Leone	Susu	86,500	Islam-Animist	-1%	1	
Svan	Soviet Russia	Svan	35,000	Unknown	0%	1	
Swaga	Zaire	Swaga	121,000	Animism	0%	1	
Swaka	Zambia	Swaka	33,000	Animism	0%	1	
Swatis	Pakistan	Swati	600,000	Islam	0%	6	79
**Swazi	South Africa	siSwati	500,000	Animism	17%	5	
**T'boli	Philippines	Tboli	150,000	Animism	3%	5	81
T'in	Thailand	T'in	25,000	Animism	-1%	5	81
Ta-Oi	Laos	Ta-Oi	15,000	Animism	-1%	5	

People	Country	Language	Population	Religion	Status
Tabasaran	Soviet Russia	Tabasaran	55,000	Islam	0% 1
Tabi	Sudan	Tabi	10,000	Animism	0% 1
Tacana	Bolivia	Tacana	3,500	Animism	-1% 1
Tadjio	Indonesia	Tadjio	100,000	Animism	-1% 1
Tadyawan	Philippines	Tadyawan	1,000	Animism	-1% 1
Tafi	Togo	Tafi	1,000	Islam-Animist	0% 1
Tagal	Malaysia	Tagal	19,000	Animism	nr 6 81
**Tagbanwa, Aborlan	Philippines	Tagbanwa	10,000	Animism	1% 5
Tagbanwa, Kalamian	Philippines	Tagbanwa, Kalamian	4,500	Christo-Paganism	1% 5
***Tagin	India	Tagin	25,000	Animism	1% 3
Tagwana	Ivory Coast	Tagwana	43,000	Islam-Animist	-1% 1
Tahit	Indonesia	Tehit	6,000	Animism	-1% 1
Taikat	Indonesia	Taikat	600	Animism	-1% 1
Taiwan-Chinese Un. Stud.	Taiwan	Mandarin	308,800	Secularism	nr 6
Tajik	Iran	Pamiri	3,600,000	Islam	0% 5
	Afghanistan	Dari	15,000	Islam	0% 5
	Soviet Russia	Persian (Tajiki)	2,500,000	Islam	-1% 1
Takankar	India	Takankar	10,960	Hindu-Animist	0% 1
Takemba	Benin	Takemba	10,000	Animism	0% 1
Takestani	Iran	Takestani	220,000	Islam	-1% 1
Tal	Nigeria	Tal	10,000	Islam	-1% 1
Talish	Iran	Talish	20,000	Islam	0% 3
*Talo	Indonesia	Talo	90,000	Islam-Animist	-1% 3
Talodi	Sudan	Talodi	1,200	Islam	0% 1
Tama	Chad	Tama	60,000	Islam-Animist	0% 1
Tamagario	Indonesia	Tamagario	3,500	Animism	-1% 1
Taman	Burma	Taman	10,000	Buddhist-Animist	0% 3
*Tamang	Nepal	Tamanq	nr	Hindu-Buddhist	nr
Tamaria in Bihar	India	Tamaria	5,050	Hindu-Buddhist	-1% 1
Tamazight	Morocco	Tamazight	1,800,000	Islam-Animist	0% 1
Tambas	Nigeria	Tambas	3,000	Animism	-1% 1
Tambo	Zambia	Tambo	7,000	Animism	0% 1
Tamil (Ceylonese)	Sri Lanka	Tamil	1,415,567	Hinduism	5% 5
*Tamil in Yellagiri Hills	India	Tamil	3,500	Hinduism	2% 5
***Tamil Plantation Workers	Malaysia	Tamil	137,150	Hinduism	1% 4
**Tamils (Indian)	Malaysia	Tamil	600,000	Hinduism	7% 5
**Tamils (Indian)	Sri Lanka	Tamil	1,195,368	Hinduism	5% 4 79
Tampulma	Ghana	Tampulensi	8,000	Animism	2% 5
Tana	Central African Empire	Tana	35,000	Animism	0% 1
Tana	Chad	Tana	3,200	Islam-Animist	-1% 1
Tanahmerah	Indonesia	Tanahmerah	1,000	Animism	-1% 1
Tandanke	Senegal	Tandanke	1,000	not reported	nr 3
Tandia	Indonesia	Tandia	350	Animism	-1% 1

NAME	COUNTRY	LANGUAGE	GROUP SIZE	PRIMARY RELIGION	% CHR	V	VOL U.P.
Tangale	Nigeria	Tangale	100,000	Islam	-1%	1	
Tangchangya	Bangladesh	Tangchangya	8,310	Islam	-1%	1	
**Tangsa	India	Tangsa	10,700	Animism	0%	3	
Tanimuca-Retuama	Colombia	Tanimuca-Retuama	300	Animism	-1%	1	
Tao't Bato	Philippines	not reported	150	Animism	-1%	4	
Taori-Kei	Indonesia	Taori-Kei	140	Animism	-1%	1	
Tara	Indonesia	Tara	125,000	Animism	0%	1	
Tarahumara, Northern	Mexico	Tarahumara, Northern	500	Christo-Paganism	0%	1	
Tarahumara, Rocoroibo	Mexico	Tarahumara, Rocoroibo	12,000	Christo-Paganism	-1%	1	
Tarahumara, Samachique	Mexico	Tarahumara, Samachique	40,000	Christo-Paganism	-1%	1	
Taram	Cameroon	Taram	3,000	Animism	0%	1	
Tarasco	Mexico	Tarasco	60,000	Christo-Paganism	-1%	1	
Targum	Israel	Targum	5,000	Judaism	-1%	1	
Tarof	Indonesia	Tarof	600	Animism	-1%	1	
Tarok	Nigeria	Tarok	60,000	Animism	-1%	1	
Tarpia	Indonesia	Tarpia	560	Animism	-1%	1	
Tat	Soviet Russia	Tat	17,000	Islam	1%	6	80
Tatars	Soviet Russia	Tatar dialects	6,000,000	Islam	-1%	1	
Tatoga	Tanzania	Tatoga	22,000	Animism	1%	5	
*Tatuyo	Colombia	Tatuyo	300	Animism	0%	5	80
Taucouleur	Senegal	Tancouleur	464,700	Islam	0%	1	
Taungyo	Burma	Taungyo	159,200	Buddhist-Animist	-1%	2	
Taungyoe	Burma	Burmese	18,000	Buddhism	0%	1	
Taurap	Indonesia	Taurap	160	Animism	-1%	1	
Tausug	Philippines	Tausug	500,000	Islam	1%	6	80
Tawr	Burma	Tawr	700	Buddhist-Animist	-1%	1	
Tayaku	Benin	Tayaku	10,000	Animism	0%	1	
Tchang	Cameroon	Tchang	100,000	Animism	0%	1	
Teda	Chad	Teda	10,000	Islam	0%	6	80
	Libya	Teda	16,000	Islam	-1%	1	
*Teenbu	Niger	Teda	120,000	Islam-Animist	-1%	1	
Tegali	Ivory Coast	Lothon	5,000	Animism	1%	4	
Teimuri	Sudan	Tegali	16,000	Islam	0%	3	
Teimurtash	Iran	Teimuri	10,000	Islam	0%	1	
Teke, Eastern	Iran	Teimurtash	7,000	Islam	0%	1	
Teke, Northern	Zaire	Teke, Eastern	71,000	Animism	0%	1	
Teke, Southwestern	Congo	Teke, Northern	24,000	Animism	-1%	1	
Tem	Congo	Teke, Southwestern	32,000	Animism	0%	1	
Tembe	Togo	Kotokoli	100,000	Islam	5%	4	
Tembo	Brazil	Tembe	250	Animism	-1%	1	
Temein	Zaire	Tembo	30,000	Animism	0%	1	
Temira	Sudan	Temein	2,300	Islam	0%	1	
	Malaysia	Temira	7,000	Animism	0%	2	

Name	Country	Language	Population	Religion	
*Temne	Sierra Leone	Temne	1,000,000	Animism	68 6 80
Tengger	Indonesia	Tengger	400,000	Hindu-Animist	18 5
*Tense	Ivory Coast	Teen	5,000	Animism	08 1
Tepehua, Huehuetla	Mexico	Tepehua, Huehuetla	2,000	Christo-Paganism	18 1
Tepehua, Pisa Flores	Mexico	Tepehua, Pisa Flores	2,500	Christo-Paganism	18 1
Tepehua, Veracruz	Mexico	Tepehua, Veracruz	900	Christo-Paganism	18 1
Tepehuan, Northern	Mexico	Tepehuan, Northern	5,000	Christo-Paganism	18 1
Tepehuan, Southeastern	Mexico	Tepehuan, Southeastern	8,000	Christo-Paganism	18 1
Tepehuan, Southwestern	Mexico	Tepehuan, Southwestern	6,000	Christo-Paganism	08 1
Tepeth	Uganda	Tepeth	4,000	Animism	08 1
Tepo	Ivory Coast	Tepo	20,000	Islam-Animist	18 1
Tera	Nigeria	Tera	46,000	Islam	18 1
Terena	Brazil	Terena	5,000	Animism	18 1
*Teribe	Panama	Teribe	1,000	Christo-Paganism	158 5
Ternatans	Indonesia	Ternate	42,000	Islam	18 1
*Tertiary Level Youth	Iran	Persian	nr	Islam	18 4
*Teso	Kenya	Luteso	110,000	Animism	88 5
Teso	Uganda	Teso	830,000	Animism	18 1
Thado in Assam	India	Thado	42,340	Hindu-Buddhist	18 1
Thai Islam (Malay)	Thailand	Mala, Pattani	1,700,000	Islam-Animist	18 6 80
*Thai Islam (Thai)	Thailand	Thai, Southern	600,000	Islam-Animist	08 4
Thai Northern	Thailand	North Thai Dialect	6,000,000	Buddhist-Animist	18 4
Thai of Bangkok	Thailand	Thai, Central	4,500,000	Buddhist-Animist	18 4
*Thai University Students	Thailand	Thai	nr	Buddhism	nr 5 81
Thai, North East	Thailand	N.E. Thai	15,500,000	Buddhist-Animist	18 4
Thai, Southern	Thailand	Southern Thai	4,000,000	Buddhist-Animist	18 4
Thai-Ney	Burma	Shan	5,000	Buddhist-Animist	08 2
Thakur	India	Thakur	99,000	Hindu-Animist	18 1
Thar in Bihar	India	Thar	8,790	Hindu-Animist	18 1
Tharu	Nepal	Bhojpuri	495,400	Hinduism	18 1
Thoi	Sudan	Thoi	400	Islam	08 1
Thuri	Sudan	Thuri	154,000	Islam	18 4
*Tibetan	India	Tibetan	nr	Buddhism	18 4
*Tibetans	China	Tibetan	3,000,000	Buddhism	18 5 81
Tibetans in Bhutan	Bhutan	Tibetan	5,000	Buddhism	18 1
Ticuna	Brazil	Ticuna	8,000	Animism	18 1
Tidorese	Indonesia	Tidore	26,500	Islam-Animist	18 1
Tiefo	Upper Volta	Tiefo	6,500	Islam-Animist	08 1
Tiene	Zaire	Tiene	24,500	Animism	18 1
Tigon	Cameroon	Tigon	25,000	Animism	18 4
Tikar	Cameroon	Tikar	12,500	Animism	18 1
Timorese	Indonesia	Timorese	300,000	Animism	08 1
Tindin	Soviet Russia	Tat	5,000	Unknown	08 1

NAME	COUNTRY	LANGUAGE	GROUP SIZE	PRIMARY RELIGION	% CHR	VOL V	U.P.
Tippera	Bangladesh	Tippera	38,000	Islam	-1%		1
Tira	Sudan	Tira	10,200	Islam	-1%		1
Tirma	Sudan	Tirma	8,500	Islam	0%		1
Tiro	Indonesia	Tiro	75,000	Animism	-1%		1
Tiruray	Philippines	Tiruray	30,000	Animism	-1%		1
Tlapaneco, Malinaltepec	Mexico	Tlapaneco, Malinaltepec	40,000	Christo-Paganism	-1%		1
Toala	Indonesia	Toala	100	Animism	-1%		1
Toba	Argentina	Toba	15,000	Animism	-1%		1
Toda in Tamil Nadu	India	Toda	770	Hindu-Animist	-1%		1
*Tofi	Benin	Tofi	33,000	Animism	3%	4	
Togbo	Zaire	Togbo	5,500	Animism	0%		1
Tojolabal	Mexico	Tojolabal	14,000	Christo-Paganism	-1%		1
Tokkaru in Tamil Nadu	India	Tokkaru	1,298,860	Hindu-Animist	-1%		1
Tol	Honduras	Tol	200	Animism	-1%		1
Tombulu	Indonesia	Tombulu	40,000	Animism	-1%		1
Tomini	Indonesia	Tomini	50,000	Animism	-1%		1
Tondanou	Indonesia	Tondanou	35,000	Animism	-1%		1
Tonga	Botswana	Tonga	6,000	Animism	0%		1
Tonga	Malawi	Tonga	62,200	Animism	-1%		1
Tonga	Mozambique	Tonga	10,000	Animism	-1%		1
*Tonga, Gwembe Valley	Rhodesia	ChiTonga	90,000	Animism	2%	5	
Tonga, Gwembe Valley	Zambia	ChiTonga	80,000	Animism	2%	7	79
Tongwe	Tanzania	Tongwe	8,000	Animism	0%		1
Tonsea	Indonesia	Tonsea	90,000	Animism	-1%		1
Tontemboa	Indonesia	Tontemboa	140,000	Animism	-1%		1
*Topotha	Sudan	Toposa	60,000	Animism	2%	4	
Toraja, Southern	Indonesia	Tae'	250,000	Animism	nr	5	81
Totis	India	Gondi	nr	Hinduism	nr	3	
Totonaco, Northern	Mexico	Totonaco, Northern	15,000	Christo-Paganism	-1%		1
Totonaco, Oxumatlan	Mexico	Totonaco, Oxumatlan	1,300	Christo-Paganism	0%		1
Totonaco, Papantla	Mexico	Totonaco, Papantla	50,000	Christo-Paganism	-1%		1
Totonaco, Sierra	Mexico	Totonaco, Sierra	100,000	Christo-paganism	-1%		1
Totonaco, Yecuatla	Mexico	Spanish	500	Christo-Paganism	0%		1
*Toussian	Upper Volta	Toussian	20,000	Islam	8%	4	
Towei	Indonesia	Towei	120	Animism	-1%		1
Trepo	Ivory Coast	Trepo	3,400	Islam-Animist	-1%		1
Trio	Surinam	Trio	800	Animism	-1%		1
Trique, San Juan Copala	Mexico	Trique, San Juan Copala	8,000	Christo-Paganism	-1%		1
Tsaangi	Congo	Tsaangi	10,000	not reported	nr		1
**Tsachila	Ecuador	Colorado	1,100	Christo-Paganism	8%	5	
Tsakhur	Soviet Russia	Tsakhur	11,000	Islam	0%		1
Tsamai	Ethiopia	Tsamai	7,000	Animism	-1%		1
Tsimane	Bolivia	Tsimane	5,500	Animism	-1%		1

Group	Country	Group	Population	Religion	
Tsogo	Gabon	Tsogo	15,000	Animism	0% 1
Tsonga	Mozambique	Tsonga	1,500,000	Animism	-1% 1
Tsou	Taiwan	Tsou	4,100	Animism	-1% 5 81
Tswa	Mozambique	Tswa	200,000	Animism	0% 1
Tswana	Rhodesia	Tswana	300,000	Animism	-1% 1
	Namibia	Tswana	11,300	Animism	0% 1
Tswana	Rhodesia	Tswana	30,000	Animism	-1% 1
Tuareg	Niger	Tamachek	200,000	Islam	-1% 6 79
Tubar	Mexico	Tubar	100	Christo-Paganism	0% 1
Tucano	Brazil	Tucano	2,000	Animism	-1% 1
Tugara	India	Tugara	43,680	Hindu-Animist	-1% 1
Tukude	Indonesia	Tukude	45,000	Christo-Paganism	-1% 1
Tula	Nigeria	Tula	19,000	Islam	-1% 1
Tulishi	Sudan	Tulishi	8,700	Islam	0% 1
Tumale	Sudan	Tumale	1,100	Islam	0% 1
Tumawo	Indonesia	Tumawo	350	Animism	-1% 1
Tumma	Sudan	Tumma	5,200	Islam	0% 1
Tumtum	Sudan	Tumtum	7,300	Islam	0% 1
Tunebo, Cobaria	Colombia	Tunebo, Cobaria	2,000	Animism	-1% 1
Tung-Chia	China	Tung	1,100,000	Animism	0% 5 81
Tunya	Central African Empire	Tunya	800	Animism	0% 1
	Chad	Tunya	800	Islam-Animism	-1% 1
Tupuri	Cameroon	Tupuri	70,000	Animism	-1% 1
	Chad	Tupuri	66,000	Islam-Animist	-1% 1
Tura	Ivory Coast	Tura	19,230	Islam-Animist	-1% 1
**Turkana Fishing Community	Kenya	Turkana	224,000	Animism	4% 5 79
Turkish Immigrant Workers	Kenya	Turkana	20,000	Animism	4% 5 79
Turkish Workers	German Federal Rep.	Turkish	1,200,000	Islam	1% 6 79
Turkomans	Belgium	Kurdish	68,000	Islam	1% 6 80
Turks, Anatolian	Iran	Turkomani	550,000	Islam	0% 6 80
Turkwam	Turkey	Turkish, Osmanli	31,000,000	Islam	-1% 1
Turu	Nigeria	Turkwam	6,000	Islam	-1% 1
	Indonesia	Turu	800	Animism	-1% 1
Tuvinian	Tanzania	Nyaturu	316,000	Animism	10% 4
Tuyuca	Soviet Russia	Tuvin	139,000	Buddhist-Animism	0% 1
Twi	Brazil	Tuyuca	500	Animism	-1% 1
	Sudan	Twi	8,800	Islam	0% 1
Tzeltal, Bachajon	Mexico	Tzeltal, Bachajon	20,000	Christo-Paganism	-1% 1
Tzeltal, Highland	Mexico	Tzeltal, Highland	25,000	Christo-Paganism	-1% 1
Tzotzil, Chenalho	Mexico	Tzotzil, Chenalho	16,000	Christo-Paganism	-1% 1
Tzotzil, Huistan	Mexico	Tzotzil, Huistan	11,000	Christo-Paganism	-1% 1
Tzutujil	Guatemala	Tzutujil	5,000	Christo-Paganism	-1% 1
Udegeis	Soviet Russia	Udegeis	1,500	Unknown	0% 1

NAME	COUNTRY	LANGUAGE	GROUP SIZE	PRIMARY RELIGION	% CHR	V	VOL U.P.
Udin	Soviet Russia	Udin	3,700	Unknown	0%	1	
Udmurt	Soviet Russia	Udmurt	704,000	Animism	0%	1	
Uduk	Sudan	Uduk	7,000	Animism	9%	4	
Uhunduni	Indonesia	Uhunduni	14,000	Animism	-1%	1	
Uighur	Afghanistan	Uighur	3,000	Islam	-1%	1	
Uigur	China	Uigur	4,800,000	Islam	-1%	5	80
Ukaan	Nigeria	Ukaan	18,000	Animism	-1%	1	
Ukpe-Bayobiri	Nigeria	Ukpe-Bayobiri	12,000	Animism	-1%	1	
Ukwuani-Aboh	Nigeria	Ukwuani-Aboh	150,000	Animism	-1%	1	
Ulchi	Soviet Russia	Ulchi	2,400	Unknown	0%	1	
Ulithi-Mall	Turks and Caicos Islands	Ulithi	2,000	Christo-Paganism	-1%	4	
Ullatan in Kerala	India	Ullatan	1,500	Hindu-Animist	-1%	1	
Umm Dorein	Sudan	Umm Dorein	460	Islam	0%	1	
Umm Gabralla	Sudan	Umm Gabralla	9,000	Islam	0%	1	
**Univ. Students of Japan	Japan	Japanese	2,000,000	Traditional Japanese	1%	4	
*University Students	France	French	850,000	Secularism	10%	6	79
Urali in Kerala	India	Urali	1,080	Hindu-Animist	-1%	1	
Urarina	Peru	Urarina	3,500	Animism	-1%	1	
**Urban Mestizos	Ecuador	Spanish	600,000	Nominal Christian	11%	5	
Urhobo	Nigeria	Urhobo	340,000	Animism	-1%	1	
Uria	Indonesia	Uria	1,200	Animism	-1%	1	
Uruangnirin	Indonesia	Uruangnirin	250	Animism	-1%	1	
Urubu	Brazil	Urubu	500	Animism	-1%	1	
Urupa	Brazil	Urupa	250	Animism	-1%	1	
Uspanteco	Guatemala	Uspanteco	15,000	Animism	-1%	1	
Utugwang	Nigeria	Utugwang	12,000	Animism	-1%	1	
Uvbie	Nigeria	Uvbie	6,000	Animism	-1%	1	
**Uzbeks	Afghanistan	Uzbeki, Turkic	1,000,000	Islam-Animist	0%	6	79
Uzekwe	Nigeria	Uzekwe	5,000	Animism	-1%	1	
Vagala	Ghana	Vagala	3,000	Animism	-1%	4	
Vagari	Pakistan	Gujarati Dialect	30,000	Hinduism	1%	5	
Vagla	Ghana	Vagla	6,000	Islam-Animist	-1%	1	
*Vai	Liberia	Vai	30,000	Islam	1%	6	80
Vai	Sierra Leone	Vai	2,800	Islam-Animist	1%	1	
Vaikino	Indonesia	Vaikino	14,000	Animism	-1%	1	
Vaiphei in Assam	India	Vaiphei	12,210	Hindu-Buddhist	-1%	1	
Vale	Central African Empire	Vale	1,400	Animism	0%	1	
Venda	Rhodesia	Venda	38,000	Animism	0%	1	
Veps	Soviet Russia	Veps	16,000	Unknown	0%	1	
Vere	Cameroon	Vere	20,000	Animism	0%	1	
***Vere	Nigeria	Vere	20,000	Animism	9%	5	
Vidunda	Tanzania	Vidunda	11,000	Animism	0%	1	

Vietnamese in the USA	Vietnamese	Laos	20,000	Buddhism	1% 4
**Vietnamese in the USA	Vietnamese	United States of America	261	Buddhism	7% 4
**Vietnamese Refugees	Vietnamese	Australia	7,800	Folk Religion	7% 4
	Vige	Thailand	140,000	Buddhism	4% 4
Vige	Vinza	Upper Volta	3,500	Islam-Animist	0% 1
Vinza	Vishavan	Tanzania	4,000	Animism	1% 1
Vishavan in Kerala	Gujarati	India	150	Hindu-Animist	-1% 1
**Vohras of Yavatmal	Woko	India	10,000	Islam	0% 4
Voko	Vute	Cameroon	1,000	Islam-Animist	1% 4
Vute	Wa	Nigeria	1,000	Animism	-1% 1
Wa	Wabo	Burma	50,000	Animism	0% 2
	Waddar	China	286,160	Traditional Chinese	1% 1
Wabo	Wagdi	Indonesia	900	Animism	-1% 1
Waddar in Andhra Pradesh	Waimiri	India	35,900	Hindu-Animist	-1% 1
Wagdi in Rajasthan	Waiwai	India	756,790	Hindu-Animist	-1% 1
Waimiri	Waja	Brazil	1,000	Animism	-1% 1
Waiwai	Kijita	Brazil	1,000	Animism	-1% 1
	Wali	Guyana	1,000	Christo-Paganism	-1% 1
Waja	Walamo	Nigeria	30,000	Islam	1% 4
**Wajita	Wambon	Tanzania	65,000	Animism	2% 5
Wala	Wanchoo	Ghana	60,000	Animism	-1% 1
Walamo	Wanda	Ethiopia	900,000	Animism	-1% 1
Wambon	Wandamen	Indonesia	2,000	Animism	-1% 1
**Wanchoo	Wandji	India	nr	Animism	0% 3
Wanda	Wanggom	Tanzania	8,000	Animism	-1% 1
Wandamen	Wanji	Indonesia	4,000	Animism	0% 1
Wandji	Wano	Gabon	6,000	Animism	0% 1
Wanggom	Wapishana	Indonesia	19,000	Animism	-1% 1
Wanji	Wapishana	Tanzania	1,700	Animism	0% 1
Wano	Wara	Indonesia	1,500	Animism	-1% 1
Wapishana		Brazil	4,000	Christo-Paganism	-1% 1
	Warao	Guyana	20,000	Animism	-1% 1
Wara	Ware	Venezuela	2,200	Islam-Animist	0% 1
Warao	Warembori	Upper Volta	15,000	Animism	-1% 1
Ware	Waris	Venezuela	2,000	Animism	-1% 1
Warembori	Warji	Mali	350	Animism	-1% 1
Waris	Warkay-Bipim	Indonesia	1,480	Animism	1% 4
*Warjawa	Waropen	Indonesia	70,000	Animism	-1% 1
Warkay-Bipim	Wasi	Nigeria	250	Animism	1% 1
Waropen	Ge	Indonesia	6,000	Animism	-1% 1
Wasi		Indonesia	13,000	Animism	0% 1
Watchi		Tanzania	1,000,000	Animism	5% 4
		Togo			

NAME	COUNTRY	LANGUAGE	GROUP SIZE	PRIMARY RELIGION	% CHR	V	VOL U.P.
Waura	Brazil	Waura	120	Animism	-1%	1	
Wayana	Surinam	Wayana	600	Animism	-1%	1	
*Wazinza	Tanzania	Kizinza	2,000	Animism	7%	4	
Weda	Indonesia	Weda	900	Islam	-1%	1	
Wetawit	Ethiopia	Wetawit	28,000	Animism	-1%	1	
Wewewa	Indonesia	Wewewa	55,000	Animism	-1%	1	
Widekum	Cameroon	Widekum	10,000	Animism	-1%	1	
**Wimbum	Cameroon	Limbum	50,000	Animism	-1%	5	
Win	Upper Volta	Win	20,000	Islam-Animist	-1%	1	
Winji-Winji	Benin	Winji-Winji	5,000	Islam	0%	3	
Wobe	Ivory Coast	Wobe	40,000	Animism	12%	4	
Wodani	Indonesia	Wodani	3,000	Animism	-1%	1	
Woi	Indonesia	Woi	1,300	Animism	-1%	1	
Woleat	Turks and Caicos Islands	Woleat	1,000	Christo-Paganism	-1%	4	
Wolio	Indonesia	Wolio	25,000	Islam-Animist	-1%	1	
Wolof	Senegal	Wolof	1,500,000	Islam-Animist	1%	6	80
Wolof, Gambian	Gambia	Wolof, Gambian	64,800	Islam-Animist	-1%	1	
Wom	Nigeria	Wom	10,000	Islam-Animist	-1%	1	
*Women Laborers	Taiwan	Amoy	1,200,000	Traditional Chinese	2%	4	
Wongo	Zaire	Wongo	8,000	Animism	-1%	1	
Woro	Sudan	Woro	400	Islam	0%	1	
Wumbvu	Gabon	Wumbvu	103	Animism	0%	1	
Wungu	Tanzania	Wungu	8,000	Animism	0%	1	
Xavante	Brazil	Xavante	2,000	Animism	-1%	1	
Xerente	Brazil	Xerente	500	Animism	-1%	1	
Xokleng	Brazil	Xokleng	250	Animism	-1%	1	
Xu	Namibia	Xu	8,000	Animism	-1%	1	
Yafi	Indonesia	Yafi	180	Animism	-1%	1	
Yaghan	Chile	Yaghan	50	Christo-Paganism	0%	1	
Yagnobi	Soviet Russia	Yagnobi	2,000	Unknown	0%	1	
Yagua	Peru	Yagua	4,000	Animism	-1%	1	
Yahadian	Indonesia	Yahadian	700	Animism	-1%	1	
Yaka	Zaire	Yaka	200,000	Animism	-1%	1	
Yakan	Philippines	Yakan	97,000	Islam-Animist	1%	6	80
Yakoma	Central African Empire	Yakoma	5,300	Animism	0%	1	
**Yala	Nigeria	Yala	60,000	Animism	6%	4	
*Yalunka	Sierra Leone	Yalunka	25,000	Islam-Animist	1%	6	80
Yaly	Indonesia	Yaly	12,000	Animism	-1%	1	
Yambasa	Cameroon	Yambasa	26,000	Animism	-1%	1	
Yaminahua	Peru	Yaminahua	1,200	Animism	-1%	1	
Yanadi in Andhra Pradesh	India	Yanadi	205,380	Hindu-Animist	0%	1	
Yandang	Nigeria	Yandang	10,000	Islam-Animist	-1%	1	
Yanga	Togo	Yanga	nr	Islam-Animist	0%	1	

Yangbye in Brazil	Yangbye	Burma	326,650	Buddhist-Animist	-1%	1
*Yanomamo in Brazil	Yanomam (Waica)	Brazil	3,000	Animism	1%	6 79
Yanomamo in Venezuela	Shamatali	Venezuela	nr	Animism	5%	5
	Yans	Zaire	165,000	Animism	0%	1
*Yanyula	Yanyula (Yanjula)	Australia	150	Other	9%	4
**Yao	Chiyao	Malawi	600,000	Islam-Animist	2%	5
**Yao	Yao (Mien Wa)	Mozambique	220,000	Islam	12%	5
*Yao Refugees from Laos	Yao	Thailand	19,867	Animism	2%	6 79
	Yao	Thailand	7,000	Animism	4%	4
Yaoure	Yaoure	Ivory Coast	14,000	Animism	-1%	4
Yaquis	Yaqui	Mexico	14,000	Christo-Paganism	-1%	5
Yaruro	Yaruro	Venezuela	5,000	Animism	-1%	1
Yasing	Yasing	Cameroon	25,000	Animism	0%	1
Yaur	Yaur	Indonesia	350	Animism	-1%	1
	Yava	Indonesia	4,500	Animism	-1%	1
Yazgulyam	Yazgulyam	Soviet Russia	2,000	Unknown	0%	5
**Yei	Yei	Botswana	10,000	Animism	4%	5
Yela	Yela	Indonesia	1,000	Animism	-1%	1
		Zaire	33,000	Animism	0%	1
Yellow Uighur	Yellow Uighur	China	4,000	Traditional Chinese	-1%	1
Yelmek	Yelmek	Indonesia	400	Animism	-1%	5 79
Yemenis	Arabic (Eastern)	Yemen, Arab Republic	5,600,000	Islam	-1%	1
Yerava in Karnataka	Yerava	India	10,870	Hindu-Animism	-1%	1
Yeretuar	Yeretuar	Indonesia	250	Animism	-1%	1
Yerukala in A.P.	Yerukala	India	67,550	Hindu-Animist	-1%	1
Yeskwa	Yeskwa	Nigeria	13,000	Islam	-1%	1
Yidinit	Yidinit	Ethiopia	600	Animism	0%	2
Yin-Kyar	Shan Dialects	Burma	2,000	Animism	0%	2
Yin-Nett	Shan Dialects	Burma	2,000	Animism	-1%	1
Yinchia	Yinchia	Burma	4,000	Buddhist-Animist	1%	4
Yinga	Yinga	Cameroon	300	Animism	0%	1
Yoabu	Yoabu	Benin	8,000	Animism	-1%	1
Yogad	Yogad	Philippines	7,000	Animism	-1%	5
Yonggom	Yonggom	Indonesia	2,000	Animism	-1%	1
Yoruk	Turkish (Danubian)	Turkey	600,000	Islam	-1%	1
Yos	Yos	Burma	4,500	Buddhist-Animist	-1%	1
Yotafa	Yotafa	Indonesia	300	Animism	-1%	1
Yuana	Yuana	Venezuela	3,000	Animism	1%	5
Yucateco	Yucateco	Guatemala	2,460	Animism	0%	1
	Yucateco	Mexico	500,000	Christo-Paganism	-1%	1
*Yucuna	Yucuna	Colombia	500	Christo-Paganism	1%	5
Yukagirs	Yukagir	Soviet Russia	nr	Unknown	0%	1
Yukpa	Yukpa	Colombia	2,500	Animism	-1%	1

NAME	COUNTRY	LANGUAGE	GROUP SIZE	PRIMARY RELIGION	% CHR	V	VOL U.P.
Yuku	Venezuela	Yukpa	3,000	Animism	0%	1	
Yulu	China	Yuku	4,000	Traditional Chinese	-1%	1	
Yulu	Sudan	Yulu	1,500	Islam	0%	1	
Yungur	Nigeria	Yungur	44,300	Islam	-1%	1	
Yuracare	Bolivia	Yuracare	2,500	Animism	-1%	1	
Yurak	Soviet Russia	Yurak	29,000	Unknown	0%	1	
Yuruti	Colombia	Yuruti	150	Animism	-1%	1	
Zaghawa	Chad	Zaghawa	61,000	Islam-Animist	-1%	1	
Zaghawa	Libya	Zaghawa	nr	Islam	-1%	1	
Zaghawa	Sudan	Zaghawa	nr	Islam	-1%	1	
Zanaki	Tanzania	Zanaki	23,000	Animism	-1%	1	
Zande	Zaire	Zande	467,000	Animism	-1%	1	
Zangskari in Kashmir	India	Zangskari	5,000	Hindu-Animist	-1%	1	
Zaramo	Tanzania	Zaramo	296,000	Islam-Animist	2%	5	
**Zaranda Hill Peoples	Nigeria	local languages	10,000	Animism	2%	4	
Zari	Nigeria	Zari	3,950	Islam	-1%	1	
Zayse	Ethiopia	Zayse	21,000	Animism	-1%	1	
Zemi Naga of Assam	India	Jeme	16,000	Animism	nr	6	81
Zenaga	Mauritania	Zenaga	112,000	Islam	0%	1	
Zigwa	Tanzania	Zigwa	3,000	Animism	0%	1	
Zilmamu	Ethiopia	Zilmamu	50,000	Animism	-1%	1	
Zimba	Zaire	Zimba	10,000	Animism	0%	1	
Zinacantecos	Mexico	Tzotzil, Chenalho	50,000	Christo-Paganism	18%	7	79
Zoliang	India	Naga, Zoliang	30,000	Animism	0%	3	
Zome	Burma	Zome	30,000	Buddhist-Animist	-1%	1	
Zome in Manipur	India	Zome	6,000	Hindu-Buddhist	-1%	1	
Zoque, Chimalapa	Mexico	Zoque, Chimalapa	10,000	Christo-Paganism	-1%	1	
Zoque, Copainala	Mexico	Zoque, Copainala	400	Christo-paganism	-1%	1	
Zoque, Francisco Leon	Mexico	Zoque, Francisco Leon	10,000	Christo-Paganism	-1%	1	
Zoque, Tabasco	Mexico	Zoque, Tabasco	37,500	Christo-paganism	-1%	1	
Zowla	Ghana	Ewe	800,000	Animism	2%	5	
Zulu	Malawi	Zulu	37,500	Animism	-1%	1	
Zuni	United States of America	Zuni	6,000	Animism	1%	4	

Index by
Receptivity

INDEX BY RECEPTIVITY

This index lists groups by their reported attitude toward the gospel. The judgment of receptivity or resistance to the gospel is a subjective and difficult question. Often times what appears to be resistance to the gospel turns out to be a rejection of the Western or foreign cultural trappings with which the gospel is offered. Or perhaps it is a resistance to the agents who bear witness because they come from a country or people not respected by those who are being asked to hear the gospel. Nonetheless, this index gives the considered judgment of those who have reported these unreached peoples. Within each category, very receptive, receptive, indifferent, reluctant, very reluctant, and unknown, peoples are listed alphabetically by group name. Their country or location is also listed.

VERY RECEPTIVE

Adi, India
Akhdam, Yemen, Arab Republic
Azteca, Mexico (79)
Bagobo, Philippines
Banaro, Papua New Guinea
Banyarwanda, Rwanda
Baoule, Ivory Coast
Basotho, Mountain, Lesotho (79)
Bipim, Indonesia
Bolinao, Philippines
Cebu, Middle-Class, Philippines
Ch'ol Sabanilla, Mexico
Citak, Indonesia
Copacabana Apt. Dwellers, Brazil
Dan, Ivory Coast
Godie, Ivory Coast
Guarani, Bolivia (79)
Halam in Tripura, India
Higi, Nigeria
Irulas in Kerala, India
Kond, India
Koreans in Germany, German Federal
  Rep.
Krahn, Liberia
Maguzawa, Nigeria (79)
Matharis, India
Mocha, Ethiopia
Nocte, India
Paez, Colombia
Pakabeti of Equator, Zaire
Prasuni, Afghanistan
Shankilla (Kazza), Ethiopia
Tagin, India
Tamil Plantation Workers, Malaysia
Vere, Nigeria

RECEPTIVE

Adja, Benin
Afo, Nigeria (80)
African Students in Cairo, Egypt
Ahl-i-Haqq in Iran, Iran (79)
Akha, Thailand (79)
Ampeeli, Papua New Guinea
Apartment Residents-Seoul, Korea,
  Republic of
Apatani in Assam, India
Apayao, Philippines
Aymara, Bolivia
Azerbaijani, Afghanistan
Babur Thali, Nigeria (80)
Bakuba, Zaire
Balangao, Philippines
Banai, Bangladesh
Bassa, Nigeria
Batangeno, Philippines
Bhil, Pakistan
Bhils, India (79)
Bidayuh of Sarawak, Malaysia (81)
Bijogo, Guinea-Bissau
Bilan, Philippines

Black Caribs, Belize, Belize (79)
Black Caribs, Guatemala, Guatemala
Black Caribs, Honduras, Honduras
Bodo Kachari, India
Boko, Benin
Bontoc, Central, Philippines (81)
Bontoc, Southern, Philippines
Boran, Kenya
Bukidnon, Philippines
Bus Drivers, South Korea, Korea,
  Republic of
Busanse, Ghana
Chayahuita, Peru
Chinese Hakka of Taiwan, Taiwan
  (79)
Chinese in Australia, Australia
Chinese in Brazil, Brazil
Chinese in Hong Kong, Hong Kong
Chinese in Indonesia, Indonesia
Chinese in Panama, Panama
Chinese in Sabah, Malaysia
Chinese in Sarawak, Malaysia
Chinese in United Kingdom, United
  Kingdom
Chinese in United States, United
  States of America
Chinese in Vancouver B.C., Canada
Chinese Refugees, France, France
  (79)
Chinese Stud., Australia, Australia
Chinese Students Glasgow, United
  Kingdom
Chiriguano, Argentina
Chrau, Viet Nam
Coreguaje, Colombia
Dagomba, Ghana
Dhodias, India
Dida, Ivory Coast
Doohwaayo, Cameroon
Dubla, India
Duka, Nigeria
Fakai, Nigeria
Falasha, Ethiopia (79)
Fali, Nigeria
Gagre, Pakistan
Ghimeera, Ethiopia
Glavda, Nigeria
Gouro, Ivory Coast
Grebo, Liberia
Hadrami, Yemen, Democratic
Hajong, Bangladesh
Hewa, Papua New Guinea (79)
High School Students, Hong Kong
Hotel Workers in Manila,
  Philippines (81)
Huave, Mexico
Huila, Angola
Hunzakut, Pakistan (79)
Iban, Malaysia (81)
Ifugao (Kalangoya), Philippines
Indians, East, Trinidad and Tobago
  (79)
Ishans, Nigeria
Izi, Nigeria
Jamaican Elite, Jamaica
Japanese Students In USA, United
  States of America
Jarawa, Nigeria '
Javanese (rural), Indonesia (79)

REGISTRY OF THE UNREACHED

Javanese of Central Java, Indonesia
Javanese of Pejompongan, Indonesia
Jimini, Ivory Coast
Jivaro (Achuara), Venezuela
K'anjobal of San Miguel, Guatemala
Kafirs, Pakistan (79)
Kalagan, Philippines
Kalinga, Tanudan, Philippines
Kalinga,Northern, Philippines (81)
Kankanay, Central, Philippines
Karbis, India
Kasena, Ghana
Kashmiri Muslims, India (79)
Kaur, Indonesia
Kekchi, Guatemala
Khmer Refugees, Thailand
Koch, Bangladesh
Kohli, Kutchi, Pakistan
Kohli, Tharadari, Pakistan
Kohli, Wadiara, Pakistan
Kohlis, Parkari, Pakistan
Kolam, India
Kono, Sierra Leone
Koranko, Sierra Leone
Korean Prisoners, Korea, Republic of
Kowaao, Liberia
Kuluis in Himachal Prades, India (81)
Kunimaipa, Papua New Guinea
Kusaasi, Ghana
Lahaulis in Punjab, India
Lambadi in Andhra Pradesh, India (81)
Lepcha, Sikkim
Lepers of Cen. Thailand, Thailand (81)
Lepers of N.E. Thailand, Thailand
Loho Loho, Indonesia
Lotuka, Sudan
Maasai, Kenya (79)
Macuxi, Brazil
Magar, Nepal
Mam Indian, Guatemala
Mamanua, Philippines (81)
Manqyan, Philippines
Manikion, Indonesia
Manjaco, Guinea-Bissau
Manobo, Cotabato, Philippines
Manobo, Salug, Philippines
Manobo, Tigwa, Philippines
Manobo, Western Bukidnon, Philippines
Mansaka, Philippines
Mawchis, India
Mazahua, Mexico
Meghwar, Pakistan (79)
Mejah, India
Melanau of Sarawak, Malaysia (80)
Meo, Thailand
Miching, India
Military Personnel, Ecuador
Mixes, Mexico
Mopan Maya, Guatemala
Mopan Maya, Belize
Mundas in Bihar, India
Muslim Immigrants in U.K., United Kingdom
Nafaara, Ghana (79)

Nambya, Rhodesia
Ndebele, Rhodesia (79)
Ndoro, Nigeria
Nepalese in India, India
Ngamo, Nigeria
Ngombe, Zaire
Nupe, Nigeria
Nyabwa, Ivory Coast
Paniyan of Kerela, India (81)
Pila, Benin
Plantation Workers, Papua New Guinea
Portuguese in France, France
Puyuma, Taiwan (81)
Quechua, Peru
Quechua, Bolivia
Quechua, Huanco, Peru
Quiche, Guatemala (79)
Quichua, Ecuador
Racetrack Residents, United States of America (79)
Saguye, Kenya
Saiva Vellala, India
Santhali, Nepal
Save, Benin
Sawi, Indonesia
Selakau of Sarawak, Malaysia
Senoi, Malaysia (81)
Serawai, Indonesia (81)
Shihu, United Arab Emirates
Shirishana, Brazil
Shluh Berbers, Morocco
Sisaala, Ghana
Somba, Benin
Subanen (Tuboy), Philippines
Subanen, Sindangan, Philippines (80)
Suena, Papua New Guinea
Sugut, Malaysia
Sundanese, Indonesia (80)
Suri, Ethiopia
Suriguenos, Philippines
Swazi, South Africa
T'boli, Philippines (81)
Tagbanwa, Aborlan, Philippines
Tamils (Indian), Sri Lanka (79)
Tangsa, India
Tatuyo, Colombia
Temne, Sierra Leone (80)
Teribe, Panama
Teso, Kenya
Tsachila, Ecuador
Turkana Fishing Community, Kenya (79)
Univ. Students of Japan, Japan
Urban Mestizos, Ecuador
Uzbeks, Afghanistan (79)
Vietnamese in the USA, United States of America
Vietnamese Refugees, Thailand
Vietnamese Refugees, Australia
Vohras of Yavatmal, India
Wajita, Tanzania
Wanchoo, India
Wimbum, Cameroon
Yala, Nigeria
Yao, Thailand (79)
Yao, Malawi
Yei, Botswana

Zaranda Hill Peoples, Nigeria

INDIFFERENT

Afawa, Nigeria (80)
Alars, India
Alawites, Syria (79)
Albanian Muslims, Albania (80)
Albanians in Yugoslavia, Yugoslavia
Americans in Geneva, Switzerland
Ami, Taiwan (81)
Arnatas, India
Asmat, Indonesia (79)
Ata of Davao, Philippines
Atta, Philippines
Atye, Ivory Coast
Bariba, Benin (80)
Bassa, Liberia
Batak, Angkola, Indonesia (80)
Bete, Ivory Coast
Bhojpuri, Nepal
Bororo, Brazil
Bosnian, Yugoslavia (80)
Bushmen (Hiechware), Rhodesia
Bushmen (Kung), Namibia (79)
Cambodians, Thailand
Casiguranin, Philippines
Central Thailand Farmers, Thailand
   (81)
Chakmas of Mizoram, India (81)
Cham (Western), Kampuchea,
   Democratic (80)
Chang-Pa of Kashmir, India (81)
Chinese in Amsterdam, Netherlands
Chinese in Austria, Austria
Chinese in Holland, Netherlands
Chinese in Japan, Japan
Chinese in Korea, Korea, Republic
   of
Chinese in Laos, Laos
Chinese in Malaysia, Malaysia
Chinese in New Zealand, New Zealand
Chinese in South Africa, South
   Africa
Chinese in Taiwan, Taiwan
Chinese in Thailand, Thailand
Chinese in West Germany, German
   Federal Rep.
Chinese Mainlanders, Taiwan
Chinese of W. Malaysia, Malaysia
Chinese Refugees in Macau, Macau
   (81)
Chinese Restaurant Wrkrs., France
Comorians, Comoros (79)
Cuna, Colombia (79)
Daka, Nigeria
Dani, Baliem, Indonesia (79)
Dewein, Liberia
Dghwede, Nigeria
Dog-Pa of Ladakh, India (81)
Dogon, Mali (79)
Dumagat , Casiguran, Philippines
   (81)
Factory Workers, Hong Kong
Fulani, Benin

Fulbe, Ghana
Gabbra, Ethiopia
Galla (Bale), Ethiopia
Gonds, India
Gorkha, India
Guajiro, Colombia
Guanano, Colombia (79)
Gypsies in Spain, Spain (79)
Havasupai, United States of America
Ibataan, Philippines
Ifugao, Philippines
Indians In Rhodesia, Rhodesia
Industrial Workers, Taiwan (81)
Industry Laborers-Japan, Japan
Inland Sea Island Peoples, Japan
Int'l Stud., Los Banos, Philippines
Iwaidja, Austria
Japanese in Korea, Korea, Republic
   of
Jeepney Drivers in Manila,
   Philippines (81)
Jeepney Drivers in Manila,
   Philippines (81)
Jewish Imgrnts.-American, Israel
Jewish Imgrnts.-Argentine, Israel
Jewish Imgrnts.-Australia, Israel
Jewish Imgrnts.-Brazilian, Israel
Jewish Imgrnts.-Mexican, Israel
Jewish Imgrnts.-Uruguayan, Israel
Jewish Immigrants, Other, Israel
Jibu, Nigeria
Jiye, Sudan
Kaffa, Ethiopia (80)
Kalanga, Botswana
Kalinga, Southern, Philippines
Kambari, Nigeria (80)
Kamuku, Nigeria (80)
Karaboro, Upper Volta
Kepas, Papua New Guinea
Khamu, Thailand
Kimyal, Indonesia
Kissi, Sierra Leone
Kissi, Liberia
Komo, Ethiopia
Konkomba, Togo
Koreans of Japan, Japan
Korku in Madhya Pradesh, India
Krahn, Ivory Coast
Kudisai Vagh Makkal, India
Kui, Thailand
Kuknas, India
Kurds of Turkey, Turkey (79)
Labourers of Jhoparpatti, India
Lahu, Thailand (81)
Lango, Ethiopia
Lao, Laos (79)
Lao Refugees, Thailand
Lisu, Thailand
Lokoro, Sudan
Mahrah, Yemen, Democratic
Malayalars, India
Manobo, Ilianen, Philippines
Masengo, Ethiopia
Meitei, India (79)
Mimika, Indonesia
Mixteco,San Juan Mixtepic, Mexico
Mokole, Benin
Molbog, Philippines
Murngin (Wulamba), Australia

REGISTRY OF THE UNREACHED

Nahua, North Pueblo, Mexico
Nepali, Nepal
Newari, Nepal
Ngen, Ivory Coast
Ningerum, Papua New Guinea
Nkoya, Zambia
Nouni, Upper Volta
Nuer, Ethiopia
Nuer, Sudan (79)
Nyantruku, Benin
Pala'wan, Philippines (81)
Parsees, India (81)
Pygmy (Mbuti), Zaire (79)
Rai, Danuwar, Nepal
Ramkamhaeng Un. Students, Thailand
Rava in Assam, India
Ryukyuan, Japan
Samo-Kubo, Papua New Guinea
Sanuma, Brazil
Sherpa, Nepal
Shourastra in Tamil Nadu, India
Sindhis of India, India
Slum Dwellers of Bangkok, Thailand
So, Thailand (81)
Somah-i, Indonesia
Talo, Indonesia
Tamang, Nepal
Tamil in Yellagiri Hills, India
Tamils (Indian), Malaysia
Teenbu, Ivory Coast
Tense, Ivory Coast
Tertiary Level Youth, Iran
Thai Islam (Thai), Thailand
Thai University Students, Thailand (81)
Tibetan Refugees, India
Tibetans, China
Tofi, Benin
Tonga, Rhodesia
Topotha, Sudan
Toussian, Upper Volta
University Students, France (79)
University Students, German Federal Rep. (79)
Vai, Liberia (80)
Warjawa, Nigeria
Wazinza, Tanzania
Women Laborers, Taiwan
Yalunka, Sierra Leone (80)
Yanomamo in Brazil, Brazil (79)
Yanyula, Australia
Yao Refugees from Laos, Thailand
Yucuna, Colombia

RELUCTANT

Afar, Ethiopia (79)
Alaba, Ethiopia
Alago, Nigeria
Arabs in Morocco, Morocco
Arabs of Khuzestan, Iran
Barasano, Southern, Colombia
Busa, Nigeria (80)
Butawa, Nigeria
Bwa, Upper Volta (80)

Chinese Fishermen, Malaysia
Chitralis, Pakistan (79)
Chola Naickans, India
Chuj of San Mateo Ixtatan, Guatemala
Digo, Kenya
Druzes, Israel (79)
Farmers of Japan, Japan
Fishing Village People, Taiwan
Fra-Fra, Ghana
Fulani, Cameroon (79)
Ga-Dang, Philippines
Galla, Harar, Ethiopia
Gilakis, Iran
Gourency, Upper Volta
Government officials, Thailand
Guarayu, Bolivia
Gujarati, United Kingdom
Gujars of Kashmir, India (81)
Gujars of Kashmir, India (81)
Hopi, United States of America
Ica, Colombia
Ifugao in Cababuyan, Philippines
Igbira, Nigeria (80)
Indians in Fiji, Fiji (79)
Indust.Workers Yongdungpo, Korea, Republic of
Iravas in Kerala, India
Ixil, Guatemala
Jama Mapun, Philippines (80)
Japanese in Brazil, Brazil (79)
Jews of Iran, Iran
Jews of Montreal, Canada
Jews, Sephardic, Canada
Kankanay, Northern, Philippines
Karen, Pwo, Thailand
Kayagar, Indonesia
Kerewe, Tanzania
Komering, Indonesia
Kotokoli, Benin
Krumen, Ivory Coast
Lamba, Togo
Lawa, Eastern, Thailand (81)
Lawa, Mountain, Thailand
Lubang Islanders, Philippines (81)
Maithili, Nepal
Malappanackers, India
Malays of Singapore, Singapore (79)
Mappillas, India
Mapuche, Chile
Mazandaranis, Iran
Miya, Nigeria
Moken, Burma (79)
Moken of Thailand, Thailand
Monpa, India
Mru, Bangladesh
Mualthuam, India
Musi, Indonesia
Nambikuara, Brazil
Ogan, Indonesia
Palaung, Burma (79)
Poouch in Kashmir, India
Purig-Pa of Kashmir, India (81)
Rabinal-Achi, Guatemala
Rajbansi, Nepal
Sabbra, Kenya
Sama Bangingi, Philippines (80)
Sama Pangutaran, Philippines (80)
Sama-Badjaw, Philippines (79)

Sangil, Philippines
Satnamis in M.P., India
Sayyids, Yemen, Arab Republic
Senufo, Ivory Coast (80)
Sinhalese, Sri Lanka
Solorese Muslims, Indonesia (81)
Somali, Ajuran, Kenya (79)
Somali, Degodia, Kenya
Somali, Gurreh, Kenya
Somali, Ogadenya, Kenya
Swatis, Pakistan (79)
T'in, Thailand (81)
Tagbanwa, Kalamian, Philippines
Tamil (Ceylonese), Sri Lanka
Tengger, Indonesia
Thai Northern, Thailand
Thai of Bangkok, Thailand
Thai, North East, Thailand
Thai, Southern, Thailand
Tibetans in Bhutan, Bhutan (81)
Tonga, Gwembe Valley, Zambia (79)
Turkana, Kenya
Turkish Immigrant Workers, German
  Federal Rep. (79)
Watchi, Togo
Winji-Winji, Benin
Woleat, Turks and Caicos Islands
Yakan, Philippines (80)
Yanomamo in Venezuela, Venezuela
Zowla, Ghana
Zuni, United States of America

Malayo, Colombia
Mandingo, Liberia (79)
Maranao, Philippines (79)
Maures, Senegal
Minangkabau, Indonesia (80)
Mirung, Bangladesh
Moor Malays, Sri Lanka (79)
Mumuye, Nigeria
Muslim Malays, Malaysia (80)
Muslims (West Nile Dist.), Uganda
Muslims in U.A.E., United Arab
  Emirates (79)
Muslims of Jordan, Jordan
North Africans in Belgium, Belgium
  (80)
Ouaddai, Chad
Paiute, Northern, United States of
  America
Redjang, Indonesia (80)
Shan, Thailand
Soka Gakkai Believers, Japan
Somali, Ethiopia
Somali, Somalia (79)
Spiritists, Brazil (79)
Tausug, Philippines (80)
Tem, Togo
Tepehuan, Southwestern, Mexico
Thai Islam (Malay), Thailand (80)
Tuareg, Niger (79)
Turkomans, Iran (80)
Turks, Anatolian, Turkey
Ulithi-Mall, Turks and Caicos
  Islands
Wolof, Senegal (80)
Yaoure, Ivory Coast
Yaquis, Mexico
Yemenis, Yemen, Arab Republic (79)
Zemi Naga of Assam, India (81)
Zinacantecos, Mexico (79)

VERY RELUCTANT

Achehnese, Indonesia (80)
Algerian (Arabs), Algeria (80)
Arawa, Nigeria
Azerbaijani Turks, Iran (80)
Balinese, Indonesia
Baluchi, Iran (80)
Bhutias, Bhutan
Bugis, Indonesia (80)
Chamula, Mexico (79)
Dawoodi Muslims, India
Dendi, Benin
Divehi, Maldives (80)
Fula, Guinea
Fula, Sierra Leone
Fulah, Upper Volta
Guaiaqui, Paraguay
Gugu-Yalanji, Australia
Gwandara, Nigeria
Jains, India
Jemez Pueblo, United States of
  America
Kabyle, Algeria (79)
Khojas, Agha Khani, India
Kotta, India
Kreen-Akakore, Brazil
Kurds in Iran, Iran (80)
Libyans, Libya
Macu, Colombia
Madurese, Indonesia (79)
Maguindano, Philippines (80)
Malakkaras of Kerela, India (81)

NOT REPORTED

"Au"ei, Botswana
Abaknon, Philippines
Abanyom, Nigeria
Abau, Indonesia
Abazin, Soviet Russia
Abe, Ivory Coast
Abialang, Sudan
Abidji, Ivory Coast
Abkhaz, Turkey
Abkhaz, Soviet Russia
Abong, Nigeria
Abou Charib, Chad
Abu Leila, Sudan
Abua, Nigeria
Abujmaria in M.P., India
Abure, Ivory Coast
Ach'ang, China
Achagua, Colombia
Acheron, Sudan
Achi, Cubulco, Guatemala
Achi, Rabinal, Guatemala
Achipa, Nigeria
Achode, Ghana

REGISTRY OF THE UNREACHED

Acholi, Uganda
Achual, Peru
Adamawa, Cameroon
Adele, Togo
Adhola, Uganda
Adiyan in Kerala, India
Adygei, Soviet Russia
Adyukru, Ivory Coast
Aeta, Philippines
Afitti, Sudan
Afshars, Iran
Agajanis, Iran
Agariya in Bihar, India
Age, Cameroon
Aghem, Cameroon
Aghu, Indonesia
Agoi, Nigeria
Aguacateco, Guatemala
Aguaruna, Peru
Agul, Soviet Russia
Agutaynon, Philippines
Agwagwune, Nigeria
Ahir in Maharashtra, India
Ahlo, Togo
Aibondeni, Indonesia
Aikwakai, Indonesia
Aimol in Assam, India
Airo-Sumaghaghe, Indonesia
Airoran, Indonesia
Aja, Sudan
Ajmeri in Rajasthan, India
Aka, India
Akan, Brong, Ivory Coast
Akawaio, Guyana
Ake, Nigeria
Akhavakh, Soviet Russia
Akpa-Yache, Nigeria
Akpafu, Ghana
Aladian, Ivory Coast
Alak, Laos
Alangan, Philippines
Alas, Indonesia
Alege, Nigeria
Algerian Arabs in France, France
Alor, Kolana, Indonesia (81)
Alur, Zaire
Alutor, Soviet Russia
Amahuaca, Peru
Amanab, Indonesia
Amar, Ethiopia
Amarakaeri, Peru
Amasi, Cameroon
Ambai, Indonesia
Amber, Indonesia
Amberbaken, Indonesia
Ambo, Zambia
Ambonese, Netherlands
Ambonese, Indonesia
Amo, Nigeria
Amsterdam Boat Dwellers,
   Netherlands
Amuesha, Peru
Amuzgo, Guerrero, Mexico
Amuzgo, Oaxaca, Mexico
Ana, Togo
Anaanq, Nigeria
Anal in Manipur, India
Andha in Andhra Pradesh, India
Andi, Soviet Russia

Andoque, Colombia
Anga in Bihar, India
Angas, Nigeria
Animere, Togo
Ankwe, Nigeria
Ansus, Indonesia
Anuak, Ethiopia
Anuak, Sudan
Anyanga, Togo
Apalai, Brazil
Apinaye, Brazil
Apurina, Brazil
Ara, Indonesia
Arab-Jabbari (Kamesh), Iran
Arab-Shaibani (Kamesh), Iran
Arabela, Peru
Aranadan in Tamil Nadu, India
Arandai, Indonesia
Arapaco, Brazil
Arawak, Guyana
Arbore, Ethiopia
Archin, Soviet Russia
Arecuna, Venezuela
Argobba, Ethiopia
Arguni, Indonesia
Arusha, Tanzania
Arutani, Venezuela
Arya in Andhra Pradesh, India
Asienara, Indonesia
Assamese, Bangladesh
Assumbo, Cameroon
Asu, Tanzania
Asuri in Bihar, India
Aten, Nigeria
Ati, Philippines
Atoc, Sudan
Atruahi, Brazil
Attie, Ivory Coast
Atuot, Sudan
Avatime, Ghana
Avikam, Ivory Coast
Avukaya, Sudan
Awngi, Ethiopia
Awutu, Ghana
Awyi, Indonesia
Awyu, Indonesia
Ayana, Kenya
Aymara, Carangas, Chile
Ayoreo, Paraguay
Ayu, Nigeria
Baali, Zaire
Babajou, Cameroon
Babri, India
Baburiwa, Indonesia
Bachama, Nigeria
Bada, Nigeria
Badagu in Nilgiri, India
Bade, Nigeria
Badyara, Guinea-Bissau
Bafut, Cameroon
Bagelkhandi in M.P., India
Baghati in H.P., India
Bagirmi, Chad
Bagri, Pakistan
Baguio Area Miners, Philippines
   (81)
Baham, Indonesia
Baharlu (Kamesh), Iran
Bahawalpuri in M.P., India

Bole, Nigeria
Bolon, Upper Volta
Bolondo, Zaire
Boma, Zaire
Bomboko, Cameroon
Bomou, Chad
Bondei, Tanzania
Bondo in Orissa, India
Bonerif, Indonesia
Bonggo, Indonesia
Bongili, Congo
Bongo, Sudan
Bonkeng-Pendia, Cameroon
Bor Gok, Sudan
Bora, Colombia
Borai, Indonesia
Boran, Ethiopia
Boran, Kenya
Botlikh, Soviet Russia
Bousansi, Upper Volta
Bovir-Ahmadi, Iran
Bowili, Togo
Boya, Sudan
Bozo, Mali
Brahui, Pakistan
Braj in Uttar Pradesh, India
Brao, Laos (79)
Brat, Indonesia
Bruneis, Malaysia
Bua, Chad
Bual, Indonesia
Bube, Equatorial Guinea
Budu, Zaire
Budug, Soviet Russia
Budugum, Cameroon
Buduma, Nigeria
Buglere, Panama
Bugombe, Zaire
Buhid, Philippines
Builsa, Ghana
Buja, Zaire
Buka-khwe, Botswana
Buli, Indonesia
Buli, Upper Volta
Bulia, Zaire
Bullom, Northern, Sierra Leone
Bullom, Southern, Sierra Leone
Bunak, Indonesia
Bunann in Kashmir, India
Bungku, Indonesia
Bunu, Nigeria
Bura, Cameroon
Burak, Nigeria
Buraka-Gbanziri, Congo
Buriat, China
Buriat, Soviet Russia
Burig, China
Burig in Kashmir, India
Burji, Ethiopia
Buru, Indonesia
Burun, Sudan
Burungi, Tanzania
Busami, Indonesia
Bushmen (Heikum), Namibia
Bushmen in Botswana, Botswana
Bushoong, Zaire
Bussa, Ethiopia
Butung, Indonesia
Buwid, Philippines (81)

Bviri, Sudan
Bwa, Zaire
Bwisi, Zaire
Cacua, Colombia
Caiwa, Brazil
Cakchiquel, Central, Guatemala
Caluyanhon, Philippines
Campa, Peru
Camsa, Colombia
Candoshi, Peru
Canela, Brazil
Capanahua, Peru
Carapana, Colombia
Cashibo, Peru
Cayapa, Ecuador
Cewa, Zambia
Ch'iang, China
Ch'ol Tila, Mexico
Chacobo, Bolivia
Chagga, Tanzania
Chaghatai, Afghanistan
Chakfem-Mushere, Nigeria
Chakossi in Ghana, Ghana
Chakossi in Togo, Togo
Chala, Ghana
Cham, Viet Nam
Chamacoco, Bahia Negra, Paraguay
Chamalin, Soviet Russia
Chamari in Madhya Pradesh, India
Chamba Daka, Nigeria
Chamba Leko, Nigeria
Chameali in H.P., India
Chami, Colombia
Chamicuro, Peru
Chamorro, Turks and Caicos Islands
Chara, Ethiopia
Chatino, Nopala, Mexico
Chatino, Panixtlahuaca, Mexico
Chatino, Tataltepec, Mexico
Chatino, Yaitepec, Mexico
Chatino, Zacatepec, Mexico
Chatino, Zenzontepec, Mexico
Chaungtha, Burma
Chawai, Nigeria
Chenchu in Andhra Pradesh, India
Cherkess, Soviet Russia
Chero in Bihar, India
Chiga, Uganda
Chik-Barik in Bihar, India
Chin, China
Chin, Asho, Burma
Chin, Falam, Burma
Chin, Haka, Burma
Chin, Khumi, Burma
Chin, Ngawn, Burma
Chin, Tiddim, Burma
Chinanteco, Tepinapa, Mexico
Chinanteco, Ayotzintepec, Mexico
Chinanteco, Chiltepec, Mexico
Chinanteco, Comaltepec, Mexico
Chinanteco, Lalana, Mexico
Chinanteco, Lealao, Mexico
Chinanteco, Ojitlan, Mexico
Chinanteco, Palantla, Mexico
Chinanteco, Quiotepec, Mexico
Chinanteco, Sochiapan, Mexico
Chinanteco, Tepetotutla, Mexico
Chinanteco, Usila, Mexico
Chinbok, Burma

Ekajuk, Nigeria
Eket, Nigeria
Ekpeye, Nigeria
El Molo, Kenya
Eleme, Nigeria
Emai-Iuleha-Ora, Nigeria
Embera, Northern, Colombia
Emumu, Indonesia
Engenni, Nigeria
Enya, Zaire
Eotile, Ivory Coast
Epie, Nigeria
Erokwanas, Indonesia
Esan, Nigeria
Eton, Cameroon
Eton, Cameroon
Etulo, Nigeria
Evant, Nigeria
Evenki, China
Evenks, Soviet Russia
Ewenkis, China (81)
Fa D'Ambu, Equatorial Guinea
Fali, Cameroon
Fali, Cameroon
Fipa, Tanzania
Foau, Indonesia
Fordat, Indonesia
Fula, Upper Volta
Fula, Cunda, Gambia
Fula, Macina, Mali
Fula, Peuhala, Mali
Fuliro, Zaire
Fulnio, Brazil
Fungom, Northern, Cameroon
Fungom, Northern, Cameroon
Fungor, Sudan
Furu, Zaire
Fyam, Nigeria
Fyer, Nigeria
Gabbra, Kenya
Gabri, Chad
Gadaban in Andhra Pradesh, India
Gaddi in Himachal Pradesh, India
Gade, Nigeria
Gagauzes, Soviet Russia
Gagu, Ivory Coast
Galambi, Nigeria
Galeshis, Iran
Galla of Bucho, Ethiopia
Galler, Laos
Galong in Assam, India
Gambai, Chad
Gamti in Gujarat, India
Gan, Upper Volta
Gane, Indonesia
Gangam, Togo
Gangte in Assam, India
Gawar-Bati, Afghanistan
Gawari in Andhra Pradesh, India
Gawwada, Ethiopia
Gayo, Indonesia (80)
Gbande, Guinea
Gbari, Nigeria (80)
Gbaya, Nigeria
Gbaya-Ndogo, Sudan
Gbazantche, Benin
Gberi, Sudan
Gedeo, Ethiopia
Geji, Nigeria

Gera, Nigeria
Geruma, Nigeria
Gesa, Indonesia
Gheko, Burma
Ghol, Sudan
Ghotuo, Nigeria
Ghulfan, Sudan
Gidar, Chad
Gidar, Cameroon
Gidar, Cameroon
Gidicho, Ethiopia
Gilyak, Soviet Russia
Gio, Liberia
Giryama, Kenya
Gisei, Cameroon
Gisiga, Cameroon
Gobato, Ethiopia
Gobeze, Ethiopia
Goemai, Nigeria
Gogo, Tanzania
Gokana, Nigeria
Gola, Liberia
Gola, Sierra Leone
Golo, Chad
Gonja, Ghana
Goroa, Tanzania
Gorontalo, Indonesia
Gosha, Kenya
Goudari, Iran
Gouin-Turka, Upper Volta
Goulai, Chad
Gouwar, Cameroon
Gouwar, Cameroon
Grasia in Gujarat, India
Grunshi, Ghana
Gu, Benin
Guajajara, Brazil
Guajibo, Colombia
Guambiano, Colombia
Guana, Paraguay
Guarojio, Mexico
Guayabero, Colombia
Guayabevo, Colombia
Gude, Cameroon
Gude, Nigeria
Gudu, Nigeria
Guduf, Nigeria
Guere, Ivory Coast
Gujuri, Afghanistan
Gula, Chad
Gulfe, Cameroon
Gulfe, Cameroon
Gumuz, Ethiopia
Gumuz, Sudan
Gurage, Ethiopia (80)
Gure-Kahugu, Nigeria
Gurensi, Ghana
Gurma, Upper Volta
Gurung, Nepal
Guruntum-Mbaaru, Nigeria
Gwa, Ivory Coast
Gwari Matai, Nigeria
Gwere, Uganda
Gypsies, Soviet Russia
Gypsies in Yugoslavia, Yugoslavia
Ha, Tanzania
Hadiyya, Ethiopia
Halbi in Madhya Pradesh, India
Hallam, Burma

REGISTRY OF THE UNREACHED

Kachin in Shan State, Burma
Kadaklan-Barlig Bontoc, Philippines
Kadar in Andhra Pradesh, India
Kadara, Nigeria
Kadazans, Malaysia
Kadiweu, Brazil
Kadugli, Sudan
Kaeti, Indonesia
Kagoma, Nigeria
Kagoro, Mali
Kagulu, Tanzania
Kahluri in Andamans, India
Kaibu, Nigeria
Kaikadi in Maharashtra, India
Kaili, Indonesia
Kaingang, Brazil
Kaiwai, Indonesia
Kajang, Indonesia
Kaka, Nigeria
Kaka, Central African Empire
Kaka, Cameroon
Kaka, Cameroon
Kakwa, Sudan
Kakwa, Uganda
Kakwa, Zaire
Kalanga, Rhodesia
Kaliko, Zaire
Kalinga, Kalagua, Philippines
Kalinga, Limus-Linan, Philippines
Kalinga, Quinaang, Philippines
Kalmytz, China
Kalmytz, Soviet Russia
Kam, China
Kamantan, Nigeria
Kamar in Madhya Pradesh, India
Kamayura, Brazil
Kambera, Indonesia
Kamberataro, Indonesia
Kami, Tanzania
Kamkam, Cameroon
Kamkam, Cameroon
Kamo, Nigeria
Kamoro, Indonesia
Kampung Baru, Indonesia
Kamtuk-Gresi, Indonesia
Kana, Nigeria
Kanauri in Uttar Pradesh, India
Kanembu, Chad
Kanembu, Niger
Kanga, Sudan
Kanikkaran in Kerala, India
Kanjari in Andhra Pradesh, India
Kanu, Zaire
Kanum, Indonesia
Kanuri, Nigeria (80)
Kao, Ethiopia
Kaonde, Zaire
Kaonde, Zambia
Kapori, Indonesia
Kapuchin, Soviet Russia
Kara, Tanzania
Karachay, Soviet Russia
Karagas, Soviet Russia
Karaim, Soviet Russia
Karakalpak, Soviet Russia (80)
Karakalpak, Soviet Russia
Karanga, Chad
Karas, Indonesia
Karatin, Soviet Russia

Karekare, Nigeria
Karen, Thailand (79)
Kari, Chad
Kari, Central African Empire
Kari, Zaire
Karipuna Creole, Brazil
Karipuna Do Guapore, Brazil
Kariya, Nigeria
Karko, Sudan
Karmali in Dihar, India
Karon Dori, Indonesia
Karon Pantai, Indonesia
Karre, Central African Empire
Kasanga, Guinea-Bissau
Kasele, Togo
Kasem, Upper Volta
Kasseng, Laos
Kasuweri, Indonesia
Katab, Nigeria
Katakari in Gujarat, India
Katcha, Sudan
Kati, Northern, Indonesia
Kati, Southern, Indonesia
Katla, Sudan
Katukina, Panoan, Brazil
Kaugat, Indonesia
Kaure, Indonesia
Kavwol, Indonesia
Kaw, Burma
Kawar in Madhya Pradesh, India
Kawe, Indonesia
Kayabi, Brazil
Kayan, Malaysia
Kayan, Burma
Kayapo, Brazil
Kaygir, Indonesia
Kayupulau, Indonesia
Kazakhs, Iran (80)
Kazakhs, China (81)
Kebu, Togo
Kebumtamp, Bhutan
Kedayanas, Malaysia
Keer in Madhya Pradesh, India
Kei, Indonesia
Keiga, Sudan
Keiga Jirru, Sudan
Kela, Zaire
Kelabit, Malaysia (81)
Kelao, China
Kele, Gabon
Kemak, Indonesia
Kembata, Ethiopia
Kemok, Malaysia
Kendari, Indonesia
Kenga, Chad
Kenyah, Indonesia
Kera, Chad
Kera, Cameroon
Kera, Cameroon
Kerinchi, Indonesia
Ket, Soviet Russia
Khakas, Soviet Russia
Khalaj, Iran
Khalka, China
Kham, China
Khamti in Assam, India
Khana, Nigeria
Khandesi, India
Khanti, Soviet Russia

Kuwaa, Liberia
Kuzamani, Nigeria
Kvanadin, Soviet Russia
Kwa, Nigeria
Kwadi, Angola
Kwakum, Cameroon
Kwambi, Namibia
Kwangali, Angola
Kwansu, Indonesia
Kwanyama, Angola
Kwanyama, Namibia
Kwaya, Tanzania
Kwe-etshori, Botswana
Kwe-Etshori, Rhodesia
Kwerba, Indonesia
Kwere, Tanzania
Kwese, Zaire
Kwesten, Indonesia
Kyibaku, Nigeria
Laamang, Nigeria
Labans, India
Labbai, India
Labhani in Andhra Pradesh, India
Lacandon, Mexico
Ladakhi in Jammu, India
Ladinos, Lebanon
Lafofa, Sudan
Lahu, Burma
Lahul, China
Laka, Cameroon
Laka, Chad
Laka, China
Laka, Central African Empire
Lakians, Soviet Russia
Lakka, Nigeria
Lala, Zambia
Lalia, Zaire
Lalung in Assam, India
Lama, Burma
Lamba, Benin
Lamba, Zaire
Lamba, Zambia
Lambi, Cameroon
Lambya, Malawi
Lambya, Tanzania
Lame, Nigeria
Lampung, Indonesia (80)
Landoma, Guinea
Landoma, Guinea-Bissau
Langi, Tanzania
Lango, Uganda
Lanoh, Malaysia
Lara, Indonesia
Laro, Sudan
Laru, Nigeria
Latdwalam, Indonesia
Lati, China
Laudje, Indonesia
Lebgo, Nigeria
Lebong, Indonesia
Leco, Bolivia
Lega, Zaire
Lele, Chad
Lele, Upper Volta
Lele, Zaire
Lelemi, Ghana
Lendu, Zaire
Lengua, Northern, Paraguay
Lenje, Zambia

Lese, Zaire
Letti, Indonesia
Li, China
Ligbi, Ivory Coast
Ligbi, Ghana
Liquri, Sudan
Liko, Zaire
Lima, Zambia
Limba, Sierra Leone
Lionese, Indonesia
Lisu, China (81)
Liv, Soviet Russia
Lo, Nigeria
Lobi, Ivory Coast
Lodhi in Bihar, India
Logba, Ghana
Logo, Zaire
Lohar, Pakistan
Loinang, Indonesia (81)
Loko, Sierra Leone
Loko, Guinea
Loko, Sierra Leone
Lolo, China (81)
Loma, Guinea
Loma, Liberia
Lombi, Zaire
Lombo, Zaire
Lomwe, Mozambique
Longuda, Nigeria
Lore, Indonesia
Lori, Sudan
Lors, Iran (80)
Lotsu-Piri, Nigeria
Loven, Laos (81)
Lozi, Rhodesia
Lozi, Zambia
Lu, China
Luac, Sudan
Luano, Zambia
Lubu, Indonesia
Luchazi, Angola
Luchazi, Zambia
Lue, Cameroon
Luqbara, Uganda
Luqbara, Zaire
Luimbi, Angola
Lumbu, Gabon
Luna, Zaire
Lunda, Angola
Lunda, Ndembu, Zambia
Lundu, Cameroon
Lungu, Nigeria
Luo, Tanzania
Lushai in Assam, India
Luwu, Indonesia
Luyana, Angola
Luyana, Zambia
Lwalu, Zaire
Lwena, Angola
Lwo, Sudan
Ma, Zaire
Maanyan, Indonesia
Maba, Chad
Maba, Sudan
Maban-Jumjum, Sudan
Maca, Paraguay
Machiguenqa, Peru
Macuna, Colombia
Madda, Nigeria

Madi, Sudan
Madi, Uganda
Madik, Indonesia
Maghi, Burma
Mahali in Assam, India
Mahri, Oman
Maiongong, Brazil
Mairasi, Indonesia
Majhwar in Madhya Pradesh, India
Maji, Ethiopia
Majingai-Ngama, Chad
Majingai-ngama, Central African
  Empire
Maka, Cameroon
Makasai, Indonesia
Makere, Uganda
Makian, West, Indonesia
Maklew, Indonesia
Makonde, Tanzania
Makua, Mozambique
Malankuravan in Kerala, India
Malapandaram in Kerala, India
Malaryan in Kerala, India
Malavedan in Kerala, India
Male, Ethiopia
Mali in Andhra Pradesh, India
Malila, Tanzania
Malki in Bihar, India
Malpaharia in Assam, India
Malvi in Madhya Pradesh, India
Mama, Nigeria
Mamasani, Iran
Mambai, Indonesia
Mambila, Cameroon
Mambwe-Lungu, Tanzania
Mambwe-Lungu, Zambia
Mamprusi, Ghana
Mamprusi, Ghana
Mamvu-Efe, Zaire
Mancang, Senegal
Manchu, China (81)
Manda, Tanzania
Mandar, Indonesia
Mandara, Nigeria
Mandaya, Philippines
Mandaya, Mansaka, Philippines
Mander, Indonesia
Manding, Senegal
Mandyak, Gambia
Manem, Indonesia
Mangbai, Chad
Mangbutu, Zaire
Manggarai Muslims, Indonesia (81)
Mangisa, Cameroon
Mangs in Maharashtra, India
Maninka, Guinea-Bissau
Maninka, Sierra Leone
Manjack, Senegal
Mankanya, Guinea-Bissau
Mankanya, Senegal
Manna-Dora in A.P., India
Mannan in Kerala, India
Mano, Liberia
Manobo, Agusan, Philippines
Manobo, Ata, Philippines
Manobo, Binokid, Philippines
Manobo, Dibabawon, Philippines
Manobo, Obo, Philippines
Manobo, Sarangani, Philippines

Manobo, Tagabawa, Philippines
Manobos, Pulangi, Philippines
Mansi, Soviet Russia
Mantera, Malaysia
Mantion, Indonesia
Manu Park Panoan, Peru
Manyika, Rhodesia
Mao, Northern, Ethiopia
Maou, Ivory Coast
Mapoyo, Venezuela
Maquiritari, Venezuela
Mara in Assam, India
Maranao, Lanad, Philippines
Mararit, Chad
Marau, Indonesia
Marba, Chad
Marghi Central, Nigeria
Mari, Soviet Russia
Maria in Andhra Pradesh, India
Marind, Indonesia
Marind, Bian, Indonesia
Marka, Upper Volta
Marubo, Brazil
Marwari in Gujarat, India
Masa, Chad
Masaba, Uganda
Masakin, Sudan
Masalit, Chad
Masalit, Sudan
Masenrempulu, Indonesia
Mashi, Zambia
Massalat, Chad
Mataco, Argentina
Matakam, Cameroon
Matakam, Nigeria
Matawari, Surinam
Matbat, Indonesia
Matengo, Tanzania
Matipuhy-Nahukua, Brazil
Matlatzinca, Atzingo, Mexico
Matumbi, Tanzania
Maure, Mali
Mauri, Niger
Maviha, Mozambique
Mawes, Indonesia
Maxakali, Brazil
Mayo, Mexico
Mayoruna, Peru
Mba, Zaire
Mbaama, Gabon
Mbai, Chad
Mbai, Central African Empire
Mbala, Zaire
Mbangwe, Zaire
Mbanja, Zaire
Mbati, Central African Empire
Mbe, Nigeria
Mbede, Gabon
Mbembe, Cameroon
Mbembe (Tigong), Nigeria
Mbimu, Cameroon
Mbo, Cameroon
Mbo, Zaire
Mboi, Nigeria
Mbole, Zaire
Mbugwe, Tanzania
Mbukushu, Angola
Mbula-Bwazza, Nigeria
Mbum, Chad

REGISTRY OF THE UNREACHED

Mbunda, Angola
Mbunga, Tanzania
Mbwela, Angola
Me'en, Ethiopia
Meax, Indonesia
Meban, Sudan
Meje, Uganda
Mekwei, Indonesia
Mende, Sierra Leone
Mende, Liberia
Menemo-Mogamo, Cameroon
Menka, Cameroon
Menri, Malaysia
Meos of Rajasthan, India (80)
Mesenqo, Ethiopia
Mesme, Chad
Mesmedje, Chad
Miao, China (81)
Midob, Sudan
Mien, China (81)
Migili, Nigeria
Mimi, Chad
Mina in Madhya Pradesh, India
Minduumo, Gabon
Mingat, Soviet Russia
Minianka, Mali
Mirdha in Orissa, India
Miri, Sudan
Mishmi in Assam, India
Miskito, Nicaragua
Mixteco, Amoltepec, Mexico
Mixteco, Apoala, Mexico
Mixteco, Central Puebla, Mexico
Mixteco, Eastern, Mexico
Mixteco, Eastern Putla, Mexico
Mixteco, Huajuapan, Mexico
Mixteco, Silacayoapan, Mexico
Mixteco, Southern Puebla, Mexico
Mixteco, Southern Putla, Mexico
Mixteco, Tututepec, Mexico
Mixteco, Yosondua, Mexico
Mo, Ghana
Mo, Ivory Coast
Moba, Ghana
Moba, Togo
Mober, Nigeria
Modo, Sudan
Mofu, Cameroon
Mogholi, Afghanistan
Mogum, Chad
Moi, Indonesia
Molof, Indonesia
Mombum, Indonesia
Momoguns, Malaysia
Mon, Burma (81)
Mona, Ivory Coast
Mongondow, Indonesia (81)
Mongour, China
Moni, Indonesia
Monjombo, Central African Empire
Mono, Zaire
Montol, Nigeria
Moors in Mauritania, Mauritania
Moqaddam, Iran
Mor, Indonesia
Moreb, Sudan
Mori, Indonesia (81)
Moru, Ivory Coast
Moru, Sudan

Morunahua, Peru
Morwap, Indonesia
Mosi, Tanzania
Mossi, Upper Volta (80)
Motilon, Colombia
Motilon, Venezuela
Movima, Bolivia
Mpoto, Malawi
Mpoto, Tanzania
Mubi, Chad
Muinane, Colombia
Mulimba, Cameroon
Multani in Punjab, India
Mumbake, Nigeria
Mun, Burma
Muna, Indonesia
Mundang, Chad
Mundari in Assam, India
Mundu, Zaire
Munduruku, Brazil
Mungaka, Cameroon
Mungqui, Indonesia
Munji-Yidgha, Afghanistan
Mura-Piraha, Brazil
Muria in Andhra Pradesh, India
Murle, Sudan
Mursi, Ethiopia
Murut, Malaysia
Musei, Chad
Musgu, Chad
Muslim Community of Bawku, Ghana
Muthuvan in A.P., India
Mutu, Venezuela
Muwasi in Madhya Pradesh, India
Mwanga, Tanzania
Mwera, Tanzania
Myaunq-Ze, Burma
Nabi, Indonesia
Nadeb Maku, Brazil
Nafar, Iran
Nafri, Indonesia
Naga, Kalyokengnyu, India
Naga, Mao, India
Naga, Nruanghmei, India
Naga, Sangtam, India
Naga, Sema, India
Naga, Tanqkhul, India
Naga, Wancho, India
Nagar in Madhya Pradesh, India
Nahsi, China
Naka, Sudan
Naltya, Indonesia
Nalu, Guinea
Nama, Namibia
Nama, South Africa
Namshi, Cameroon
Nanai, China
Nanai, Soviet Russia
Nancere, Chad
Nandi, Zaire
Nandu-Tari, Nigeria
Nao, Ethiopia
Naoudem, Togo
Nara, Ethiopia
Naraguta, Nigeria
Nata, Tanzania
Natemba, Togo
Natioro, Upper Volta
Nawuri, Ghana

Nchimburu, Ghana
Nchumbulu, Ghana
Nchumunu, Ghana
Ndaaka, Zaire
Ndali, Tanzania
Ndam, Central African Empire
Ndamba, Tanzania
Ndaonese, Indonesia
Ndau, Rhodesia
Nde-Nsele-Nta, Nigeria
Ndengereko, Tanzania
Ndjem, Cameroon
Ndo, Zaire
Ndoe, Nigeria
Ndogo, Central African Empire
Ndogo, Sudan
Ndom, Indonesia
Ndomde, Tanzania
Ndoolo, Zaire
Ndop-Bamessing, Cameroon
Ndoro, Cameroon
Nduga, Indonesia
Ndunga, Zaire
Ndunpa Duupa, Cameroon
Nentsy, Soviet Russia
Neyo, Ivory Coast
Ngada, Indonesia
Ngalik, North, Indonesia
Ngalik, Southern, Indonesia
Ngalum, Indonesia
Nganasan, Soviet Russia
Ngando, Central African Empire
Ngando, Zaire
Ngasa, Tanzania
Ngayaba, Cameroon
Ngbaka, Zaire
Ngbaka Ma'bo, Central African
  Empire
Ngbaka Ma'bo, Zaire
Ngbandi, Zaire
Ngbee, Zaire
Ngemba, Cameroon
Ngeq, Laos
Ngere, Ivory Coast
Ngi, Cameroon
Ngindo, Tanzania
Nginyukwur, Sudan
Ngirere, Sudan
Ngiri, Zaire
Ngizim, Nigeria
Ngok, Sudan
Ngoni, Tanzania
Ngoni, Zambia
Ngulu, Malawi
Ngulu, Tanzania
Ngumba, Cameroon
Ngumbi, Equatorial Guinea
Ngunduna, Sudan
Nguqwurang, Sudan
Ngurimi, Tanzania
Nguu, Tanzania
Ngwo, Cameroon
Ngwoi, Nigeria
Nharon, Botswana
Nhengatu, Brazil
Nias, Indonesia
Nielim, Chad
Nihali in Madhya Pradesh, India
Nilamba, Tanzania

Nimadi in Madhya Pradesh, India
Nimboran, Indonesia
Ninam, Brazil
Ninggrum, Indonesia
Ninzam, Nigeria
Nisa, Indonesia
Nivkhi, Soviet Russia
Njadu, Indonesia
Njalgulgule, Sudan
Nkem-Nkum, Nigeria
Nkom, Cameroon
Nkonya, Ghana
Nkutu, Zaire
Nohu, Cameroon
Norra, Burma
Northern Cagayan Negrito,
  Philippines
Nosu, China
Nsenga, Rhodesia
Nsenga, Zambia
Nso, Cameroon
Nsongo, Angola
Ntomba, Zaire
Ntrubo, Ghana
Ntrubo, Togo
Ntrubs, Ghana
Numana-Nunku-Gwantu, Nigeria
Nung, China
Nungu, Nigeria
Nunuma, Upper Volta
Nuristani, Afghanistan (80)
Nyaheun, Laos
Nyakyusa, Malawi
Nyakyusa, Tanzania
Nyambo, Tanzania
Nyamusa, Sudan
Nyamwezi, Tanzania (80)
Nyaneka, Angola
Nyang, Cameroon
Nyanga-Li, Zaire
Nyangbo, Ghana
Nyanja, Rhodesia
Nyankole, Uganda
Nyarueng, Sudan
Nyemba, Angola
Nyiha, Tanzania
Nyiha, Zambia
Nyoro, Uganda
Nyuli, Uganda
Nyungwe, Mozambique
Nyzatom, Sudan
Nzakara, Central African Empire
Nzanyi, Nigeria
Nzebi, Congo
Nzema, Ivory Coast
Nzema, Ghana
O'ung, Angola
Obanliku, Nigeria
Obolo, Nigeria
Ocaina, Peru
Od, Pakistan
Odual, Nigeria
Odut, Nigeria
Ogbia, Nigeria
Oi, Laos
Oirat, China
Ojhi in Madhya Pradesh, India
Okobo, Nigeria
Okpamheri, Nigeria

Ollari in Orissa, India
Olulumo-Ikom, Nigeria
Ong in Andamans, India
Onin, Indonesia
Orang Kanak, Malaysia
Orang Laut, Malaysia
Orang Ulu, Malaysia
Orejon, Peru
Oring, Nigeria
Ormu, Indonesia
Oroch, Soviet Russia
Orok, Soviet Russia
Oron, Nigeria
Oronchon, China
Oso, Cameroon
Ot Danum, Indonesia
Otank, Nigeria
Otomi, Eastern, Mexico
Otomi, Mezquital, Mexico
Otomi, Northwestern, Mexico
Otomi, Southeastern, Mexico
Otomi, State of Mexico, Mexico
Otomi, Tenango, Mexico
Otomi, Texcatepec, Mexico
Otoro, Sudan
Oubi, Ivory Coast
Oyampipuku, Brazil
Oyda, Ethiopia
Pacu, Brazil
Pahari Garhwali in U.P., India
Pai, Nigeria
Pai, China (81)
Paipai, Mexico
Paite in Assam, India
Pakaasnovos, Brazil
Palara, Ivory Coast
Palawano, Philippines
Palawano, Central, Philippines
Palembang, Indonesia
Palenquero, Colombia
Palikur, Brazil
Paloc, Sudan
Pambia, Central African Empire
Pame, Central Chichimeca, Mexico
Pame, Chichimeca-Jonaz, Mexico
Pame, Northern, Mexico
Pana, Central African Empire
Panare, Venezuela
Pande, Congo
Pangwa, Tanzania
Panika, India
Pankararu, Brazil
Pankhu, Bangladesh
Pantu, Indonesia
Pao, Burma
Pao in Madhya Pradesh, India
Paongan, China
Pape, Cameroon
Papel, Guinea-Bissau
Papuma, Indonesia
Parakanan, Brazil
Paranan, Philippines
Pardhan in Andhra Pradesh, India
Pare, Tanzania
Parenqi in Orissa, India
Paresi, Brazil
Parintintin, Brazil
Pashayi, Afghanistan
Pashtuns, Iran (80)

Patamona, Guyana
Patelia in Gujarat, India
Pato Tapuia, Brazil
Paumari, Brazil
Paya, Honduras
Penan, Western, Malaysia (81)
Pende, Zaire
Pengo in Orissa, India
Peri, Zaire
Pero, Nigeria
Persians of Iran, Iran (80)
Phu Thai, Laos
Piapoco, Colombia
Piaroa, Venezuela
Pilaga, Argentina
Pima Bajo, Mexico
Pimbwe, Tanzania
Piratapuyo, Brazil
Piro, Peru
Pisa, Indonesia
Pishagchi, Iran
Piti, Nigeria
Pitu Uluna Salu, Indonesia
Piya, Nigeria
Pnar in Assam, India
Pocomchi, Eastern, Guatemala
Pocomchi, Western, Guatemala
Podokwo, Cameroon
Podzo, Mozambique
Pogolo, Tanzania
Poke, Zaire
Pokot, Uganda
Pol, Congo
Polci, Nigeria
Pom, Indonesia
Pongu, Nigeria
Popoloca, Ahuatempan, Mexico
Popoloca, Coyotepec, Mexico
Popoloca, Eastern, Mexico
Popoloca, Northern, Mexico
Popoloca, Southern, Mexico
Popoloca, Western, Mexico
Popoluca, Oluta, Mexico
Popoluca, Sayula, Mexico
Popoluca, Sierra, Mexico
Popoluca, Texistepec, Mexico
Porohanon, Philippines
Prang, Ghana
Pu-I, China
Puquli, Upper Volta
Puku-Geeri-Keri-Wipsi, Nigeria
Pular, Senegal
Punjabis, Pakistan (80)
Punu, China
Punu, Congo
Puragi, Indonesia
Purum, Burma
Pye, Ivory Coast
Pygmy (Binga), Burundi
Pygmy (Binga), Central African
  Empire
Pyu, Indonesia
Qajars, Iran
Qara'i, Iran
Qaragozlu, Iran
Qashqa'i, Iran (80)
Quaiquer, Colombia
Quarequena, Brazil
Rabha in Assam, India

REGISTRY OF THE UNREACHED

Soli, Zambia
Somahai, Indonesia
Somrai, Chad
Somrai, Central African Empire
Sondwari in M.P., India
Songe, Zaire
Songhai, Mali
Songhai, Niger
Songhai, Upper Volta
Songomeno, Zaire
Songoora, Zaire
Soninke, Gambia
Soninke, Mali
Soninke, Mauritania
Sonjo, Tanzania
Sopi, Sudan
Sora in Orissa, India
Soruba, Benin
Sowanda, Indonesia
Students in Cuiaba, Brazil
Su, Cameroon
Suba, Tanzania
Subanun,Lapuyan, Philippines
Subi, Tanzania
Suga, Cameroon
Sui, China
Suk, Kenya
Suku, Zaire
Sukur, Nigeria
Sulung, India
Sumba, Indonesia
Sumbawa, Indonesia
Sumbwa, Tanzania
Sumu, Nicaragua
Sungor, Chad
Suppire, Mali
Sura, Nigeria
Surubu, Nigeria
Surui, Brazil
Susu, Guinea-Bissau
Susu, Sierra Leone
Svan, Soviet Russia
Swaga, Zaire
Swaka, Zambia
Ta-Oi, Laos
Tabasaran, Soviet Russia
Tabi, Sudan
Tacana, Bolivia
Tadjio, Indonesia
Tadyawan, Philippines
Tafi, Togo
Tagal, Malaysia (81)
Tagwana, Ivory Coast
Tahit, Indonesia
Taikat, Indonesia
Taiwan-Chinese Un. Stud., Taiwan
Tajik, Iran (80)
Tajik, Afghanistan
Tajik, Soviet Russia
Takankar, India
Takemba, Benin
Takestani, Iran
Tal, Nigeria
Talish, Iran
Talodi, Sudan
Tama, Chad
Tamagario, Indonesia
Taman, Burma
Tamaria in Bihar, India

Tamazight, Morocco
Tambas, Nigeria
Tambo, Zambia
Tampulma, Ghana
Tana, Chad
Tana, Central African Empire
Tanahmerah, Indonesia
Tandanke, Senegal
Tandia, Indonesia
Tangale, Nigeria
Tangchangya, Bangladesh
Tanimuca-Retuama, Colombia
Tao't Bato, Philippines
Taori-Kei, Indonesia
Tara, Indonesia
Tarahumara, Northern, Mexico
Tarahumara, Rocoroibo, Mexico
Tarahumara, Samachique, Mexico
Taram, Cameroon
Tarasco, Mexico
Targum, Israel
Tarof, Indonesia
Tarok, Nigeria
Tarpia, Indonesia
Tat, Soviet Russia
Tatars, Soviet Russia (80)
Tatoga, Tanzania
Taucouleur, Senegal (80)
Taungyo, Burma
Taungyoe, Burma
Taurap, Indonesia
Tawr, Burma
Tayaku, Benin
Tchanq, Cameroon
Teda, Chad (80)
Teda, Libya
Teda, Niger
Tegali, Sudan
Teimuri, Iran
Teimurtash, Iran
Teke, Eastern, Zaire
Teke, Northern, Congo
Teke, Southwestern, Congo
Tembe, Brazil
Tembo, Zaire
Temein, Sudan
Temira, Malaysia
Tepehua, Huehuetla, Mexico
Tepehua, Pisa Flores, Mexico
Tepehua, Veracruz, Mexico
Tepehuan, Northern, Mexico
Tepehuan, Southeastern, Mexico
Tepeth, Uganda
Tepo, Ivory Coast
Tera, Nigeria
Terena, Brazil
Ternatans, Indonesia
Teso, Uganda
Thado in Assam, India
Thai-Ney, Burma
Thakur, India
Thar in Bihar, India
Tharu, Nepal
Thoi, Sudan
Thuri, Sudan
Ticuna, Brazil
Tidorese, Indonesia
Tiefo, Upper Volta
Tiene, Zaire

REGISTRY OF THE UNREACHED

Wapishana, Guyana
Wapishana, Venezuela
Wara, Upper Volta
Warao, Venezuela
Ware, Mali
Warembori, Indonesia
Waris, Indonesia
Warkay-Bipim, Indonesia
Waropen, Indonesia
Wasi, Tanzania
Waura, Brazil
Wayana, Surinam
Weda, Indonesia
Wetawit, Ethiopia
Wewewa, Indonesia
Widekum, Cameroon
Win, Upper Volta
Wobe, Ivory Coast
Wodani, Indonesia
Woi, Indonesia
Wolio, Indonesia
Wolof, Gambian, Gambia
Wom, Nigeria
Wongo, Zaire
Woro, Sudan
Wumbvu, Gabon
Wungu, Tanzania
Xavante, Brazil
Xerente, Brazil
Xokleng, Brazil
Xu, Namibia
Yafi, Indonesia
Yaghan, Chile
Yagnobi, Soviet Russia
Yagua, Peru
Yahadian, Indonesia
Yaka, Zaire
Yakoma, Central African Empire
Yaly, Indonesia
Yambasa, Cameroon
Yaminahua, Peru
Yanadi in Andhra Pradesh, India
Yandang, Nigeria
Yanga, Togo
Yangbye, Burma
Yans, Zaire
Yao, Mozambique
Yaruro, Venezuela
Yasing, Cameroon
Yaur, Indonesia
Yava, Indonesia
Yazgulyam, Soviet Russia
Yei, Indonesia
Yela, Zaire
Yellow Uighur, China
Yelmek, Indonesia
Yerava in Karnataka, India
Yeretuar, Indonesia
Yerukala in A.P., India
Yeskwa, Nigeria
Yidinit, Ethiopia
Yin-Kyar, Burma
Yin-Nett, Burma
Yinchia, Burma
Yinga, Cameroon
Yoabu, Benin
Yogad, Philippines
Yonggom, Indonesia
Yoruk, Turkey

Yos, Burma
Yotafa, Indonesia
Yuana, Venezuela
Yucateco, Guatemala
Yucateco, Mexico
Yukaqirs, Soviet Russia
Yukpa, Colombia
Yukpa, Venezuela
Yuku, China
Yulu, Sudan
Yungur, Nigeria
Yuracare, Bolivia
Yurak, Soviet Russia
Yuruti, Colombia
Zaghawa, Chad
Zaghawa, Libya
Zaghawa, Sudan
Zanaki, Tanzania
Zande, Zaire
Zangskari in Kashmir, India
Zaramo, Tanzania
Zari, Nigeria
Zayse, Ethiopia
Zenaga, Mauritania
Zigwa, Tanzania
Zilmamu, Ethiopia
Zimba, Zaire
Zoliang, India
Zome, Burma
Zome in Manipur, India
Zoque, Chimalapa, Mexico
Zoque, Copainala, Mexico
Zoque, Francisco Leon, Mexico
Zoque, Tabasco, Mexico
Zulu, Malawi

Index by
Religion

INDEX BY PRINCIPLE PROFESSED RELIGION

This list indicates predominant professed religion, whether or not a majority of those who profess the religion are active practitioners. Many of the groups have more than one professed religion present but only the one with the largest percentage of followers is indicated in this section.

AFRICAN INDEPENDENT

**Dida, Ivory Coast

ANCESTOR WORSHIP

**Akha, Thailand (79)
**K'anjobal of San Miguel,
Guatemala

ANIMISM

"Au"ei, Botswana
Abanyom, Nigeria
Abau, Indonesia
Abua, Nigeria
Achagua, Colombia
Achi, Cubulco, Guatemala
Achi, Rabinal, Guatemala
Acholi, Uganda
Achual, Peru
Adamawa, Cameroon
Adhola, Uganda
***Adi, India
**Adja, Benin
*Afawa, Nigeria (80)
**Afo, Nigeria (80)
Age, Cameroon
Aghem, Cameroon
Aghu, Indonesia
Agoi, Nigeria
Aguacateco, Guatemala
Aguaruna, Peru
Agwagwune, Nigeria
Aibondeni, Indonesia
Aikwakai, Indonesia
Airo-Sumaghaghe, Indonesia
Airoran, Indonesia
Aka, India
Ake, Nigeria
Akpa-Yache, Nigeria
Alago, Nigeria
Alak, Laos
Alege, Nigeria
Alor, Kolana, Indonesia (81)
Alur, Zaire
Amahuaca, Peru
Amanab, Indonesia
Amar, Ethiopia
Amarakaeri, Peru
Amasi, Cameroon
Ambai, Indonesia
Amber, Indonesia
Amberbaken, Indonesia
Ambo, Zambia
Ambonese, Netherlands
Ambonese, Indonesia
Amo, Nigeria
Amuesha, Peru

Anaang, Nigeria
Anal in Manipur, India
Andha in Andhra Pradesh, India
Andoque, Colombia
Angas, Nigeria
Ankwe, Nigeria
Ansus, Indonesia
Anuak, Ethiopia
Anuak, Sudan
Apalai, Brazil
**Apatani in Assam, India
Apinaye, Brazil
Apurina, Brazil
Arabela, Peru
Arandai, Indonesia
Arapaco, Brazil
Arbore, Ethiopia
Arecuna, Venezuela
Argobba, Ethiopia
Arguni, Indonesia
*Arnatas, India
Arusha, Tanzania
Arutani, Venezuela
Asienara, Indonesia
*Asmat, Indonesia (79)
Assumbo, Cameroon
Asu, Tanzania
Asuri in Bihar, India
*Ata of Davao, Philippines
Atruahi, Brazil
*Atta, Philippines
*Atye, Ivory Coast
Awyi, Indonesia
Awyu, Indonesia
**Aymara, Bolivia
Ayoreo, Paraguay
Baali, Zaire
Babajou, Cameroon
**Babur Thali, Nigeria (80)
Baburiwa, Indonesia
Bada, Nigeria
Badagu in Nilgiri, India
Bafut, Cameroon
Baghati in H.P., India
Baham, Indonesia
Bahawalpuri in M.P., India
Baiga in Bihar, India
Baka, Cameroon
Baka, Zaire
Bakairi, Brazil
**Bakuba, Zaire
Bakwele, Congo
Balangaw, Philippines
Balante, Guinea-Bissau
Balong, Cameroon
Balti in Jammu, India
Bamougoun-Bamenjou, Cameroon
***Banaro, Papua New Guinea
Bandi, Liberia
Bandjoun, Cameroon
Banen, Cameroon
Bangba, Zaire
Baniwa, Brazil
***Banyarwanda, Rwanda
Banyun, Guinea-Bissau
***Baoule, Ivory Coast
Barabaig, Tanzania (79)
Barasano, Colombia
Barasano, Northern, Colombia

Barasano, Southern, Colombia
Barau, Indonesia
Bare'e, Indonesia
*Bariba, Benin (80)
Basakomo, Nigeria
Basari, Togo
Basari, Senegal
Basari, Guinea
Basari, Senegal
Bashar, Nigeria
Basketo, Ethiopia
***Basotho, Mountain, Lesotho (79)
*Bassa, Liberia
**Bassa, Nigeria
Batak, Karo, Indonesia
Batak, Simalungun, Indonesia
Batak, Toba, Indonesia
Batanga-Ngolo, Cameroon
Bateg, Malaysia
Bazigar in Gujarat, India
Bediya in Bihar, India
Bedoanas, Indonesia
Bekwarra, Nigeria
Bembe, Zaire
Bena, Tanzania
Bencho, Ethiopia
Bende, Tanzania
Bene, Cameroon
Benga, Gabon
Berba, Benin
Berik, Indonesia
Berom, Nigeria
Besisi, Malaysia
Bete, India
*Bete, Ivory Coast
Bethen, Cameroon
Betsinga, Cameroon
Bette-Bende, Nigeria
Bharia in Madhya Pradesh, India
**Bhils, India (79)
Bhuiya in Bihar, India
Biafada, Guinea-Bissau
Biak, Indonesia
Biduanda, Malaysia
**Bijogo, Guinea-Bissau
Biksi, Indonesia
**Bilan, Philippines
Binji, Zaire
Bira, Zaire
Birifor, Ghana
Bisa, Zambia
Bisaya, Malaysia (81)
Bitare, Cameroon
Bobe, Cameroon
Bobo Fing, Mali
Bobo Wule, Mali
Bodo in Assam, India
Boghom, Nigeria
**Boko, Benin
Bokyi, Nigeria
Bokyi, Cameroon
Bolondo, Zaire
Boma, Zaire
Bomboko, Cameroon
Bonerif, Indonesia
Bonggo, Indonesia
Bongili, Congo
Bonkeng-Pendia, Cameroon
**Bontoc, Central, Philippines
   (81)

Bora, Colombia
Borai, Indonesia
*Bororo, Brazil
Boya, Sudan
Bozo, Mali
Braj in Uttar Pradesh, India
Brao, Laos (79)
Brat, Indonesia
Bruneis, Malaysia
Bua, Chad
Bube, Equatorial Guinea
Budu, Zaire
Budugum, Cameroon
Bugombe, Zaire
Builsa, Ghana
Buja, Zaire
Buka-khwe, Botswana
**Bukidnon, Philippines
Bulia, Zaire
Bunak, Indonesia
Bunann in Kashmir, India
Bungku, Indonesia
Bunu, Nigeria
Bura, Cameroon
Buraka-Gbanziri, Congo
Buriq in Kashmir, India
Burji, Ethiopia
Buru, Indonesia
Burunqi, Tanzania
Busami, Indonesia
**Busanse, Ghana
Bushmen (Heikum), Namibia
*Bushmen (Hiechware), Rhodesia
*Bushmen (Kung), Namibia (79)
Bushmen in Botswana, Botswana
Bushoong, Zaire
Bussa, Ethiopia
Buwid, Philippines (81)
Bwa, Upper Volta (80)
Bwa, Zaire
Bwisi, Zaire
Cacua, Colombia
Caiwa, Brazil
Cakchiquel, Central, Guatemala
Campa, Peru
Camsa, Colombia
Candoshi, Peru
Canela, Brazil
Capanahua, Peru
Carapana, Colombia
Cashibo, Peru
Cayapa, Ecuador
Cewa, Zambia
Ch'ol Tila, Mexico
Chacobo, Bolivia
Chagga, Tanzania
Chakfem-Mushere, Nigeria
Chakossi in Ghana, Ghana
Chakossi in Togo, Togo
Chamacoco, Bahia Negra, Paraguay
Chami, Colombia
Chamicuro, Peru
Chara, Ethiopia
Chawai, Nigeria
Chero in Bihar, India
Chiga, Uganda
Chik-Barik in Bihar, India
Chinga, Cameroon
Chinga, Cameroon

Chip, Nigeria
Chipaya, Bolivia
Chiquitano, Bolivia
**Chiriguano, Argentina
Chokobo, Nigeria
Chokwe, Zambia
Chokwe (Lunda), Angola
Chola Naickans, India
Chopi, Mozambique
Chorote, Argentina
Chorote, Paraguay
Chorti, Guatemala
**Chrau, Viet Nam
Chuabo, Mozambique
Chuang, China (81)
Chuj, Guatemala
Chuj of San Mateo Ixtatan,
   Guatemala
Cinta Larga, Brazil
***Citak, Indonesia
Citak, Indonesia
Cocama, Peru
Cofan, Colombia
Cogui, Colombia
**Coreguaje, Colombia
Coreguaje, Colombia
Cubeo, Colombia
Cuiba, Colombia
Cujareno, Peru
Culina, Brazil
*Cuna, Colombia (79)
Cuna, Colombia
Curipaco, Colombia
Daba, Cameroon
Daba, Cameroon
Dabra, Indonesia
Dagada, Indonesia
Daqari, Ghana
Daju of Dar Fur, Sudan
*Daka, Nigeria
***Dan, Ivory Coast
*Dani, Baliem, Indonesia (79)
Dathanik, Ethiopia
Day, Central African Empire
Degema, Nigeria
Dem, Indonesia
Demta, Indonesia
Dengese, Zaire
Deori in Assam, India
Desano, Brazil
*Dghwede, Nigeria
Dghwede, Cameroon
Dghwede, Cameroon
Dhaiso, Tanzania
Dhanka in Gujarat, India
Dhanwar in Madhya Pradesh, India
Didinga, Sudan
Digo, Tanzania
Dimasa in Cachar, India
Dime, Ethiopia
Dinka, Sudan
Doe, Tanzania
*Dog-Pa of Ladakh, India (81)
*Dogon, Mali (79)
Dompago, Benin
Dongo, Zaire
**Doohwaayo, Cameroon
Dorobo, Kenya
Dorobo, Tanzania

Dorze, Ethiopia
Dubu, Indonesia
**Duka, Nigeria
Duma, Gabon
*Dumagat , Casiguran, Philippines
   (81)
Duru, Cameroon
Dusun, Malaysia (81)
Duvele, Indonesia
Edo, Nigeria
Efik, Nigeria
Efutop, Nigeria
Eggon, Nigeria
Ejagham, Nigeria
Ekagi, Indonesia
Ekajuk, Nigeria
Eket, Nigeria
Ekpeye, Nigeria
El Molo, Kenya
Eleme, Nigeria
Emai-Iuleha-Ora, Nigeria
Embera, Northern, Colombia
Emumu, Indonesia
Engenni, Nigeria
Enya, Zaire
Epie, Nigeria
Erokwanas, Indonesia
Esan, Nigeria
Eton, Cameroon
Eton, Cameroon
Etulo, Nigeria
Evant, Nigeria
Ewenkis, China (81)
Fa D'Ambu, Equatorial Guinea
**Fakai, Nigeria
**Fali, Nigeria
Fipa, Tanzania
Foau, Indonesia
Fordat, Indonesia
Fra-Fra, Ghana
Fula, Macina, Mali
Fula, Peuhala, Mali
Fulio, Zaire
Fulnio, Brazil
Fungom, Northern, Cameroon
Fungom, Northern, Cameroon
Furu, Zaire
Fyam, Nigeria
Fyer, Nigeria
Ga-Dang, Philippines
Gade, Nigeria
**Gagre, Pakistan
Gagu, Ivory Coast
Galler, Laos
Gane, Indonesia
Gawwada, Ethiopia
Gbande, Guinea
Gbari, Nigeria (80)
Gedeo, Ethiopia
Gesa, Indonesia
**Ghimeera, Ethiopia
Ghotuo, Nigeria
Gidar, Cameroon
Gidar, Cameroon
Gidicho, Ethiopia
Gio, Liberia
Giryama, Kenya
Gisei, Cameroon
Gisiga, Cameroon

REGISTRY OF THE UNREACHED

**Glavda, Nigeria
Gobato, Ethiopia
Gobeze, Ethiopia
***Godie, Ivory Coast
Goemai, Nigeria
Gogo, Tanzania
Gokana, Nigeria
*Gonds, India
Goroa, Tanzania
Gourency, Upper Volta
**Gouro, Ivory Coast
Gouwar, Cameroon
Gouwar, Cameroon
**Grebo, Liberia
Grunshi, Ghana
Gu, Benin
Guaiaqui, Paraguay
Guajajara, Brazil
Guajibo, Colombia
*Guajiro, Colombia
Guambiano, Colombia
Guana, Paraguay
***Guarani, Bolivia (79)
Guayabero, Colombia
Guayabevo, Colombia
Gude, Cameroon
Gude, Nigeria
Gudu, Nigeria
Guduf, Nigeria
Gugu-Yalanji, Australia
Gulfe, Cameroon
Gulfe, Cameroon
Gumuz, Ethiopia
Gurensi, Ghana
Gwandara, Nigeria
Gwere, Uganda
Ha, Tanzania
Hadiyya, Ethiopia
***Halam in Tripura, India
Hangaza, Tanzania
Hatsa, Tanzania
Havu, Zaire
Havunese, Indonesia
Haya, Tanzania
Hehe, Tanzania
Helong, Indonesia
Herero, Botswana
Herero, Namibia
Heso, Zaire
**Hewa, Papua New Guinea (79)
***Higi, Nigeria
Hixkaryana, Brazil
Hohodene, Brazil
Holoholo, Tanzania
Holu, Angola
Hopi, United States of America
Huachipaire, Peru
Huambisa, Peru
**Huila, Angola
Huitoto, Meneca, Colombia
Huitoto, Murui, Peru
Hukwe, Angola
Hunde, Zaire
Hupda Maku, Colombia
Ibaji, Nigeria
**Iban, Malaysia (81)
Ibanag, Philippines
Ibibio, Nigeria
Ica, Colombia

Idoma, Nigeria
Idoma, North, Nigeria
Ifuago, Antipolo, Philippines
*Ifugao, Philippines
**Ifugao (Kalangoya), Philippines
Ifugao in Cababuyan, Philippines
Ifugao, Ambanad, Philippines
Ifugao, Kiangan, Philippines
Ifumu, Congo
Igala, Nigeria
Igede, Nigeria
Ignaciano, Bolivia
Igorot, Philippines
Iha, Indonesia
Ihceve, Nigeria
Ijo, Central-Western, Nigeria
Ijo, Northeast, Nigeria
Ijo, Northeast Central, Nigeria
Ikalahan, Philippines
Ikizu, Tanzania
Ikwere, Nigeria
Ila, Zambia
Ilongot, Philippines
Inanwatan, Indonesia
Ingassana, Sudan
Insinai, Philippines
Iquito, Peru
Irahutu, Indonesia
Iraqw, Tanzania
Iraqw, Tanzania
Iresim, Indonesia
Iria, Indonesia
Irigwe, Nigeria
Isanzu, Tanzania
Isekiri, Nigeria
Isneg, Dibagat-Kabugao,
   Philippines
Isneg, Karagawan, Philippines
Isoko, Nigeria
Itik, Indonesia
Itonama, Bolivia
Ivbie North-Okpela-Atte, Nigeria
Iwa, Zambia
*Iwaidja, Austria
Iwur, Indonesia
Iyon, Nigeria
Iyon, Cameroon
Iyon, Cameroon
Izarek, Nigeria
**Izi, Nigeria
Jaba, Nigeria
Jacalteco, Guatemala
Jamamadi, Brazil
Jamden, Indonesia
Janjero, Ethiopia
Janjo, Nigeria
Jaqaru, Peru
**Jarawa, Nigeria
Jebero, Peru
Jeng, Laos
Jerawa, Nigeria
*Jibu, Nigeria
Jiji, Tanzania
Jinja, Tanzania
Jinuos, China (81)
Jita, Tanzania
Jiye, Uganda
*Jiye, Sudan
Juhai, Malaysia

Jukun, Nigeria
Kaalong, Cameroon
Kaalong, Cameroon
Kaba, Central African Empire
Kaba Dunjo, Central African
  Empire
Kabixi, Brazil
Kabre, Togo
Kabre, Benin
Kachama, Ethiopia
Kadaklan-Barlig Bontoc,
  Philippines
Kadara, Nigeria
Kadazans, Malaysia
Kadiweu, Brazil
Kaeti, Indonesia
**Kafirs, Pakistan (79)
Kagoro, Mali
Kagulu, Tanzania
Kaili, Indonesia
Kaiwai, Indonesia
Kajang, Indonesia
Kaka, Central African Empire
Kaka, Cameroon
Kaka, Cameroon
Kakwa, Uganda
Kakwa, Zaire
**Kalagan, Philippines
*Kalanga, Botswana
Kalanga, Rhodesia
Kaliko, Zaire
Kalinga, Kalagua, Philippines
Kalinga, Limus-Linan,
  Philippines
Kalinga, Quinaang, Philippines
*Kalinga, Southern, Philippines
Kamantan, Nigeria
Kamayura, Brazil
*Kambari, Nigeria (80)
Kambera, Indonesia
Kamberataro, Indonesia
Kami, Tanzania
Kamkam, Cameroon
Kamkam, Cameroon
Kamoro, Indonesia
Kampung Baru, Indonesia
Kamtuk-Gresi, Indonesia
*Kamuku, Nigeria (80)
Kana, Nigeria
**Kankanay, Central, Philippines
Kankanay, Northern, Philippines
Kanu, Zaire
Kanum, Indonesia
Kao, Ethiopia
Kaonde, Zaire
Kaonde, Zambia
Kapori, Indonesia
Kara, Tanzania
*Karaboro, Upper Volta
Karas, Indonesia
Karen, Thailand (79)
Karen, Pwo, Thailand
Kari, Central African Empire
Kari, Zaire
Karipuna Creole, Brazil
Karipuna Do Guapore, Brazil
Karon Dori, Indonesia
Karon Pantai, Indonesia
Karre, Central African Empire

**Kasena, Ghana
Kasseng, Laos
Kasuweri, Indonesia
Kati, Northern, Indonesia
Kati, Southern, Indonesia
Katukina, Panoan, Brazil
Kaugat, Indonesia
Kaure, Indonesia
Kavwol, Indonesia
Kaw, Burma
Kawe, Indonesia
Kayabi, Brazil
Kayagar, Indonesia
Kayan, Malaysia
Kayan, Burma
Kayapo, Brazil
Kaygir, Indonesia
Kayupulau, Indonesia
Kedayanas, Malaysia
Kei, Indonesia
Kela, Zaire
Kelabit, Malaysia (81)
Kele, Gabon
Kemak, Indonesia
Kembata, Ethiopia
Kemok, Malaysia
Kenyah, Indonesia
*Kepas, Papua New Guinea
Kera, Cameroon
Kera, Cameroon
Kerewe, Tanzania
*Khamu, Thailand
Kichepo, Sudan
Kim, Central African Empire
Kimaghama, Indonesia
Kimbu, Tanzania
*Kimyal, Indonesia
Kinga, Tanzania
Kisankasa, Tanzania
Kisi, Tanzania
*Kissi, Sierra Leone
Kissi, Guinea
*Kissi, Liberia
Koalib, Sudan (79)
Kodi, Indonesia
Koenoem, Nigeria
Kofyar, Nigeria
Kohoroxitari, Brazil
Kohumono, Nigeria
Kole, Cameroon
Kole, Cameroon
Koma, Ghana
Koma, Nigeria
Koma, Cameroon
Koma, Cameroon
*Komo, Ethiopia
Konabem, Cameroon
Konabem, Cameroon
***Kond, India
Koneraw, Indonesia
*Konkomba, Togo
Konkomba, Ghana
**Kono, Sierra Leone
Konongo, Tanzania
Konso, Ethiopia
Korapun, Indonesia
*Korku in Madhya Pradesh, India
Koro, Nigeria
Koroma, Sudan

Korop, Nigeria
Korop, Cameroon
Korop, Cameroon
Kota, Gabon
Kotogut, Indonesia
Kotoko, Cameroon
Kotoko, Cameroon
Kotopo, Cameroon
Kotta, India
**Kowaao, Liberia
Koyra, Ethiopia
Kpa, Cameroon
Kpa, Cameroon
Kpelle, Liberia
***Krahn, Liberia
*Krahn, Ivory Coast
Kreen-Akakore, Brazil
Krongo, Sudan
Krumen, Ivory Coast
Kuatinema, Brazil
Kubu, Indonesia (80)
Kugbo, Nigeria
Kuikuro, Brazil
Kukele, Nigeria
Kukwa, Congo
Kulango, Ivory Coast
Kulere, Nigeria
Kumam, Uganda
Kumu, Zaire
Kunda, Mozambique
Kunda, Rhodesia
Kunda, Zambia
Kunda, Zambia
Kupsabiny, Uganda
Kurfei, Niger
Kuria, Tanzania
Kurudu, Indonesia
**Kusaasi, Ghana
Kusu, Zaire
Kutin, Cameroon
Kutu, Tanzania
Kwadi, Angola
Kwakum, Cameroon
Kwambi, Namibia
Kwangali, Angola
Kwansu, Indonesia
Kwanyama, Angola
Kwanyama, Namibia
Kwaya, Tanzania
Kwe-etshori, Botswana
Kwe-Etshori, Rhodesia
Kwerba, Indonesia
Kwere, Tanzania
Kwese, Zaire
Kwesten, Indonesia
*Lahu, Thailand (81)
Lahu, Burma
Laka, Cameroon
Laka, Central African Empire
Lala, Zambia
Lalia, Zaire
Lamba, Togo
Lamba, Benin
Lamba, Zaire
Lamba, Zambia
**Lambadi in Andhra Pradesh, India
    (81)
Lambi, Cameroon
Lambya, Malawi

Lambya, Tanzania
Langi, Tanzania
*Lango, Ethiopia
Lango, Uganda
Lanoh, Malaysia
Lara, Indonesia
Latdwalam, Indonesia
Laudje, Indonesia
Lebgo, Nigeria
Leco, Bolivia
Lega, Zaire
Lele, Zaire
Lendu, Zaire
Lengua, Northern, Paraguay
Lenje, Zambia
Lese, Zaire
Letti, Indonesia
Liko, Zaire
Lima, Zambia
Limba, Sierra Leone
*Lisu, Thailand
Lisu, China (81)
Lo, Nigeria
Lobi, Ivory Coast
Logo, Zaire
**Loho Loho, Indonesia
Loinang, Indonesia (81)
Loko, Sierra Leone
Lolo, China (81)
Loma, Guinea
Loma, Liberia
Lombi, Zaire
Lombo, Zaire
Lomwe, Mozambique
Lore, Indonesia
Lozi, Rhodesia
Lozi, Zambia
Luano, Zambia
Luchazi, Angola
Luchazi, Zambia
Lue, Cameroon
Luqbara, Zaire
Luimbi, Angola
Lumbu, Gabon
Luna, Zaire
Lunda, Angola
Lundu, Cameroon
Lungu, Nigeria
Luo, Tanzania
Luyana, Angola
Luyana, Zambia
Lwalu, Zaire
Lwena, Angola
Ma, Zaire
Maanyan, Indonesia
**Maasai, Kenya (79)
Maca, Paraguay
Machiguenga, Peru
Macu, Colombia
Macuna, Colombia
**Macuxi, Brazil
Madda, Nigeria
Madi, Uganda
Madik, Indonesia
***Maguzawa, Nigeria (79)
Mahri, Oman
Maiongong, Brazil
Mairasi, Indonesia
Maji, Ethiopia

Majingai-ngama, Central African
  Empire
Maka, Cameroon
Makasai, Indonesia
Makere, Uganda
Makian, West, Indonesia
Maklew, Indonesia
Makua, Mozambique
Malappanackers, India
*Malayalars, India
Malayo, Colombia
Male, Ethiopia
Malila, Tanzania
Mama, Nigeria
Mambai, Indonesia
Mambila, Cameroon
Mambwe-Lungu, Tanzania
Mambwe-Lungu, Zambia
Mamprusi, Ghana
Mamvu-Efe, Zaire
Manda, Tanzania
Mandaya, Philippines
Mandaya, Mansaka, Philippines
Mander, Indonesia
Manem, Indonesia
Mangbutu, Zaire
Mangisa, Cameroon
**Mangyan, Philippines
**Manikion, Indonesia
**Manjaco, Guinea-Bissau
Mano, Liberia
Manobo, Agusan, Philippines
Manobo, Ata, Philippines
Manobo, Binokid, Philippines
**Manobo, Cotabato, Philippines
Manobo, Dibabawon, Philippines
*Manobo, Ilianen, Philippines
Manobo, Obo, Philippines
**Manobo, Salug, Philippines
Manobo, Sarangani, Philippines
Manobo, Tagabawa, Philippines
**Manobo, Tigwa, Philippines
**Manobo, Western Bukidnon,
  Philippines
Manobos, Pulangi, Philippines
Mantera, Malaysia
Mantion, Indonesia
Manu Park Panoan, Peru
Manyika, Rhodesia
Mao, Northern, Ethiopia
Mapoyo, Venezuela
Maquiritari, Venezuela
Marau, Indonesia
Marind, Indonesia
Marind, Bian, Indonesia
Marubo, Brazil
Masa, Chad
Masaba, Uganda
*Masengo, Ethiopia
Mashi, Zambia
Mataco, Argentina
Matakam, Cameroon
Matawari, Surinam
Matbat, Indonesia
Matengo, Tanzania
Matipuhy-Nahukua, Brazil
Mauri, Niger
Maviha, Mozambique
Mawes, Indonesia

Maxakali, Brazil
Mayoruna, Peru
Mba, Zaire
Mbaama, Gabon
Mbai, Central African Empire
Mbala, Zaire
Mbangwe, Zaire
Mbanja, Zaire
Mbati, Central African Empire
Mbe, Nigeria
Mbede, Gabon
Mbembe, Cameroon
Mbembe (Tigong), Nigeria
Mbimu, Cameroon
Mbo, Cameroon
Mbo, Zaire
Mbole, Zaire
Mbugwe, Tanzania
Mbukushu, Angola
Mbunda, Angola
Mbunga, Tanzania
Mbwela, Angola
Me'en, Ethiopia
Meax, Indonesia
Meban, Sudan
**Mejah, India
Meje, Uganda
Mekwei, Indonesia
**Melanau of Sarawak, Malaysia
  (80)
Mende, Sierra Leone
Menemo-Mogamo, Cameroon
Menka, Cameroon
Menri, Malaysia
**Meo, Thailand
Miao, China (81)
Mien, China (81)
Migili, Nigeria
Minduumo, Gabon
Minianka, Mali
Mirung, Bangladesh
Miya, Nigeria
Mo, Ghana
Moba, Ghana
Moba, Togo
***Mocha, Ethiopia
Mofu, Cameroon
Moi, Indonesia
Moken, Burma (79)
Moken of Thailand, Thailand
*Mokole, Benin
Molof, Indonesia
Mombum, Indonesia
Momoguns, Malaysia
Mongondow, Indonesia (81)
Moni, Indonesia
Monjombo, Central African Empire
Mono, Zaire
Mor, Indonesia
Morunahua, Peru
Morwap, Indonesia
Mosi, Tanzania
Mossi, Upper Volta (80)
Motilon, Colombia
Motilon, Venezuela
Movima, Bolivia
Mpoto, Malawi
Mpoto, Tanzania
Mru, Bangladesh

Mualthuam, India
Muinane, Colombia
Mumuye, Nigeria
**Mundas in Bihar, India
Mundu, Zaire
Munduruku, Brazil
Mungaka, Cameroon
Munggui, Indonesia
Mura-Piraha, Brazil
Murle, Sudan
*Murngin (Wulamba), Australia
Mursi, Ethiopia
Murut, Malaysia
Mwanga, Tanzania
Mwera, Tanzania
Myaung-Ze, Burma
Nabi, Indonesia
Nadeb Maku, Brazil
**Nafaara, Ghana (79)
Nafri, Indonesia
Naltya, Indonesia
Nama, Namibia
Nama, South Africa
Nambikuara, Brazil
**Nambya, Rhodesia
Namshi, Cameroon
Nandi, Zaire
Nao, Ethiopia
Naraguta, Nigeria
Nata, Tanzania
Nawuri, Ghana
Nchimburu, Ghana
Ndaaka, Zaire
Ndali, Tanzania
Ndam, Central African Empire
Ndamba, Tanzania
Ndaonese, Indonesia
Ndau, Rhodesia
Nde-Nsele-Nta, Nigeria
**Ndebele, Rhodesia (79)
Ndengereko, Tanzania
Ndjem, Cameroon
Ndo, Zaire
Ndoe, Nigeria
Ndogo, Central African Empire
Ndom, Indonesia
Ndomde, Tanzania
Ndoolo, Zaire
Ndop-Bamessing, Cameroon
**Ndoro, Nigeria
Ndoro, Cameroon
Nduga, Indonesia
Ndunga, Zaire
Neyo, Ivory Coast
Ngalik, North, Indonesia
Ngalik, Southern, Indonesia
Ngalum, Indonesia
**Ngamo, Nigeria
Ngando, Central African Empire
Ngando, Zaire
Ngasa, Tanzania
Ngayaba, Cameroon
Ngbaka, Zaire
Ngbaka Ma'bo, Central African Empire
Ngbaka Ma'bo, Zaire
Ngbandi, Zaire
Ngbee, Zaire
Ngemba, Cameroon

*Ngen, Ivory Coast
Ngeq, Laos
Ngere, Ivory Coast
Ngi, Cameroon
Ngindo, Tanzania
Ngiri, Zaire
**Ngombe, Zaire
Ngoni, Tanzania
Ngoni, Zambia
Ngulu, Malawi
Ngulu, Tanzania
Ngumba, Cameroon
Ngumbi, Equatorial Guinea
Ngurimi, Tanzania
Nguu, Tanzania
Ngwo, Cameroon
Nharon, Botswana
Nhengatu, Brazil
Nias, Indonesia
Nilamba, Tanzania
Nimboran, Indonesia
Ninam, Brazil
*Ningerum, Papua New Guinea
Ninggrum, Indonesia
Nisa, Indonesia
Njadu, Indonesia
Nkem-Nkum, Nigeria
Nkom, Cameroon
*Nkoya, Zambia
Nkutu, Zaire
***Nocte, India
Nohu, Cameroon
*Nouni, Upper Volta
Nsenga, Rhodesia
Nsenga, Zambia
Nso, Cameroon
Nsongo, Angola
Ntomba, Zaire
Ntrubo, Ghana
Ntrubs, Ghana
*Nuer, Ethiopia
*Nuer, Sudan (79)
Nungu, Nigeria
**Nyabwa, Ivory Coast
Nyaheun, Laos
Nyakyusa, Malawi
Nyakyusa, Tanzania
Nyambo, Tanzania
Nyamwezi, Tanzania (80)
Nyaneka, Angola
Nyang, Cameroon
Nyanga-Li, Zaire
Nyanja, Rhodesia
Nyankole, Uganda
*Nyantruku, Benin
Nyemba, Angola
Nyiha, Tanzania
Nyiha, Zambia
Nyoro, Uganda
Nyuli, Uganda
Nyungwe, Mozambique
Nyzatom, Sudan
Nzakara, Central African Empire
Nzebi, Congo
O'ung, Angola
Obanliku, Nigeria
Obolo, Nigeria
Ocaina, Peru
Odual, Nigeria

Serere, Senegal (79)
Serui-Laut, Indonesia
Seuci, Brazil
Sha, Nigeria
Shambala, Tanzania
Shanga, Nigeria
Sharanahua, Peru
Sheko, Ethiopia
Shinasha, Ethiopia
Shipibo, Peru
**Shirishana, Brazil
Shua, Botswana
Siagha-Yenimu, Indonesia
Sikanese, Indonesia
Sikhule, Indonesia
Simaa, Zambia
Siona, Colombia
Sira, Gabon
Siriano, Colombia
Siriono, Bolivia
**Sisaala, Ghana
So, Laos
*So, Thailand (81)
So, Cameroon
Sobei, Indonesia
Soga, Uganda
Soli, Zambia
*Somahai, Indonesia
Somahai, Indonesia
**Somba, Benin
Somrai, Central African Empire
Songe, Zaire
Songhai, Mali
Songomeno, Zaire
Songoora, Zaire
Sonjo, Tanzania
Soruba, Benin
Sowanda, Indonesia
Su, Cameroon
Suba, Tanzania
**Subanen (Tuboy), Philippines
**Subanen, Sindangan, Philippines (80)
Subi, Tanzania
Suga, Cameroon
**Sugut, Malaysia
Suk, Kenya
Suku, Zaire
Sumbwa, Tanzania
Suppire, Mali
**Suri, Ethiopia
Surui, Brazil
Swaga, Zaire
Swaka, Zambia
**Swazi, South Africa
**T'boli, Philippines (81)
T'in, Thailand (81)
Ta-Oi, Laos
Tabi, Sudan
Tacana, Bolivia
Tadjio, Indonesia
Tadyawan, Philippines
Tagal, Malaysia (81)
**Tagbanwa, Aborlan, Philippines
***Tagin, India
Tahit, Indonesia
Taikat, Indonesia
Takemba, Benin
Tamagario, Indonesia

Tambas, Nigeria
Tambo, Zambia
Tampulma, Ghana
Tana, Central African Empire
Tanahmerah, Indonesia
Tandia, Indonesia
**Tangsa, India
Tanimuca-Retuama, Colombia
Tao't Bato, Philippines
Taori-Kei, Indonesia
Tara, Indonesia
Taram, Cameroon
Tarof, Indonesia
Tarok, Nigeria
Tarpia, Indonesia
Tatoga, Tanzania
**Tatuyo, Colombia
Taurap, Indonesia
Tayaku, Benin
Tchang, Cameroon
*Teenbu, Ivory Coast
Teke, Eastern, Zaire
Teke, Northern, Congo
Teke, Southwestern, Congo
Tembe, Brazil
Tembo, Zaire
Temira, Malaysia
**Temne, Sierra Leone (80)
*Tense, Ivory Coast
Tepeth, Uganda
Terena, Brazil
Teso, Uganda
**Teso, Kenya
Ticuna, Brazil
Tiene, Zaire
Tigon, Cameroon
Tikar, Cameroon
Timorese, Indonesia
Tiro, Indonesia
Tiruray, Philippines
Toala, Indonesia
Toba, Argentina
*Tofi, Benin
Togbo, Zaire
Tol, Honduras
Tombulu, Indonesia
Tomini, Indonesia
Tondanou, Indonesia
*Tonga, Rhodesia
Tonga, Botswana
Tonga, Malawi
Tonga, Mozambique
Tonga, Gwembe Valley, Zambia (79)
Tongwe, Tanzania
Tonsea, Indonesia
Tontemboa, Indonesia
*Topotha, Sudan
Toraja, Southern, Indonesia (81)
Towei, Indonesia
Trio, Surinam
Tsamai, Ethiopia
Tsimane, Bolivia
Tsogo, Gabon
Tsonga, Mozambique
Tsou, Taiwan (81)
Tswa, Mozambique
Tswa, Rhodesia
Tswana, Namibia

Tswana, Rhodesia
Tucano, Brazil
Tumawo, Indonesia
Tunebo, Cobaria, Colombia
Tung-Chia, China (81)
Tunya, Central African Empire
Tupuri, Cameroon
Turkana, Kenya
**Turkana Fishing Community, Kenya (79)
Turu, Tanzania
Turu, Indonesia
Tuyuca, Brazil
Udmurt, Soviet Russia
Uduk, Sudan
Uhunduni, Indonesia
Ukaan, Nigeria
Ukpe-Bayobiri, Nigeria
Ukwuani-Aboh, Nigeria
Urarina, Peru
Urhobo, Nigeria
Uria, Indonesia
Uruangnirin, Indonesia
Urubu, Brazil
Urupa, Brazil
Uspanteco, Guatemala
Utugwang, Nigeria
Uvbie, Nigeria
Uzekwe, Nigeria
Vagala, Ghana
Vaikino, Indonesia
Vale, Central African Empire
Venda, Rhodesia
***Vere, Nigeria
Vere, Cameroon
Vidunda, Tanzania
Vinza, Tanzania
Vute, Nigeria
Wa, Burma
Wabo, Indonesia
Waimiri, Brazil
Waiwai, Brazil
**Wajita, Tanzania
Wala, Ghana
Walamo, Ethiopia
Wambon, Indonesia
**Wanchoo, India
Wanda, Tanzania
Wandamen, Indonesia
Wandji, Gabon
Wanggom, Indonesia
Wanji, Tanzania
Wano, Indonesia
Wapishana, Brazil
Wapishana, Venezuela
Warao, Venezuela
Ware, Mali
Warembori, Indonesia
Waris, Indonesia
*Warjawa, Nigeria
Warkay-Bipim, Indonesia
Waropen, Indonesia
Wasi, Tanzania
Watchi, Togo
Waura, Brazil
Wayana, Surinam
*Wazinza, Tanzania
Wetawit, Ethiopia
Wewewa, Indonesia

Widekum, Cameroon
**Wimbum, Cameroon
Wobe, Ivory Coast
Wodani, Indonesia
Woi, Indonesia
Wonqo, Zaire
Wumbvu, Gabon
Wungu, Tanzania
Xavante, Brazil
Xerente, Brazil
Xoklenq, Brazil
Xu, Namibia
Yafi, Indonesia
Yaqua, Peru
Yahadian, Indonesia
Yaka, Zaire
Yakoma, Central African Empire
**Yala, Nigeria
Yaly, Indonesia
Yambasa, Cameroon
Yaminahua, Peru
*Yanomamo in Brazil, Brazil (79)
Yanomamo in Venezuela, Venezuela
Yans, Zaire
**Yao, Thailand (79)
*Yao Refugees from Laos, Thailand
Yaoure, Ivory Coast
Yaruro, Venezuela
Yasing, Cameroon
Yaur, Indonesia
Yava, Indonesia
**Yei, Botswana
Yei, Indonesia
Yela, Zaire
Yelmek, Indonesia
Yeretuar, Indonesia
Yidinit, Ethiopia
Yin-Kyar, Burma
Yin-Nett, Burma
Yinga, Cameroon
Yoabu, Benin
Yogad, Philippines
Yonqgom, Indonesia
Yotafa, Indonesia
Yuana, Venezuela
Yucateco, Guatemala
Yukpa, Colombia
Yukpa, Venezuela
Yuracare, Bolivia
Yuruti, Colombia
Zanaki, Tanzania
Zande, Zaire
**Zaranda Hill Peoples, Nigeria
Zayse, Ethiopia
Zemi Naga of Assam, India (81)
Ziqwa, Tanzania
Zilmamu, Ethiopia
Zimba, Zaire
Zoliang, India
Zowla, Ghana
Zulu, Malawi
Zuni, United States of America

BUDDHISM

REGISTRY OF THE UNREACHED

Bhutias, Bhutan
*Chinese in Thailand, Thailand
Danu, Burma
Government officials, Thailand
Hkun, Burma
Japanese in Brazil, Brazil (79)
Kachin in Shan State, Burma
Kalmytz, Soviet Russia
Koreans in Manchuria, China (81)
**Lahaulis in Punjab, India
*Lao, Laos (79)
**Lepers of N.E. Thailand,
     Thailand
 Palaung, Burma (79)
 Pao, Burma
*Ramkamhaeng Un. Students,
     Thailand
 Shan, Burma
*Sherpa, Nepal
 Sinhalese, Sri Lanka
*Slum Dwellers of Bangkok,
     Thailand
 Soka Gakkai Believers, Japan
 Taungyoe, Burma
*Thai University Students,
     Thailand (81)
*Tibetan Refugees, India
*Tibetans, China
 Tibetans in Bhutan, Bhutan (81)
 Vietnamese, Laos
**Vietnamese in the USA, United
     States of America
**Vietnamese Refugees, Thailand

 Lawa, Mountain, Thailand
**Lepers of Cen. Thailand,
     Thailand (81)
 Loven, Laos (81)
 Lu, China
 Maghi, Burma
 Mon, Burma (81)
 Monpa, India
 Mun, Burma
 Norra, Burma
 Pai, China (81)
 Phu Thai, Laos
 Purum, Burma
 Ralte, Burma
 Riang-Lang, Burma
 Senthang, Burma
 Shan, Thailand
 Shan Chinese, Burma
 Sharchagpakha, Bhutan
 Taman, Burma
 Taungyo, Burma
 Tawr, Burma
 Thai Northern, Thailand
 Thai of Bangkok, Thailand
 Thai, North East, Thailand
 Thai, Southern, Thailand
 Thai-Ney, Burma
 Tuvinian, Soviet Russia
 Yangbye, Burma
 Yinchia, Burma
 Yos, Burma
 Zome, Burma

BUDDHIST-ANIMIST

*Ami, Taiwan (81)
**Banai, Bangladesh
 Buriat, Soviet Russia
*Cambodians, Thailand
*Central Thailand Farmers,
     Thailand (81)
*Chakmas of Mizoram, India (81)
*Chang-Pa of Kashmir, India (81)
 Chaungtha, Burma
 Chin, Asho, Burma
 Chin, Falam, Burma
 Chin, Haka, Burma
 Chin, Khumi, Burma
 Chin, Nqawn, Burma
 Chin, Tiddim, Burma
 Chinbok, Burma
 Dai, Burma
 Evenks, Soviet Russia
 Gheko, Burma
 Hallam, Burma
 Hrangkhol, Burma
 Intha, Burma
 Kebumtamp, Bhutan
**Khmer Refugees, Thailand
 Kokant, Burma
*Kui, Thailand
 Lama, Burma
*Lao Refugees, Thailand
 Lawa, Eastern, Thailand (81)

CHRISTO-PAGANISM

 Abaknon, Philippines
 Aeta, Philippines
 Akawaio, Guyana
 Alangan, Philippines
**Ampeeli, Papua New Guinea
 Amuzgo, Guerrero, Mexico
 Amuzgo, Oaxaca, Mexico
**Apayao, Philippines
 Arawak, Guyana
 Ati, Philippines
 Aymara, Carangas, Chile
***Azteca, Mexico (79)
***Bagobo, Philippines
**Balangao, Philippines
 Bantuanon, Philippines
 Batak, Palawan, Philippines
**Bidayuh of Sarawak, Malaysia
     (81)
***Bipim, Indonesia
**Black Caribs, Belize, Belize
     (79)
**Black Caribs, Guatemala,
     Guatemala
**Black Caribs, Honduras, Honduras
**Bontoc, Southern, Philippines
 Buglere, Panama
 Buhid, Philippines
 Caluyanhon, Philippines
***Cebu, Middle-Class, Philippines
***Ch'ol Sabanilla, Mexico

**Suena, Papua New Guinea
Sumba, Indonesia
Sumu, Nicaragua
Tagbanwa, Kalamian, Philippines
Tarahumara, Northern, Mexico
Tarahumara, Rocoroibo, Mexico
Tarahumara, Samachique, Mexico
Tarasco, Mexico
Tepehua, Huehuetla, Mexico
Tepehua, Pisa Flores, Mexico
Tepehua, Veracruz, Mexico
Tepehuan, Northern, Mexico
Tepehuan, Southeastern, Mexico
Tepehuan, Southwestern, Mexico
**Teribe, Panama
Tlapaneco, Malinaltepec, Mexico
Tojolabal, Mexico
Totonaco, Northern, Mexico
Totonaco, Oxumatlan, Mexico
Totonaco, Papantla, Mexico
Totonaco, Sierra, Mexico
Totonaco, Yecuatla, Mexico
Trique, San Juan Copala, Mexico
**Tsachila, Ecuador
Tubar, Mexico
Tukude, Indonesia
Tzeltal, Bachajon, Mexico
Tzeltal, Highland, Mexico
Tzotzil, Chenalho, Mexico
Tzotzil, Huistan, Mexico
Tzutujil, Guatemala
Ulithi-Mall, Turks and Caicos
  Islands
Waiwai, Guyana
Wapishana, Guyana
Woleat, Turks and Caicos Islands
Yaghan, Chile
Yaquis, Mexico
Yucateco, Mexico
*Yucuna, Colombia
Zinacantecos, Mexico (79)
Zoque, Chimalapa, Mexico
Zoque, Copainala, Mexico
Zoque, Francisco Leon, Mexico
Zoque, Tabasco, Mexico

FOLK RELIGION

*Alars, India
**Apartment Residents-Seoul,
  Korea, Republic of
Druzes, Israel (79)
*Gabbra, Ethiopia
Gabbra, Kenya
*Gypsies in Spain, Spain (79)
Indust.Workers Yongdungpo,
  Korea, Republic of
*Koreans of Japan, Japan
Romany, Turkey
Spiritists, Brazil (79)
**Vietnamese Refugees, Australia

HINDU-ANIMIST

Abujmaria in M.P., India
Aimol in Assam, India
Ajmeri in Rajasthan, India
Aranadan in Tamil Nadu, India
Bagelkhandi in M.P., India
Balinese, Indonesia
Bangaru in Punjab, India
Bhakta, India
Bhattri, India
Bhilala, India
Bhoyari in Maharashtra, India
Bhumij in Assam, India
Bhunjia in Madhya Pradesh, India
Bijori in Bihar, India
Binjhwari in Bihar, India
Birhor in Bihar, India
**Bodo Kachari, India
Cham, Viet Nam
Chamari in Madhya Pradesh, India
Chameali in H.P., India
Chenchu in Andhra Pradesh, India
Chodhari in Gujarat, India
Churahi in H.P., India
**Dhodias, India
Dhurwa, India
Dorlin in Andhra Pradesh, India
**Dubla, India
Gadaban in Andhra Pradesh, India
Gaddi in Himachal Pradesh, India
Galong in Assam, India
Gamti in Gujarat, India
Gangte in Assam, India
Gawari in Andhra Pradesh, India
Grasia in Gujarat, India
**Hajong, Bangladesh
Halbi in Madhya Pradesh, India
Harauti in Rajasthan, India
Ho in Bihar, India
Holiya in Madhya Pradesh, India
Jagannathi in A.P., India
Jatapu in Andhra Pradesh, India
Jaunsari in Uttar Pradesh, India
Kadar in Andhra Pradesh, India
Kahluri in Andamans, India
Kaikadi in Maharashtra, India
Kamar in Madhya Pradesh, India
Kanikkaran in Kerala, India
Kanjari in Andhra Pradesh, India
**Karbis, India
Karmali in Dihar, India
Katakari in Gujarat, India
Kawar in Madhya Pradesh, India
Keer in Madhya Pradesh, India
Khandesi, India
Kharia in Bihar, India
Khirwar in Madhya Pradesh, India
Khowar, India
Kisan in Bihar, India
Kishanganjia in Bihar, India
Kishtwari in Jammu, India
**Koch, Bangladesh
Koda in Bihar, India
**Kohli, Wadiara, Pakistan
Kol in Assam, India
**Kolam, India

Kom in Manipur, India
Konda-Dora in A.P., India
Konkani in Gujarat, India
Koraga in Kerala, India
Korwa in Bihar, India
Kota in Tamil Nadu, India
Kotia in Andhra Pradesh, India
Koya in Andhra Pradesh, India
Kudiya, India
*Kuknas, India
Kumauni in Assam, India
Kupia in Andhra Pradesh, India
Kurichiya in Kerala, India (81)
Kuruba in Tamil Nadu, India
Kurux in Bihar, India
Kuvi in Orissa, India
Lodhi in Bihar, India
Lushai in Assam, India
**Magar, Nepal
Mahali in Assam, India
Maithili, Nepal
Majhwar in Madhya Pradesh, India
Malakkaras of Kerela, India (81)
Malankuravan in Kerala, India
Malapandaram in Kerala, India
Malaryan in Kerala, India
Mali in Andhra Pradesh, India
Malki in Bihar, India
Malpaharia in Assam, India
Malvi in Madhya Pradesh, India
Manna-Dora in A.P., India
Mannan in Kerala, India
Mara in Assam, India
Maria in Andhra Pradesh, India
Marwari in Gujarat, India
**Mawchis, India
**Miching, India
Mina in Madhya Pradesh, India
Mirdha in Orissa, India
Mishmi in Assam, India
Multani in Punjab, India
Mundari in Assam, India
Muria in Andhra Pradesh, India
Muthuvan in A.P., India
Muwasi in Madhya Pradesh, India
Naga, Kalyokengnyu, India
Nagar in Madhya Pradesh, India
Nihali in Madhya Pradesh, India
Ojhi in Madhya Pradesh, India
Ollari in Orissa, India
Ong in Andamans, India
Pahari Garhwali in U.P., India
Paite in Assam, India
Panika, India
Pardhan in Andhra Pradesh, India
Parengi in Orissa, India
Patelia in Gujarat, India
Pengo in Orissa, India
Pnar in Assam, India
Rabha in Assam, India
*Rai, Danuwar, Nepal
Rajbansi, India
Sadan in Andamans, India
Sondwari in M.P., India
Takankar, India
Tengger, Indonesia
Thakur, India
Thar in Bihar, India
Toda in Tamil Nadu, India

Tokkaru in Tamil Nadu, India
Tugara, India
Ullatan in Kerala, India
Urali in Kerala, India
Vishavan in Kerala, India
Waddar in Andhra Pradesh, India
Waqdi in Rajasthan, India
Yanadi in Andhra Pradesh, India
Yerava in Karnataka, India
Yerukala in A.P., India
Zangskari in Kashmir, India

HINDU-BUDDHIST

Kanauri in Uttar Pradesh, India
Khamti in Assam, India
Labans, India
Labhani in Andhra Pradesh, India
Ladakhi in Jammu, India
Lalung in Assam, India
**Lepcha, Sikkim
Naga, Mao, India
Naga, Nruanghmei, India
Naga, Sangtam, India
Naga, Tangkhul, India
Naga, Wancho, India
*Newari, Nepal
Nimadi in Madhya Pradesh, India
Pao in Madhya Pradesh, India
Rai, Nepal
Riang in Assam, India
Sikkimese, India
Sulung, India
*Tamang, Nepal
Tamaria in Bihar, India
Thado in Assam, India
Vaiphei in Assam, India
Zome in Manipur, India

HINDUISM

Adiyan in Kerala, India
Agariya in Bihar, India
Anga in Bihar, India
Arya in Andhra Pradesh, India
Babri, India
Baqri, Pakistan
Bajania, Pakistan (79)
Balmiki, Pakistan
Bareli in Madhya Pradesh, India
Bathudi in Bihar, India
**Bhil, Pakistan
*Bhojpuri, Nepal
Bondo in Orissa, India
*Gorkha, India
Gujarati, United Kingdom
Gurung, Nepal
Indians in Fiji, Fiji (79)
*Indians In Rhodesia, Rhodesia
**Indians, East, Trinidad and
    Tobago (79)

Iravas in Kerala, India
***Irulas in Kerala, India
Jharia in Orissa, India
Juang in Orissa, India
Kachchi in Andhra Pradesh, India
Khasi in Assam, India
**Kohli, Kutchi, Pakistan
**Kohli, Tharadari, Pakistan
**Kohlis, Parkari, Pakistan
*Kudisai Vagh Makkal, India
**Kuluis in Himachal Prades, India (81)
*Labourers of Jhoparpatti, India
Lohar, Pakistan
Malavedan in Kerala, India
Mangs in Maharashtra, India
***Matharis, India
**Meghwar, Pakistan (79)
*Meitei, India (79)
**Nepalese in India, India
*Nepali, Nepal
Od, Pakistan
*Rava in Assam, India
**Saiva Vellala, India
*Shourastra in Tamil Nadu, India
*Sindhis of India, India
Sochi, Pakistan
Sora in Orissa, India
Tamil (Ceylonese), Sri Lanka
*Tamil in Yellagiri Hills, India
***Tamil Plantation Workers, Malaysia
*Tamils (Indian), Malaysia
**Tamils (Indian), Sri Lanka (79)
Tharu, Nepal
Totis, India
Vagari, Pakistan

ISLAM

Abazin, Soviet Russia
Abialang, Sudan
Abkhaz, Turkey
Abong, Nigeria
Abu Leila, Sudan
Achehnese, Indonesia (80)
Acheron, Sudan
Achipa, Nigeria
Adygei, Soviet Russia
Afitti, Sudan
**African Students in Cairo, Egypt
Afshars, Iran
Agajanis, Iran
Agul, Soviet Russia
Ahir in Maharashtra, India
**Ahl-i-Haqq in Iran, Iran (79)
Aja, Sudan
Alaba, Ethiopia
*Alawites, Syria (79)
*Albanian Muslims, Albania (80)
*Albanians in Yugoslavia, Yugoslavia
Algerian (Arabs), Algeria (80)
Algerian Arabs in France, France
Ara, Indonesia

Arab-Jabbari (Kamesh), Iran
Arab-Shaibani (Kamesh), Iran
Arabs in Morocco, Morocco
Arabs of Khuzestan, Iran
Arawa, Nigeria
Assamese, Bangladesh
Aten, Nigeria
Atoc, Sudan
Atuot, Sudan
Avukaya, Sudan
Awngi, Ethiopia
Ayu, Nigeria
**Azerbaijani, Afghanistan
Azerbaijani Turks, Iran (80)
Bachama, Nigeria
Bade, Nigeria
Badyara, Guinea-Bissau
Baharlu (Kamesh), Iran
Bai, Sudan
Bajau, Indonesian, Indonesia
Bakhtiaris, Iran (80)
Balkars, Soviet Russia
Baluchi, Iran (80)
Bambara, Mali
Bambuka, Nigeria
Bandawa-Minda, Nigeria
Banga, Nigeria
Banggai, Indonesia
Barambu, Sudan
Bari, Sudan
Bashgali, Afghanistan
Bashkir, Soviet Russia (80)
*Batak, Angkola, Indonesia (80)
Batu, Nigeria
Baushi, Nigeria
Bawm, Bangladesh
Bayats, Iran
Beja, Ethiopia
Beja, Sudan
Bengali, Bangladesh (80)
Bhatneri, India
Bilen, Ethiopia
Bimanese, Indonesia
Binawa, Nigeria
Binga, Sudan
Bingkokak, Indonesia
Biti, Sudan
Bole, Nigeria
Bondei, Tanzania
Bongo, Sudan
Bor Gok, Sudan
*Bosnian, Yugoslavia (80)
Bovir-Ahmadi, Iran
Brahui, Pakistan
Bual, Indonesia
Buduma, Nigeria
Burak, Nigeria
Burun, Sudan
Busa, Nigeria (80)
Butawa, Nigeria
Bviri, Sudan
Chaghatai, Afghanistan
*Cham (Western), Kampuchea, Democratic
Cherkess, Soviet Russia
Chinese in Saudi Arabia, Saudi Arabia
Chinese Muslims, Taiwan (81)
Chitralis, Pakistan (79)

Maban-Jumjum, Sudan
Madi, Sudan
Madurese, Indonesia (79)
Maguindano, Philippines (80)
*Mahrah, Yemen, Democratic
Makonde, Tanzania
Malays of Singapore, Singapore (79)
Mamasani, Iran
Mandar, Indonesia
Mandara, Nigeria
Mandingo, Liberia (79)
Manggarai Muslims, Indonesia (81)
Mappillas, India
Maranao, Philippines (79)
Marghi Central, Nigeria
Marka, Upper Volta
Masakin, Sudan
Masalit, Sudan
Masenrempulu, Indonesia
Matakam, Nigeria
Matumbi, Tanzania
Maures, Senegal
Mazandaranis, Iran
Mboi, Nigeria
Mbula-Bwazza, Nigeria
Meos of Rajasthan, India (80)
Midob, Sudan
Minangkabau, Indonesia (80)
Miri, Sudan
Mober, Nigeria
Modo, Sudan
Mogholi, Afghanistan
Montol, Nigeria
Moor Malays, Sri Lanka (79)
Moors in Mauritania, Mauritania
Mogaddam, Iran
Moreb, Sudan
Mori, Indonesia (81)
Moru, Sudan
Mumbake, Nigeria
Munji-Yidgha, Afghanistan
Muslim Community of Bawku, Ghana
**Muslim Immigrants in U.K., United Kingdom
Muslim Malays, Malaysia (80)
Muslims (West Nile Dist.), Uganda
Muslims in U.A.E., United Arab Emirates (79)
Muslims of Jordan, Jordan
Nafar, Iran
Naka, Sudan
Nandu-Tari, Nigeria
Nginyukwur, Sudan
Ngirere, Sudan
Ngizim, Nigeria
Ngok, Sudan
Ngunduna, Sudan
Nquqwurang, Sudan
Ngwoi, Nigeria
Ninzam, Nigeria
Njalgulgule, Sudan
North Africans in Belgium, Belgium (80)
Numana-Nunku-Gwantu, Nigeria
**Nupe, Nigeria
Nuristani, Afghanistan (80)

Nyamusa, Sudan
Nyarueng, Sudan
Nzanyi, Nigeria
Otoro, Sudan
Ouaddai, Chad
Palembang, Indonesia
Paloc, Sudan
Pankhu, Bangladesh
Pashtuns, Iran (80)
Pero, Nigeria
Persians of Iran, Iran (80)
Pishagchi, Iran
Piti, Nigeria
Piya, Nigeria
Polci, Nigeria
Ponqu, Nigeria
Poouch in Kashmir, India
***Prasuni, Afghanistan
Puku-Geeri-Keri-Wipsi, Nigeria
Punjabis, Pakistan (80)
Puriq-Pa of Kashmir, India (81)
Qajars, Iran
Qara'i, Iran
Qaragozlu, Iran
Qashqa'i, Iran (80)
Redjang, Indonesia (80)
Rukuba, Nigeria
Rumaya, Nigeria
Ruruma, Nigeria
Rut, Sudan
Rutul, Soviet Russia
**Saguye, Kenya
Sama Panqutaran, Philippines (80)
Sanqa, Nigeria
Sanqil, Philippines
Sarakole, Senegal (80)
Sasanis, Iran
Sau, Afghanistan
Saya, Nigeria
Sayyids, Yemen, Arab Republic
Sere, Sudan
Shahsavans, Iran (80)
Shatt, Sudan
Shawiya, Algeria
**Shihu, United Arab Emirates
Shilluk, Sudan
Shughni, Afghanistan
Shuwa Arabic, Nigeria
Shwai, Sudan
Siri, Nigeria
Solorese Muslims, Indonesia (81)
Somali, Ethiopia
Somali, Somalia (79)
Somali, Ajuran, Kenya (79)
Somali, Deqodia, Kenya
Somali, Gurreh, Kenya
Somali, Ogadenya, Kenya
Soninke, Gambia
Soninke, Mali
Soninke, Mauritania
Sopi, Sudan
Sukur, Nigeria
Sumbawa, Indonesia
Sura, Nigeria
Surubu, Nigeria
Swatis, Pakistan (79)
Tabasaran, Soviet Russia
Tajik, Iran (80)

Tajik, Afghanistan
Tajik, Soviet Russia
Takestani, Iran
Tal, Nigeria
Talish, Iran
Talodi, Sudan
Tangale, Nigeria
Tangchangya, Bangladesh
Tat, Soviet Russia
Tatars, Soviet Russia (80)
Taucouleur, Senegal (80)
Tausug, Philippines (80)
Teda, Chad (80)
Teda, Libya
Tegali, Sudan
Teimuri, Iran
Teimurtash, Iran
Tem, Togo
Temein, Sudan
Tera, Nigeria
Ternatans, Indonesia
*Tertiary Level Youth, Iran
Thoi, Sudan
Thuri, Sudan
Tippera, Bangladesh
Tira, Sudan
Tirma, Sudan
*Toussian, Upper Volta
Tsakhur, Soviet Russia
Tuareg, Niger (79)
Tula, Nigeria
Tulishi, Sudan
Tumale, Sudan
Tumma, Sudan
Tumtum, Sudan
Turkish Immigrant Workers,
  German Federal Rep. (79)
Turkish Workers, Belgium (80)
Turkomans, Iran (80)
Turks, Anatolian, Turkey
Turkwam, Nigeria
Twi, Sudan
Uighur, Afghanistan
Uigur, China (80)
Umm Dorein, Sudan
Umm Gabralla, Sudan
*Vai, Liberia (80)
**Vohras of Yavatmal, India
Waja, Nigeria
Weda, Indonesia
Winji-Winji, Benin
Woro, Sudan
Yao, Mozambique
Yemenis, Yemen, Arab Republic
  (79)
Yeskwa, Nigeria
Yoruk, Turkey
Yulu, Sudan
Yungur, Nigeria
Zaghawa, Libya
Zaghawa, Sudan
Zari, Nigeria
Zenaga, Mauritania

ISLAM-ANIMIST

Abe, Ivory Coast
Abidji, Ivory Coast
Abou Charib, Chad
Abure, Ivory Coast
Achode, Ghana
Adele, Togo
Adyukru, Ivory Coast
Afar, Ethiopia (79)
Aqutaynon, Philippines
Ahlo, Togo
Akan, Brong, Ivory Coast
***Akhdam, Yemen, Arab Republic
Akpafu, Ghana
Aladian, Ivory Coast
Alas, Indonesia
Ana, Togo
Animere, Togo
Anyanga, Togo
Attie, Ivory Coast
Avatime, Ghana
Avikam, Ivory Coast
Awutu, Ghana
Ayana, Kenya
Baqirmi, Chad
Bajau, Land, Malaysia
Bakwe, Ivory Coast
Balantak, Indonesia
Bali, Nigeria
Bambara, Ivory Coast
Banyum, Senegal
Bariba, Nigeria
Basila, Togo
Bata, Nigeria
Bayot, Gambia
Bayot, Guinea-Bissau
Bayot, Senegal
Bidyogo, Guinea-Bissau
Bilala, Chad
Bile, Nigeria
Bimoba, Ghana
Bimoba, Togo
Bira, Indonesia
Birifor, Upper Volta
Bitare, Nigeria
Bolon, Upper Volta
Bomou, Chad
Boran, Ethiopia
**Boran, Kenya
Boran, Kenya
Bousansi, Upper Volta
Bowili, Togo
Buqis, Indonesia (80)
Buli, Indonesia
Buli, Upper Volta
Bullom, Northern, Sierra Leone
Bullom, Southern, Sierra Leone
Butunq, Indonesia
Chala, Ghana
Chamba Daka, Nigeria
Chamba Leko, Nigeria
Cirebon, Indonesia
Dagari, Upper Volta
**Dagomba, Ghana
Daju of Dar Dadju, Chad
Daju of Dar Sila, Chad
Dan, Liberia
Dangaleat, Chad
Dass, Nigeria
Dida, Ivory Coast

REGISTRY OF THE UNREACHED

Diola, Senegal
Dirim, Nigeria
Doghosie, Upper Volta
Dyan, Upper Volta
Dyerma, Niger (80)
Dyola, Gambia
Dyola, Guinea-Bissau
Dyola, Senegal
Ebira, Nigeria
Ebrie, Ivory Coast
Eotile, Ivory Coast
Fula, Upper Volta
Fula, Cunda, Gambia
Fulani, Cameroon (79)
*Fulani, Benin
*Fulbe, Ghana
Gabri, Chad
*Galla (Bale), Ethiopia
Gambai, Chad
Gan, Upper Volta
Gangam, Togo
Gayo, Indonesia (80)
Gidar, Chad
Gola, Liberia
Gola, Sierra Leone
Golo, Chad
Gonja, Ghana
Gosha, Kenya
Gouin-Turka, Upper Volta
Goulai, Chad
Guere, Ivory Coast
Gujars of Kashmir, India (81)
Gujars of Kashmir, India (81)
Gula, Chad
Gurage, Ethiopia (80)
Gurma, Upper Volta
Gwa, Ivory Coast
Hwela-Numu, Ivory Coast
Icen, Nigeria
Igbira, Nigeria (80)
Jama Mapun, Philippines (80)
Jambi, Indonesia
**Javanese (rural), Indonesia (79)
**Javanese of Central Java,
   Indonesia
Jongor, Chad
Kanembu, Chad
Kanembu, Niger
Karachay, Soviet Russia
Karanga, Chad
Kari, Chad
Kasanga, Guinea-Bissau
Kasele, Togo
Kasem, Upper Volta
**Kaur, Indonesia
Kazakhs, China (81)
Kebu, Togo
Kendari, Indonesia
Kenga, Chad
Kera, Chad
Kerinchi, Indonesia
Kibet, Chad
Kim, Chad
Kirgiz, Soviet Russia (80)
Kissi, Southern, Sierra Leone
Klaoh, Liberia
Kobiana, Guinea
Koke, Chad
Kolbila, Cameroon

Komering, Indonesia
Komono, Upper Volta
Konyagi, Guinea
**Koranko, Sierra Leone
Kotoko, Chad
Kotokoli, Togo
Kouya, Ivory Coast
Kpelle, Guinea
Kposo, Togo
Krachi, Ghana
Krim, Sierra Leone
Krio, Gambia
Krobou, Ivory Coast
Kubu, Indonesia (81)
Kuka, Chad
Kulele, Ivory Coast
Kullo, Ethiopia
Kulung, Nigeria
Kunante, Guinea-Bissau
Kurumba, Upper Volta
Kuwaa, Liberia
Laka, Chad
Lampung, Indonesia (80)
Landoma, Guinea
Landoma, Guinea-Bissau
Lele, Chad
Lele, Upper Volta
Lelemi, Ghana
Liguri, Sudan
Logba, Ghana
Loko, Guinea
Loko, Sierra Leone
Maba, Chad
Majingai-Ngama, Chad
Mamprusi, Ghana
Mandyak, Gambia
Mangbai, Chad
Maninka, Guinea-Bissau
Maninka, Sierra Leone
Mankanya, Guinea-Bissau
Mankanya, Senegal
Maou, Ivory Coast
Maranao, Lanad, Philippines
Mararit, Chad
Marba, Chad
Masalit, Chad
Massalat, Chad
Maure, Mali
Mbai, Chad
Mbum, Chad
Mende, Liberia
Mesengo, Ethiopia
Mesme, Chad
Mesmedje, Chad
Mimi, Chad
Mo, Ivory Coast
Mogum, Chad
*Molbog, Philippines
Mona, Ivory Coast
Moru, Ivory Coast
Mubi, Chad
Muna, Indonesia
Mundang, Chad
Musei, Chad
Musqu, Chad
Musi, Indonesia
Nalu, Guinea
Nancere, Chad
Naoudem, Togo

Nara, Ethiopia
Natemba, Togo
Natioro, Upper Volta
Nchumbulu, Ghana
Nchumunu, Ghana
Ndunpa Duupa, Cameroon
Nielim, Chad
Nkonya, Ghana
Ntrubo, Togo
Nunuma, Upper Volta
Nyangbo, Ghana
Nzema, Ivory Coast
Nzema, Ghana
Ogan, Indonesia
Oubi, Ivory Coast
Palara, Ivory Coast
Papel, Guinea-Bissau
Pashayi, Afghanistan
Prang, Ghana
Puguli, Upper Volta
Pye, Ivory Coast
Rataning, Chad
Rendille, Kenya
Runga, Chad
Safaliba, Ghana
Sakuye, Kenya
Sama Banginqi, Philippines (80)
Sama, Siasi, Philippines
Sama, Sibuku, Philippines
Sama-Badjaw, Philippines (79)
Samo, Northern, Upper Volta
Santrokofi, Ghana
Sarwa, Chad
Sasak, Indonesia (80)
Sekayu, Indonesia
Sekpele, Ghana
**Serawai, Indonesia (81)
Serere-Non, Senegal
Serere-Sine, Senegal
Shilha, Morocco
Shina, Afghanistan
**Shluh Berbers, Morocco
Sidamo, Ethiopia
Sisala, Upper Volta
Siwu, Ghana
Somrai, Chad
Songhai, Niger
Songhai, Upper Volta
Subanun,Lapuyan, Philippines
**Sundanese, Indonesia (80)
Sungor, Chad
Susu, Guinea-Bissau
Susu, Sierra Leone
Tafi, Togo
Tagwana, Ivory Coast
*Talo, Indonesia
Tama, Chad
Tamazight, Morocco
Tana, Chad
Teda, Niger
Tepo, Ivory Coast
Thai Islam (Malay), Thailand
  (80)
*Thai Islam (Thai), Thailand
Tidorese, Indonesia
Tiefo, Upper Volta
Trepo, Ivory Coast
Tunya, Chad
Tupuri, Chad

Tura, Ivory Coast
**Uzbeks, Afghanistan (79)
Vagla, Ghana
Vai, Sierra Leone
Vige, Upper Volta
Voko, Cameroon
Wara, Upper Volta
Win, Upper Volta
Wolio, Indonesia
Wolof, Senegal (80)
Wolof, Gambian, Gambia
Wom, Nigeria
Yakan, Philippines (80)
*Yalunka, Sierra Leone (80)
Yandang, Nigeria
Yanga, Togo
**Yao, Malawi
Zaghawa, Chad
Zaramo, Tanzania

JAIN

Jains, India

JUDAISM

**Falasha, Ethiopia (79)
*Jewish Imgrnts.-American, Israel
*Jewish Imgrnts.-Argentine,
  Israel
*Jewish Imgrnts.-Australia,
  Israel
*Jewish Imgrnts.-Brazilian,
  Israel
*Jewish Imgrnts.-Mexican, Israel
*Jewish Imgrnts.-Uruguayan,
  Israel
*Jewish Immigrants, Other, Israel
Jews of Iran, Iran
Jews of Montreal, Canada
Jews, Sephardic, Canada
Ladinos, Lebanon
Targum, Israel

NOMINAL CHRISTIAN

Baguio Area Miners, Philippines
  (81)
**Batangeno, Philippines
***Bolinao, Philippines
*Casiguranin, Philippines
***Copacabana Apt. Dwellers,
  Brazil
**Hotel Workers in Manila,
  Philippines (81)
**Ishans, Nigeria
*Jeepney Drivers in Manila,
  Philippines (81)

*Jeepney Drivers in Manila,
  Philippines (81)
**Kalinga, Tanudan, Philippines
**Military Personnel, Ecuador
**Urban Mestizos, Ecuador

PEYOTE RELIGION

Paiute, Northern, United States
  of America

SECULARISM

*Americans in Geneva, Switzerland
Amsterdam Boat Dwellers,
  Netherlands
*Chinese in Korea, Korea,
  Republic of
*Chinese in West Germany, German
  Federal Rep.
*Chinese Mainlanders, Taiwan
**Chinese Stud., Australia,
  Australia
*Industrial Workers, Taiwan (81)
**Jamaican Elite, Jamaica
*Japanese Students In USA, United
  States of America
**Korean Prisoners, Korea,
  Republic of
*Parsees, India (81)
**Portuguese in France, France
**Racetrack Residents, United
  States of America (79)
Seychellois, Seychelles
Students in Cuiaba, Brazil
**Suriguenos, Philippines
Taiwan-Chinese Un. Stud.,
  Taiwan
*University Students, France (79)
*University Students, German
  Federal Rep. (79)

TRADITIONAL CHINESE

Ach'ang, China
Buriat, China
Burig, China
Ch'iang, China
Chin, China
Chinese Businessmen, Hong Kong
  (81)
Chinese Factory Workers, Hong
  Kong
Chinese Fishermen, Malaysia
**Chinese Hakka of Taiwan, Taiwan
  (79)
**Chinese in Australia, Australia

*Chinese in Austria, Austria
**Chinese in Brazil, Brazil
Chinese in Burma, Burma
**Chinese in Hong Kong, Hong Kong
**Chinese in Indonesia, Indonesia
*Chinese in Japan, Japan
*Chinese in Laos, Laos
*Chinese in Malaysia, Malaysia
*Chinese in New Zealand, New
  Zealand
**Chinese in Panama, Panama
Chinese in Puerto Rico, Puerto
  Rico
**Chinese in Sabah, Malaysia
**Chinese in Sarawak, Malaysia
*Chinese in South Africa, South
  Africa
*Chinese in Taiwan, Taiwan
**Chinese in United Kingdom,
  United Kingdom
**Chinese in United States, United
  States of America
**Chinese in Vancouver B.C.,
  Canada
*Chinese of W. Malaysia,
  Malaysia
*Chinese Refugees in Macau, Macau
  (81)
**Chinese Refugees, France, France
  (79)
*Chinese Restaurant Wrkrs.,
  France
**Chinese Students Glasgow, United
  Kingdom
Chinese Villagers, Hong Kong
Chingp'o, China
Chungchia, China
Chwang, China
Daqur, China
Evenki, China
Fishing Village People, Taiwan
Hani, China
**High School Students, Hong Kong
Jyarung, China
Kalmytz, China
Kam, China
Kelao, China
Khalka, China
Kham, China
Lahul, China
Laka, China
Lati, China
Li, China
Manchu, China (81)
Mongour, China
Nahsi, China
Nanai, China
Nosu, China
Nung, China
Oirat, China
Oronchon, China
Paongan, China
Pu-I, China
Punu, China
Rawang, China
Salar, China
Santa, China
Sibo, China
Sui, China

Wa, China
*Women Laborers, Taiwan
Yellow Uighur, China
Yuku, China

TRADITIONAL JAPANESE

Farmers of Japan, Japan
*Industry Laborers-Japan, Japan
*Inland Sea Island Peoples, Japan
*Japanese in Korea, Korea,
   Republic of
*Ryukyuan, Japan
**Univ. Students of Japan, Japan

OTHER

**Lotuka, Sudan
*Yanyula, Australia

UNKNOWN

Abkhaz, Soviet Russia
Akhavakh, Soviet Russia
Alutor, Soviet Russia
Andi, Soviet Russia
Archin, Soviet Russia
Bangangte, Cameroon
Basaa, Cameroon
Batsi, Soviet Russia
Botlikh, Soviet Russia
Budug, Soviet Russia
**Bus Drivers, South Korea, Korea,
   Republic of
Chamalin, Soviet Russia
*Chinese in Amsterdam,
   Netherlands
Chinese in Costa Rica, Costa
   Rica
*Chinese in Holland, Netherlands
Chinese Merchants, Ghana
Chukot, Soviet Russia
Didoi, Soviet Russia
Dolgans, Soviet Russia
*Factory Workers, Hong Kong
Gilyak, Soviet Russia
*Havasupai, United States of
   America
Itelmen, Soviet Russia
Izhor, Soviet Russia
Kapuchin, Soviet Russia
Karagas, Soviet Russia
Karaim, Soviet Russia
Karakalpak, Soviet Russia
Karatin, Soviet Russia
Ket, Soviet Russia
Khakas, Soviet Russia

Khana, Nigeria
Khanti, Soviet Russia
Khinalug, Soviet Russia
Khvarshin, Soviet Russia
Kongo, Angola
***Koreans in Germany, German
   Federal Rep.
Koryak, Soviet Russia
Kryz, Soviet Russia
Kvanadin, Soviet Russia
Liv, Soviet Russia
Lugbara, Uganda
Mansi, Soviet Russia
Mingat, Soviet Russia
Naga, Sema, India
Nanai, Soviet Russia
Nentsy, Soviet Russia
Nganasan, Soviet Russia
Nivkhi, Soviet Russia
Oroch, Soviet Russia
Orok, Soviet Russia
Saams, Soviet Russia
Selkup, Soviet Russia
Shor, Soviet Russia
Svan, Soviet Russia
Tindin, Soviet Russia
Udegeis, Soviet Russia
Udin, Soviet Russia
Ulchi, Soviet Russia
Veps, Soviet Russia
Yagnobi, Soviet Russia
Yazgulyam, Soviet Russia
Yukagirs, Soviet Russia
Yurak, Soviet Russia

NOT REPORTED

Balanta, Senegal
Bamum, Cameroon
Lunda, Ndembu, Zambia
Mancang, Senegal
Manding, Senegal
Manjack, Senegal
Mulimba, Cameroon
Ndogo, Sudan
Pular, Senegal
Tandanke, Senegal
Tsaangi, Congo

Index by
Language

INDEX BY LANGUAGE

Groups are listed according to their primary vernacular language. In many cases, groups are bilingual or trilingual, speaking several languages including a more commonly known trade language.

"Au"ei	"Au"ei, Botswana
Abaknon	Abaknon, Philippines
Abanyom	Abanyom, Nigeria
Abau	Abau, Indonesia
Abazin	Abazin, Soviet Russia
Abe	Abe, Ivory Coast
Abialang	Abialang, Sudan
Abkhaz	Abkhaz, Turkey
	Abkhaz, Soviet Russia
Abong	Abong, Nigeria
Abou Charib	Abou Charib, Chad
Abu Leila	Abu Leila, Sudan
Abua	Abua, Nigeria
Abujmaria	Abujmaria in M.P., India
Abure	Abure, Ivory Coast
Ach'ang	Ach'ang, China
Achagua	Achagua, Colombia
Achehnese	Achehnese, Indonesia (80)
Acheron	Acheron, Sudan
Achi, Cubulco	Achi, Cubulco, Guatemala
Achi, Rabinal	Achi, Rabinal, Guatemala
Achipa	Achipa, Nigeria
Achode	Achode, Ghana
Acholi	Acholi, Uganda
Achual	Achual, Peru
Adele	Adele, Togo
Adhola	Adhola, Uganda
Adi	***Adi, India
Adidji	Abidji, Ivory Coast
Adiyan	Adiyan in Kerala, India
Adygei	Adygei, Soviet Russia
Adyukru	Adyukru, Ivory Coast
Aeta	Aeta, Philippines
Afanci	*Afawa, Nigeria (80)
Afar	Afar, Ethiopia (79)
Afitti	Afitti, Sudan
Afshari	Afshars, Iran
	Inallu, Iran
Agajanis	Agajanis, Iran
Agariya	Agariya in Bihar, India
Agau	**Falasha, Ethiopia (79)
Age	Age, Cameroon
Aghem	Aghem, Cameroon
Aghu	Aghu, Indonesia
Agoi	Agoi, Nigeria
Aguacateco	Aguacateco, Guatemala
Aguaruna	Aguaruna, Peru
Agul	Agul, Soviet Russia
Agutaynon	Agutaynon, Philippines
Agwagwune	Agwagwune, Nigeria
Ahir	Ahir in Maharashtra, India
Ahlo	Ahlo, Togo
Aibondeni	Aibondeni, Indonesia
Aikwakai	Aikwakai, Indonesia
Aimol	Aimol in Assam, India
Airo-Sumaghaghe	Airo-Sumaghaghe, Indonesia
Airoran	Airoran, Indonesia
Aja	Aja, Sudan
Ajmeri	Ajmeri in Rajasthan, India
Aka	Aka, India
Akan, Brong	Akan, Brong, Ivory Coast
Akawaio	Akawaio, Guyana
Ake	Ake, Nigeria
Akha	**Akha, Thailand (79)
Akhavakh	Akhavakh, Soviet Russia
Akpa-Yache	Akpa-Yache, Nigeria
Akpafu	Akpafu, Ghana
Alaban	Alaba, Ethiopia
Aladian	Aladian, Ivory Coast

Alago	Alago, Nigeria
Alak	Alak, Laos
Alangan	Alangan, Philippines
Albanian (Gheg)	*Albanians in Yugoslavia, Yugoslavia
Albanian Tosk	*Albanian Muslims, Albania (80)
Aledjo	*Nyantruku, Benin
Alege	Alege, Nigeria
Allar	*Alars, India
Alor, Kolana	Alor, Kolana, Indonesia (81)
Altaic	Ewenkis, China (81)
Alur	Alur, Zaire
Alutor	Alutor, Soviet Russia
Amahuaca	Amahuaca, Peru
Amanab	Amanab, Indonesia
Amar	Amar, Ethiopia
Amarakaeri	Amarakaeri, Peru
Amasi	Amasi, Cameroon
Ambai	Ambai, Indonesia
Amber	Amber, Indonesia
Amberbaken	Amberbaken, Indonesia
Ambo	Ambo, Zambia
Ambonese	Ambonese, Netherlands
	Ambonese, Indonesia
Ami	*Ami, Taiwan (81)
Amo	Amo, Nigeria
Amoy	Fishing Village People, Taiwan
	*Women Laborers, Taiwan
Ampale	**Ampeeli, Papua New Guinea
Amuesha	Amuesha, Peru
Amuzgo, Guerrero	Amuzgo, Guerrero, Mexico
Amuzgo, Oaxaca	Amuzgo, Oaxaca, Mexico
Ana	Ana, Togo
Anaang	Anaang, Nigeria
Anal	Anal in Manipur, India
Andha	Andha in Andhra Pradesh, India
Andi	Andi, Soviet Russia
Andoque	Andoque, Colombia
Anga	Anga in Bihar, India
Angas	Angas, Nigeria
Animere	Animere, Togo
Ankwai	Ankwe, Nigeria
Ansus	Ansus, Indonesia
Anuak	Anuak, Ethiopia
	Anuak, Sudan
Anyanga	Anyanga, Togo
Apalai	Apalai, Brazil
Apartani	**Apatani in Assam, India
Apinaye	Apinaye, Brazil
Apurina	Apurina, Brazil
Ara	Ara, Indonesia
Arabela	Arabela, Peru
Arabic	***Akhdam, Yemen, Arab Republic
	*Alawites, Syria (79)
	Algerian (Arabs), Algeria (80)
	Algerian Arabs in France, France
	Arab-Jabbari (Kamesh), Iran
	Arab-Shaibani (Kamesh), Iran
	Arabs of Khuzestan, Iran
	Chinese in Saudi Arabia, Saudi Arabia
	Druzes, Israel (79)
	**Hadrami, Yemen, Democratic
	Libyans, Libya
	Masalit, Sudan
	Maures, Senegal
	Muslims in U.A.E., United Arab Emirates (79)
	Muslims of Jordan, Jordan
	North Africans in Belgium, Belgium (80)
	Sayyids, Yemen, Arab Republic

Bakairi	Bakairi, Brazil
Bakhtiaris	Bakhtiaris, Iran (80)
Bakwe	Bakwe, Ivory Coast
Bakwele	Bakwele, Congo
Balangao	**Balangao, Philippines
Balangaw	Balangaw, Philippines
Balanta	Balanta, Senegal
	Balante, Guinea-Bissau
Balantak	Balantak, Indonesia
Bali	Bali, Nigeria
Balinese	Balinese, Indonesia
Balkar	Balkars, Soviet Russia
Balti	Balti in Jammu, India
Baluchi	Baluchi, Iran (80)
Bambara	Bambara, Mali
	Bambara, Ivory Coast
Bambuka	Bambuka, Nigeria
Bamougoun-Bamenjou	Bamougoun-Bamenjou, Cameroon
Bamum	Bamum, Cameroon
Banaro	***Banaro, Papua New Guinea
Bandawa-Minda	Bandawa-Minda, Nigeria
Bandi	Bandi, Liberia
	Gbande, Guinea
Bandjoun	Bandjoun, Cameroon
Banen	Banen, Cameroon
Banga	Banga, Nigeria
Bangba	Bangba, Zaire
Banggai	Banggai, Indonesia
Bangri	Bangaru in Punjab, India
Baniwa	Baniwa, Brazil
Bantuanon	Bantuanon, Philippines
Banyum	Banyum, Senegal
Banyun	Banyun, Guinea-Bissau
Barambu	Barambu, Sudan
Barasano	Barasano, Colombia
Barasano, Northern	Barasano, Northern, Colombia
Barau	Barau, Indonesia
Bare'e	Bare'e, Indonesia
Bareli	Bareli in Madhya Pradesh, India
Bari	Bari, Sudan
Bariba	*Bariba, Benin (80)
	Bariba, Nigeria
Basaa	Basaa, Cameroon
Basari	Basari, Togo
	Basari, Guinea
	Basari, Senegal
Bashar	Bashar, Nigeria
Bashgali	Bashgali, Afghanistan
Basila	Basila, Togo
Basketo	Basketo, Ethiopia
Bassa	*Bassa, Liberia
	**Bassa, Nigeria
Bata	Bata, Nigeria
Batak, Angkola	*Batak, Angkola, Indonesia (80)
Batak, Karo	Batak, Karo, Indonesia
Batak, Palawan	Batak, Palawan, Philippines
Batak, Simalungun	Batak, Simalungun, Indonesia
Batak, Toba	Batak, Toba, Indonesia
Batanga-Ngolo	Batanga-Ngolo, Cameroon
Bateg	Bateg, Malaysia
Bathudi	Bathudi in Bihar, India
Batsi	Batsi, Soviet Russia
Batu	Batu, Nigeria
Baule	***Baoule, Ivory Coast
Baushi	Baushi, Nigeria
Bawm	Bawm, Bangladesh
Bayat	Bayats, Iran
Bayot	Bayot, Gambia
	Bayot, Guinea-Bissau

Bitare	Bitare, Nigeria
	Bitare, Cameroon
Biti	Biti, Sudan
Bobe	Bobe, Cameroon
Bobo Fing	Bobo Fing, Mali
Bobo Wule	Bobo Wule, Mali
Bodo	Bodo in Assam, India
	**Bodo Kachari, India
Boghom	Boghom, Nigeria
Boko (Busa)	**Boko, Benin
Bokyi	Bokyi, Nigeria
	Bokyi, Cameroon
Bole	Bole, Nigeria
Bolinao	***Bolinao, Philippines
Bolon	Bolon, Upper Volta
Bolondo	Bolondo, Zaire
Boma	Boma, Zaire
Bomboko	Bomboko, Cameroon
Bomou	Bomou, Chad
Bondei	Bondei, Tanzania
Bondo	Bondo in Orissa, India
Bonerif	Bonerif, Indonesia
Bonggo	Bonggo, Indonesia
Bongili	Bongili, Congo
Bongo	Bongo, Sudan
Bonkeng-Pendia	Bonkeng-Pendia, Cameroon
Bontoc, Central	**Bontoc, Central, Philippines (81)
Bor Gok	Bor Gok, Sudan
Bora	Bora, Colombia
Borai	Borai, Indonesia
Boran	Boran, Ethiopia
	**Boran, Kenya
	Boran, Kenya
	Sabbra, Kenya
Bororo	*Bororo, Brazil
Botlikh	Botlikh, Soviet Russia
Bowili	Bowili, Togo
Boya	Boya, Sudan
Bozo	Bozo, Mali
Brahui	Brahui, Pakistan
Braj	Braj in Uttar Pradesh, India
Brao	Brao, Laos (79)
Brat	Brat, Indonesia
Bruneis	Bruneis, Malaysia
Bua	Bua, Chad
Bual	Bual, Indonesia
Buamu (Bobo Wule)	Bwa, Upper Volta (80)
Bube	Bube, Equatorial Guinea
Budu	Budu, Zaire
Budug	Budug, Soviet Russia
Buduma	Buduma, Nigeria
Bugis	Bugis, Indonesia (80)
Buglere	Buglere, Panama
Bugombe	Bugombe, Zaire
Buhid	Buhid, Philippines
Buja	Buja, Zaire
Buka-khwe	Bushmen in Botswana, Botswana
Buli	Builsa, Ghana
	Buli, Indonesia
	Buli, Upper Volta
Bulia	Bulia, Zaire
Bullom, Northern	Bullom, Northern, Sierra Leone
Bullom, Southern	Bullom, Southern, Sierra Leone
Bunak	Bunak, Indonesia
Bunan	Bunann in Kashmir, India
Bungku	Bungku, Indonesia
Bunu	Bunu, Nigeria
Bura	Bura, Cameroon
Bura (Babur)	**Babur Thali, Nigeria (80)

REGISTRY OF THE UNREACHED

Chamalin	Chamalin, Soviet Russia
Chamari	Chamari in Madhya Pradesh, India
Chamba Daka	Chamba Daka, Nigeria
Chamba Leko	Chamba Leko, Nigeria
Chameali	Chameali in H.P., India
Chami	Chami, Colombia
Chamicuro	Chamicuro, Peru
Chamorro	Chamorro, Turks and Caicos Islands
Chara	Chara, Ethiopia
Chatino, Nopala	Chatino, Nopala, Mexico
Chatino, Panixtlahuaca	Chatino, Panixtlahuaca, Mexico
Chatino, Tataltepec	Chatino, Tataltepec, Mexico
Chatino, Zacatepec	Chatino, Zacatepec, Mexico
Chatino, Zenzontepec	Chatino, Zenzontepec, Mexico
Chaungtha	Chaungtha, Burma
Chawai	Chawai, Nigeria
Chayawita	**Chayahuita, Peru
Chenchu	Chenchu in Andhra Pradesh, India
Cherkes	Cherkess, Soviet Russia
Chero	Chero in Bihar, India
Chhattisgarhi	Satnamis in M.P., India
Chiga	Chiga, Uganda
Chik-Barik	Chik-Barik in Bihar, India
ChiKalanga	*Kalanga, Botswana
Chin	Chin, China
Chin, Asho	Chin, Asho, Burma
Chin, Falam	Chin, Falam, Burma
Chin, Haka	Chin, Haka, Burma
Chin, Khumi	Chin, Khumi, Burma
Chin, Ngawn	Chin, Ngawn, Burma
Chin, Tiddim	Chin, Tiddim, Burma
Chinanteco, Ayotzintepec	Chinanteco, Ayotzintepec, Mexico
Chinanteco, Chiltepec	Chinanteco, Chiltepec, Mexico
Chinanteco, Comaltepec	Chinanteco, Comaltepec, Mexico
Chinanteco, Lalana	Chinanteco, Lalana, Mexico
Chinanteco, Lealao	Chinanteco, Lealao, Mexico
Chinanteco, Ojitlan	Chinanteco, Ojitlan, Mexico
Chinanteco, Palantla	Chinanteco, Palantla, Mexico
Chinanteco, Quiotepec	Chinanteco, Quiotepec, Mexico
Chinanteco, Sochiapan	Chinanteco, Sochiapan, Mexico
Chinanteco, Tepetotutla	Chinanteco, Tepetotutla, Mexico
Chinanteco, Tepinapa	Chinanteco, Tepinapa, Mexico
Chinanteco, Usila	Chinanteco, Usila, Mexico
Chinbok	Chinbok, Burma
Chinese dialects	*Chinese in Malaysia, Malaysia
	Chinese Merchants, Ghana
	**Chinese Stud., Australia, Australia
Chinga	Chinga, Cameroon
	Chinga, Cameroon
Chingp'o	Chingp'o, China
Chip	Chip, Nigeria
Chipaya	Chipaya, Bolivia
Chiquitano	Chiquitano, Bolivia
ChiTonga	*Tonga, Rhodesia
	Tonga, Gwembe Valley, Zambia (79)
Chiyao	**Yao, Malawi
Chodhari	Chodhari in Gujarat, India
Chokobo	Chokobo, Nigeria
Chokwe	Chokwe, Zambia
	Chokwe (Lunda), Angola
Chopi	Chopi, Mozambique
Chorote	Chorote, Argentina
	Chorote, Paraguay
Chorti	Chorti, Guatemala
Chuang	Chuang, China (81)
Chuj	Chuj, Guatemala
	Chuj of San Mateo Ixtatan, Guatemala
Chuj, San Mateo Ixtatan	Chuj, San Mateo Ixtatan, Mexico
Chukot	Chukot, Soviet Russia

366

Deori	Deori in Assam, India
Dera	Dera, Nigeria
Desano	Desano, Brazil
Dghwede	Dghwede, Cameroon
	Dghwede, Cameroon
Dhaiso	Dhaiso, Tanzania
Dhanka	Dhanka in Gujarat, India
Dhanwar	Dhanwar in Madhya Pradesh, India
Dhimba	Herero, Namibia
Dhodia Dialects	**Dhodias, India
Dhuwal	*Murngin (Wulamba), Australia
Dida	Dida, Ivory Coast
	**Dida, Ivory Coast
Didinga	Didinga, Sudan
	Didinga, Sudan
Didoi	Didoi, Soviet Russia
Digo	Digo, Tanzania
	Digo, Kenya
Dimasa	Dimasa in Cachar, India
Dime	Dime, Ethiopia
Dinka	Dinka, Sudan
Dinka, Agar	Dinka, Agar, Sudan
Diola	Diola, Senegal
	Diola, Guinea-Bissau (80)
Dirim	Dirim, Nigeria
Dirya	Dirya, Nigeria
Divehi	Divehi, Maldives (80)
Djuka	Djuka, Surinam
Doe	Doe, Tanzania
Doghosie	Doghosie, Upper Volta
Dogon	*Dogon, Mali (79)
Dolgan	Dolgans, Soviet Russia
Dompago	Dompago, Benin
Dongjoi	Dongjoi, Sudan
Dongo	Dongo, Sudan
	Dongo, Zaire
Doohyaayo	**Doohwaayo, Cameroon
Dorli	Dorlin in Andhra Pradesh, India
Dorze	Dorze, Ethiopia
Duala	Balong, Cameroon
Dubu	Dubu, Indonesia
Duguri	Duguir, Nigeria
Duguza	Duguza, Nigeria
Dukanci	**Duka, Nigeria
Duma	Duma, Gabon
Dumagat	*Dumagat , Casiguran, Philippines (81)
Dungan	Dungan, Soviet Russia
Duru	Duru, Cameroon
Dusun	**Sugut, Malaysia
Dutch	Amsterdam Boat Dwellers, Netherlands
Duvele	Duvele, Indonesia
Dyan	Dyan, Upper Volta
Dyerma	Dyerma, Niger (80)
	Dyerma, Nigeria
Dyola	Dyola, Gambia
	Dyola, Guinea-Bissau
	Dyola, Senegal
Ebira	Ebira, Nigeria
Ebrie	Ebrie, Ivory Coast
Edo	Edo, Nigeria
Efik	Efik, Nigeria
Efutop	Efutop, Nigeria
Eggon	Eggon, Nigeria
Ejagham	Ejagham, Nigeria
Ekagi	Ekagi, Indonesia
Ekajuk	Ekajuk, Nigeria
Eket	Eket, Nigeria
Ekpeye	Ekpeye, Nigeria
Eleme	Eleme, Nigeria

	*Galla (Bale), Ethiopia
	**Saguye, Kenya
Galler	Galler, Laos
Gallinya	Galla, Harar, Ethiopia
Gallinya (Oromo)	Galla of Bucho, Ethiopia
Galong	Galong in Assam, India
Gambai	Gambai, Chad
Gamti	Gamti in Gujarat, India
Gan	Gan, Upper Volta
Gane	Gane, Indonesia
Gangam	Gangam, Togo
Gangte	Gangte in Assam, India
Gasari	Basari, Senegal
Gawar-Bati	Gawar-Bati, Afghanistan
Gawari	Gawari in Andhra Pradesh, India
Gawwada	Gawwada, Ethiopia
Gayo	Alas, Indonesia
	Gayo, Indonesia (80)
Gbari	Gbari, Nigeria (80)
Gbaya	Gbaya, Nigeria
Gbaya-Ndogo	Gbaya-Ndogo, Sudan
Gbazantche	Gbazantche, Benin
Gberi	Gberi, Sudan
Ge	**Adja, Benin
	Watchi, Togo
Gedeo	Gedeo, Ethiopia
Geji	Geji, Nigeria
Gera	Gera, Nigeria
German	*University Students, German Federal Rep. (79)
Geruma	Geruma, Nigeria
Gesa	Gesa, Indonesia
Gheko	Gheko, Burma
Ghol	Ghol, Sudan
Ghotuo	Ghotuo, Nigeria
Ghulfan	Ghulfan, Sudan
Gidar	Gidar, Chad
	Gidar, Cameroon
	Gidar, Cameroon
Gidicho	Gidicho, Ethiopia
Gilaki	Gilakis, Iran
Gilyak	Gilyak, Soviet Russia
Gimira	**Ghimeera, Ethiopia
Giryama	Giryama, Kenya
Gisiga	Gisiga, Cameroon
Glavda	**Glavda, Nigeria
Gobato	Gobato, Ethiopia
Gobeze	Gobeze, Ethiopia
Godie	***Godie, Ivory Coast
Goemai	Goemai, Nigeria
Gogo	Gogo, Tanzania
Gokana	Gokana, Nigeria
Gola	Gola, Liberia
Golo	Golo, Chad
Gondi	*Gonds, India
	Totis, India
Gonja	Gonja, Ghana
Goroa	Goroa, Tanzania
Gorontalo	Gorontalo, Indonesia
Gosha	Gosha, Kenya
Goudari	Goudari, Iran
Gouin-Turka	Gouin-Turka, Upper Volta
Goulai	Goulai, Chad
Gourendi	Gourency, Upper Volta
Gouro	**Gouro, Ivory Coast
Gouwar	Gouwar, Cameroon
	Gouwar, Cameroon
Grasia	Grasia in Gujarat, India
Grebo Dialects	**Grebo, Liberia

Hausa	Arawa, Nigeria
	Kurfei, Niger
	***Maguzawa, Nigeria (79)
	Mauri, Niger
Hausa, Ghana	Muslim Community of Bawku, Ghana
Havu	Havu, Zaire
Havunese	Havunese, Indonesia
Haya	Haya, Tanzania
Hebrew	*Jewish Imgrnts.-American, Israel
	*Jewish Imgrnts.-Argentine, Israel
	*Jewish Imgrnts.-Australia, Israel
	*Jewish Imgrnts.-Brazilian, Israel
	*Jewish Imgrnts.-Mexican, Israel
	*Jewish Imgrnts.-Uruguayan, Israel
	*Jewish Immigrants, Other, Israel
Hehe	Hehe, Tanzania
Heiban	Heiban, Sudan
Heikum	Bushmen (Heikum), Namibia
Helong	Helong, Indonesia
Herero	Herero, Botswana
Heso	Heso, Zaire
Hewa	**Hewa, Papua New Guinea (79)
Hezara'i	Hezareh, Iran
Higi	***Higi, Nigeria
Hindi	Jains, India
Hindustani	Balmiki, Pakistan
	Indians in Fiji, Fiji (79)
Hixkaryana	Hixkaryana, Brazil
Ho	Ho in Bihar, India
Hohodene	Hohodene, Brazil
Hokkien	Chinese Fishermen, Malaysia
Holiya	Holiya in Madhya Pradesh, India
Holoholo	Holoholo, Tanzania
Holu	Holu, Angola
Hopi	Hopi, United States of America
Hrangkhol	Hrangkhol, Burma
Huachipaire	Huachipaire, Peru
Huambisa	Huambisa, Peru
Huasteco	Huasteco, Mexico
Huave	**Huave, Mexico
Hui-hui-yu	Hui, China (80)
Huichol	Huichol, Mexico
Huila	**Huila, Angola
Huitoto, Meneca	Huitoto, Meneca, Colombia
Huitoto, Murui	Huitoto, Murui, Peru
Hukwe	Hukwe, Angola
Hunde	Hunde, Zaire
Hupda Maku	Hupda Maku, Colombia
Hwana	Hwana, Nigeria
Hwela-Numu	Hwela-Numu, Ivory Coast
Hyam	Hyam, Nigeria
Ibaji	Ibaji, Nigeria
Iban	**Iban, Malaysia (81)
Ibanag	Ibanag, Philippines
Ibataan	*Ibataan, Philippines
Ibibio	Ibibio, Nigeria
Ica	Ica, Colombia
Icen	Icen, Nigeria
Icheve	Ihceve, Nigeria
Idoma	Idoma, Nigeria
Idoma, North	Idoma, North, Nigeria
Ifugao	*Ifugao, Philippines
	Ifugao in Cababuyan, Philippines
Ifugao, Ambanad	Ifugao, Ambanad, Philippines
Ifugao, Kiangan	Ifugao, Kiangan, Philippines
Ifumu	Ifumu, Congo
Igala	Igala, Nigeria
Igbirra	Igbira, Nigeria (80)
Igede	Igede, Nigeria

Ignaciano	Ignaciano, Bolivia
Igorot	Igorot, Philippines
Iha	Iha, Indonesia
Ijo	Ijo, Central-Western, Nigeria
	Ijo, Northeast, Nigeria
	Ijo, Northeast Central, Nigeria
Ikalahan	Ikalahan, Philippines
Ikulu	Ikulu, Nigeria
Ikwere	Ikwere, Nigeria
Ila	Ila, Zambia
Ilianen Manobo	*Manobo, Ilianen, Philippines
Ilocano	Baguio Area Miners, Philippines (81)
Ilongot	Ilongot, Philippines
Inanwatan	Inanwatan, Indonesia
Indonesian	**Chinese in Indonesia, Indonesia
	Jambi, Indonesia
	Musi, Indonesia
	Ogan, Indonesia
	Sekayu, Indonesia
Inga	Inga, Colombia
Ingush	Ingushes, Soviet Russia
Insinai	Insinai, Philippines
Intha	Intha, Burma
Irahutu	Irahutu, Indonesia
Iraqw	Iraqw, Tanzania
	Iraqw, Tanzania
Iraya	Iraya, Philippines
Iresim	Iresim, Indonesia
Iria	Iria, Indonesia
Irigwe	Irigwe, Nigeria
Irula	***Irulas in Kerala, India
Isaalin	**Sisaala, Ghana
Isanzu	Isanzu, Tanzania
Isekiri	Isekiri, Nigeria
Isneg	**Apayao, Philippines
Isneg, Dibagat-Kabugao	Isneg, Dibagat-Kabugao, Philippines
Isneg, Karagawan	Isneg, Karagawan, Philippines
Isoko	Isoko, Nigeria
Itawit	Itawit, Philippines
Itelmen	Itelmen, Soviet Russia
Itik	Itik, Indonesia
Itneg, Adasen	Itneg, Adasen, Philippines
Itneg, Binongan	Itneg, Binongan, Philippines
Itneg, Masadiit	Itneg, Masadiit, Philippines
Itonama	Itonama, Bolivia
Ivbie North-Okpela-Atte	Ivbie North-Okpela-Atte, Nigeria
Iwa	Iwa, Zambia
Iwaidja	*Iwaidja, Austria
Iwur	Iwur, Indonesia
Iyon	Iyon, Nigeria
	Iyon, Cameroon
	Iyon, Cameroon
Izarek	Izarek, Nigeria
Izhor	Izhor, Soviet Russia
Izi	**Izi, Nigeria
Jaba	Jaba, Nigeria
Jacalteco	Jacalteco, Guatemala
Jagannathi	Jagannathi in A.P., India
Jamaican Patois	**Jamaican Elite, Jamaica
Jamamadi	Jamamadi, Brazil
Jamden	Jamden, Indonesia
Jamshidi	Jamshidis, Iran
Janena	Barasano, Southern, Colombia
Janjero	Janjero, Ethiopia
Janjo	Janjo, Nigeria
Japanese	Farmers of Japan, Japan
	*Industry Laborers-Japan, Japan
	*Inland Sea Island Peoples, Japan
	Japanese in Brazil, Brazil (79)

	*Japanese in Korea, Korea, Republic of
	**Japanese Students In USA, United States of America
	Soka Gakkai Believers, Japan
	**Univ. Students of Japan, Japan
Jaqaru	Jaqaru, Peru
Jara	Jara, Nigeria
Jaranchi	**Jarawa, Nigeria
Jatapu	Jatapu in Andhra Pradesh, India
Jati	Jati, Afghanistan
Jaunsari	Jaunsari in Uttar Pradesh, India
Javanese	**Javanese (rural), Indonesia (79)
	**Javanese of Central Java, Indonesia
Javanese, Tjirebon	Cirebon, Indonesia
Jeme	Zemi Naga of Assam, India (81)
Jeng	Jeng, Laos
Jera	Jera, Nigeria
Jharia	Jharia in Orissa, India
Jibu, Jibanci	*Jibu, Nigeria
Jiji	Jiji, Tanzania
Jimbin	Jimbin, Nigeria
Jimini	**Jimini, Ivory Coast
Jinja	Jinja, Tanzania
Jita	Jita, Tanzania
Jivaro	**Jivaro (Achuara), Venezuela
Jiye	Jiye, Uganda
Jiye (Karamojong)	*Jiye, Sudan
Jongor	Jongor, Chad
Jro	**Chrau, Viet Nam
Juang	Juang in Orissa, India
Juhai	Juhai, Malaysia
Jyarung	Jyarung, China
K'anjobal	**K'anjobal of San Miguel, Guatemala
Kaagan	Kaagan, Philippines
Kaalong	Kaalong, Cameroon
	Kaalong, Cameroon
Kaba	Kaba, Central African Empire
Kaba Dunjo	Kaba Dunjo, Central African Empire
Kabixi	Kabixi, Brazil
Kabre	Kabre, Togo
	Kabre, Benin
Kabyle	Kabyle, Algeria (79)
Kachama	Kachama, Ethiopia
Kachchi	Kachchi in Andhra Pradesh, India
Kadaklan-Barlig Bontoc	Kadaklan-Barlig Bontoc, Philippines
Kadar	Kadar in Andhra Pradesh, India
Kadara	Kadara, Nigeria
	Kamantan, Nigeria
Kadazan	Dusun, Malaysia (81)
Kadazans	Kadazans, Malaysia
Kadiweu	Kadiweu, Brazil
Kadugli	Kadugli, Sudan
Kaeti	Kaeti, Indonesia
Kaffenya (Kefa)	*Kaffa, Ethiopia (80)
Kafiristani (Bashgali)	**Kafirs, Pakistan (79)
Kagoma	Kagoma, Nigeria
Kagulu	Kagulu, Tanzania
Kahluri	Kahluri in Andamans, India
Kaibu	Kaibu, Nigeria
Kaikadi	Kaikadi in Maharashtra, India
Kaili	Kaili, Indonesia
Kaingang	Kaingang, Brazil
Kaiwai	Kaiwai, Indonesia
Kajang	Kajang, Indonesia
Kaka	Kaka, Nigeria
	Kaka, Central African Empire
	Kaka, Cameroon
	Kaka, Cameroon
Kakwa	Kakwa, Sudan

	**Kasena, Ghana
Kashmiri	**Kashmiri Muslims, India (79)
Kasseng	Kasseng, Laos
Kasuweri	Kasuweri, Indonesia
Katab	Katab, Nigeria
Katakari	Katakari in Gujarat, India
Katcha	Katcha, Sudan
Kati, Northern	Kati, Northern, Indonesia
Kati, Southern	Kati, Southern, Indonesia
Katla	Katla, Sudan
Katukina, Panoan	Katukina, Panoan, Brazil
Kaugat	Kaugat, Indonesia
Kaur	**Kaur, Indonesia
Kaure	Kaure, Indonesia
Kavwol	Kavwol, Indonesia
Kaw	Kaw, Burma
Kawar	Kawar in Madhya Pradesh, India
Kawe	Kawe, Indonesia
Kayabi	Kayabi, Brazil
Kayagar	Kayagar, Indonesia
Kayan	Kayan, Malaysia
Kayapo	Kayapo, Brazil
Kaygir	Kaygir, Indonesia
Kayupulau	Kayupulau, Indonesia
Kazakh	Kazakhs, China (81)
Kazakhi	Kazakhs, Iran (80)
Kebu	Kebu, Togo
Kebumtamp	Kebumtamp, Bhutan
Kedayanas	Kedayanas, Malaysia
Keer	Keer in Madhya Pradesh, India
Kei	Kei, Indonesia
Keiga	Keiga, Sudan
Keiga Jirru	Keiga Jirru, Sudan
Kekchi	**Kekchi, Guatemala
Kela	Kela, Zaire
Kelabit	Kelabit, Malaysia (81)
Kelao	Kelao, China
Kele	Kele, Gabon
Keley-i	Ifuago, Antipolo, Philippines
Kemak	Kemak, Indonesia
Kembata	Kembata, Ethiopia
Kemok	Kemok, Malaysia
Kendari	Kendari, Indonesia
Kenga	Kenga, Chad
Kenyah	Kenyah, Indonesia
Kera	Kera, Chad
	Kera, Cameroon
	Kera, Cameroon
Kerinchi	Kerinchi, Indonesia
Ket	Ket, Soviet Russia
Kewa	*Kepas, Papua New Guinea
Khakas	Khakas, Soviet Russia
Khalaj	Khalaj, Iran
Khalka	Khalka, China
Kham	Kham, China
Khamti	Khamti in Assam, India
Khamu	*Khamu, Thailand
Khana	Khana, Nigeria
Khandesi	Khandesi, India
Khanti	Khanti, Soviet Russia
Kharia	Kharia in Bihar, India
Khasi	Khasi in Assam, India
Khasonke	Khasonke, Mali
Khinalug	Khinalug, Soviet Russia
Khirwar	Khirwar in Madhya Pradesh, India
Khowar	Khowar, India
Khuwar	Chitralis, Pakistan (79)
Khvarshin	Khvarshin, Soviet Russia
Kibet	Kibet, Chad

Korapun	Korapun, Indonesia
Korean	**Apartment Residents-Seoul, Korea, Republic of
	**Bus Drivers, South Korea, Korea, Republic of
	Indust.Workers Yonqdunqpo, Korea, Republic of
	**Korean Prisoners, Korea, Republic of
	***Koreans in Germany, German Federal Rep.
	Koreans in Manchuria, China (81)
	*Koreans of Japan, Japan
Korku	*Korku in Madhya Pradesh, India
Koro	Koro, Nigeria
Koroma	Koroma, Sudan
Korop	Korop, Nigeria
	Korop, Cameroon
	Korop, Cameroon
Korwa	Korwa in Bihar, India
Koryak	Koryak, Soviet Russia
Kota	Kota, Gabon
	Kota in Tamil Nadu, India
	Kotta, India
Kotia	Kotia in Andhra Pradesh, India
Kotogut	Kotogut, Indonesia
Kotoko	Kotoko, Chad
	Kotoko, Cameroon
	Kotoko, Cameroon
Kotokoli	Kotokoli, Benin
	Kotokoli, Toqo
	Tem, Toqo
Kotopo	Kotopo, Cameroon
Kouya	Kouya, Ivory Coast
Kowaao	**Kowaao, Liberia
Koya	Koya in Andhra Pradesh, India
Koyra	Koyra, Ethiopia
Kpa	Kpa, Cameroon
	Kpa, Cameroon
Kpelle	Kpelle, Liberia
	Kpelle, Guinea
Kposo	Kposo, Toqo
Krachi	Krachi, Ghana
Krahn	***Krahn, Liberia
Kreen-Akakore	Kreen-Akakore, Brazil
Krifi	Kirifi, Niqeria
Krio	Krio, Gambia
Krobou	Krobou, Ivory Coast
Krongo	Krongo, Sudan
Krumen	Krumen, Ivory Coast
Kryz	Kryz, Soviet Russia
Kubu	Kubu, Indonesia (81)
Kuda-Chamo	Kuda-Chamo, Nigeria
Kudiya	Kudiya, India
Kugbo	Kuqbo, Niqeria
Kui	***Kond, India
	*Kui, Thailand
Kuikuro	Kuikuro, Brazil
Kuka	Kuka, Chad
Kukele	Kukele, Niqeria
Kukni	*Kuknas, India
Kukwa	Kukwa, Congo
Kulango	Kulango, Ivory Coast
Kulele	Kulele, Ivory Coast
Kulere	Kulere, Niqeria
Kullo	Kullo, Ethiopia
Kului	**Kuluis in Himachal Prades, India (81)
Kulung	Kulunq, Nigeria
Kumam	Kumam, Uqanda
Kumauni	Kumauni in Assam, India
Kumu	Kumu, Zaire

Kunama	Kunama, Ethiopia
Kunante	Kunante, Guinea-Bissau
Kunda	Kunda, Mozambique
	Kunda, Rhodesia
	Kunda, Zambia
	Kunda, Zambia
Kunimaipa	**Kunimaipa, Papua New Guinea
Kupia	Kupia in Andhra Pradesh, India
Kupsabiny	Kupsabiny, Uganda
Kuranko (Maninka)	**Koranko, Sierra Leone
Kurdish	Kurds in Kuwait, Kuwait
	Turkish Workers, Belgium (80)
Kurdish (Kirmancho)	*Kurds of Turkey, Turkey (79)
Kurdish dialects	**Ahl-i-Haqq in Iran, Iran (79)
	Kurds in Iran, Iran (80)
Kuria	Kuria, Tanzania
Kurichiya	Kurichiya in Kerala, India (81)
Kuruba	Kuruba in Tamil Nadu, India
Kurudu	Kurudu, Indonesia
Kurumba	Kurumba, Upper Volta
Kurux	Kurux in Bihar, India
Kusaal	**Kusaasi, Ghana
Kushi	Kushi, Nigeria
Kusso	Mbukushu, Angola
Kusu	Kusu, Zaire
Kuteb	Kuteb, Nigeria
Kutin	Kutin, Cameroon
Kutu	Kutu, Tanzania
Kuturmi	Kuturmi, Nigeria
Kuvi	Kuvi in Orissa, India
Kuwaa	Kuwaa, Liberia
Kuzamani	Kuzamani, Nigeria
Kvanadin	Kvanadin, Soviet Russia
Kwa	Kwa, Nigeria
Kwadi	Kwadi, Angola
Kwakum	Kwakum, Cameroon
Kwambi	Kwambi, Namibia
Kwangali	Kwangali, Angola
Kwansu	Kwansu, Indonesia
Kwanyama	Kwanyama, Angola
	Kwanyama, Namibia
Kwaya	Kwaya, Tanzania
Kwe-Etshari	*Bushmen (Hiechware), Rhodesia
Kwe-etshori	Kwe-etshori, Botswana
	Kwe-Etshori, Rhodesia
Kwerba	Kwerba, Indonesia
Kwere	Kwere, Tanzania
Kwese	Kwese, Zaire
Kwesten	Kwesten, Indonesia
Kyibaku	Kyibaku, Nigeria
Laamang	Laamang, Nigeria
Labaani	Labans, India
Labhani	Labhani in Andhra Pradesh, India
Lacandon	Lacandon, Mexico
Ladakhi	Ladakhi in Jammu, India
Ladinos	Ladinos, Lebanon
Lafofa	Lafofa, Sudan
Lahouli	**Lahaulis in Punjab, India
Lahu	*Lahu, Thailand (81)
	Lahu, Burma
Lahul	Lahul, China
Laka	Laka, Cameroon
	Laka, China
	Laka, Central African Empire
Lakal	Laka, Chad
Lakian	Lakians, Soviet Russia
Lakka	Lakka, Nigeria
Lala	Lala, Zambia
Lalia	Lalia, Zaire

Lalung	Lalung in Assam, India
Lama	Lama, Burma
Lamba	Lamba, Togo
	Lamba, Benin
	Lamba, Zaire
	Lamba, Zambia
Lambadi	**Lambadi in Andhra Pradesh, India (81)
Lambi	Lambi, Cameroon
Lambya	Lambya, Malawi
	Lambya, Tanzania
Lame	Lame, Nigeria
Landoma	Landoma, Guinea
	Landoma, Guinea-Bissau
Langi	Langi, Tanzania
Lango	*Lango, Ethiopia
	Lango, Uganda
Lanoh	Lanoh, Malaysia
Lao	*Lao, Laos (79)
	*Lao Refugees, Thailand
Lara	Lara, Indonesia
Laro	Laro, Sudan
Laru	Laru, Nigeria
Latdwalam	Latdwalam, Indonesia
Lati	Lati, China
Latuka	**Lotuka, Sudan
Laudje	Laudje, Indonesia
Lawa	Lawa, Mountain, Thailand
Lebgo	Lebgo, Nigeria
Leco	Leco, Bolivia
Leqa	Leqa, Zaire
Lele	Lele, Chad
	Lele, Upper Volta
	Lele, Zaire
Lelemi	Lelemi, Ghana
Lendu	Lendu, Zaire
Lengua, Northern	Lengua, Northern, Paraguay
Lenje	Lenje, Zambia
Lepcha	**Lepcha, Sikkim
Lese	Lese, Zaire
Letti	Letti, Indonesia
Li	Li, China
Ligbi	Ligbi, Ivory Coast
	Ligbi, Ghana
Liguri	Liguri, Sudan
Liko	Liko, Zaire
Lima	Lima, Zambia
Limba	Limba, Sierra Leone
Limbum	**Wimbum, Cameroon
Lio	Lionese, Indonesia
Lisu	*Lisu, Thailand
Liv	Liv, Soviet Russia
Lo	Lo, Nigeria
Lobi	Lobi, Ivory Coast
Local Dialects	Bangangte, Cameroon
	Buka-khwe, Botswana
	Kubu, Indonesia (80)
	*Mahrah, Yemen, Democratic
	Moken of Thailand, Thailand
	Nuristani, Afghanistan (80)
	**Plantation Workers, Papua New Guinea
	Pygmy (Binga), Burundi
	Pygmy (Binga), Central African Empire
local languages	*Pygmy (Mbuti), Zaire (79)
	**Zaranda Hill Peoples, Nigeria
Lodhi	Lodhi in Bihar, India
Logba	Logba, Ghana
Logo	Logo, Zaire
Logoro (Bambara)	Kagoro, Mali
Loinang	Loinang, Indonesia (81)

REGISTRY OF THE UNREACHED

Mairasi	Mairasi, Indonesia
Maithili	Maithili, Nepal
Majangiir	*Masengo, Ethiopia
Majhwar	Majhwar in Madhya Pradesh, India
Maji	Maji, Ethiopia
Majingai-Ngama	Majingai-Ngama, Chad
	Majingai-ngama, Central African Empire
Maka	Maka, Cameroon
Makasai	Makasai, Indonesia
Makere	Makere, Uganda
Makian, West	Makian, West, Indonesia
Maklew	Maklew, Indonesia
Makua	Makua, Mozambique
Mala, Pattani	Thai Islam (Malay), Thailand (80)
Malamutha	Malakkaras of Kerela, India (81)
Malankuravan	Malankuravan in Kerala, India
Malapandaram	Malapandaram in Kerala, India
Malappanackan	Malappanackers, India
Malaryan	Malaryan in Kerala, India
Malavedan	Malavedan in Kerala, India
Malay	Malays of Singapore, Singapore (79)
Malayalam	*Malayalars, India
Malayalan	Mappillas, India
Malayo	Malayo, Colombia
Male	Male, Ethiopia
Mali	Mali in Andhra Pradesh, India
Malila	Malila, Tanzania
Malinke, Senegalese	Manding, Senegal
Malki	Malki in Bihar, India
Malpaharia	Malpaharia in Assam, India
Malvi	Malvi in Madhya Pradesh, India
Mam	**Mam Indian, Guatemala
Mama	Mama, Nigeria
Mambai	Mambai, Indonesia
Mambila	Mambila, Cameroon
Mambwe-Lungu	Mambwe-Lungu, Tanzania
	Mambwe-Lungu, Zambia
Mampruli	Mamprusi, Ghana
Mamvu-Efe	Mamvu-Efe, Zaire
Manchu	Manchu, China (81)
Manda	Manda, Tanzania
Mandar ·	Mandar, Indonesia
Mandara	Mandara, Nigeria
Mandarin	*Chinese in Austria, Austria
	*Chinese in Holland, Netherlands
	*Chinese in Japan, Japan
	*Chinese in Korea, Korea, Republic of
	*Chinese in Laos, Laos
	**Chinese in United Kingdom, United Kingdom
	**Chinese in United States, United States of America
	*Chinese in West Germany, German Federal Rep.
	*Chinese Mainlanders, Taiwan
	Chinese Muslims, Taiwan (81)
	**Chinese Students Glasgow, United Kingdom
	Taiwan-Chinese Un. Stud., Taiwan
Mandarin and dialects	Chinese in Burma, Burma
	**Chinese in Sarawak, Malaysia
Mandaya	Mandaya, Philippines
Mandaya, Mansaka	Mandaya, Mansaka, Philippines
Mander	Mander, Indonesia
Mandingo	Mandingo, Liberia (79)
Mandyak	Mandyak, Gambia
Mandyako	**Manjaco, Guinea-Bissau
Mandyale	Manjack, Senegal
Manem	Manem, Indonesia
Mangbai	Mangbai, Chad
Mangbutu	Mangbutu, Zaire

Matbat	Matbat, Indonesia
Matengo	Matengo, Tanzania
Matipuhy-Nahukua	Matipuhy-Nahukua, Brazil
Matlatzinca, Atzingo	Matlatzinca, Atzingo, Mexico
Matumbi	Matumbi, Tanzania
Maure	Maure, Mali
Maviha	Maviha, Mozambique
Mawchi	**Mawchis, India
Mawes	Mawes, Indonesia
Maxakali	Maxakali, Brazil
Mayo	Mayo, Mexico
Mayoruna	Mayoruna, Peru
Mazahua	**Mazahua, Mexico
Mazandarani	Mazandaranis, Iran
Mba	Mba, Zaire
Mbaama	Mbaama, Gabon
Mbai	Mbai, Chad
	Mbai, Central African Empire
Mbala	Mbala, Zaire
Mbanqwe	Mbanqwe, Zaire
Mbanja	Mbanja, Zaire
Mbati	Mbati, Central African Empire
Mbe	Mbe, Nigeria
Mbede	Mbede, Gabon
Mbembe	Mbembe, Cameroon
	Mbembe (Tigong), Nigeria
Mbimu	Mbimu, Cameroon
Mbo	Mbo, Cameroon
	Mbo, Zaire
Mboi	Mboi, Nigeria
Mbole	Mbole, Zaire
Mbugwe	Mbuqwe, Tanzania
Mbula-Bwazza	Mbula-Bwazza, Nigeria
Mbum	Mbum, Chad
Mbunda	Mbunda, Angola
Mbunga	Mbunga, Tanzania
Mbwela	Mbwela, Angola
Me'en	Me'en, Ethiopia
Meax	Meax, Indonesia
Mejah	**Mejah, India
Meje	Meje, Uganda
Mekwei	Mekwei, Indonesia
Melanau	**Melanau of Sarawak, Malaysia (80)
Mende	Gola, Sierra Leone
	Krim, Sierra Leone
	Mende, Sierra Leone
	Mende, Liberia
Menemo-Mogamo	Menemo-Mogamo, Cameroon
Menka	Menka, Cameroon
Menri	Menri, Malaysia
Meo	**Meo, Thailand
Mesengo	Mesengo, Ethiopia
Mesme	Mesme, Chad
Mesmedje	Mesmedje, Chad
Miao	Miao, China (81)
Miching	**Miching, India
Midob	Midob, Sudan
Mien	Mien, China (81)
Migili	Migili, Nigeria
Mikir	**Karbis, India
Mimi	Mimi, Chad
Mimika	*Mimika, Indonesia
Mina	Mina in Madhya Pradesh, India
Minamanwa	**Mamanua, Philippines (81)
Minangkabau	Minangkabau, Indonesia (80)
Minduumo	Minduumo, Gabon
Mingat	Mingat, Soviet Russia
Mirdha	Mirdha in Orissa, India
Miri	Miri, Sudan

Mirung	Mirung, Bangladesh
Mishmi	Mishmi in Assam, India
Miskito	Miskito, Nicaragua
Mixe	**Mixes, Mexico
Mixteco	*Mixteco,San Juan Mixtepic, Mexico
Mixteco, Amoltepec	Mixteco, Amoltepec, Mexico
Mixteco, Apoala	Mixteco, Apoala, Mexico
Mixteco, Eastern	Mixteco, Eastern, Mexico
Mixteco, Eastern Putla	Mixteco, Eastern Putla, Mexico
Mixteco, Huajuapan	Mixteco, Huajuapan, Mexico
Mixteco, Silacayoapan	Mixteco, Silacayoapan, Mexico
Mixteco, Southern Puebla	Mixteco, Southern Puebla, Mexico
Mixteco, Southern Putla	Mixteco, Southern Putla, Mexico
Mixteco, Tututepec	Mixteco, Tututepec, Mexico
Mixteco, Yosondua	Mixteco, Yosondua, Mexico
Miya	Miya, Nigeria
Mo	Mo, Ivory Coast
Mo (Degha)	Mo, Ghana
Mober	Mober, Nigeria
Mocha	***Mocha, Ethiopia
Modo	Modo, Sudan
Mofu	Mofu, Cameroon
Mogholi	Mogholi, Afghanistan
Mogum	Mogum, Chad
Moi	Moi, Indonesia
Moken	Moken, Burma (79)
Mokole	*Mokole, Benin
Molbog	*Molbog, Philippines
Mole	Mossi, Upper Volta (80)
Molof	Molof, Indonesia
Mombum	Mombum, Indonesia
Momoguns	Momoguns, Malaysia
Mon	Mon, Burma (81)
Mona	Mona, Ivory Coast
Mongondow	Mongondow, Indonesia (81)
Mongour	Mongour, China
Moni	Moni, Indonesia
Monjombo	Monjombo, Central African Empire
Mono	Mono, Zaire
Monpa	Monpa, India
Montol	Montol, Nigeria
Mopan Maya	**Mopan Maya, Guatemala
	**Mopan Maya, Belize
Moqaddam	Moqaddam, Iran
Mor	Mor, Indonesia
Moreb	Moreb, Sudan
Moreno	**Black Caribs, Belize, Belize (79)
	**Black Caribs, Guatemala, Guatemala
	**Black Caribs, Honduras, Honduras
Mori	Mori, Indonesia (81)
Moru	Moru, Ivory Coast
	Moru, Sudan
Morunahua	Morunahua, Peru
Morwap	Morwap, Indonesia
Mosi	Mosi, Tanzania
Motilon	Motilon, Colombia
	Motilon, Venezuela
Movima	Movima, Bolivia
Mpoto	Mpoto, Malawi
	Mpoto, Tanzania
Mualthuam	Mualthuam, India
Mubi	Mubi, Chad
Muinane	Muinane, Colombia
Mulimba	Mulimba, Cameroon
Multani	Multani in Punjab, India
Mumbake	Mumbake, Nigeria
Mumuye	Mumuye, Nigeria
Mun	Mun, Burma
Muna	Muna, Indonesia

Munda	**Mundas in Bihar, India
Mundang	Mundang, Chad
Mundari	Mundari in Assam, India
Mundu	Mundu, Zaire
Munduruku	Munduruku, Brazil
Mungaka	Mungaka, Cameroon
Mungqui	Munqqui, Indonesia
Munji-Yidgha	Munji-Yidgha, Afghanistan
Mura-Piraha	Mura-Piraha, Brazil
Muria	Muria in Andhra Pradesh, India
Murle	Murle, Sudan
Mursi	Mursi, Ethiopia
Murung	Mru, Bangladesh
Murut	Murut, Malaysia
Musei	Musei, Chad
Musgu	Musgu, Chad
Muthuvan	Muthuvan in A.P., India
Muwasi	Muwasi in Madhya Pradesh, India
Mwanga	Mwanga, Tanzania
Mwera	Mwera, Tanzania
Myaung-Ze	Myaung-Ze, Burma
N.E. Thai	Thai, North East, Thailand
Nabi	Nabi, Indonesia
Nadeb Maku	Nadeb Maku, Brazil
Nafri	Nafri, Indonesia
Naga, Kalyokenqnyu	Naga, Kalyokenqnyu, India
Naga, Mao	Naga, Mao, India
Naga, Nruanghmei	Naga, Nruanghmei, India
Naga, Sangtam	Naga, Sangtam, India
Naga, Sema	Naga, Sema, India
Naga, Tangkhul	Naga, Tangkhul, India
Naga, Wancho	Naga, Wancho, India
Naga, Zoliang	Zoliang, India
Nagar	Nagar in Madhya Pradesh, India
Nahsi	Nahsi, China
Nahua	*Nahua, North Pueblo, Mexico
Nahuatl, Hidalgo	***Azteca, Mexico (79)
Naka	Naka, Sudan
Naltya	Naltya, Indonesia
Nalu	Nalu, Guinea
Nama	Nama, Namibia
	Nama, South Africa
Nambikuara	Nambikuara, Brazil
Nambya	**Nambya, Rhodesia
Namshi	Namshi, Cameroon
Nanai	Nanai, China
	Nanai, Soviet Russia
Nancere	Nancere, Chad
Nandi	Dorobo, Kenya
	Nandi, Zaire
Nandu-Tari	Nandu-Tari, Nigeria
Nao	Nao, Ethiopia
Naoudem	Naoudem, Togo
Napali	*Gorkha, India
Nara	Nara, Ethiopia
Naraguta	Naraguta, Nigeria
Nata	Nata, Tanzania
Natemba	Natemba, Togo
Natioro	Natioro, Upper Volta
Native Senoi	**Senoi, Malaysia (81)
Nawuri	Nawuri, Ghana
Nchumbulu	Nchumbulu, Ghana
Nchumburu	Nchimburu, Ghana
Nchumunu	Nchumunu, Ghana
Ndaaka	Ndaaka, Zaire
Ndali	Ndali, Tanzania
Ndam	Ndam, Central African Empire
Ndamba	Ndamba, Tanzania
Ndao	Ndaonese, Indonesia

Ndau   Ndau, Rhodesia
Nde-Nsele-Nta   Nde-Nsele-Nta, Nigeria
Ndengereko   Ndengereko, Tanzania
Ndjem   Ndjem, Cameroon
Ndo   Ndo, Zaire
Ndoe   Ndoe, Nigeria
Ndogo   Ndogo, Central African Empire
    Ndogo, Sudan
Ndom   Ndom, Indonesia
Ndomde   Ndomde, Tanzania
Ndoolo   Ndoolo, Zaire
Ndop-Bamessing   Ndop-Bamessing, Cameroon
Ndoro   **Ndoro, Nigeria
    Ndoro, Cameroon
Nduga   Nduga, Indonesia
Ndunga   Ndunga, Zaire
Ndunpa Duupa   Ndunpa Duupa, Cameroon
Nentsy   Nentsy, Soviet Russia
Nepali   **Nepalese in India, India
    *Nepali, Nepal
Nevo   Neyo, Ivory Coast
Newari   *Newari, Nepal
Ngada   Ngada, Indonesia
Ngalik, North   Ngalik, North, Indonesia
Ngalik, Southern   Ngalik, Southern, Indonesia
Ngalum   Ngalum, Indonesia
Ngamo   **Ngamo, Nigeria
Nganasan   Nganasan, Soviet Russia
Ngando   Ngando, Central African Empire
    Ngando, Zaire
Ngasa   Ngasa, Tanzania
Ngayaba   Ngayaba, Cameroon
Ngbaka   Ngbaka, Zaire
Ngbaka Ma'bo   Ngbaka Ma'bo, Central African Empire
    Ngbaka Ma'bo, Zaire
Ngbandi   Ngbandi, Zaire
Ngbee   Ngbee, Zaire
Ngemba   Ngemba, Cameroon
Ngen   *Ngen, Ivory Coast
Ngeq   Ngeq, Laos
Ngi   Ngi, Cameroon
Ngindo   Ngindo, Tanzania
Nginyukwur   Nginyukwur, Sudan
Ngirere   Ngirere, Sudan
Ngiri   Ngiri, Zaire
Ngizim   Ngizim, Nigeria
Ngok   Ngok, Sudan
Ngombe   **Ngombe, Zaire
Ngoni   Ngoni, Tanzania
    Ngoni, Zambia
Ngulu   Ngulu, Malawi
    Ngulu, Tanzania
Ngumba   Ngumba, Cameroon
Ngumbi   Ngumbi, Equatorial Guinea
Ngunduna   Ngunduna, Sudan
Nguqwurang   Nguqwurang, Sudan
Ngurimi   Ngurimi, Tanzania
Nguu   Nguu, Tanzania
Ngwo   Ngwo, Cameroon
Ngwoi   Ngwoi, Nigeria
Nharon   Nharon, Botswana
Nhengatu   Nhengatu, Brazil
Nias   Nias, Indonesia
Nielim   Nielim, Chad
Nihali   Nihali in Madhya Pradesh, India
Nilamba   Nilamba, Tanzania
Nimadi   Nimadi in Madhya Pradesh, India
Nimboran   Nimboran, Indonesia
Ninam   Ninam, Brazil

Ningerum	*Ningerum, Papua New Guinea
Ninggrum	Ninggrum, Indonesia
Ninzam	Ninzam, Nigeria
Nisa	Nisa, Indonesia
Nivkhi	Nivkhi, Soviet Russia
Njadu	Njadu, Indonesia
Njalgulqule	Njalgulqule, Sudan
Nkem-Nkum	Nkem-Nkum, Nigeria
Nkom	Nkom, Cameroon
Nkonya	Nkonya, Ghana
Nkutu	Nkutu, Zaire
Nocte	***Nocte, India
Nohu	Nohu, Cameroon
Norra	Norra, Burma
North Thai Dialect	Thai Northern, Thailand
Northeast Thai	**Lepers of N.E. Thailand, Thailand
Northern Cagayan Negrito	Northern Cagayan Negrito, Philippines
Northern Kamer	*Cambodians, Thailand
Northern Kankanay	Kankanay, Northern, Philippines
Nosu	Nosu, China
Nouni	*Nouni, Upper Volta
Nsenga	Nsenga, Rhodesia
	Nsenga, Zambia
Nso	Nso, Cameroon
Nsongo	Nsongo, Angola
Ntomba	Ntomba, Zaire
Ntrubo	Ntrubo, Ghana
	Ntrubo, Togo
	Ntrubs, Ghana
Nuer	*Nuer, Ethiopia
	*Nuer, Sudan (79)
Numana-Nunku-Gwantu	Numana-Nunku-Gwantu, Nigeria
Nung	Nung, China
Nungu	Nungu, Nigeria
Nunuma	Nunuma, Upper Volta
Nupe	**Nupe, Nigeria
Nyabwa	**Nyabwa, Ivory Coast
Nyaheun	Nyaheun, Laos
Nyakyusa	Nyakyusa, Malawi
	Nyakyusa, Tanzania
Nyambo	Nyambo, Tanzania
Nyamusa	Nyamusa, Sudan
Nyamwezi	Nyamwezi, Tanzania (80)
Nyaneka	Nyaneka, Angola
Nyang	Nyang, Cameroon
Nyanga-Li	Nyanga-Li, Zaire
Nyangbo	Nyangbo, Ghana
Nyanja	Nyanja, Rhodesia
Nyankole	Nyankole, Uganda
Nyaruenq	Nyaruenq, Sudan
Nyaturu	Turu, Tanzania
Nyemba	Nyemba, Angola
Nyiha	Nyiha, Tanzania
	Nyiha, Zambia
Nyoro	Nyoro, Uganda
Nyuli	Nyuli, Uganda
Nyunqwe	Nyunqwe, Mozambique
Nzakara	Nzakara, Central African Empire
Nzanyi	Nzanyi, Nigeria
Nzebi	Nzebi, Congo
Nzema	Nzema, Ivory Coast
	Nzema, Ghana
O'ung	O'ung, Angola
Obanliku	Obanliku, Nigeria
Obolo	Obolo, Nigeria
Ocaina	Ocaina, Peru
Odki	Od, Pakistan
Odual	Odual, Nigeria
Odut	Odut, Nigeria

Paranan	Paranan, Philippines
Pardhan	Pardhan in Andhra Pradesh, India
Pare	Pare, Tanzania
Parengi	Parengi in Orissa, India
Paresi	Paresi, Brazil
Parintintin	Parintintin, Brazil
Parji	Dhurwa, India
Pashayi	Pashayi, Afghanistan
Pashtu	Pashtuns, Iran (80)
Patamona	Patamona, Guyana
Patelia	Patelia in Gujarat, India
Pato Tapuia	Pato Tapuia, Brazil
Paumari	Paumari, Brazil
Penan	Penan, Western, Malaysia (81)
Pende	Pende, Zaire
Pengo	Pengo in Orissa, India
Peri	Peri, Zaire
Pero	Pero, Nigeria
Persian	Persians of Iran, Iran (80)
	*Tertiary Level Youth, Iran
Persian (Tajiki)	Tajik, Soviet Russia
Phu Thai	Phu Thai, Laos
Piapoco	Piapoco, Colombia
Piaroa	Piaroa, Venezuela
Pila-Pila	**Pila, Benin
Pilaga	Pilaga, Argentina
Pilipino	**Hotel Workers in Manila, Philippines (81)
	*Jeepney Drivers in Manila, Philippines (81)
	Lubang Islanders, Philippines (81)
Pima Bajo	Pima Bajo, Mexico
Pimbwe	Pimbwe, Tanzania
Pisa	Pisa, Indonesia
Pishagchi	Pishagchi, Iran
Piti	Piti, Nigeria
Pitu Uluna Salu	Pitu Uluna Salu, Indonesia
Piya	Piya, Nigeria
Pnar	Pnar in Assam, India
Pocomchi, Eastern	Pocomchi, Eastern, Guatemala
Pocomchi, Western	Pocomchi, Western, Guatemala
Podokwo	Podokwo, Cameroon
Podzo	Podzo, Mozambique
Pogolo	Pogolo, Tanzania
Poke	Poke, Zaire
Pokot	Pokot, Uganda
Pol	Pol, Congo
Polci	Polci, Nigeria
Pom	Pom, Indonesia
Pongu	Pongu, Nigeria
Poochi	Poouch in Kashmir, India
Popoloca, Eastern	Popoloca, Eastern, Mexico
Popoloca, Northern	Popoloca, Northern, Mexico
Popoloca, Western	Popoloca, Western, Mexico
Popoluca, Sayula	Popoluca, Sayula, Mexico
Popoluca, Sierra	Popoluca, Sierra, Mexico
Porohanon	Porohanon, Philippines
Portuguese	***Copacabana Apt. Dwellers, Brazil
	Pankararu, Brazil
	**Portuguese in France, France
	Spiritists, Brazil (79)
	Students in Cuiaba, Brazil
Prang	Prang, Ghana
Prasuni	***Prasuni, Afghanistan
Pu-I	Pu-I, China
Puguli	Puguli, Upper Volta
Puku-Geeri-Keri-Wipsi	Puku-Geeri-Keri-Wipsi, Nigeria
Punjabi	**Gagre, Pakistan
Punu	Punu, China
	Punu, Congo

Saliba	Saliba, Colombia
Sama Panqutaran	Sama Panqutaran, Philippines (80)
Sama, Mapun	Sama, Mapun, Philippines
Sama, Siasi	Sama, Siasi, Philippines
Sama, Sibuku	Sama, Sibuku, Philippines
Samal dialects	Sama-Badjaw, Philippines (79)
Samarkena	Samarkena, Indonesia
Samburu	El Molo, Kenya
Samo	*Samo-Kubo, Papua New Guinea
Samo, Northern	Samo, Northern, Mali
	Samo, Northern, Upper Volta
Samogho	Samogho, Mali
San	San, Namibia
Sanapana	Sanapana, Paraguay
Sandawe	Sandawe, Tanzania
Sanga	Sanga, Nigeria
	Sanga, Zaire
Sangil	Sangil, Philippines
Sangir	Sangir, Indonesia
Sangke	Sangke, Indonesia
Sangu	Sangu, Gabon
	Sangu, Tanzania
Santa	Santa, China
Santhali	**Santhali, Nepal
Sanuma	*Sanuma, Brazil
	Sanuma, Venezuela
Sanza	Sanza, Zaire
Saramaccan	Saramaccan, Surinam
Sarwa	Sarwa, Chad
Sasak	Sasak, Indonesia (80)
Sasani	Sasanis, Iran
Sasaru-Enwan Igwe	Sasaru-Enwan Igwe, Nigeria
Satere	Satere, Brazil
Sau	Sau, Afghanistan
Sause	Sause, Indonesia
Save (Yoruba)	**Save, Benin
Sawi	**Sawi, Indonesia
Saya	Saya, Nigeria
Secoya	Secoya, Ecuador
Sekar	Sekar, Indonesia
Seko	Seko, Indonesia
Sekpele	Sekpele, Ghana
Selakau	**Selakau of Sarawak, Malaysia
Sele	Santrokofi, Ghana
Selkup	Selkup, Soviet Russia
Semelai	Semelai, Malaysia
Sempan	Sempan, Indonesia
Sena	Sena, Malawi
	Sena, Mozambique
Senari	Senufo, Ivory Coast (80)
Senggi	Senggi, Indonesia
Sentani	Sentani, Indonesia
Senthang	Senthang, Burma
Serawai (Pasemah)	**Serawai, Indonesia (81)
Serbo-Croation	*Bosnian, Yugoslavia (80)
Sere	Sere, Sudan
Serere	Serere, Senegal (79)
Serere-Non	Serere-Non, Senegal
Serere-Sine	Serere-Sine, Senegal
Seri	Seri, Mexico
Serui-Laut	Serui-Laut, Indonesia
Sgaw Karen	Karen, Thailand (79)
Sha	Sha, Nigeria
Shamatali	Yanomamo in Venezuela, Venezuela
Shambala	Shambala, Tanzania
Shan	Hkun, Burma
	Shan, Thailand
	Shan, Burma
	Shan Chinese, Burma

	Songhai, Upper Volta
Songomeno	Songomeno, Zaire
Songoora	Songoora, Zaire
Soninke	Sarakole, Senegal (80)
	Soninke, Gambia
	Soninke, Mali
	Soninke, Mauritania
Sonjo	Sonjo, Tanzania
Sopi	Sopi, Sudan
Sora	Sora in Orissa, India
Soruba	Soruba, Benin
Sough	**Manikion, Indonesia
Southern Bontoc	**Bontoc, Southern, Philippines
Southern Sesotho	***Basotho, Mountain, Lesotho (79)
Southern Thai	Thai, Southern, Thailand
Sowanda	Sowanda, Indonesia
Spanish	Arutani, Venezuela
	Chatino, Yaitepec, Mexico
	**Chinese in Panama, Panama
	Chocho, Mexico
	Iquito, Peru
	Jebero, Peru
	**Military Personnel, Ecuador
	Mixteco, Central Puebla, Mexico
	Mutu, Venezuela
	Paipai, Mexico
	Palenquero, Colombia
	Pame, Chichimeca-Jonaz, Mexico
	Paya, Honduras
	Popoloca, Ahuatempan, Mexico
	Popoloca, Coyotepec, Mexico
	Popoloca, Southern, Mexico
	Popoluca, Oluta, Mexico
	Popoluca, Texistepec, Mexico
	Totonaco, Yecuatla, Mexico
	**Urban Mestizos, Ecuador
Su	Su, Cameroon
Suba	Suba, Tanzania
Subanen, Tuboy	**Subanen (Tuboy), Philippines
Subanun	**Subanen, Sindangan, Philippines (80)
Subanun, Lapuyan	Subanun,Lapuyan, Philippines
Subi	Subi, Tanzania
Suena	**Suena, Papua New Guinea
Suga	Suga, Cameroon
Sui	Sui, China
Suku	Suku, Zaire
Sukur	Sukur, Nigeria
Sulung	Sulung, India
Sumba	Sumba, Indonesia
Sumbawa	Sumbawa, Indonesia
Sumbwa	Sumbwa, Tanzania
Sumu	Sumu, Nicaragua
Sundanese	**Sundanese, Indonesia (80)
Sungor	Sungor, Chad
Suppire	Minianka, Mali
	Suppire, Mali
Sura	Sura, Nigeria
Suri	**Suri, Ethiopia
Surigueno	**Suriquenos, Philippines
Surubu	Surubu, Nigeria
Surui	Surui, Brazil
Susu	Susu, Guinea-Bissau
	Susu, Sierra Leone
Svan	Svan, Soviet Russia
Swaga	Swaga, Zaire
Swahili	Ikizu, Tanzania
Swaka	Swaka, Zambia
Swati	Swatis, Pakistan (79)
T'in	T'in, Thailand (81)

Tatar dialects	Tatars, Soviet Russia (80)
Tatoga	Barabaig, Tanzania (79)
	Tatoga, Tanzania
Tatuyo	***Tatuyo, Colombia
Taungyo	Taungyo, Burma
Taurap	Taurap, Indonesia
Tausug	Tausug, Philippines (80)
Tawr	Tawr, Burma
Tayaku	Tayaku, Benin
Tboli	**T'boli, Philippines (81)
Tchang	Tchang, Cameroon
Teda	Teda, Chad (80)
	Teda, Libya
	Teda, Niger
Teen	*Tense, Ivory Coast
Tegali	Tegali, Sudan
Tehit	Tahit, Indonesia
Teimuri	Teimuri, Iran
Teimurtash	Teimurtash, Iran
Teke, Eastern	Teke, Eastern, Zaire
Teke, Northern	Teke, Northern, Congo
Teke, Southwestern	Teke, Southwestern, Congo
Telugu	***Matharis, India
Tembe	Tembe, Brazil
Tembo	Tembo, Zaire
Temein	Temein, Sudan
Temira	Temira, Malaysia
Temne	**Temne, Sierra Leone (80)
Tengqerese	Tengqer, Indonesia
Tepehua, Huehuetla	Tepehua, Huehuetla, Mexico
Tepehua, Pisa Flores	Tepehua, Pisa Flores, Mexico
Tepehua, Veracruz	Tepehua, Veracruz, Mexico
Tepehuan, Northern	Tepehuan, Northern, Mexico
Tepehuan, Southeastern	Tepehuan, Southeastern, Mexico
Tepehuan, Southwestern	Tepehuan, Southwestern, Mexico
Tepeth	Tepeth, Uganda
Tepo	Tepo, Ivory Coast
Tera	Tera, Nigeria
Terena	Terena, Brazil
Teribe	**Teribe, Panama
Ternate	Ternatans, Indonesia
Teso	Teso, Uganda
Tewa (Jemez)	Jemez Pueblo, United States of America
Thado	Thado in Assam, India
Thai	*Central Thailand Farmers, Thailand (81)
	Government officials, Thailand
	**Lepers of Cen. Thailand, Thailand (81)
	*Ramkamhaeng Un. Students, Thailand
	*Slum Dwellers of Bangkok, Thailand
	*Thai University Students, Thailand (81)
Thai, Central	Thai of Bangkok, Thailand
Thai, Southern	*Thai Islam (Thai), Thailand
Thakur	Thakur, India
Thar	Thar in Bihar, India
Thoi	Thoi, Sudan
Thuri	Thuri, Sudan
Tibetan	*Tibetan Refugees, India
	*Tibetans, China
	Tibetans in Bhutan, Bhutan (81)
Tibetan Dialect	*Chang-Pa of Kashmir, India (81)
Tibeto-Burman	Jinuos, China (81)
	Lisu, China (81)
Tibeto-Burman Dialect	Lawa, Eastern, Thailand (81)
Ticuna	Ticuna, Brazil
Tidore	Tidorese, Indonesia
Tiefo	Tiefo, Upper Volta
Tien-Chiu	**Chinese Refugees, France, France (79)
Tiene	Tiene, Zaire
Tigon	Tigon, Cameroon

Tupuri	Tupuri, Chad
	Tupuri, Cameroon
Tura	Tura, Ivory Coast
Turkana	Turkana, Kenya
	**Turkana Fishing Community, Kenya (79)
Turkish	Baharlu (Kamesh), Iran
	Nafar, Iran
	Turkish Immigrant Workers, German Federal
	Rep. (79)
Turkish (Danubian)	Yoruk, Turkey
Turkish, Osmanli	Turks, Anatolian, Turkey
Turkomani	Turkomans, Iran (80)
Turkwam	Turkwam, Nigeria
Turu	Turu, Indonesia
Tuvin	Tuvinian, Soviet Russia
Tuyuca	Tuyuca, Brazil
Twi	Twi, Sudan
Tzeltal, Bachajon	Tzeltal, Bachajon, Mexico
Tzeltal, Highland	Tzeltal, Highland, Mexico
Tzotzil (Chamula)	Chamula, Mexico (79)
Tzotzil, Chenalho	Tzotzil, Chenalho, Mexico
	Zinacantecos, Mexico (79)
Tzotzil, Huistan	Tzotzil, Huistan, Mexico
Tzutujil	Tzutujil, Guatemala
Udegeis	Udegeis, Soviet Russia
Udin	Udin, Soviet Russia
Udmurt	Udmurt, Soviet Russia
Uduk	Uduk, Sudan
Uhunduni	Uhunduni, Indonesia
Uighur	Uighur, Afghanistan
Uigur	Uigur, China (80)
Ukaan	Ukaan, Nigeria
Ukpe-Bayobiri	Ukpe-Bayobiri, Nigeria
Ukwuani-Aboh	Ukwuani-Aboh, Nigeria
Ulchi	Ulchi, Soviet Russia
Ulithi	Ulithi-Mall, Turks and Caicos Islands
Ullatan	Ullatan in Kerala, India
Umm Dorein	Umm Dorein, Sudan
Umm Gabralla	Umm Gabralla, Sudan
Urali	Urali in Kerala, India
Urarina	Urarina, Peru
Urhobo	Urhobo, Nigeria
Uria	Uria, Indonesia
Uruangnirin	Uruangnirin, Indonesia
Urubu	Urubu, Brazil
Urupa	Urupa, Brazil
Uspanteco	Uspanteco, Guatemala
Utugwang	Utuqwang, Nigeria
Uvbie	Uvbie, Nigeria
Uzbeki, Turkic	**Uzbeks, Afghanistan (79)
Uzekwe	Uzekwe, Nigeria
Vagala	Vagala, Ghana
Vaqla	Vagla, Ghana
Vai	*Vai, Liberia (80)
	Vai, Sierra Leone
Vaikino	Vaikino, Indonesia
Vaiphei	Vaiphei in Assam, India
Vale	Vale, Central African Empire
Various dialects	**African Students in Cairo, Egypt
	**Mangyan, Philippines
Venda	Venda, Rhodesia
Veps	Veps, Soviet Russia
Vere	***Vere, Nigeria
	Vere, Cameroon
Vidunda	Vidunda, Tanzania
Vietnamese	*Int'l Stud., Los Banos, Philippines
	Vietnamese, Laos
	**Vietnamese in the USA, United States of
	America

Yahadian	Yahadian, Indonesia
Yaka	Yaka, Zaire
Yakan	Yakan, Philippines (80)
Yakoma	Yakoma, Central African Empire
Yala	**Yala, Nigeria
Yalunka	*Yalunka, Sierra Leone (80)
Yaly	Yaly, Indonesia
Yambasa	Yambasa, Cameroon
Yaminahua	Yaminahua, Peru
Yanadi	Yanadi in Andhra Pradesh, India
Yandang	Yandang, Nigeria
Yanga	Yanga, Togo
Yangbye	Yangbye, Burma
Yanomam (Waica)	*Yanomamo in Brazil, Brazil (79)
Yans	Yans, Zaire
Yanyula (Yanjula)	*Yanyula, Australia
Yao	Yao, Mozambique
	*Yao Refugees from Laos, Thailand
Yao (Mien Wa)	**Yao, Thailand (79)
Yaoure	Yaoure, Ivory Coast
Yaqui	Yaquis, Mexico
Yaruro	Yaruro, Venezuela
Yasing	Yasing, Cameroon
Yaur	Yaur, Indonesia
Yava	Yava, Indonesia
Yazgulyam	Yazgulyam, Soviet Russia
Yei	**Yei, Botswana
	Yei, Indonesia
Yela	Yela, Zaire
Yellow Uighur	Yellow Uighur, China
Yelmek	Yelmek, Indonesia
Yerava	Yerava in Karnataka, India
Yeretuar	Yeretuar, Indonesia
Yerukala	Yerukala in A.P., India
Yeskwa	Yeskwa, Nigeria
Yi	Lolo, China (81)
	Pai, China (81)
Yidinit	Yidinit, Ethiopia
Yinchia	Yinchia, Burma
Yinga	Yinga, Cameroon
Yoabu	Yoabu, Benin
Yogad	Yogad, Philippines
Yonggom	Yonggom, Indonesia
Yos	Yos, Burma
Yotafa	Yotafa, Indonesia
Yuana	Yuana, Venezuela
Yucateco	Yucateco, Guatemala
	Yucateco, Mexico
Yucuna	*Yucuna, Colombia
Yukagir	Yukagirs, Soviet Russia
Yukpa	Yukpa, Colombia
	Yukpa, Venezuela
Yuku	Yuku, China
Yulu	Yulu, Sudan
Yungur	Yungur, Nigeria
Yuracare	Yuracare, Bolivia
Yurak	Yurak, Soviet Russia
Yuruti	Yuruti, Colombia
Zaghawa	Zaghawa, Chad
	Zaghawa, Libya
	Zaghawa, Sudan
Zanaki	Zanaki, Tanzania
Zande	Zande, Zaire
Zangskari	Zangskari in Kashmir, India
Zaramo	Zaramo, Tanzania
Zari	Zari, Nigeria
Zayse	Zayse, Ethiopia
Zenaga	Zenaga, Mauritania
Zighvana (Dghwede)	*Dghwede, Nigeria

Index by
Country

INDEX BY COUNTRY

Groups are listed by the countries for which information has been reported by questionnaires. In most cases, this means they are listed in the country where they are primarily located. Many peoples are found in several countries. This listing is limited to the country for which the MARC files have information. Groups are listed alphabetically under each country listed. Please note that not all countries will be found in this index. Peoples have not been reported from every country. Cambodia is listed under its new name Kampuchea. The Republic of China is listed as Taiwan. Dahomey is listed under its current name, Benin. The population estimate given is an indication of the size of that people in that one country. In some cases, it is only a part of a large people to be found in several other countries as well.

Afghanistan	**Azerbaijani	5,000
	Bashgali	10,000
	Chaghatai	300,000
	Gawar-Bati	8,000
	Gujuri	10,000
	Jati	1,000
	Kirghiz	45,000
	Mogholi	2,000
	Munji-Yidgha	14,000
	Nuristani (80)	67,000
	Pashayi	96,000
	***Prasuni	2,000
	Sau	1,000
	Shina	50,000
	Shughni	3,000
	Tajik	3,600,000
	Uighur	3,000
	**Uzbeks (79)	1,000,000
Albania	*Albanian Muslims (80)	1,700,000
Algeria	Algerian (Arabs) (80)	8,000,000
	Kabyle (79)	1,000,000
	Shawiya	150,000
Angola	Chokwe (Lunda)	400,000
	Holu	12,000
	**Huila	200,000
	Hukwe	9,000
	Kongo	756,000
	Kwadi	15,000
	Kwangali	25,000
	Kwanyama	100,000
	Luchazi	60,000
	Luimbi	20,000
	Lunda	50,000
	Luyana	3,500
	Lwena	90,000
	Mbukushu	6,000
	Mbunda	59,000
	Mbwela	100,000
	Nsongo	15,000
	Nyaneka	40,000
	Nyemba	100,000
	O'ung	5,000
Argentina	**Chiriguano	15,000
	Chorote	500
	Mataco	10,000
	Pilaga	4,000
	Toba	15,000
Australia	**Chinese in Australia	30,000
	**Chinese Stud., Australia	5,500
	Guqu-Yalanji	5,400
	*Murngin (Wulamba)	3,500
	**Vietnamese Refugees	7,800
	*Yanyula	150
Austria	*Chinese in Austria	1,000
	*Iwaidja	150
Bangladesh	Assamese	10,000,000
	**Banai	2,000
	Bawm	7,000
	Bengali (80)	80,000,000
	**Hajong	17,000
	**Koch	35,000
	Mirung	12,000
	Mru	50,000
	Pankhu	630
	Tangchangya	8,310
	Tippera	38,000
Belgium	North Africans in Belgium (80)	90,000
	Turkish Workers (80)	60,000
Belize	**Black Caribs, Belize (79)	10,000

Benin	**Mopan Maya	4,000
	**Adja	250,000
	*Bariba (80)	400,000
	Berba	44,000
	**Boko	40,000
	Dendi	40,000
	Dompago	19,000
	*Fulani	70,000
	Gbazantche	9,000
	Gu	173,000
	Kabre	35,000
	Kotokoli	75,000
	Lamba	29,000
	*Mokole	7,000
	*Nyantruku	4,000
	**Pila	50,000
	**Save	15,000
	**Somba	60,000
	Soruba	5,000
	Takemba	10,000
	Tayaku	10,000
	*Tofi	33,000
	Winji-Winji	5,000
	Yoabu	8,000
Bhutan	Bhutias	780,000
	Kebumtamp	400,000
	Sharchagpakha	400,000
	Tibetans in Bhutan (81)	5,000
Bolivia	**Aymara	850,000
	Chacobo	250
	Chipaya	850
	Chiquitano	20,000
	***Guarani (79)	15,000
	Guarayu	5,000
	Ignaciano	5,000
	Itonama	110
	Leco	200
	Movima	1,000
	**Quechua	1,000,000
	Reyesano	1,000
	Siriono	500
	Tacana	3,500
	Tsimane	5,500
	Yuracare	2,500
Botswana	"Au"ei	5,000
	Buka-khwe	9,000
	Bushmen in Botswana	30,000
	Herero	10,000
	*Kalanga	150,000
	Kwe-etshori	3,000
	Nharon	3,000
	Shua	400
	Tonga	6,000
	**Yei	10,000
Brazil	Apalai	100
	Apinaye	210
	Apurina	1,000
	Arapaco	310
	Atruahi	500
	Bakairi	300
	Baniwa	2,440
	*Bororo	500
	Caiwa	7,000
	Canela	1,400
	**Chinese in Brazil	45,000
	Cinta Larga	500
	***Copacabana Apt. Dwellers	400,000
	Culina	800
	Desano	1,040

	Chin, Khumi	30,000
	Chin, Ngawn	5,000
	Chin, Tiddim	38,000
	Chinbok	21,000
	Chinese in Burma	600,000
	Dai	10,000
	Danu	70,000
	Gheko	4,000
	Hallam	11,000
	Hkun	20,000
	Hrangkhol	8,500
	Intha	80,000
	Kachin in Shan State	80,000
	Kaw	30,000
	Kayan	18,000
	Kokant	50,000
	Lahu	40,000
	Lama	3,000
	Maghi	300,000
	Moken (79)	5,000
	Mon (81)	350,000
	Mun	10,000
	Myaung-Ze	7,000
	Norra	10,000
	Palaung (79)	150,000
	Pao	100,000
	Purum	300
	Ralte	17,000
	Riang-Lang	20,000
	Senthang	10,000
	Shan	800,000
	Shan Chinese	20,000
	Taman	10,000
	Taungyo	150,200
	Taungyoe	18,000
	Tawr	700
	Thai-Ney	5,000
	Wa	50,000
	Yangbye	326,650
	Yin-Kyar	2,000
	Yin-Nett	2,000
	Yinchia	4,000
	Yos	4,500
	Zome	30,000
Burundi	Pygmy (Binga)	30,000
Cameroon	Adamawa	380,000
	Age	5,000
	Aghem	7,000
	Amasi	10,000
	Assumbo	10,000
	Babajou	500
	Bafut	25,000
	Baka	15,000
	Balong	4,500
	Bamougoun-Bamenjou	31,000
	Bamum	75,000
	Bandjoun	60,000
	Banen	28,000
	Banganqte	475,000
	Basaa	170,000
	Batanga-Ngolo	9,000
	Bene	60,000
	Bethen	10,000
	Betsinga	10,000
	Bitare	50,000
	Bobe	600
	Bokyi	87,000
	Bomboko	2,500
	Bonkeng-Pendia	1,500

	Ndjem	25,000
	Ndop-Bamessing	17,000
	Ndoro	10,000
	Ndunpa Duupa	1,000
	Ngayaba	1,000
	Ngemba	33,500
	Ngi	10,000
	Ngumba	10,000
	Ngwo	10,000
	Nkom	30,000
	Nohu	6,500
	Nso	100,000
	Nyang	10,000
	Oso	25,000
	Pape	1,000
	Podokwo	25,000
	So	6,000
	Su	500
	Suga	10,000
	Taram	3,000
	Tchang	100,000
	Tigon	25,000
	Tikar	12,500
	Tupuri	70,000
	Vere	20,000
	Voko	1,000
	Widekum	10,000
	**Wimbum	50,000
	Yambasa	26,000
	Yasing	25,000
	Yinga	300
Canada	**Chinese in Vancouver B.C.	80,000
	Jews of Montreal	120,000
	Jews, Sephardic	26,000
Central African Empire	Day	1,600
	Kaba	11,000
	Kaba Dunjo	17,000
	Kaka	37,000
	Kari	4,000
	Karre	40,000
	Kim	5,000
	Laka	40,000
	Majingai-ngama	47,000
	Mbai	73,000
	Mbati	15,000
	Monjombo	11,000
	Ndam	670
	Ndogo	3,500
	Ngando	2,000
	Ngbaka Ma'bo	17,000
	Nzakara	3,000
	Pambia	2,000
	Pana	20,000
	Pygmy (Binga)	2,000
	Runga	13,000
	Somrai	50,000
	Tana	35,000
	Tunya	800
	Vale	1,400
	Yakoma	5,300
Chad	Abou Charib	25,000
	Bagirmi	40,000
	Bilala	42,000
	Bomou	15,000
	Bua	20,000
	Daju of Dar Dadju	27,000
	Daju of Dar Sila	33,000
	Dangaleat	20,000
	Daza	159,000

	Jyarung	70,000
	Kalmytz	70,000
	Kam	825,320
	Kazakhs (81)	700,000
	Kelao	23,000
	Khalka	68,000
	Kham	11,400
	Kirgiz	90,000
	Koreans in Manchuria (81)	3,000,000
	Lahul	1,600
	Laka	6,000
	Lati	450
	Li	1,000,000
	Lisu (81)	470,000
	Lolo (81)	4,800,000
	Lu	400,000
	Manchu (81)	200,000
	Miao (81)	2,800,000
	Mien (81)	740,000
	Mongour	50,000
	Nahsi	155,750
	Nanai	1,000
	Nosu	556,000
	Nung	100,000
	Oirat	60,000
	Oronchon	2,400
	Pai (81)	1,000,000
	Paongan	8,000
	Pu-I	1,311,020
	Punu	220,000
	Rawang	60,000
	Salar	31,000
	Santa	155,500
	Sibo	21,000
	Sui	160,310
	*Tibetans	3,000,000
	Tung-Chia (81)	1,100,000
	Uigur (80)	4,800,000
	Wa	286,160
	Yellow Uighur	4,000
	Yuku	4,000
Colombia	Achagua	100
	Andoque	100
	Barasano	400
	Barasano, Northern	450
	Barasano, Southern	400
	Bora	400
	Cacua	150
	Camsa	2,000
	Carapana	200
	Chami	3,000
	Cofan	250
	Coqui	4,000
	**Coreguaje	500
	Coreguaje	500
	Cubeo	2,000
	Cuiba	2,000
	*Cuna (79)	600
	Cuna	600
	Curipaco	2,500
	Embera, Northern	2,000
	Guajibo	15,000
	*Guajiro	60,000
	Guambiano	9,000
	*Guanano (79)	800
	Guayabero	700
	Guayabevo	600
	Huitoto, Meneca	600
	Hupda Maku	150

	Gedeo	250,000
	**Ghimeera	50,000
	Gidicho	500
	Gobato	1,000
	Gobeze	22,000
	Gumuz	53,000
	Gurage (80)	750,000
	Hadiyya	700,000
	Harari	13,000
	Janjero	1,000
	Kachama	500
	*Kaffa (80)	320,000
	Kao	600
	Kembata	250,000
	*Komo	20,000
	Konso	30,000
	Koyra	5,000
	Kullo	82,000
	Kunama	70,000
	*Lango	8,000
	Maji	15,000
	Male	12,000
	Mao, Northern	13,000
	*Masengo	7,000
	Me'en	38,000
	Mesengo	28,000
	***Mocha	170,000
	Mursi	6,000
	Nao	5,000
	Nara	25,000
	*Nuer	70,000
	Oyda	3,000
	Reshiat	10,000
	***Shankilla (Kazza)	20,000
	Sheko	23,000
	Shinasha	4,000
	Sidamo	857,000
	Somali	1,000,000
	**Suri	30,000
	Tsamai	7,000
	Walamo	988,000
	Wetawit	28,000
	Yidinit	600
	Zayse	21,000
	Zilmamu	3,000
Fiji	Indians in Fiji (79)	265,000
France	Algerian Arabs in France	804,000
	**Chinese Refugees, France (79)	100,000
	*Chinese Restaurant Wrkrs.	50,000
	**Portuguese in France	150,000
	*University Students (79)	800,000
Gabon	Benga	nr
	Duma	10,000
	Kele	15,000
	Kota	nr
	Lumbu	12,000
	Mbaama	12,000
	Mbede	45,000
	Minduumo	4,000
	Sangu	18,000
	Sira	17,000
	Tsogo	15,000
	Wandji	6,000
	Wumbvu	103
Gambia	Bayot	4,000
	Dyola	216,000
	Fula, Cunda	70,200
	Krio	3,000
	Mandyak	85,000

	**Kekchi	270,000
	**Mam Indian	470,000
	**Mopan Maya	2,000
	Pocomchi, Eastern	20,000
	Pocomchi, Western	25,000
	**Quiche (79)	500,000
	Rabinal-Achi	21,000
	Tzutujil	5,000
	Uspanteco	15,000
	Yucateco	3,000
Guinea	Basari	3,500
	Fula	1,500,000
	Gbande	66,000
	Kissi	266,000
	Kobiana	300
	Konyagi	85,000
	Kpelle	250,000
	Landoma	4,000
	Loko	16,000
	Loma	180,000
	Nalu	10,000
Guinea-Bissau	Badyara	10,000
	Balante	100,000
	Banyun	15,000
	Bayot	3,000
	Biafada	15,000
	Bidyogo	10,000
	**Bijogo	25,000
	Diola (80)	15,000
	Dyola	nr
	Kasanga	420
	Kunante	6,000
	Landoma	5,000
	Maninka	65,000
	**Manjaco	80,000
	Mankanya	35,000
	Papel	36,300
	Susu	2,000
Guyana	Akawaio	3,000
	Arawak	5,000
	Patamona	1,000
	Waiwai	1,000
	Wapishana	4,000
Honduras	**Black Caribs, Honduras	20,000
	Paya	300
	Tol	200
Hong Kong	Chinese Businessmen (81)	10,000
	Chinese Factory Workers	500,000
	**Chinese in Hong Kong	4,135,000
	Chinese Villagers	500,000
	*Factory Workers	40,000
	**High School Students	453,000
India	Abujmaria in M.P.	11,000
	***Adi	80,300
	Adiyan in Kerala	2,500
	Agariya in Bihar	11,790
	Ahir in Maharashtra	132,520
	Aimol in Assam	110
	Ajmeri in Rajasthan	580
	Aka	2,257
	*Alars	400
	Anal in Manipur	6,590
	Andha in Andhra Pradesh	64,650
	Anga in Bihar	423,500
	**Apatani in Assam	11,000
	Aranadan in Tamil Nadu	600
	*Arnatas	700
	Arya in Andhra Pradesh	2,590
	Asuri in Bihar	4,540

Iravas in Kerala	3,700,000
***Irulas in Kerala	10,000
Jagannathi in A.P.	1,310
Jains	2,000,000
Jatapu in Andhra Pradesh	36,450
Jaunsari in Uttar Pradesh	56,560
Jharia in Orissa	2,060
Juang in Orissa	12,170
Kachchi in Andhra Pradesh	470,990
Kadar in Andhra Pradesh	800
Kahluri in Andamans	66,190
Kaikadi in Maharashtra	11,850
Kamar in Madhya Pradesh	10,110
Kanauri in Uttar Pradesh	28,500
Kanikkaran in Kerala	10,000
Kanjari in Andhra Pradesh	55,390
**Karbis	300,000
Karmali in Dihar	69,620
**Kashmiri Muslims (79)	3,060,000
Katakari in Gujarat	4,950
Kawar in Madhya Pradesh	33,770
Keer in Madhya Pradesh	2,890
Khamti in Assam	300
Khandesi	14,700
Kharia in Bihar	88,900
Khasi in Assam	384,010
Khirwar in Madhya Pradesh	34,250
Khojas, Agha Khani	175,000
Khowar	6,960
Kisan in Bihar	73,850
Kishanganjia in Bihar	56,920
Kishtwari in Jammu	12,170
Koda in Bihar	14,140
Kol in Assam	82,900
**Kolam	60,000
Kom in Manipur	6,970
***Kond	900,000
Konda-Dora in A.P.	15,650
Konkani in Gujarat	1,522,680
Koraqa in Kerala	1,500
*Korku in Madhya Pradesh	250,000
Korwa in Bihar	14,250
Kota in Tamil Nadu	860
Kotia in Andhra Pradesh	15,000
Kotta	1,200
Koya in Andhra Pradesh	211,880
*Kudisai Vagh Makkal	1,000,000
Kudiya	100
*Kuknas	125,000
**Kuluis in Himachal Prades (81)	200,000
Kumauni in Assam	1,234,940
Kupia in Andhra Pradesh	4,000
Kurichiya in Kerala (81)	12,130
Kuruba in Tamil Nadu	7,900
Kurux in Bihar	1,240,400
Kuvi in Orissa	190,000
Labans	nr
Labbai	nr
Labhani in Andhra Pradesh	1,203,340
*Labourers of Jhoparpatti	1,500
Ladakhi in Jammu	56,740
**Lahaulis in Punjab	18,000
Lalung in Assam	10,650
**Lambadi in Andhra Pradesh (81)	1,300,000
Lodhi in Bihar	44,070
Lushai in Assam	270,310
Mahali in Assam	14,300
Majhwar in Madhya Pradesh	27,960
Malakkaras of Kerela (81)	1,000

	Sikkimese	36,580
	*Sindhis of India	3,000,000
	Sondwari in M.P.	31,490
	Sora in Orissa	221,710
	Sulung	nr
	***Tagin	25,000
	Takankar	10,960
	Tamaria in Bihar	5,050
	*Tamil in Yellagiri Hills	3,500
	**Tangsa	10,700
	Thado in Assam	42,340
	Thakur	99,000
	Thar in Bihar	8,790
	*Tibetan Refugees	nr
	Toda in Tamil Nadu	770
	Tokkaru in Tamil Nadu	1,298,860
	Totis	nr
	Tugara	43,680
	Ullatan in Kerala	1,500
	Urali in Kerala	1,080
	Vaiphei in Assam	12,210
	Vishavan in Kerala	150
	**Vohras of Yavatmal	10,000
	Waddar in Andhra Pradesh	35,900
	Wagdi in Rajasthan	756,790
	**Wanchoo	nr
	Yanadi in Andhra Pradesh	205,380
	Yerava in Karnataka	10,870
	Yerukala in A.P.	67,550
	Zangskari in Kashmir	5,000
	Zemi Naga of Assam (81)	16,000
	Zoliang	50,000
	Zome in Manipur	30,000
Indonesia	Abau	3,390
	Achehnese (80)	2,200,000
	Aghu	3,000
	Aibondeni	150
	Aikwakai	400
	Airo-Sumaghaghe	2,000
	Airoran	350
	Alas	30,000
	Alor, Kolana (81)	90,000
	Amanab	2,800
	Ambai	6,000
	Amber	300
	Amberbaken	5,000
	Ambonese	80,000
	Ansus	3,000
	Ara	75,000
	Arandai	2,000
	Arguni	200
	Asienara	700
	*Asmat (79)	30,000
	Awyi	400
	Awyu	18,000
	Baburiwa	160
	Baham	500
	Bajau, Indonesian	50,000
	Balantak	125,000
	Balinese	2,000,000
	Banggai	200,000
	Barau	150
	Bare'e	325,000
	*Batak, Angkola (80)	nr
	Batak, Karo	400,000
	Batak, Simalungun	800,000
	Batak, Toba	1,600,000
	Bedoanas	250
	Berik	800

Kaugat	1,000
**Kaur	50,000
Kaure	800
Kavwol	500
Kawe	300
Kayagar	9,000
Kaygir	4,000
Kayupulau	570
Kei	30,000
Kemak	50,000
Kendari	500,000
Kenyah	37,500
Kerinchi	170,000
Kimaghama	3,000
*Kimyal	7,000
Kodi	25,000
Komering	400,000
Koneraw	300
Korapun	4,000
Kotogut	1,000
Kubu (80)	6,000
Kubu (81)	25,000
Kurudu	1,100
Kwansu	350
Kwerba	2,000
Kwesten	2,480
Lampung (80)	1,500,000
Lara	12,000
Latdwalam	860
Laudje	125,000
Lebong	nr
Letti	6,000
Lionese	100,000
**Loho Loho	10,000
Loinang (81)	100,000
Lore	140,000
Lubu	1,000,000
Luwu	500,000
Maanyan	15,000
Madik	1,000
Madurese (79)	7,000,000
Mairasi	1,000
Makasai	70,000
Makian, West	12,000
Maklew	120
Mambai	80,000
Mandar	302,000
Mander	100
Manem	400
Manggarai Muslims (81)	25,000
**Manikion	8,000
Mantion	12,000
Marau	1,200
Marind	7,000
Marind, Bian	900
Masenrempulu	250,000
Matbat	550
Mawes	690
Meax	10,000
Mekwei	1,200
*Mimika	10,000
Minangkabau (80)	5,000,000
Moi	4,000
Molof	200
Mombum	250
Mongondow (81)	400,000
Moni	20,000
Mor	1,000
Mori (81)	200,000

	Tara	125,000
	Tarof	600
	Tarpia	560
	Taurap	160
	Tengger	400,000
	Ternatans	42,000
	Tidorese	26,000
	Timorese	300,000
	Tiro	75,000
	Toala	100
	Tombulu	40,000
	Tomini	50,000
	Tondanou	35,000
	Tonsea	90,000
	Tontemboa	140,000
	Toraja, Southern (81)	250,000
	Towei	120
	Tukude	45,000
	Tumawo	350
	Turu	800
	Uhunduni	14,000
	Uria	1,200
	Uruangnirin	250
	Vaikino	14,000
	Wabo	900
	Wambon	2,000
	Wandamen	4,000
	Wanggom	1,000
	Wano	1,700
	Warembori	350
	Waris	1,480
	Warkay-Bipim	250
	Waropen	6,000
	Weda	900
	Wewewa	55,000
	Wodani	3,000
	Woi	1,300
	Wolio	25,000
	Yafi	180
	Yahadian	700
	Yaly	12,000
	Yaur	350
	Yava	4,500
	Yei	1,000
	Yelmek	400
	Yeretuar	250
	Yonggom	2,000
	Yotafa	2,460
Iran	Afshars	290,000
	Agajanis	1,000
	**Ahl-i-Haqq in Iran (79)	500,000
	Arab-Jabbari (Kamesh)	13,000
	Arab-Shaibani (Kamesh)	16,000
	Arabs of Khuzestan	520,000
	Azerbaijani Turks (80)	6,000,000
	Baharlu (Kamesh)	7,500
	Bakhtiaris (80)	590,000
	Baluchi (80)	1,100,000
	Bayats	nr
	Bovir-Ahmadi	110,000
	Galeshis	2,000
	Gilakis	1,950,000
	Goudari	2,000
	Hezareh	nr
	Inallu	5,000
	Jamshidis	1,000
	Jews of Iran	93,000
	Kazakhs (80)	3,000
	Khalaj	20,000

	Kurds in Iran (80)	2,000,000
	Lors (80)	600,000
	Mamasani	110,000
	Mazandaranis	1,620,000
	Moqaddam	1,000
	Nafar	3,500
	Pashtuns (80)	3,000
	Persians of Iran (80)	2,000,000
	Pishagchi	1,000
	Qajars	3,000
	Qara'i	2,000
	Qaragozlu	2,000
	Qashqa'i (80)	350,000
	Sasanis	1,000
	Shahsavans (80)	180,000
	Tajik (80)	15,000
	Takestani	220,000
	Talish	20,000
	Teimuri	10,000
	Teimurtash	7,000
	*Tertiary Level Youth	nr
	Turkomans (80)	550,000
Israel	Druzes (79)	33,000
	*Jewish Imgrnts.-American	25,797
	*Jewish Imgrnts.-Argentine	17,686
	*Jewish Imgrnts.-Australia	1,257
	*Jewish Imgrnts.-Brazilian	4,005
	*Jewish Imgrnts.-Mexican	1,065
	*Jewish Imgrnts.-Uruguayan	2,720
	*Jewish Immigrants, Other	5,520
	Targum	5,000
Ivory Coast	Abe	28,500
	Abidji	23,000
	Abure	25,000
	Adyukru	50,450
	Akan, Brong	50,000
	Aladian	14,770
	Attie	160,000
	*Atye	210,000
	Avikam	7,940
	Bakwe	5,060
	Bambara	1,000,000
	***Baoule	1,200,000
	*Bete	300,000
	***Dan	270,000
	Dida	115,000
	**Dida	120,000
	Ebrie	50,000
	Eotile	4,000
	Gagu	25,000
	***Godie	20,000
	**Gouro	200,000
	Guere	117,870
	Gwa	8,300
	Hwela-Numu	50,000
	**Jimini	42,000
	Kouya	5,690
	*Krahn	250,000
	Krobou	3,400
	Krumen	17,000
	Kulango	60,000
	Kulele	15,000
	Ligbi	20,000
	Lobi	40,000
	Maou	80,000
	Mo	800
	Mona	5,570
	Moru	10,000
	Neyo	5,000

425

	*Ngen	20,000
	Ngere	150,000
	**Nyabwa	30,000
	Nzema	24,080
	Oubi	1,340
	Palara	10,000
	Pye	6,120
	Senufo (80)	300,000
	Tagwana	43,000
	*Teenbu	5,000
	*Tense	5,000
	Tepo	20,000
	Trepo	3,400
	Tura	19,230
	Wobe	40,000
	Yaoure	14,000
Jamaica	**Jamaican Elite	800,000
Japan	*Chinese in Japan	50,000
	Farmers of Japan	24,988,740
	*Industry Laborers-Japan	21,000,000
	*Inland Sea Island Peoples	1,000,000
	*Koreans of Japan	600,000
	*Ryukyuan	1,000,000
	Soka Gakkai Believers	6,500,000
	**Univ. Students of Japan	2,000,000
Jordan	Muslims of Jordan	1,000,000
Kampuchea, Democratic	*Cham (Western) (80)	90,000
Kenya	Ayana	5,000
	**Boran	37,000
	Boran	40,000
	Digo	168,000
	Dorobo	22,000
	El Molo	1,000
	Gabbra	12,000
	Giryama	335,900
	Gosha	3,000
	**Maasai (79)	100,000
	Rendille	20,000
	Sabbra	18,000
	**Saguye	30,000
	Sakuye	8,000
	Samburu	60,500
	Somali, Ajuran (79)	25,374
	Somali, Degodia	68,667
	Somali, Gurreh	54,165
	Somali, Ogadenya	99,129
	Suk	133,200
	**Teso	110,000
	Turkana	224,000
	**Turkana Fishing Community (79)	20,000
Korea, Republic of	**Apartment Residents-Seoul	87,000
	**Bus Drivers, South Korea	26,000
	*Chinese in Korea	20,000
	Indust.Workers Yongdungpo	140,000
	*Japanese in Korea	5,000
	**Korean Prisoners	45,000
Kuwait	Kurds in Kuwait	145,000
Laos	Alak	8,000
	Brao (79)	18,000
	*Chinese in Laos	25,000
	Galler	50,000
	Jeng	500
	Kasseng	15,000
	*Lao (79)	1,908,600
	Loven (81)	25,000
	Ngeq	50,000
	Nyaheun	15,000
	Oi	10,000
	Phu Thai	100,000

	So	15,000
	Ta-Oi	15,000
	Vietnamese	20,000
Lebanon	Ladinos	7,300
Lesotho	***Basotho, Mountain (79)	70,000
Liberia	Bandi	32,000
	*Bassa	200,000
	Dan	94,000
	*Dewein	5,000
	Gio	92,000
	Gola	47,000
	**Grebo	65,000
	*Kissi	35,000
	Klaoh	81,000
	**Kowaao	7,000
	Kpelle	200,000
	***Krahn	55,000
	Kuwaa	5,500
	Loma	60,000
	Mandingo (79)	30,000
	Mano	65,000
	Mende	5,000
	Sapo	30,000
	*Vai (80)	30,000
Libya	Libyans	2,300,000
	Teda	16,000
	Zaghawa	nr
Macau	*Chinese Refugees in Macau (81)	100,000
Malawi	Lambya	18,600
	Mpoto	22,000
	Ngulu	476,000
	Nyakyusa	34,000
	Sena	115,000
	Tonga	62,200
	**Yao	600,000
	Zulu	37,500
Malaysia	Bajau, Land	90,000
	Bateg	400
	Besisi	7,000
	**Bidayuh of Sarawak (81)	110,000
	Biduanda	4,000
	Bisaya (81)	2,800
	Bruneis	25,000
	Chinese Fishermen	4,000
	*Chinese in Malaysia	3,555,879
	**Chinese in Sabah	180,000
	**Chinese in Sarawak	330,000
	*Chinese of W. Malaysia	3,500,000
	Dusun (81)	160,000
	**Iban (81)	30,000
	Juhai	400
	Kadazans	110,000
	Kayan	12,000
	Kedayanas	25,000
	Kelabit (81)	17,000
	Kemok	400
	Lanoh	400
	Mantera	4,000
	**Melanau of Sarawak (80)	61,000
	Menri	400
	Momoguns	110,000
	Murut	37,500
	Muslim Malays (80)	5,500,000
	Orang Kanak	4,000
	Orang Laut	4,000
	Orang Ulu	4,000
	Penan, Western (81)	2,600
	**Selakau of Sarawak	5,300
	Semelai	3,000

	**Senoi (81)	337,400
	**Sugut	10,000
	Tagal (81)	19,000
	***Tamil Plantation Workers	137,150
	*Tamils (Indian)	600,000
	Temira	7,000
Maldives	Divehi (80)	120,000
Mali	Bambara	1,000,000
	Bobo Fing	3,000
	Bobo Wule	366,000
	Bozo	nr
	*Dogon (79)	312,000
	Fula, Macina	50,000
	Fula, Peuhala	450,000
	Kagoro	30,000
	Khasonke	71,000
	Kita	150,000
	Maure	58,000
	Minianka	300,000
	Samo, Northern	50,000
	Samogho	10,000
	Songhai	125,100
	Soninke	283,000
	Suppire	300,000
Mauritania	Ware	2,000
	Moors in Mauritania	1,000,000
	Soninke	22,000
Mexico	Zenaga	16,000
	Amuzgo, Guerrero	20,000
	Amuzgo, Oaxaca	5,000
	***Azteca (79)	250,000
	***Ch'ol Sabanilla	20,000
	Ch'ol Tila	38,000
	Chamula (79)	50,000
	Chatino, Nopala	7,500
	Chatino, Panixtlahuaca	4,500
	Chatino, Tataltepec	2,000
	Chatino, Yaitepec	2,000
	Chatino, Zacatepec	500
	Chatino, Zenzontepec	4,000
	Chinanteco, Tepinapa	3,000
	Chinanteco, Ayotzintepec	2,000
	Chinanteco, Chiltepec	3,000
	Chinanteco, Comaltepec	1,500
	Chinanteco, Lalana	10,000
	Chinanteco, Lealao	5,000
	Chinanteco, Ojitlan	10,000
	Chinanteco, Palantla	10,600
	Chinanteco, Quiotepec	7,000
	Chinanteco, Sochiapan	2,000
	Chinanteco, Tepetotutla	1,000
	Chinanteco, Usila	5,000
	Chocho	2,500
	Chuj, San Mateo Ixtatan	3,000
	Cocopa	900
	Cora	8,000
	Cuicateco, Tepeuxila	10,000
	Cuicateco, Teutila	6,000
	Guarojio	5,000
	Huasteco	80,000
	**Huave	18,000
	Huichol	8,000
	Kikapoo	5,001
	Lacandon	200
	Matlatzinca, Atzingo	1,700
	Mayo	30,000
	**Mazahua	150,000
	**Mixes	60,000
	Mixteco, Amoltepec	6,000

	Mixteco, Apoala	6,000
	Mixteco, Central Puebla	3,000
	Mixteco, Eastern	15,000
	Mixteco, Eastern Putla	7,000
	Mixteco, Huajuapan	3,000
	Mixteco, Silacayoapan	15,000
	Mixteco, Southern Puebla	12,000
	Mixteco, Southern Putla	2,500
	Mixteco, Tututepec	2,000
	Mixteco, Yosondua	15,000
	*Mixteco,San Juan Mixtepic	15,000
	*Nahua, North Pueblo	55,000
	Otomi, Eastern	20,000
	Otomi, Mezquital	100,000
	Otomi, Northwestern	40,000
	Otomi, Southeastern	1,500
	Otomi, State of Mexico	70,000
	Otomi, Tenango	10,000
	Otomi, Texcatepec	8,000
	Paipai	300
	Pame, Central Chichimeca	2,500
	Pame, Chichimeca-Jonaz	1,200
	Pame, Northern	2,000
	Pima Bajo	1,000
	Popoloca, Ahuatempan	6,000
	Popoloca, Coyotepec	500
	Popoloca, Eastern	2,000
	Popoloca, Northern	6,000
	Popoloca, Southern	1,000
	Popoloca, Western	8,000
	Popoluca, Oluta	200
	Popoluca, Sayula	6,000
	Popoluca, Sierra	18,000
	Popoluca, Texistepec	2,000
	Seri	400
	Tarahumara, Northern	500
	Tarahumara, Rocoroibo	12,000
	Tarahumara, Samachique	40,000
	Tarasco	60,000
	Tepehua, Huehuetla	2,000
	Tepehua, Pisa Flores	2,500
	Tepehua, Veracruz	900
	Tepehuan, Northern	5,000
	Tepehuan, Southeastern	8,000
	Tepehuan, Southwestern	6,000
	Tlapaneco, Malinaltepec	40,000
	Tojolabal	14,000
	Totonaco, Northern	15,000
	Totonaco, Oxumatlan	1,300
	Totonaco, Papantla	50,000
	Totonaco, Sierra	100,000
	Totonaco, Yecuatla	500
	Trique, San Juan Copala	8,000
	Tubar	100
	Tzeltal, Bachajon	20,000
	Tzeltal, Highland	25,000
	Tzotzil, Chenalho	16,000
	Tzotzil, Huistan	11,000
	Yaquis	14,000
	Yucateco	500,000
	Zinacantecos (79)	10,000
	Zoque, Chimalapa	6,000
	Zoque, Copainala	10,000
	Zoque, Francisco Leon	12,000
	Zoque, Tabasco	400
Morocco	Arabs in Morocco	5,250,000
	Shilha	3,000,000
	**Shluh Berbers	2,000,000
	Tamazight	1,800,000

REGISTRY OF THE UNREACHED

Mozambique	Chopi	400,000
	Chuabo	250,000
	Kunda	60,000
	Lomwe	1,000,000
	Makua	1,200,000
	Maviha	70,000
	Nyungwe	700,000
	Podzo	45,000
	Ronga	400,000
	Sena	85,000
	Tonga	10,000
	Tsonga	1,500,000
	Tswa	200,000
	Yao	220,000
Namibia	Bushmen (Heikum)	16,000
	*Bushmen (Kung) (79)	10,000
	Herero	40,000
	Kwambi	30,000
	Kwanyama	150,000
	Nama	10,000
	San	6,000
	Tswana	11,300
	Xu	8,000
Nepal	*Bhojpuri	806,480
	Gurung	172,000
	**Magar	300,000
	Maithili	1,000,000
	*Nepali	6,060,758
	*Newari	500,000
	Rai	232,000
	*Rai, Danuwar	12,000
	Rajbansi	15,000
	**Santhali	nr
	*Sherpa	20,000
	*Tamang	nr
	Tharu	495,000
Netherlands	Ambonese	30,000
	Amsterdam Boat Dwellers	7,500
	*Chinese in Amsterdam	15,000
	*Chinese in Holland	35,000
New Zealand	*Chinese in New Zealand	12,500
Nicaragua	Miskito	20,000
	Sumu	2,000
Niger	Dyerma (80)	1,000,000
	Kanembu	1,500
	Kurfei	50,000
	Mauri	100,000
	Songhai	93,000
	Teda	120,000
	Tuareg (79)	200,000
Nigeria	Abanyom	3,850
	Abong	1,000
	Abua	24,000
	Achipa	3,600
	*Afawa (80)	10,000
	**Afo (80)	25,000
	Agoi	3,650
	Agwagwune	20,000
	Ake	300
	Akpa-Yache	15,000
	Alago	35,000
	Alege	1,200
	Amo	3,550
	Anaang	246,000
	Angas	100,000
	Ankwe	10,000
	Arawa	200,000
	Aten	4,000
	Ayu	4,000

430

Galambi	1,000
Gbari (80)	500,000
Gbaya	350,000
Geji	2,650
Gera	13,300
Geruma	4,700
Ghotuo	9,000
**Glavda	19,000
Goemai	80,000
Gokana	54,000
Gude	40,000
Gudu	1,200
Guduf	21,300
Gure-Kahugu	5,000
Guruntum-Mbaaru	10,000
Gwandara	25,000
Gwari Matai	200,000
***Higi	150,000
Hwana	20,000
Hyam	60,000
Ibaji	20,000
Ibibio	2,000,000
Icen	7,000
Idoma	300,000
Idoma, North	56,000
Igala	350,000
Igbira (80)	400,000
Igede	70,000
Ihceve	5,000
Ijo, Central-Western	338,700
Ijo, Northeast	395,300
Ijo, Northeast Central	8,400
Ikulu	6,000
Ikwere	200,000
Irigwe	15,000
Isekiri	33,000
**Ishans	25,000
Isoko	20,000
Ivbie North-Okpela-Atte	20,000
Iyon	2,000
Izarek	30,000
**Izi	200,000
Jaba	60,000
Janjo	6,100
Jara	40,000
**Jarawa	150,000
Jera	23,000
Jerawa	70,000
*Jibu	20,000
Jimbin	1,500
Jukun	20,000
Kadara	40,000
Kagoma	6,250
Kaibu	650
Kaka	2,000
Kamantan	5,000
*Kambari (80)	100,000
Kamo	3,000
*Kamuku (80)	20,000
Kana	90,000
Kanuri (80)	3,000,000
Karekare	39,000
Kariya	2,200
Katab	32,370
Khana	90,000
Kilba	80,000
Kirifi	14,000
Koenoem	3,000
Kofyar	40,000

	Piya	2,500
	Polci	6,150
	Pongu	3,680
	Puku-Geeri-Keri-Wipsi	15,000
	Reshe	30,000
	Rukuba	50,000
	Rumaya	1,800
	Ruruma	2,200
	Sanga	5,000
	Sasaru-Enwan Igwe	3,780
	Saya	50,000
	Sha	500
	Shanga	5,000
	Shuwa Arabic	100,000
	Siri	2,000
	Sukur	10,000
	Sura	40,000
	Surubu	1,950
	Tal	10,000
	Tambas	3,000
	Tangale	100,000
	Tarok	60,000
	Tera	46,000
	Tula	19,000
	Turkwam	6,000
	Ukaan	18,000
	Ukpe-Bayobiri	12,000
	Ukwuani-Aboh	150,000
	Urhobo	340,000
	Utugwang	12,000
	Uvbie	6,000
	Uzekwe	5,000
	***Vere	20,000
	Vute	1,000
	Waja	30,000
	*Warjawa	70,000
	Wom	10,000
	**Yala	60,000
	Yandang	10,000
	Yeskwa	13,000
	Yungur	44,300
	**Zaranda Hill Peoples	10,000
	Zari	3,950
Oman	Mahri	50,000
Pakistan	Bagri	20,000
	Bajania (79)	20,000
	Balmiki	20,000
	**Bhil	800,000
	Brahui	745,000
	Chitralis (79)	120,000
	**Gagre	40,000
	**Hunzakut (79)	10,000
	**Kafirs (79)	3,000
	**Kohli, Kutchi	50,000
	**Kohli, Tharadari	40,000
	**Kohli, Wadiara	40,000
	**Kohlis, Parkari	100,000
	Lohar	nr
	**Meghwar (79)	100,000
	Od	40,000
	Punjabis (80)	49,000,000
	Sochi	nr
	Swatis (79)	600,000
	Vagari	30,000
Panama	Buglere	2,000
	**Chinese in Panama	25,000
	**Teribe	1,000
Papua New Guinea	**Ampeeli	1,000
	***Banaro	2,500

**Bontoc, Southern	12,000
Buhid	6,000
**Bukidnon	100,000
Buwid (81)	6,000
Caluyanhon	30,000
*Casiguranin	10,000
***Cebu, Middle-Class	500,000
Cuyonon	49,000
Davaweno	13,000
*Dumagat , Casiguran (81)	1,000
Ga-Dang	5,500
Hanonoo	6,000
**Hotel Workers in Manila (81)	11,000
Ibanag	319
*Ibataan	500
Ifuago, Antipolo	5,000
*Ifugao	95,000
**Ifugao (Kalangoya)	35,000
Ifugao in Cababuyan	4,000
Ifugao, Ambanad	15,000
Ifugao, Kiangan	25,000
Igorot	20,000
Ikalahan	40,000
Ilongot	7,640
Insinai	10,000
*Int'l Stud., Los Banos	nr
Iraya	6,000
Isneg, Dibagat-Kabugao	10,000
Isneg, Karagawan	8,000
Itawit	15,000
Itneg, Adasen	4,000
Itneg, Binongan	7,000
Itneg, Masadiit	7,500
Jama Mapun (80)	15,000
*Jeepney Drivers in Manila (81)	20,000
Kaagan	20,000
Kadaklan-Barlig Bontoc	4,000
**Kalagan	19,000
Kalinga, Kalagua	3,600
Kalinga, Limus-Linan	20,000
Kalinga, Quinaang	41,000
*Kalinga, Southern	11,000
**Kalinga, Tanudan	5,700
**Kalinga,Northern (81)	20,000
**Kankanay, Central	40,000
Kankanay, Northern	40,000
Kinaray-A	288,000
Lubang Islanders (81)	18,000
Maguindano (80)	700,000
**Mamanua (81)	1,000
Mandaya	3,000
Mandaya, Mansaka	35,400
**Mangyan	60,000
Manobo, Agusan	15,000
Manobo, Ata	7,000
Manobo, Binokid	40,550
**Manobo, Cotabato	10,000
Manobo, Dibabawon	1,790
*Manobo, Ilianen	5,000
Manobo, Obo	4,000
**Manobo, Salug	4,000
Manobo, Sarangani	15,000
Manobo, Tagabawa	9,900
**Manobo, Tigwa	4,000
**Manobo, Western Bukidnon	12,000
Manobos, Pulangi	5,000
**Mansaka	25,000
Maranao (79)	500,000

437

	Bullom, Southern	40,000
	Fula	250,000
	Gola	1,400
	*Kissi	48,000
	Kissi, Southern	58,000
	**Kono	133,000
	**Koranko	103,000
	Krim	3,400
	Limba	233,000
	Loko	80,000
	Loko	60,700
	Maninka	64,200
	Mende	600,000
	Susu	86,500
	**Temne (80)	1,000,000
	Vai	2,800
	*Yalunka (80)	25,000
Sikkim	**Lepcha	18,000
Singapore	Malays of Singapore (79)	300,000
Somalia	Somali (79)	2,500,000
South Africa	*Chinese in South Africa	9,000
	Nama	15,000
	Ronga	600,000
	**Swazi	500,000
Soviet Russia	Abazin	25,000
	Abkhaz	83,000
	Adygei	100,000
	Agul	8,800
	Akhavakh	5,000
	Alutor	2,000
	Andi	9,000
	Archin	900
	Balkars	60,000
	Bashkir (80)	1,200,000
	Batsi	3,000
	Botlikh	3,500
	Budug	2,000
	Buriat	315,000
	Chamalin	5,500
	Cherkess	40,000
	Chukot	14,000
	Dargin	231,000
	Didoi	7,000
	Dolgans	4,900
	Dungan	39,000
	Evenks	25,000
	Gagauzes	157,000
	Gilyak	4,400
	Gypsies	175,000
	Ingushes	158,000
	Itelmen	1,300
	Izhor	1,100
	Kalmytz	137,000
	Kapuchin	2,500
	Karachay	173,000
	Karagas	600
	Karaim	1,000
	Karakalpak (80)	277,000
	Karakalpak	236,000
	Karatin	6,000
	Ket	1,200
	Khakas	67,000
	Khanti	21,000
	Khinalug	1,500
	Khvarshin	1,800
	Kirgiz (80)	1,700,000
	Komi-Permyat	153,000
	Komi-Zyrian	322,000
	Koryak	7,500

Gbaya-Ndogo	1,800
Gberi	600
Ghol	2,000
Ghulfan	3,300
Gumuz	40,000
Heiban	25,000
Ingassana	35,000
*Jiye	7,000
Kadugli	19,000
Kakwa	84,000
Kanga	6,400
Karko	2,200
Katcha	6,000
Katla	8,700
Keiga	6,000
Keiga Jirru	1,400
Kichepo	16,000
Koalib (79)	320,000
Koma, Central	3,000
Koroma	30,000
Krongo	121,000
Lafofa	2,000
Laro	3,000
Liguri	2,000
*Lokoro	22,000
Lori	1,000
**Lotuka	150,000
Luac	700
Lwo	20,000
Maba	9,000
Maban-Jumjum	20,000
Madi	6,000
Masakin	16,000
Masalit	27,000
Meban	130,000
Midob	1,800
Miri	8,000
Modo	1,700
Moreb	560
Moru	23,000
Murle	40,000
Naka	3,600
Ndogo	3,500
Nginyukwur	3,800
Ngirere	4,200
Ngok	21,000
Ngunduna	9,000
Nguqwurang	8,000
Njalgulgule	900
*Nuer (79)	844,000
Nyamusa	1,200
Nyarueng	2,000
Nyzatom	80,000
Otoro	28,000
Paloc	13,500
Rut	515
Sere	3,500
Shatt	9,000
Shilluk	110,000
Shwai	2,800
Sopi	1,600
Tabi	10,000
Talodi	1,200
Tegali	16,000
Temein	2,300
Thoi	400
Thuri	154,000
Tira	10,200
Tirma	8,500

	Kutu	17,000
	Kwaya	35,000
	Kwere	63,000
	Lambya	7,000
	Langi	95,000
	Luo	1,522,000
	Makonde	550,000
	Malila	175,000
	Mambwe-Lungu	16,000
	Manda	10,000
	Matengo	58,000
	Matumbi	72,000
	Mbugwe	8,000
	Mbunga	10,000
	Mosi	240,000
	Mpoto	36,000
	Mwanga	27,000
	Mwera	110,000
	Nata	9,500
	Ndali	57,000
	Ndamba	19,000
	Ndengereko	53,000
	Ndomde	12,000
	Ngasa	1,000
	Ngindo	85,000
	Ngoni	85,000
	Ngulu	12,800
	Ngurimi	11,800
	Nguu	46,000
	Nilamba	210,000
	Nyakyusa	193,000
	Nyambo	4,000
	Nyamwezi (80)	590,000
	Nyiha	64,000
	Pangwa	26,000
	Pare	99,000
	Pimbwe	13,000
	Pogolo	65,000
	Ruihi	71,000
	Rungi	95,000
	Rungwa	5,000
	Rusha	54,000
	Safwa	102,000
	Sagala	20,000
	Sandawe	38,000
	Sangu	30,000
	Shambala	152,000
	Sonjo	7,400
	Suba	17,000
	Subi	74,000
	Sumbwa	64,000
	Tatoga	22,000
	Tongwe	8,000
	Turu	316,000
	Vidunda	11,000
	Vinza	4,000
	**Wajita	65,000
	Wanda	8,000
	Wanji	19,000
	Wasi	13,000
	*Wazinza	2,000
	Wungu	8,000
	Zanaki	23,000
	Zaramo	296,000
	Zigwa	112,000
Thailand	**Akha (79)	9,916
	*Cambodians	1,000,000
	*Central Thailand Farmers (81)	5,000,000
	*Chinese in Thailand	3,600,000

	Gwere	162,000
	Jiye	34,000
	Kakwa	573,000
	Kumam	100,000
	Kupsabiny	60,000
	Lango	560,000
	Lugbara	260,000
	Madi	114,000
	Makere	17,500
	Masaba	110,000
	Meje	13,200
	Muslims (West Nile Dist.)	45,000
	Nyankole	810,000
	Nyoro	620,000
	Nyuli	140,000
	Pokot	170,000
	Rwamba	60,000
	Saamia	124,000
	Soga	780,000
	Tepeth	4,000
	Teso	830,000
United Arab Emirates	Muslims in U.A.E. (79)	202,000
	**Shihu	10,000
United Kingdom	**Chinese in United Kingdom	105,000
	**Chinese Students Glasgow	1,000
	Gujarati	300,000
	**Muslim Immigrants in U.K.	500,000
United States of America	**Chinese in United States	550,000
	*Havasupai	300
	Hopi	6,000
	**Japanese Students In USA	nr
	Jemez Pueblo	1,800
	Paiute, Northern	5,000
	**Racetrack Residents (79)	50,000
	**Vietnamese in the USA	261
	Zuni	6,000
Upper Volta	Birifor	50,000
	Bolon	4,000
	Bousansi	140,000
	Buli	60,000
	Bwa (80)	140,000
	Dagari	150,000
	Doghosie	7,900
	Dyan	8,000
	Fula	250,000
	Fulah	300,000
	Gan	4,000
	Gouin-Turka	25,000
	Gourency	300,000
	Gurma	250,000
	*Karaboro	40,000
	Kasem	28,000
	Komono	6,000
	Kurumba	86,000
	Lele	61,000
	Marka	39,000
	Mossi (80)	3,300,000
	Natioro	1,100
	*Nouni	50,000
	Nunuma	43,000
	Puguli	5,000
	Samo, Northern	70,000
	Sisala	4,000
	Songhai	35,000
	Tiefo	6,500
	*Toussian	20,000
	Vige	3,500
	Wara	2,200
	Win	20,000

Venezuela	Arecuna	14,000
	Arutani	100
	**Jivaro (Achuara)	20,000
	Mapoyo	200
	Maquiritari	5,000
	Motilon	3,000
	Mutu	300
	Panare	1,200
	Piaroa	12,000
	Sanuma	4,000
	Wapishana	20,000
	Warao	15,000
	Yanomamo in Venezuela	nr
	Yaruro	5,000
	Yuana	300
	Yukpa	3,000
Viet Nam	Cham	45,000
	**Chrau	15,000
Yemen, Arab Republic	***Akhdam	nr
	Sayyids	nr
	Yemenis (79)	5,600,000
Yemen, Democratic	**Hadrami	151,000
	*Mahrah	50,000
Yugoslavia	*Albanians in Yugoslavia	1,500,000
	*Bosnian (80)	1,740,000
	Gypsies in Yugoslavia	800,000
Zaire	Alur	19,000
	Baali	38,000
	Baka	2,600
	**Bakuba	75,000
	Bangba	29,000
	Bembe	50,000
	Binji	64,000
	Bira	35,000
	Bolondo	1,000
	Boma	15,000
	Budu	83,000
	Bugombe	12,000
	Buja	200,000
	Bulia	45,000
	Bushoong	100,000
	Bwa	35,000
	Bwisi	6,000
	Dengese	4,000
	Dongo	5,000
	Enya	7,000
	Fuliro	56,000
	Furu	5,000
	Havu	262,000
	Heso	6,000
	Hunde	33,500
	Kakwa	20,000
	Kaliko	18,000
	Kanu	3,500
	Kaonde	20,000
	Kari	1,000
	Kela	100,000
	Kumu	60,000
	Kusu	26,000
	Kwese	60,000
	Lalia	30,000
	Lamba	80,000
	Lega	150,000
	Lele	26,000
	Lendu	250,000
	Lese	20,000
	Liko	26,000
	Logo	54,000
	Lombi	8,100

	Lombo	10,000
	Lugbara	350,000
	Luna	50,000
	Lwalu	21,000
	Ma	4,700
	Mamvu-Efe	40,000
	Mangbutu	8,000
	Mba	20,000
	Mbala	200,000
	Mbangwe	2,000
	Mbanja	81,000
	Mbo	2,000
	Mbole	100,000
	Mono	30,000
	Mundu	5,000
	Nandi	310,000
	Ndaaka	4,700
	Ndo	13,000
	Ndoolo	5,000
	Ndunga	2,500
	Ngando	121,000
	Ngbaka	700,000
	Ngbaka Ma'bo	17,000
	Ngbandi	137,000
	Ngbee	30,000
	Ngiri	6,000
	**Ngombe	5,000
	Nkutu	40,000
	Ntomba	50,000
	Nyanga-Li	25,000
	***Pakabeti of Equator	3,000
	Pende	200,000
	Peri	40,000
	Poke	46,000
	*Pygmy (Mbuti) (79)	40,000
	Rwamba	48,000
	Sakata	75,000
	Salampasu	60,000
	Sanga	35,000
	Sanza	15,000
	Songe	500,000
	Songomeno	40,000
	Songoora	1,300
	Suku	74,000
	Swaga	121,000
	Teke, Eastern	71,000
	Tembo	30,000
	Tiene	24,500
	Togbo	5,500
	Wongo	8,000
	Yaka	200,000
	Yans	165,000
	Yela	33,000
	Zande	467,000
	Zimba	50,000
Zambia	Ambo	1,000
	Bisa	83,000
	Cewa	200,000
	Chokwe	25,000
	Ila	39,000
	Iwa	15,000
	Kaonde	116,000
	Kunda	21,000
	Kunda	8,000
	Lala	125,000
	Lamba	89,000
	Lenje	79,000
	Lima	12,000
	Lozi	215,000

Appendices

ACHING THE UNREACHED

of a program being carried out jointly by the Strategy Working Group of the
anne Committee for World Evangelization and MARC, the Missions Advanced
arch and Communication Center, which is a ministry of World Vision International.

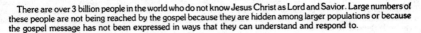

919 West Huntington Drive, Monrovia, California, USA

There are over 3 billion people in the world who do not know Jesus Christ as Lord and Savior. Large numbers of these people are not being reached by the gospel because they are hidden among larger populations or because the gospel message has not been expressed in ways that they can understand and respond to.

They are unreached people.

It has been estimated that there are at least 15,000 major unreached people groups, the vast majority of which have not been identified as to where they are and how they can be reached. This is a task for Christ's Church throughout the world. This is *your* task.

In order to understand and locate these unreached people the Strategy Working Group of the Lausanne Committee for World Evangelization has been working with the Missions Advanced Research and Communication Center (MARC). The early results of this research were presented at the Lausanne Congress on World Evangelization in 1974. Since then this worldwide effort has continued.

The on-going results are published annually in a directory entitled *Unreached Peoples*. As new information comes in from around the world, basic data about each group is listed and some 80 to 100 groups are described in detail. Information on each group is available for your use from MARC.

By publishing whatever information is available, the *Unreached Peoples* directory acts as a bridge between those who are discovering new unreached people, and those whom God has chosen to seek them out with the good news. Your contribution is important!

This questionnaire has been designed to make that task as simple as possible. We ask that you supply whatever information you can, trusting that the Lord of the Harvest has others who will supply what is missing.

Thank you for being a part of this grand vision that every person in the world may have an opportunity to know Jesus Christ.

52478A

FINDING THE UNREACHED: YOU CAN HELP!

You can help locate unreached people groups

You are part of a worldwide network of concerned Christians. There are millions upon millions of people in the world who have had little or no contact with the gospel of Jesus Christ. Because of this, we are asking you to help the Church locate and identify these peoples so it can reach them.

Within each country there are distinct and unique groups of people who may be unreached. This questionnaire is designed to help you describe such groups so that Christians everywhere may pray and consider how these groups might be reached with the gospel. This information will be continuously compiled and made available to the Church and her mission agencies. It appears each year in an annual directory, *Unreached Peoples*, produced by David C. Cook.

There are many different groups of people in the world. How varied they are! Consequently, this questionnaire may not always ask the best questions for understanding a particular people. The questions have been asked in a way that will give comparative information to as large a number of Christians as possible. Where you feel another form of question would better suit your situation, please feel free to comment.

What is a "people group"?

A people group is a part of a society that has some basic characteristics in common that cause it to feel a sense of oneness, and set it apart from other groups. It may be unified by language, religion, economic status, occupation, ethnic origin, geographic location, or social position. For example, a distinct group based on ethnic, language and geographic characteristics might be the Quechua of Bolivia; a sociological group might be the urban university and college students of Colombia, or the urban industrial workers of France. It is important to see that groups may share a common way of life and sense of oneness because of social, occupational or economic characteristics, as well as because of language or ethnic origin. Therefore, whenever possible, *describe the smallest number of persons who make up a distinct group;* that is, don't say that all persons in a region or province are a group, rather describe the specific subgroups within that region or province.

Who are the "unreached and unevangelized people"?

Christians have different definitions of the terms "unreached" or "unevangelized." For the purposes of this worldwide effort, we describe an unreached or unevangelized people as a people who has not received or responded to the gospel. This unresponsiveness may be due to lack of opportunity, to lack of understanding, or because the people has not received enough information about the gospel message in its own language through the eyes of its own culture so that it can truly respond to Christ.

We consider a people "unreached" when less than 20 percent of the members of the group are *practicing* Christians, that is, are active members of the Christian community. By "Christian" we mean adherents (church members, families and followers) of the historic Christian communions; Protestant, Anglican, Roman Catholic, Orthodox and such independent groups as may claim the Bible as the basis of faith and Jesus Christ as Lord and Savior. A group less than 20 percent Christian may yet need Christians from outside the group to help with the evangelism task.

How you can provide information

The attached questionnaire has two parts. If you only have information for the first part, send that in now.

Please fill in one questionnaire for *each* people group with which you are familiar. Do not put several groups on one questionnaire. (If you need more questionnaires, ask for extra copies or photocopy this one, or typewrite the questions you are answering on a separate sheet of paper.) We realize that one person may not have all the answers to these questions. Just answer what you can. PLEASE DO NOT WAIT UNTIL YOU HAVE ALL THE INFORMATION REQUESTED ON THIS QUESTIONNAIRE. SEND WHAT YOU HAVE. Other people may provide information that you do not have. Thank you for your help!

When you have completed this questionnaire, please return it to:

Unreached Peoples Program Director
c/o MARC, 919 W. Huntington Drive, Monrovia, CA 91016 U.S.A.

SURVEY QUESTIONNAIRE FOR UNEVANGELIZED AND UNREACHED PEOPLES

Do you see a group of people who are unreached or unevangelized? Identify them! As the Lord spoke to Ezekiel of old, so He speaks to us today. "Son of man, What do you see"?

Answers to the questions on these two pages will provide the minimum information needed to list this people group in the *Unreached Peoples* annual.

After you have read the directions, type or print your answers so they can be easily read. It is unlikely that you will have all the information requested. Do the best you can. What information you are lacking others may supply. If your information is a best guess or estimate, merely place an "E" after it. Send in what you have as soon as possible. Please ignore the small numbers next to the answers. They help others prepare your answers for the *Unreached Peoples* annual.

*this reason I bow
y knees before the
ather, from whom
y family in heaven
and on earth is
named . . ."
sians 3:14-15 (RSV)*

1. Name of the group or people:_____

2. Alternate name(s) or spelling: _____

3. Country where located: _____

4. Approximate size of the group in this country: _____

5. Vernacular or common language: _____

6. Lingua franca or trade language: _____

7. Name of religious groups found among this people:

	% who are adherents of this religion	% who practice this religion
CHRISTIAN GROUPS:		
Protestant	_____ %	_____ %
Roman Catholic	_____ %	_____ %
Eastern Orthodox	_____ %	_____ %
Other Christian: _____ (name)	_____ %	_____ %
NON-CHRISTIAN GROUPS OR SECULARISM:		
_____	_____ %	_____ %
_____	_____ %	_____ %
_____	_____ %	_____ %
_____	_____ %	_____ %
TOTAL FOR ALL GROUPS:	100 %	

*ethren, My heart's
esire and prayer to
for them is that
hey may be saved."
Romans 10:1
(RSV)*

8. In your opinion, what is the attitude of this people toward Christianity?

(01)□ Strongly favorable   (02)□ Somewhat favorable   (03)□ Indifferent   (04)□ Somewhat opposed   (05)□ Strongly opposed

TURN THIS SHEET OVER FOR PAGE 2

s2479B

9. Questionnaire completed by:

Name: _____ Date: _____

Organization: _____

Address: _____

_____

10. Who else might be able to provide information about this people?

Name	Organization (if any)	Address

11. If you are aware of any publications describing this people, please give title and author.

_____

12. What other information do you have that could help others to understand this people better? What do you would help in evangelizing them?   *(Use additional sheet if necessary.)*

"And how are they to believe in him of whom they have never heard? And how are they to hear without a preacher?"
Romans 10:14 (RSV)

13. Are you also sending in pages 3 and 4? ☐ Yes   ☐ No

Please send whatever information you have immediately. Do not wait until you have every answer.

Mail to:

Unreached Peoples Program Director
c/o MARC, 919 W. Huntington Drive, Monrovia, CA 91016 USA

If you have any more information about this people group, please complete the following two pages as best you can. If not, please send in pages one and two now. If you can obtain more information later, send it in as soon as possible.

PEOPLE DISTINCTIVES—What makes them different? Why are they a people group?

14. A number of different things contribute to create a distinctive people or group, one that in some way shares a common way of life, sees itself as a particular group having an affinity toward one another, and differs to some extent from other groups or peoples. What would you say makes the people you are describing distinctive? Check the appropriate box of as many of the following descriptions as *are important* in making this people distinctive. Use the following scale: "High" importance, "Medium" importance, "Low" importance. For example, if you thought that the fact that they had a common political loyalty was of medium importance in unifying and making a group distinctive, you would place an "X" in the middle box under "Medium".

Importance

High Medium Low

(01)☐ ☐ ☐ Same language
(02)☐ ☐ ☐ Common political loyalty
(03)☐ ☐ ☐ Similar occupation
(04)☐ ☐ ☐ Racial or ethnic similarity
(05)☐ ☐ ☐ Shared religious customs
(06)☐ ☐ ☐ Common kinship ties
(07)☐ ☐ ☐ Strong sense of unity
(08)☐ ☐ ☐ Similar education level
(09)☐ ☐ ☐ Other(s) _____
(please write in)

Importance

High Medium Low

(10)☐ ☐ ☐ Common residential area
(11)☐ ☐ ☐ Similar social class or caste
(12)☐ ☐ ☐ Similar economic status
(13)☐ ☐ ☐ Shared hobby or special interest
(14)☐ ☐ ☐ Discrimination from other groups
(15)☐ ☐ ☐ Unique health situation
(16)☐ ☐ ☐ Distinctive legal status
(17)☐ ☐ ☐ Similar age
(18)☐ ☐ ☐ Common significant problems

15. How rapidly would you say the lifestyle of this people is changing? (check one)

(01)☐ Very Slow Change   (02)☐ Slow Change   (03)☐ Moderate Change   (04)☐ Rapid Change   (05)☐ Very Rapid Change

PEOPLE LANGUAGES—What do they speak?

Please list the various languages used by the members of this people:

LANGUAGE TYPE	Primary name(s) of their language(s)	Approximate % who speak this language	Approximate % of people over 15 years of age who read this language
16. Vernacular or common language:	_____	_____ %	_____ %
17. Lingua franca or trade language:	_____	_____ %	_____ %
18. Language used for instruction in schools:	_____	_____ %	_____ %
19. Language suitable for presentation of the gospel:	_____	_____ %	_____ %

20. If there is Christian witness at present, what language(s) is being used? _____

21. Place an "x" in the boxes that indicate the status of Scripture translation *in the language you consider most suitable for communicating the gospel* (question 19):

	CURRENT STATUS				AVAILABLE		
	Not available	In process	Completed		In oral form	In print	On cassette or records
(POR)New Testament portions	☐	☐	☐		☐	☐	☐
(NT)Complete New Testament	☐	☐	☐		☐	☐	☐
(OT)Complete Old Testament	☐	☐	☐		☐	☐	☐

22. Of the <u>Christians</u> present among this people, what percent *over 15 years of age can* and *do read any language?*

_____ %

9347BC

CHRISTIAN WITNESS TO THIS PEOPLE—Who is trying to reach them?

23. If there are Christian churches or missions (national or foreign) now active *within the area or region where people is concentrated,* please give the following information:

(If there are none, check here: ☐)

"... with an eternal gospel to proclaim to those who dwell on earth, to every nation and tribe and tongue, and people."
Revelation 14:6 (RSV)

CHURCH OR MISSION Name of church, denomination	YEAR Year work began in this area	MEMBERS Approximate number of full members from this people	ADHERENTS Approximate number of adherents (community including children)	WORKERS Approximate numbers of trained pastors and evangelists from this people
_____	_____	_____	_____	_____
_____	_____	_____	_____	_____
_____	_____	_____	_____	_____

24. What is the growth rate of the total Christian community among this people group?

(01)☐ Rapid growth   (02)☐ Slow growth   (03)☐ Stable   (04)☐ Slow decline   (05)☐ Rapid decline

25. In your opinion, what is the attitude of this people to religious change of any kind?

(01)☐ Very open   (02)☐ Somewhat open   (03)☐ Indifferent   (04)☐ Somewhat closed   (05)☐ Very closed

26. In your opinion, what is the attitude of this people toward Christianity?

(01)☐ Strongly favorable   (02)☐ Somewhat favorable   (03)☐ Indifferent   (04)☐ Somewhat opposed   (05)☐ Strongly opposed

27. Most people move through a series of more or less well-defined stages in their attitude toward Christianity. Parts people group will be further along than other parts. Here are ten categories that attempt to show this progress. However, locating people in some of these categories can be difficult, so to make things simpler some categol are combined in the questions that follow.

In your estimation, what percentage of this people can be described as those who: (These percentages exclusive. Do not include people more than once. Your total should add up to 100%.)

"And you he made alive when you were dead, through the trespasses and sins in which you once walked . . ."
Ephesians 2:1-2 (RSV)

Have no awareness of Christianity... _____

Have awareness of the existence of Christianity....................................... _____

Have some knowledge of the gospel .... _____

Understand the message of the gospel .... _____

See the personal implications of the gospel ....
Recognize a personal need that the gospel can meet................................. } _____
Are being challenged to receive Christ ....

Have decided for Christ, but are not incorporated into a fellowship
(may be evaluating their decision) .... _____

Are incorporated into a fellowship of Christians .... _____

Are active propagators of the gospel... _____

TOTAL 10(

28. On the whole, how accurate is the information you have given us?

(V)☐ Very accurate   (F)☐ Fairly accurate   (E)☐ Good estimate   (G)☐ Mainly guesses

29. Are you willing to have your name publically associated with this information?

☐ No   ☐ Yes   ☐ Yes, with qualifications: _____

APPENDIX B

Recommended Bibliography

Background Notes, U.S. Government Printing Office

Beaver, R. Pierce, ed. *The Gospel and Frontier Peoples.* Pasadena: William Carey Library, 1973.

Dayton, Edward R. *That Everyone May Hear.* Monrovia: MARC, 1979.

Dayton, Edward R. *Planning Strategies for Evangelism* (6th Edition). Monrovia: MARC, 1979.

Dayton, Edward R. and Fraser, David A. *Planning Strategies for World Evangelization.* Grand Rapids: William B. Eerdmans Publishing Company, 1980.

Douglas, J., ed. *Let the Earth Hear His Voice.* Minneapolis: World Wide Publications, 1975.

Europa Publications, Ltd. *Europa World Year Book.* London.

Grimes, Barbara, ed. *Ethnologue.* Huntington Beach: Wycliffe Bible Translators, 1978.

Hedlund, Roger E., ed. *World Christianity: South Asia.* Monrovia: MARC, 1980.

Holland, Clifford, ed. *World Christianity: Central America.* Monrovia: MARC, 1980.

Johnstone, Patrick St. G. *World Handbook for the World Christian.* South Pasadena: World Christian Book Shelf.

Kane, J. Herbert. *Global View of Christian Mission.* Grand Rapids: Baker Book Co., 1971.

Lebar, Frank M., ed. *Ethnic Groups of Insular Southeast Asia* (Vol. 1). New Haven: Human Relations Area Files Press, 1972.

Lebar, Frank M., ed. *Ethnic Groups of Insular Southeast Asia* (Vol. 2). New Haven: Human Relations Area Files Press, 1975.

Lebar, Frank M., Hickey, G. C.; and Musgrave, J. K. *Ethnic Groups of Mainland Southeast Asia.* New Haven: Human Relations Area Files Press, 1964.

Luzbetak, Louis J. *The Church and Cultures.* Illinois: Divine Word Publications, 1963.

Maloney, Clarence. *People of South Asia.* New York: Holt, Reinhart and Wilson, 1974.

McCurry, Don M., ed. *The Gospel and Islan: A 1978 Compendium.* Monrovia: MARC, 1979.

McCurry, Don M., ed. *World Christianity: Middle East.* Monrovia: MARC, 1979.

Murdock, George P. *Africa: Its Peoples and Their Culture History.* New York: McGraw-Hill, 1959.

Nida, Eugene A., ed. *The Book of a Thousand Tongues.* New York: United Bible Societies, 1972.

Pentecost, Edward C. *Reaching the Unreached.* South Pasadena: William Carey Library, 1974.

Read, William R., and Ineson, Frank A. *Brazil 1980: The Protestant Handbook.* Monrovia: MARC, 1973.

Steward, Julian H. *Handbook of South American Indians.* New York: Cooper Square Pub., 1959.

Tindale, Norman B. *Aboriginal Tribes of Australia.* Berkeley: Univ. of Calif. Press, 1975.

Wagner, C. Peter. *Frontiers in Missionary Strategy.* Chicago: Moody Press, 1971.

Wagner, C. Peter, and Dayton, Edward R., eds. *Unreached Peoples '79: The Challenge of the Church's Unfinished Business.* Illinois: David C. Cook Pub. Co., 1978.

Wagner, C. Peter, and Dayton, Edward R., eds. *Unreached Peoples '80: The Challenge of the Church's Unfinished Business.* Illinois: David C. Cook Pub. Co., 1980.

Wauchope, Robert, ed. *Handbook of Middle American Indians: Guide to Ethnohistorical Sources* (Vols. 1-15). Austin: Univ. of Texas Press, 1964.

Weekes, Richard V. *Muslim Peoples: A World Ethnographic Survey.* Connecticut: Greenwood Press, 1978.

Wilson, Samuel, ed. *Mission Handbook: North American Protestant Ministries Overseas* (12th Edition). Monrovia: MARC, 1980.

Wong, James; Larson, Peter; and Pentecost, Edward. *Missions from the Third World.* Singapore: Church Growth Study Center, 1973.

Audiovisual

Dayton, Edward R. "That Everyone May Hear." Audiovisual, Monrovia: MARC, 1979.

APPENDIX C

**Expanded Descriptions in
Unreached Peoples '79 and '80**

**INDEX OF PEOPLE GROUPS WITH EXPANDED
DESCRIPTIONS IN** *UNREACHED PEOPLES '79*

APPENDIX C

INDEX OF PEOPLE GROUPS WITH DESCRIPTIONS
IN *UNREACHED PEOPLES '80*

APPENDIX C

APPENDIX D

FOLLOW-UP INFORMATION

It appears that there is the following error/omission on page_____

of *Unreached Peoples '81:* _____

_____

_____

_____

_____

_____

I would like to receive more information on the _____

_____(name of people group).

Additional Comments: _____

_____

_____

Name_____

Date _____

Address _____

Please detach, insert in an envelope, and mail to:

Missions Advanced Research and
Communication Center
919 West Huntington Drive
Monrovia, CA 91016
U.S.A.

I would like to order a copy of the laser operation tape
(or cassette) Psalms by _____

_____

_____

_____

_____

_____

_____

_____

I would like to receive more information on the _____

_____ Number of people in group

Additional Code Info _____

_____

_____

Name _____

Org _____

Address _____

For a free detailed printed form, envelope, or write to:

Applied Laboratory Research, Inc.
Communication Group
c/o William Riffle Drive
Mandan, CA 91101
USA